D0894438

HYPNOTIC AND STRATEGIC INTERVENTIONS: PRINCIPLES AND PRACTICE

Hypnotic and Strategic Interventions: Principles and Practice

Edited by
Michael D. Yapko, Ph.D.

RC
490.5
H97
1986

Copyright © 1986 by Michael D. Yapko, Ph.D.

All rights reserved. No part of this book may be reproduced in any manner whatever, including information storage or retrieval, in whole or in part (except for brief quotations in critical articles or
reviews), without written permission from the pub-
lisher. For information write to Irvington
Publishers, Inc., 740 Broadway, New York, New
York 10003.

ISBN 0-8290-1803-4

3-25-88

Acknowledgments

Organizing a conference and having it run successfully to the satisfaction of all involved was a project that consumed most of our collective energies. I would like to express my appreciation to those people who helped make the conference possible.

Diane Yapko, Beverly Hershfield, Linda Griebel, and Judy Robinson all made huge contributions to the organizing and running of the conference, attending to every detail from scheduling events to processing registrations to keeping the bagel table amply supplied. Mitchell Harris and John Koriath also gave generously of their time and energy, which is greatly appreciated. Wendy and Richard Horowitz also deserve special recognition for their enthusiasm and support.

The faculty for the conference was primarily comprised of local clinicians whose work has been recognized as innovative and skilled. Jeffrey Zeig and Ernest Rossi were particularly gracious in their willingness to travel to San Diego in order to participate. All of the faculty members deserve recognition for their fine contributions to this event.

Michael D. Yapko, Ph.D., Director
The Milton H. Erickson
Institute of San Diego
2525 Camino Del Rio South,
Suite 225
San Diego, Ca. 92108
(619) 295-1010

This volume is dedicated with love to my parents, Gerda and Benjamin Yapko, and Madeline and Gerald Harris. That you have survived the trials and tribulations associated with my varied growth experiences is a tribute to your higher consciousness.

Preface

This volume contains papers presented at The San Diego Conference on Hypnotic and Strategic Interventions, held February 8-10, 1985. The conference was organized by The Milton H. Erickson Institute of San Diego for the major purposes of advancing general awareness of hypnotic and strategic approaches to psychotherapy and to bring together qualified professionals with a common interest in these approaches.

The three day conference featured presentations on applications of brief methods of psychotherapy, and principles of communication helpful in diagnosing and treating disorders effectively. Presentations included readings of prepared papers, panel discussions, participatory workshops, and demonstrations. The conference drew attendees from as far away as Canada and Europe, and yet still managed to maintain the intimacy of a small group sharing a special experience. Held in San Diego at the edge of Mission Bay, the atmosphere of a marina in the foreground and the ocean in the background provided attendees with an inspiring (and trance-inducing) view at all times.

The Milton H. Erickson Institute of San Diego

The Milton H. Erickson Institute of San Diego has been authorized by the Board of Directors of the Milton H. Erickson Foundation in Phoenix, Arizona, to practice and promote the concepts and techniques of the late Dr. Erickson. Toward that end, the Institute has several functions:

— To provide high quality clinical services to the community of which we are a part
— To provide clinical training for health care professionals in clinical hypnosis and techniques of psychotherapy
— To provide educational opportunities to the public in a variety of areas, each designed to enhance the quality of life
— To stimulate a cohesiveness in the professional community for those interested in Ericksonian approaches to hypnosis and psychotherapy
— To stimulate research in the areas of clinical hypnosis and strategic psychotherapy

The Milton H. Erickson Institute of San Diego has an important name to live up to and a valuable reputation to preserve. We have earned our own good reputation as well, based on skill and accomplishment, and we invite you to make good use of the resources we have to share.

The San Diego Conference on Hypnotic and Strategic Interventions was the first of what will become an annual tradition for the Institute. Future conferences will continue to feature skilled presenters providing "hands-on" learning opportunities in an atmosphere conducive to such meaningful interaction. If you would like to be notified of future conferences and other training events, please contact the Institute.

TABLE OF CONTENTS

Conceptual Frameworks

Issues In Treatment

Tools for Facilitating Treatment

Therapy with Specific Populations

Special Applications

Invited Address

INTRODUCTION

This book presents the proceedings of the First Annual San Diego Conference on Hypnotic and Strategic Interventions held February 8-10, 1985. Organized by Michael D. Yapko, Ph.D., Director of the Milton H. Erickson Institute of San Diego, this meeting offered attendees a chance to experience the work of some top practitioners of Ericksonian therapy—mostly from Southern California. The Conference consisted of both workshops and papers. By making the papers available in book form, the impact of the meeting is extended and practitioners can avail themselves of some of the important advances presented in San Diego.

Theoretical and clinical findings are presented. Those looking for new conceptual understandings will be pleased. For example, Ernest Rossi's important chapter presents a scale to standardize Erickson's approaches so that research of his methods can be facilitated. Also, key concepts of Erickson's methods are developed by J. Adrian Williams, Michal Samko and Christopher Beletsis. A methodological overview is presented by John Koriath.

Clinical issues include diagnosis, supervision, treatment techniques, comparisons to other methods, and hypnosis in school settings and with families. Authors are Beverlee Hockenstein, Neil Simon, Waleed Salameh, Neil Ribner, Timothy Wolf, Mark Reese, Fritz Klein & Sally Cutler-Huntington, and Diane Yapko. Michael Yapko, the editor of this book, presents valuable new ideas for using strategic hypnotherapy with depressive patients.

Contained herein is a growing edge of Ericksonian therapy which itself is a growing edge of the entire field of psychotherapy. In great numbers, practitioners are attending training programs and delving into the literature to learn about the effective, often baffling, approaches of Milton H. Erickson, M.D.

There are a number of important events in the evolution of Ericksonian therapy. Certainly, many of us came to know Erickson through the seminal work of Jay Haley, the architect of the interpersonal/strategic approach. Subsequently, Rossi presented Erickson through the lens of his intrapsychic orientation. Others followed and views about Erickson proliferated.

In 1979, the Milton H. Erickson Foundation was formed to administer the December, 1980 International Congress on Ericksonian Approaches to Hypnosis and Psychotherapy. The original Board of Directors of the Foundation was: Milton H. Erickson, M.D., Elizabeth Erickson, Sherron S. Peters and myself, Jeffrey K. Zeig. When Dr. Erickson died, Kristina K. Erickson, M.D., Erickson's youngest daughter, took his place on the Board of Directors.

The Foundation has developed a number of functions including Congresses, training programs, and its archives of audio- and videotapes of Dr. Erickson. Recently the Foundation organized a landmark training event, The Evolution of Psychotherapy Conference which featured 26 master practitioners from diverse schools within the field of psychotherapy.

Also, the Foundation certifies institutes to use the Erickson name. Yapko's institute, the Milton H. Erickson Institute of San Diego, applied to the Erickson Foundation. It is one of 25 existent institutes. Of the institutes, 10 are located outside of the United States. There is one in Canada, one in Italy, two in France, two in Australia, two in Germany, one in England and one in Argentina. The institutes are an important extension of the Foundation and foster its purpose of promoting and advancing the important contributions of Milton H. Erickson, M.D.

The Milton H. Erickson Institute of San Diego provides clinical services and training in the local community. It also organizes the annual San Diego Conferences on Hypnotic and Strategic Interventions. It is the first institute to hold such an annual meeting. These efforts are of great value in adding positive impetus to the young field of Ericksonian psychotherapy.

The work of Yapko and his contributors will be appreciated by serious students of Ericksonian therapy. We look forward with great anticipation to their future contributions.

It was a pleasure to present the keynote address for the 1985 Conference. It is an equal pleasure to introduce this valuable book.

> Jeffrey K. Zeig, Ph.D., Director
> Milton H. Erickson Foundation
> May, 1986

AUTHORS' BIOGRAPHIES

(in alphabetical order)

CHRISTOPHER BELETSIS, PH.D.   LA JOLLA, CALIFORNIA

Chris has been conducting training programs on Erickson's approaches to hypnosis and therapy for the past six years. He presented a paper on his work entitled "An Ericksonian Approach in the Treatment of Alcoholism" at the *Second International Congress on Ericksonian Approaches to Hypnosis and Psychotherapy* in Phoenix in December, 1983. Chris is well known and respected for his outstanding ability to teach Ericksonian theory and practice in a comprehensive, exciting, humorous, and caring fashion.

PAUL M. CARTER, PH.D.   ENCINITAS, CALIFORNIA

Paul Carter received his doctorate in psychology from International College and trained extensively with Milton H. Erickson, M.D. His studies also included work with Virginia Satir and Gregory Bateson, integrating a variety of fields into his research of psychotherapy and communication.

Dr. Carter is internationally known for conducting outstanding training seminars on the psychotherapeutic techniques of the late Dr. Erickson. In addition, he was among the most well-received presenters at the First International Congress on Ericksonian Hypnosis and Psychotherapy in Phoenix in 1980 and at the Erickson Congress in San Francisco in 1981.

Paul is in the process of completing his book, *THE PARTS MODEL: A FORMULA FOR INTEGRITY*, containing an explication and expansion of the reframing model and presenting specific applications of Erickson's work in transforming clinical symptoms into therapeutic resources.

In addition to his teaching activities, Dr. Carter maintains a private practice in San Diego.

BEVERLEE HOCKENSTEIN, PH.D. LA JOLLA, CALIFORNIA
Beverlee works privately in San Diego emphasizing Ericksonian hypnosis and N.L.P. techniques in her practice. She is a certified trainer and consultant in the field of business management for Process Communication Management. Beverlee teaches classes on communication, relationships, stress management and self-esteem.

SALLY CUTLER-HUNTINGTON, M.A. SAN DIEGO, CALIFORNIA
Sally received her M.A. in marriage and family therapy from United States International University in 1981 and is licensed as a Marriage Family and Child Therapist. She is on the staff of the Clinical Institutes in San Diego, the staff of the Institute for Sexual Behavior, the therapy staff of UCSD Gender Identity Program, and is in private practice.

FRITZ (FRED) KLEIN, M.D. SAN DIEGO, CALIFORNIA
Fritz is on the Board of Certified Psychiatrists and has a private practice in San Diego. He is also director of the Institute of Sexual Behavior, Inc. Fritz uses Ericksonian hypnosis, N.L.P., and specializes in short term therapies. He has written several books on sexual orientation, including the **Bisexual Option**.

JOHN JAY KORIATH, PH.D. PHOENIX, ARIZONA
John is currently involved in psychophysiological research at Arizona State University. His perspectives represent a blending of an undergraduate degree in philosophy, clinical experience with biofeedback, and other self-management techniques for treating the psychological aspects of serious illness (especially cancer). He is especially interested in the application of research methods in describing the multiple levels of human experience.

MARK REESE, M.A., PH.D. Candidate ENCINITAS, CALIFORNIA
Mark is a Feldenkrais Practitioner and leader of professional training programs in the Feldenkrais Method. His paper on parallels between the work of Feldenkrais and Erickson, presented at the *Second International Congress on Ericksonian Hypnosis and Psychotherapy,* is included in the published Congress proceedings.

NEIL G. RIBNER, PH.D. LA JOLLA, CALIFORNIA
Neil is a Clinical Psychologist in private practice in La Jolla. He is also on the faculties of the California School of Professional Psychology

and National University. His professional interests include the nature and treatment of depression and the functional nature of symptoms within a system. He specializes in working with depressives and also with families and stepfamilies.

ERNEST L. ROSSI, PH.D.   LOS ANGELES, CALIFORNIA

Ernie is a Clinical Psychologist practicing in the Los Angeles area. He is on the faculty of the C.G. Jung Institute in Southern California and is a member of the Editorial Boards of **The American Journal of Clinical Hypnosis, Psychological Perspectives,** and **Ericksonian Monographs.** He co-authored three volumes with Milton H. Erickson: **Hypnotic Realities** (1976), **Hypnotherapy: An Exploratory Casebook** (1979), and **Experiencing Hypnosis: Therapeutic Approaches to Altered States** (New York: Irvington Publishers); and edited **The Collected Papers of Milton H. Erickson on Hypnosis** (4 volumes, 1980, New York: Irvington Publishers). He is currently co-editing 4 to 5 volumes of Erickson's lectures given during the 1950's and 1960's. In addition to his work with Erickson, Ernie has written extensively in the areas of dreams, consciousness, and altered states. In 1974 he authored his first volume entitled, **Dreams and the Growth of Personality: Expanding Awareness in Psychotherapy.** Recently he has been investigating possible neurophysiological factors involved in hypnosis, altered states, and psychotherapeutic change and healing.

WALEED A. SALAMEH, PH.D.   SAN DIEGO, CALIFORNIA

Waleed is a licensed Clinical Psychologist and consultant in private practice in San Diego. Waleed's practice focuses on using his psychotherapeutic approach, and Integractive Short Term Therapy (I.S.T.T.), in working with individuals, couples, families, and groups, as well as conducting clinical and Humor Immersion Training experiences. He has published extensively in the area of psychotherapy and is a recognized authority on the strategic uses of humor in psychotherapy. Waleed is co-author of the forthcoming **Handbook of Humor and Therapy.**

MICHAEL R. SAMKO, PH.D.   DEL MAR, CALIFORNIA

Michael is a licensed Clinical Psychologist in private practice in Del Mar and Carlsbad. Much of his therapeutic work involves the utilization of hypnosis and strategic interventions. Michael's work in the area of hypnosis has been published and he has lectured on hypnosis in various countries including the Peoples Republic of China, Yugoslavia, and Mexico. Michael studied under Milton Erickson over a period of four years.

NEIL SIMON, M.A.   YPSILANTI, MICHIGAN

Neil is actively involved in professional training, clinical practice and consulting. Currently, Neil is developing specialized brief intervention programs for health care organizations and local industries, teaching strategic patterns of intervention to professionals. Neil has authored several training manuals in the field of clinical hypnosis.

J. ADRIAN WILLIAMS, PH.D.   CHARLESTON, ILLINOIS

Adrian is a Clinical Psychologist and founder and director of Psychotherapeutic Systems Institute in Charleston. He is noted for his creative applications of hypnosis in the fields of psychotherapy and pain control. Adrian has written a number of professional articles on Erickson's work, and is a frequent lecturer on Ericksonian approaches to hypnosis and psychotherapy.

TIMOTHY J. WOLF, PH.D.   SAN DIEGO, CALIFORNIA

Tim is a Marriage, Family and Child Therapist in private practice. He is also director of counseling at Blessed Sacrament Elementary School and a consultant for the San Diego Unified School District. Concerned with the welfare of children, Tim is also involved in the evaluation and treatment of sexually abused children at the Institute of Sexual Behavior in San Diego.

DIANE YAPKO, M.A.   SAN DIEGO, CALIFORNIA

Diane is on the Board of Directors of *The Milton H. Erickson Institute of San Diego* and functions as the speech-language consultant for the Institute. She works as a Speech-Language Pathologist at the UCSD Medical Center's Communicative Disorders Center where she specializes in speech and language disorders of young children. Diane obtained her B.A. and M.A. degrees in Speech Pathology and Audiology from San Diego State University.

MICHAEL D. YAPKO, PH.D.   SAN DIEGO, CALIFORNIA

Michael is director of *The Milton H. Erickson Institute of San Diego*. He is a recognized expert on patterns of clinical hypnosis, having authored numerous articles on the subject, as well as the textbook **Trancework: An Introduction to Clinical Hypnosis** (1984, Irvington Publishers). Michael is a founding member of the Editoral Board of the **Ericksonian Monographs,** and has been a presenter at national and international meetings sponsored by The Milton H. Erickson Foundation and the American Society of Clinical Hypnosis. In additon to his private clinical practice, Michael is on the faculties of National University and United States International University in San Diego.

JEFFREY K. ZEIG, PH.D.   **PHOENIX, ARIZONA**
Jeff is a Clinical Psychologist engaged in private practice and consulting. He spent over six years studyng with Dr. Erickson, and now conducts workshops on Ericksonian techniques in North America, South America, Europe and Australia. Jeff edited and wrote commmentary for **A Teaching Seminar with Milton H. Erickson** and edited **Ericksonian Approaches to Hypnosis and Psychotherapy,** and **Ericksonian Psychotherapy (Volumes I & II),** four distinguished landmark volumes in the field. Jeff has organized the two international congresses on Ericksonian approaches, and serves as a member of the Editoral Boards of the **American Journal of Clinical Hypnosis** and **The Ericksonian Monographs.** Jeff is the founding president of the Phoenix Society of Clinical Hypnosis, and is adjunct assistant professor of clinical psychology at Arizona State University. Jeff is director of the Milton H. Erickson Foundation, Inc. in Phoenix.

The Indirect Trance Assessment Scale (ITAS): A Preliminary Outline And Learning Tool

by
Ernest L. Rossi, Ph.D.

Introduction: Erickson and Hull in Hypnosis Research

The history of hypnosis research during the past fifty years, beginning with the pioneering efforts of Milton H. Erickson (1980c) and Clark Hull (1933), is a record of concerted efforts to assess and validate the characteristics and parameters of hypnotic phenomena. This research has taken two classical forms: (1) The laboratory experiment with carefully designed controls and a standardized methodology that permits replication by other investigators; and (2) the so-called "field experiment" wherein an investigator took advantage of naturally occurring situations to make some interesting observations and infer something new about the phenomena under study. The precision of statistically verifiable hypothesis testing is the scientific virtue of the laboratory approach, while the generation of unique insights and new hypotheses is the virtue of the field experiment. When Hull and Erickson parted company more than fifty years ago (Erickson, 1980a, p. 3), they and their followers took the two classical but divergent paths. Hull inspired the academic experimental approach that led to the work of modern laboratory workers (Fromm & Shor, 1972; Sheehan & Perry, 1976). When Erickson, after an extensive initial period of laboratory studies in the 1930s and 1940s began to demonstrate and teach hypnosis to clinicians, the field experiment became more important to him. During the latter half of the 1950s, the 1960s, and the 1970s, his demonstrations and teaching via the "field experiment" became his dominant mode of investigation and therapy (Erickson, 1980b). Neisser's work (1982) on memory is an excellent illustration of how the laboratory and field experiments can be integrated. Furthermore, The Indirect Trance Assessment Scale (ITAS) is being developed to facilitate this ideal of combining the laboratory and field approaches. The ITAS is described in this paper.

Indirect Approaches and the ITAS

One reason Erickson developed and used indirect approaches was to avoid the problems of simulation and "cooperative complaisance" wherein subjects either faked hypnotic effects in order to deceive the operator, or consciously strove too hard to please him. Both alternatives were a trap for the investigator who sought to explore the nature of unconscious processes in hypnosis without the intervention of conscious intentionality.

Erickson's *Collected Papers* (1980d) (particularly the first and fourth volumes) are a record of his ingenious field experiments using indirect forms of suggestion. So ingenious were the hypnotic effects that he reported, however, that there are those who imply that he was more of a showman interested in drama than a respectable scientist interested in verifiable replication. Thus Hilgard (1984) wrote in a recent review of Erickson's *Collected Papers*:

> Erickson often wrote as a sage or a dramatist rather than as a scientist. Whatever one feels about him, it must be acknowledged that he was a healer, and that—after careful winnowing—there is much to be learned from his writings. (p. 263)

The preliminary outline of the Indirect Trance Assessment Scale (ITAS), as presented here for the first time, represents a twelve-year effort by the author to do a bit of this "winnowing" of Erickson's voluminous writings in order to make some of his most ingenious discoveries and approaches available to both researchers and clinicians—novices and experienced alike.

This scale has not yet been standardized with the normative data and all the statistical "bells and whistles" that are required before it can become a proper scientific instrument. Its current form is simply a first-stage effort to sort out which of Erickson's indirect approaches could be used in comparison and contrast to the direct induction and suggestion scales that have been the standard of all academic and experimental research to date. The values and limitations of these scales of direct suggestion are well known (Gruenwald, 1982; Hilgard, 1982; Weitzenhoffer, 1980) and cannot be detailed here. It is sufficient to note that many investigators acknowledge that something new is needed (Frankel, 1982; Sacerdote, 1982). This first-stage outline of the ITAS is presented here to help and encourage these investigators to take up the necessary work of developing it further.

The ITAS as a Learning Tool

The basic problem in researching Erickson's indirect approaches is that well-developed skills in observation and communication are required to use them effectively. To facilitate the development of these skills, the current form of ITAS can be used as a guide to the most relevant Ericksonian literature in these areas. Most of the 15 items (hypnotic phenomena) of ITAS have references to the key papers wherein Erickson described the clinical nuances of "how to do" them. Very little theory is involved—the development of special clinical skills is the primary requirement for learning to administer and evaluate the ITAS. In its current form the ITAS can thus be used as a learning tool to focus on the acquisition of Ericksonian approaches to the classical hypnotic phenomena as well as hypnotherapy. The author is using it in this way at this time.

The ITAS in Hypnotic Demonstrations: Its Use and Limitations

The author has also found that the ITAS is particularly useful in professional demonstrations wherein the nature of hypnotic phenomena is being explored with volunteer subjects from the audience. For example, at The Second International Congress on Ericksonian Approaches to Hypnosis and Psychotherapy in Phoenix, 1983, the ITAS approach was used to demonstrate with varying degress of success (Rossi, 1983), ideomotor signaling, catalepsy, contractures, literalism, the watch hallucination, stopped vision, and the Picture Hanging Experiment.* The demonstration of the Picture Hanging Experiment (Erickson, 1980h) was of special

*A video tape of this demonstration is available from The Milton H. Erickson Foundation, 3606 North 24th Street, Phoenix, Arizona, 85016.

interest because it was the first publicly recorded documentation of this rare hypnotic phenomenon since Erickson first developed it more than a generation ago. It was fascinating to note that the subject's responses in this case were of the same class as described by Erickson yet differed in their particular manifestations from anything he had reported.

A more recent effort using the ITAS for demonstrations with professionals in a hypnosis workshop in Rome, Italy (1984), however, illustrated its limitations. In this situation a young psychologist who was apparently in a somnambulistic state by all other criteria took an unusually long time to give a response to the Picture Hanging Experiment. When he finally gave his response it was of an apparently conventional, reality-oriented type that would not be scored as a positive example of the Picture Hanging Hypnotic Response. After the demonstration the psychologist admitted that his initial hypnotic response was one characteristic of a somnambulistic subject. He was aware of the "right response" from his reading of the Italian translation of the *Collected Papers*, however, and did not want to give such "obviously correct responses," so he took his time and figured out a good, reality-oriented response. He apologized for "ruining the demonstration." Apologies were not necessary. He had demonstrated the more important truth that even in somnambulistic states, people retain their personality and pride in choice and free will. Nonetheless, this was also an illustration of the fact that ITAS can be faked if the subject has prior knowledge about it.

The best of the clinical and research traditions will be required to further develop the ITAS. Once the ITAS is standardized, however, many basic issues about altered states, healing, and the nature of consciousness and personality will be open to more informative, systematic, and ingenious study.

References for Introduction

Erickson, M. (1980a). Initial experiments investigating the nature of hypnosis. In E. Rossi (Ed.), *The collected papers of Milton H. Erickson on hypnosis: Vol. 1. The nature of hypnosis and suggestion.* (3–17). New York: Irvington.

Erickson, M. (1980b). Further experimental investigation of hypnotic and nonhypnotic realities. In E. Rossi, (Ed.), *The collected papers of Milton H. Erickson on hypnosis: Vol. 1. The nature of hypnosis and suggestion.* (pp. 18–82). New York: Irvington.

Erickson, M. (1980c). *Innovative hypnotherapy: Vol. 4. The collected papers of Milton H. Erickson on hypnosis.* Edited by E. Rossi. New York: Irvington.

Erickson, M. (1980d). Possible detrimental effects of experimental hypnosis. In E. Rossi (Ed.), *The collected papers of Milton H. Erickson on hypnosis: Vol. 1. The nature of hypnosis and suggestion (493–497). New York: Irvington.*

Erickson, M. (1980e). The collected papers of Milton H. Erickson on hypnosis: 4 volumes. Edited by E. Rossi. New York: Irvington.

Frankel, F. (1982) Hypnosis and hypnotizability scales: A reply. The International Journal of Clinical & Experimental Hypnosis, 30(4), 377–392.

Fromm, E., & Shor, R. (Eds.) (1972). *Hypnosis: Research developments and perspectives.* Chicago: Aldine.

Gruenewald, D. (1982). Problems of relevance in the application of laboratory data to clinical situations. *The International Journal of Clinical & Experimental Hypnosis, 30*(4), 345–353.

Hilgard, E. (1982). Hypnotic susceptibility and implications for measurement. *The International Journal of Clinical & Experimental Hypnosis, 30*(4), 394–403.

Hilgard, E. (1984). *The collected papers of Milton H. Erickson: A review. The International Journal of Clinical & Experimental Hypnosis, 32*(2), 257–265.

Hull, C. (1933). *Hypnosis and suggestibility.* New York: Appleton-Century.

Neisser, U. (1982). *Memory observed.* San Francisco: Freeman & Co.

Rossi, E. (1983). Demonstration given at The Second International Congress on Ericksonian Approaches to Hypnosis and Psychotherapy. Phoenix, Arizona.

Sacerdote, P. (1982). Further reflections on the hypnotizability scales: A comment. *The International Journal of Clinical & Experimental Hypnosis, 30*(4), 393.

Sheehan, P., & Perry, C. (1976). *Methodologies of hypnosis.* New Jersey: Erlbaum Associates.

Weitzenhoffer, A. (1980) Hypnotic susceptibility revisited. *The American Journal of Clinical Hypnosis, 22*(3), 130–146.

The Indirect Trance Assessment Scale (ITAS)

By
Ernest L. Rossi, Ph.D.

General Rationale

1. Most altered states and hypnotic phenomena were originally discovered as natural and spontaneous manifestations of unusual behavior. Once discovered, investigators then tried to evoke the altered state or "suggest" the hypnotic phenomenon artificially.

2. The problem with directly suggesting any altered state or hypnotic phenomenon is that subjects may simulate the desired response; the investigator may have no way of determining whether a hypnotic phenomenon was genuine or faked.

3. THE INDIRECT TRANCE ASSESSMENT SCALE (ITAS) is an effort to avoid the problem of simulating hypnotic phenomena or any behavioral manifestation of an altered state of consciousness. Responses are assessed indirectly so that the average uninformed subject does not know what to simulate.

4. This project is essentially a continuation of Milton Erickson's pioneering efforts to differentiate between hypnotic and nonhypnotic realities, particularly those described in his paper, "Further Experimental Investigation Of Hypnotic And Nonhypnotic Realities" (Erickson, 1980h).

General Administration Procedures
Rationale for Indirect Suggestion

1. Indirect suggestion is a means of assessing and facilitating a subject's behavior and potentials in a manner that is as unobtrusive as possible.

Ideally the subject does not have any conscious awareness that his behavior is being assessed or facilitated. In this way the traditional problem of faking behavior, whatever the motivation, can be minimized if not entirely eliminated.

2. Indirect suggestion is most effective when it utilizes the subject's own beliefs, motivations, and behavior. The subject wants to have his needs and goals facilitated, not those of the operator.

3. Any goals the operator may have (such as using this scale) can only be fulfilled secondarily and incidentally to the subject's goals.

Practical Administration Procedure

1. This scale consists of a series of non-directive questions and approaches to assess the degree to which a subject is experiencing hypnotic realities, altered states, or departures from normal, everyday reality orientation.

2. The ideal administration is to casually weave the scale questions into the fabric of an apparently ordinary conversation or interview situation. It is especially appropriate to use this scale in medical or psychological examinations and during therapeutic encounters.

3. The questions can be asked in any order with any variation in wording that is appropriate to the situation.

4. The administration should be so unobtrusive that subjects do not consciously realize their current reality orientation is being assessed.

General Scoring Principles

1. Scoring of the scale is simply the sum total of the number of different categories of "hypnotic responses" obtained. For example, if literalism and catalepsy were present at any time during the assessment period, the score would be "two."

2. There are fifteen items in the full scale but only fourteen are scoreable. Thus the highest possible score for the full scale is fourteen.

3. Each category of hypnotic response may be assessed as often as desired during the assessment period.

4. Momentary variations in trance depth and responsiveness are characteristic of hypnosis so that continuous evaluation is necessary throughout the assessment period.

5. Ideally there should be a qualitative evaluation of the assessment written independently by the operator and the subject (in those cases in which the subject was later made aware of the fact that an assessment was made).

Therapeutic "Trance" Induction

1. There is no formal or set pattern for hypnotic induction with this scale.
2. The first two items of the scale (ideomotor signaling and catalepsy), however, introduce special approaches to focusing attention and facilitating creative problem solving that set the tone for the entire scale.
3. Whether this special problem solving approach is described as functioning via any or all of the following descriptive phrases is immaterial, since current research efforts cannot distinguish between them:
a) therapeutic trance work
b) hypnosis
c) altered states
d) deep reflection
e) focusing
f) sensitivity training
g) active imagination
h) guided inner work
i) utilizing the creative unconscious
j) etc.
4. In using this scale it is best to use whichever of the above descriptions best fits the subject or patient's needs and frames of reference.

1. Ideomotor Signaling
Rationale for Ideomotor Signaling

1. Ideomotor signaling has been known since ancient times as an approach to trance and the "truth". Erickson (1980i) recounted how he rediscovered it in his early student days as a method of hypnotic induction.
2. Erickson's approach was indirect in that he suggested ideomotor signaling by implication and usually in the form of "a double or triple bind" (Erickson, 1980c).
3. Erickson always utilized a subject's own vocabulary, interests, motivations and expectancies to introduce the topic of ideomotor signaling and to facilitate an experience of learning it.

Assessing Ideomotor Signaling

Begin with an exploration to determine the subject's interests and motivations for accessing his "creative unconscious."
When the subject admits that his conscious mind is "stuck" and does not know the answer to some absorbing issue, proceed as follows:

1. "Sometimes when we listen to a person we may be *nodding or shaking the head not knowing it* in either agreement or disagreement. *It would be just as easy to do it with the finger or the hand.* Now I would like to ask your unconscious mind a question that can be answered with a simple yes or no. It's a question that *only your unconscious mind can answer.* Neither your conscious mind nor my conscious mind, nor, for that matter, even my unconscious mind knows the answers. *Only your unconscious mind knows* which *answer can be communicated,* and it *will have to think either a yes or no answer. It could be by a nod or shake of the head, a lifting of the index finger . . . or the right hand could lift or the left hand could lift. But only your unconscious mind knows* what the answer will be when I ask for that yes or no answer."

2. "And not even your unconscious mind will know, when the question is asked, whether *it will answer with a head movement, or a finger movement,* and *your unconscious mind will have to think through that question* and *to decide, after it has formulated its own answer, just how it will answer."* (Erickson, 1980c p 303)

3. "In other words I will ask a question to which *only your unconscious mind can give the answer,* and concerning which your conscious mind can only guess if it does at all; maybe correctly, maybe wrongly, or maybe have only some kind of an opinion, but, if so, only an opinion, *not an answer."* (Erickson, 1980c, p. 304)

4. "My question is (said slowly, intently, gravely), 'Does your unconscious mind *think* it will raise your hand or your finger or move your head?' "

5. "Just wait patiently, wonderingly, and let the answer happen." (Erickson, 1980c, p. 307)

Scoring Ideomotor Signaling

1. Erickson (1980c, p. 305) described the perseveration criteria for a genuine ideomotor signaling response as follows:

a) ". . . One never tells the patient that an unconscious reply is almost always characterized by a strong element of perseveration. Apparently an altered time sense in hypnotic subjects, possibly deriving from their altered reality relationships, prevents even experienced subjects from appreciating this point, and it constitutes an excellent criterion of the character of the response. This perseveration of ideomotor activity, however, is much briefer in duration if the unconscious mind wishes the conscious mind to know; the time lag and dissociated character are greatly reduced, although the unconscious answer may be considerably delayed as the unconscious mind goes through the process of formulating its reply and the decision to share or not to share."

b) Score ideomotor signaling "positive" only if the movement lasts ten seconds or more with no further reinforcing suggestions.

2. Catalepsy
Rationale for Catalepsy

1. Erickson developed many methods of facilitating and assessing catalepsy as a criterion of trance. He described it as a form of balanced muscle tonicity such that "In this trance state the subject's arm may be lifted and it will remain fixed in any position. The subject appears to be unable to move the arm, nor does he seem to experience any fatigue." (Erickson, 1980a, p. 9)

2. "Catalepsy is a general phenomenon that can be used as:
- a testing procedure for assessing hypnotic susceptibility.
- an induction procedure.
- an index for the continuation of the hypnotic state.
- a reinduction procedure.
- a trance deepening procedure.

3. Absolutely requisite for the successful facilitation and utilization of catalepsy are:
- a willingness of the subject to be approached.
- an appropriate situation.
- suitableness of the situation for the continuation of the experience. (Erickson and Rossi, 1981, p. 47)

Procedures for Assessing Catalepsy
Catalepsy #1: Sensitivity Assessment

1. The assessment of catalepsy can be described as a form of sensitivity test or training with the following verbalizations:
"May I evaluate your arm's sensitivity by guiding it up as lightly and gently as possible?"
The operator guides the arm up (as described in Erickson and Rossi, 1981, p. 33–62).

2. Supportive remarks can be given such as the following:
"Is it possible for that arm to respond to the most subtle, guiding touch?"
"How comfortably can it remain there?"
"And I'm not telling you to put it down."
"And you don't have to move it, do you?"

Catalepsy #2: Therapy Facilitation

1. Catalepsy can be assessed as part of a therapeutic process as follows:
"We know there is an important relationship between the muscle tonus

of the body and your general degree of alertness. The reticular activating system at the base of your brain converts muscle sensations and stimuli into signals that activate your higher cortical centers and increase your alertness."

"We can use this relationship to help you focus your mental energy on that question (problem) that you are interested in answering (resolving).

"Will it be all right for me to very lightly and gently guide your arm up to increase your muscle tonus and thereby demonstrate how you can intensify your mental focus to get an answer to that question?"

2. Proceed with the induction of catalepsy as described in Catalepsy #1.

Catalepsy #3: Handshake Induction
Rationale of the Handshake Induction

1. The handshake induction of catalepsy has the advantage of surprise and confusion as factors facilitating trance induction.

2. The entire procedure for the handshake induction together with a variety of its uses has been described elsewhere (Erickson and Rossi, 1981, p 49–51).

Procedure of the Handshake Induction

Erickson described his approach to the handshake induction as follows (Erickson & Rossi, 1981):

"When I begin by shaking hands, I do so normally. The 'hypnotic touch' then begins when I let loose. The letting loose becomes transformed from a firm grip into a gentle touch by the thumb, a lingering drawing away of the little finger, a faint brushing of the subject's hand with the middle finger—just enough vague sensation to attract the attention. As the subject gives attention to the touch of your thumb, you shift to a touch of your little finger. As your subject's attention follows that, you shift to a touch with your middle finger and then again to the thumb . . .

"the subject's withdrawal from the handshake is arrested by this attention arousal, which establishes a waiting set, an expectancy. . . .

"if you don't want your subjects to know what you are doing, you simply distract their attention, usually by some appropriate remark, and casually terminate." (p. 49)

Scoring Catalepsy

1. All three of the above approaches to catalepsy may be scored by the same criteria.

2. A positive score has three criteria:
a) The arm moves easily to the operator's guiding touch and movements;
b) The arm and hand remain fixed in any position they are left in;
c) The arm remains fixed for at least ten seconds while the operator goes on to other apparently unrelated things.

3. Literalism
Rationale for Literalism

1. The usual answer to questions in this category from subjects in the normal awake state is a response to the implication of the question. Thus if we ask people, "Do you mind telling me your name?", the awake subject will respond with his actual name. The subject experiencing literalism, however, will respond with "Yes" or "No."
2. The trance subject almost invariably responds with "a simple affirmative reply without any movement to acquiesce to the behavioral implications of the inquiry. This was particularly true with somnambulistic subjects, somewhat less so with medium subjects, and slighly less so with subjects in the light trance. On rare occasions the reply would be complete inaction, explained upon request by the statement that they were comfortable as they were or that there was no need to do so. On the other hand, the waking subject would explain a negative response with the challenging, 'Why should I?' or 'I don't want to,' or 'It doesn't make sense to do that.' " (Erickson, 1980k, p. 92)

Questions Assessing Literalism

1. "*Do you mind* telling me your name?"
2. "*Do you mind* doing it now?"
3. "*Do you mind* standing up?"
4. "*Do you mind* taking a step forward?"
5. "*Do you mind* sitting in the other chair?"
6. "*Are you willing* to tell me where you are?" (Answer examples indicating literalism: *Yes. Here. I don't know. A little in front of you. With you.* In general all responses are related to the operator but not the surrounding environment. Deeply somnambulistic subjects behave as if nothing exists apart from their relation to the operator.)
7. "*Are you willing* to tell me what you are doing here?" (*Yes. Sitting. Talking to you.* In general any response literally descriptive of the subject's actual concrete behavior or the relation to the operator is scored positively.)

9. *"Say something."* (*"Something,"* would be the literal response).

Scoring Literalism

1. Any literal response of "yes" or "no" without any further effort to give a fuller cognitive elaboration (telling one's name, for example) is scored as a positive manifestation of literalism. The yes or no response may be verbal or nonverbal (e.g., head nodding or shaking).

2. Take care to score as positive other literal responses regarding the subject's actual concrete behavior or his relation to the operator as noted above.

Contractures

Rationale for Contractures

1. A contracture is an unusual rigidification of any part or the entire body.

2. It is of great significance because it is very rare in modern work though it was mentioned more often in the past.

3. The author noticed it only once in a stage demonstration when the subject also manifested positive responses to visual hallucinations and the Picture Hanging Experiment. This subject appeared frightened and complained that she feared being hurt. Great caution should be excercised, then, should such contractures appear.

4. It is most unfortunate that stage hypnotists persist in using a full body contracture to position a subject between chairs and then sit on the subject. Erickson (1980d) reported how serious spinal damage can result from such unethical procedures.

Assessing Contractures

1. When a subject's arm remains in a perfect cataleptic position for two minutes or more, contractures may be assessed by taking hold of the subject's wrist and applying a force as if to move it very gently.

2. A contracture is present if the wrist, fingers, and arm feel stiff and do not bend. A total body contracture is present if by very carefully persisting in applying force to the arm it is found that the whole body remains stiff so that it will actually rock back and forth like a pendulum. The operator should position himself carefully in order to catch the subject should he be pushed off balance entirely.

3. It is sometimes found that when the operator has an assistant (who

is out of rapport with the subject) try to move the subject's cataleptic arm, the arm will rigidify into a contracture. Erickson usually had his assistant quietly enter the situation after the subject had developed somnambulism.

Scoring Contractures

1. A positive score is given only for the spontaneous appearance of a contracture when assessed as described above.

2. When contractures have been verbally suggested by the use of words like "rigid," "fixed," "immobile," and "you can't move it," no positive score can be given. The subject could be simulating or trying to cooperate consciously.

3. It is possible to suggest a contracture nonverbally by holding a subject's arm firmly and stroking it. Contractures can also be suggested if the operator visibly stiffens his own body as if modeling nonverbally for the subject. Such maneuvers are not scored as a spontaneous contracture in this scale.

5. Startle Reflex Loss

Rationale for Startle Reflex Loss

1. Erickson has used a lack of a startle response as an indicator of trance development (Erickson, Rossi and Rossi, 1976, p. 306). Apparently the normal response to disruptive stimuli is dissociated during the intense focus of trance.

Assessing Loss of Startle Reflex

1. Erickson would arrange little "accidents" such as the falling of a book or paperweight from a desk to assess the loss of the startle reflex.

2. The loss of the startle reflex is assessed by knocking over an average size book from a table so that it falls between three and four feet in front of or toward the side of the subject. This should NOT be done in back of the subject.

3. The book should be perched near the edge of the table in full sight before the subject enters the assessment situation so that the subject's unconscious has had an opportunity to record it, and, if necessary, correctly interpret the essentially innocuous nature of the situation.

Scoring Loss of Startle Reflex

1. A lack of a startle reflex to any sudden little "accident" as described above is scored as positive.

6. Anesthesia-Analgesia
Rationale for Anesthesia-Analgesia

1. A spontaneous anesthesia for all or most body sensation often exists in somnambulistic subjects. Erickson has attributed this to the "dissociated" character of their state (1980g, p. 320).

Assessing Anesthesia-Analgesia

1. Erickson often assessed anesthesia indirectly by having an accomplice pinch or yank a subject's hair while standing outside the subject's line of sight (1980I, p. 343)

Scoring Anesthesia-Analgesia

1. Any lack of normal responsiveness to the accomplice's pinch or hair yank is scored as positive for anesthesia-analgesia.
2. Another typically valid response occurs when the subject responds to the accomplice's stimulus as if it were an irritatating fly or some other adversive stimulus. If, under these circumstances, the subject responds to the operator's question, *"What are you doing?"*, with a rationalization such as, "Damned fly," one could also score a point for a hallucinatory response.

7. Age Regression
Rationale for Age Regression

1. Methods of direct suggestion for age regression are especially vulnerable to simulation wherein the subject tries to consciously help the suggestion. This, of course, confounds conscious and unconscious processes so that the resulting age regression is of an uncertain sort. During his student days Erickson (1980h) accidentally found that the appropriate use of a childhood word in the right context of expectation could by itself evoke a more genuine age regression free from conscious intentionality and adult associations.

Questions Assessing Age Regression

Age regression can be induced via implication by intently looking at a spot on the floor within the subject's line of sight and saying one of the following slowly and deliberately as seems appropriate:

"Do you like that little doggie (kitty)?"

"Which one of those little doggies (kitties) do you like? I like the brown one with white spots."

3. *"Oh, there is that mother dog; she has got two puppies! (pause) I think I like the black and white one best. Which one do you like best?"* (Erickson, 1980m, p. 144)

Age regression can then be verified by asking non directive questions such as:

"Where are we?"

"What are you going to do today?"

"How old will you be next year?"

Scoring Age Regression

1. Any response indicating that the subject is experiencing an earlier age level via two criteria is scored as positive:

a) Verbal behavior (vocabulary and appropriate associations) characteristic of a younger age level;

b) Nonverbal behavior and manner characteristic of a younger age level.

2. Both of the above must be present for a positive score indicating a genuine age revivification experience rather than a mere reliance on memories of past behavior.

8. Visual Hallucinations—Negative

Rationale for MHE's Stopped Vision

1. While Erickson used many approaches to negative hallucinations, the phenomenon he discovered and named "stopped vision" will be used in this scale because it seems to hold the most promise as a paradigm for further research.

2. "Stopped vision" is a kind of negative visual hallucination in which subjects "have given the remarkable reply signifying that there had occurred for them, from a trance induction resulting in somnambulism with the eyes open, *definite linear limitations of vision.*" (Erickson, 1980h, p. 31)

Assessing Stopped Vision: MHE Method

Erickson (1980h, p. 31) described his method of assessing stopped vision as follows.

1. "In using these naive subjects to demonstrate negative visual hallucinations, the author has asked such subjects, gesturing toward the audience, *'What do you see there?'*
In reply he would be given the answer, 'Your hand.' I mean back part of your hand.' 'Oh, part of the ring on your finger in back of your hand.' "When Erickson asked, *"I mean further back?"*, The reply might be, "Nothing."
2. "Suggestion would be offered to them that they see the speaker's platform on which they sat, and they would be asked what they saw beyond that. In several hundred such instances the answer was they saw nothing, that they 'stopped seeing' where the platform ended.
3. "When instructed to see the audience, they would do so, and simple inquiry about what was beyond the audience would elicit the reply of 'Nothing.'
4. "When they were questioned why they saw nothing beyond the audience, they would explain that they looked at the audience but had 'stopped seeing further.' "

Scoring Stopped Vision: MHE Method

1. Any response like the above indicating a stoppage of the linear extent of vision is scored positively.
2. Another scoreable type of question and answer is as follows (Erickson, 1980h, p. 32):
Q: *"Is someone sitting to my right?"*
A: "I don't know."
Q: *"Why?"*
A: "I haven't looked that far."
Q: *"Can you see my right arm?"*
A: "Yes."
Q: *"Do you see anything else?"*
A: "No."
Q: *"Why not?"*
A: "I haven't looked any further."
Q: *"Is there anything to see if you looked further?"*
A: "I don't know, I haven't looked."
Note the literalism in these responses: they are exact answers to the questions; they do not respond to any implications of the questions.

Rationale for Rossi's Approach

1. Since there is as yet no experimental data or general agreement about the nature of "stopped vision," Rossi has developed the following line of questioning to assess it as nondirectively as possible.

Rossi's Scale for Stopped Vision

The following series of questions assesses the degree of stopped vision that may be present. Each successive question provides more hints to see something other than the operator. If the subject still cannot report seeing anything other than the operator in response to question #5, then one can say that the highest degree of stopped vision is being experienced. Thus stopped vision can be scored on a scale of one to five, with five being the highest score.

This one to five score is of special research interest only and is not included as part of the general ITAS score.

1. "What do you see as you look *at* me?"

All responses which describe the operator and nothing else indicate that at least there is a *narrowing of attention* to the operator. There is a *literalness of response* and at least the suggestion of a profound *rapport*. If the subject describes anything besides the operator, (anything in the backround, lights, others present, etc.) one can immediately conclude that stopped vision is not present.

2. "Tell me more about what you see as you look *toward* me?"

A response supplying more details about the operator is now more presumptive of a genuine experience of stopped vision.

Subjects not experiencing stopped vision will describe other features in the room.

3. "What else do you see as you look *in my direction?*"

a response still confined to the operator is stronger evidence of stopped vision.

4. "Is there anyting else as you look *in my direction?*"

a response still confined to the person of the operator is very strong evidence of stopped vision.

5. "What is to my right? (to my left? in back of me?)"

A response of "I don't know," or something similar indicating that the subject looks no further than the operator, is Erickson's evidence for stopped vision.

9. Visual Hallucinations—Positive

Rationale for Visual Hallucinations

Three types of positive visual hallucinations are currently assessed in this scale.

1. Questioning for spontaneous hallucinations that have not been suggested in any way whatsoever.
2. Substituting memories for real objects.
3. The Picture Hanging Experiment.

Spontaneous Visual Hallucinations
Rationale for Spontaneous Hallucinations

1. Spontaneous visual hallucinations are a common occurrence in somnambulism, i.e., deep trance when the subject has eyes open. The subject typically has a fixed stare in one direction or appears to be watching or interacting with something of interest. The most nondirective questioning, as indicated below, is usually sufficient to elicit the fact that the subject is hallucinating.

Assessing Visual Hallucinations

Whenever the operator suspects the subject may be in an altered state the following questions may be asked.
"What are you looking at? (As subject sits quietly and passively apparently staring into space)
"What do you see there?" (Operator gestures toward a blank wall.)

Scoring Visual Hallucinations

1. Any response wherein the subject mentions or describes what is being watched is scored as positive.

Replacing Memory for Real Object: #1
Rationale for Watch Hallucination

1. Substituting a memory for a real object is characteristic of somnambulism.
2. For this preliminary item the operator briefly holds his arm with his wristwatch plainly evident, about a foot in front of the subject's face (only for the length of time required to administer the instruction to "continue seeing the watch *right there!*").
3. This is a preparation for the more demanding "twins hallucination" described in the next item of this scale.

Assessing the Watch Hallucination

1. "Continue looking at my watch (or whatever) *right there*".
2. After removing the watch from the subject's line of sight, ask for details about it, *"Describe every detail of my watch to me."*

3. The somnambulistic subject apparently will continue hallucinating the watch in its previous position while describing it. The subject is thus literally continuing to see the memory image of the watch *"right there"* as suggested.

Scoring the Watch Hallucination

1. Score positive if the subject accurately describes at least four possible details while staring at the former position of the watch. For example, color of watch, details about its face and hands, presence of a second hand, type of crystal, watch band, actual time, etc.

Replacing Memory for Real Object: #2
Rationale for Twins Hallucination

1. The ability to substitute a memory for a real object is characteristic of somnambulism. Subjects resort to this device to solve puzzling problems in most unusual ways leading Orne to postulate a "trance logic" (Orne, 1959, 1972).

Assessing the Twins Hallucination

1. *"I want you to continue seeing me right here."*
2. Have subject close eyes and then step out of subject's line of sight and say, *"Open your eyes and tell me what do you see?"*
3. If the subject responds as if the operator is still standing directly in front of him, a number of other interesting questions can be asked to assess *"trance logic."*
"Point to where you see me standing."
"Point to where my voice is coming from."
If the subject points in different directions he may then be questioned as follows.
"How can that be?"
"Are there two of us?"
"Are we twins?"
"Are we both real?"
"Which one of us is real?"

Scoring the Twins Hallucination

1. Score positive for any pointing response that indicates subject continues to see the operator in the original position in front of the subject.

Picture Hanging Experiment

Rationale for Picture Hanging Experiment

1. Somnambulistic subjects apparently experience an intense rapport with the hypnotist and a corresponding restriction or impoverishment of the remainder of their environment. The picture hanging experiment demonstrates this because the hallucinated picture is always hung in relation to the hypnotist or the subject's own body, regardless of the inappropriateness of that location from the point of view of the surrounding environment. For example, the picture may be hung right above and in back of the hypnotist even though there is no wall there.

Assessing Picture Hanging Experiment

1. In the context of some other aspect of the demonstration, ask the subject or hand him a card on which the following is typed:
"While we are waiting, where in this room if you had a three-by-four picture of—(a person actually present, a small snapshot of a person known by the subject, an actual small item nearby like a bowl of fruit, or a picture of something like a bowl of fruit—*where in this room would you hang it? Consider carefully, and when you have made up your mind, specify exactly."*

Scoring Picture Hanging Experiment

1. "Without fail each subject in the trance state slowly, thoughtfully surveyed the room and then placed the picture above and slightly behind the selected person (or other reality item present), regardless of the absurdity of the reality background." (Erickson, 1980h, p. 58)
2. In a videotaped demonstration at The Second International Congress On Ericksonian Approaches To Hypnosis and Psychotherapy (1983), Rossi's subject said she would hang the picture about a foot behind Rossi, in the small space between the subject and Rossi's leg level, and right behind the subject. All such locations were impossible since there was no wall. When asked how far behind her she would hang the picture, she said, "Don't matter!"
3. Score positive any response that is made by hanging the picture in relation to the real object rather than in response to the realities of the surrounding environment.
4. To make the inappropriateness of hanging the picture in relation to the reality object most evident, the reality object should be placed in the middle of a room or in front of a window—anyplace where one could not ordinarily hang a picture.

10. Reversable Amnesia
Rationale for Reversable Amnesia

1. The ability to experience an amnesia and then remove it has been a historically important criterion for a genuine hypnotic altered state. A reversible amnesia is also important as a modern criterion of the "state bound" nature of hypnotic amnesia and, indeed, all states of consciousness (Erickson, Rossi and Rossi, 1976, p299).

Assessing Amnesia: Available-Request

After a satisfactory period of hypnotic experience a reversible amnesia can be explored by the following procedure.
1. "Feel rested and comfortable, feel a need to establish an increasing contact with my voice, with me, . . *and leave behind but available on request* practically everything of importance, *knowing but not knowing* that it is *available upon request*. And now, let us see, that's right, you are sitting there, wide awake, rested, comfortable, and *ready for discussion of what little there is*." (Erickson, 1980b, p. 100)
2. After assessing the degree of amnesia present the operator can then reverse the amnesia to make memories of the content of the hypnotic experience available by specifying the following with quiet emphasis:
"Well, perhaps now matters will *become available*."
"Now, it can *become available on request. Now!*"

Scoring Reversible Amnesia

1. Score positive only if (a) an initial amnesia is evident and (b) it is reversed with the appropriate suggestion so that full recall is present.

11. Posthypnotic Suggestion
Rationale: Posthypnotic Suggestion

1. The posthypnotic suggestion used in this scale is not scored because a subject could respond "correctly" to it in an effort to simulate trance.
2. Instead, what is actually scored is whether or not the subject manifests behavior characteristic of the "posthypnotic trance" which is item #15 of ITAS.
3. Thus this item of the ITAS exists only to set up an adequate assessment of the posthypnotic trance.

Assessing Posthypnotic Suggestion

1. Any posthypnotic suggestion requiring several steps and at least a minute or two to be completed is satisfactory. It is always best to use typical and fairly casual patterns of behavior that are more or less inevitable in the real-life situation.

2. Example: *"As I ask you, 'How are you feeling (pause) right now?', you will share with me something you can feel comfortable talking about in this situation."*

3. *The careful wording and implications of such suggestions have been discussed by Erickson (see particularly 1980e, p. 398).*

Scoring Posthypnotic Suggestion

1. No score is given for this item regardless of the subject's response.

2. Rather, the subject's responsive behavior is carefully observed for indications of the development of the "Posthypnotic Trance" described in item #15 of this scale.

12. Space Depth Alterations
Rationale of Space Depth Alterations

1. Spontaneous alterations in depth perception that have not been suggested in any way are reliable indirect indicators of genuine trance experience (Erickson, 1980j, p. 147).

Assessing Space Depth Alterations

When a subject opens his or her eyes during trance (or after awakening from trance), note whether there is a blinking or special effort to reorient the visual sense by looking about. Space depth alterations can then be assessed with the following questions.

"How do things look to you?"
"What's different?"
"How are you seeing things?"

Scoring Space Depth Alterations

1. Score positive for space-depth alterations if subject reports that "the world seems flatter in two dimensions," or "things seem to be deeper in three dimensions," etc.

13. Post Trance Body Reorientation

Rationale: Post Trance Reorientation

1. Awakening from any extended period of trance is invariably accompanied by characteristic patterns of behavior that can serve to validate that an altered state has been experienced.

Assessing Post Trance Reorientation

1. A spontaneous body reorientation after awakening from trance is characterized by stretching, body and facial adjustments (usually accompanied by a tentative touching and "rubbing awake" of different parts of the body and face), blinking and/or rubbing of eyes, looking about, a clearing of the throat and often an initial reluctance to speak that may be masking a psycholinguistic retardation (possibly due to a cerebral hemispheric shift away from the speech centers during trance).

Scoring Post Trance Reorientation

1. The occurrence of any two or more of the above mentioned behaviors yields a positive score.

14. Time Distortion

Rationale for Time Distortion

1. The presence of time distortion is the easiest and perhaps most sensitive indicator of trance experience.
2. Even when trance is so "light" that the subject does not believe an altered state was experienced, time distortion is usually present. Erickson used it continually to ratify the experience of trance when he was training new or skeptical subjects (Erickson, Rossi and Rossi, 1976).
3. For experimental purposes two indirect approaches have been included. Type #1 is the typical approach used by Erickson in which no suggestion whatsoever for time distortion is given, while type #2 has a very subtle, embedded, indirect suggestion for time distortion.

Time Distortion #1: No Suggestion

1. At any time during the assessment period (or immediately after trance) the subject may be asked, *"How long have we been talking together?"* or *"How long have we been together here today?"*

2. The usual response to this question (particularly when administered after trance is over) is one of time contraction: subjective time seems shorter than real clock time.

Time Distortion #2: Suggestion

1. "While you consider the implications of that question (or whatever) *for just a moment or two*, will it be all right if I very gently guide your arm up?"
2. Continue to demonstrate catalepsy and whatever else may be appropriate for about ten or fifteen minutes and then test for the presence of time distortion by asking, *"And how long have you been considering that question?"*
3. *"How long have we been here together?"*
4. The usual response to item #3 (particularly when administered during trance) is one of time contraction: subjective time seems shorter than real clock time.

Scoring Time Distortion

1. At least 100% time distortion is required for a positive score. Thus if the subject has been in trance for twenty minutes, an estimate of no more than ten minutes is required to score positive for time distortion type #1.
2. For time distortion type #2 the subject should evidence at least 100% time distortion by responding that he has been considering the question for no more than a moment or two or, at most, five minutes, with a real clock time of ten minutes.

15. Posthypnotic Trance
Rationale for Posthypnotic Trance

1. Erickson (1980e, p. 391) discovered that when a posthypnotic suggestion is carried out the subject invariably enters a spontaneous *posthypnotic trance*.
2. *The presence of this posthypnotic trance is assessed by blocking the completion of the posthypnotic suggestion. This results in an obvious arrest of the subject's behavior as he awaits further instruction.*
3. *Erickson described it as follows: "The spontaneous posthypnotic trance is usually single in appearance, develops at the moment of initiation of the posthypnotic act, and persists usually for only a moment or*

two; hence it is easily overlooked despite certain residual effects it has upon general behavior." (1980e, p. 389)

4. While the posthypnotic trance requires the most sophisticated observational skills to be assessed correctly, Erickson regarded it as a most effective way of differentiating between genuine trance and the simulaton of trance (1980e, p. 399).

Assessing Posthypnotic Trance

1. Block the completion of the posthypnotic suggestion by some vague verbal suggestion such as:

"Wait a moment, just a moment;"
"Don't let anything change now;"
"Stay as you are right now, never mind that;"
"I'd rather talk to you now;"
"I'll be waiting as soon as you have done it."

2. Erickson (1980e, p. 390) described the actual behaviors characteristic of the posthypnotic trance as follows:

"A slight pause in the subject's immediate activity, a facial expression of distraction and detachment, a peculiar glassiness of the eyes with dilation of the pupils and a failure to focus, a condition of catalepsy, a fixity and narrowing of attention, an intentness of purpose, a marked loss of contact with the general environment, and an unresponsiveness to any external stimulus until the posthypnotic act is either in progress or has been completed, depending upon the actual duration of the trance state itself and the demands of the posthypnotic task."

Scoring Posthypnotic Trance

1. Score positive for the presence of a posthypnotic trance if interference with the posthypnotic suggestion results in a complete arrest of the subject's behavior with an apparent waiting for further instructions.

2. The appearance and manner of subjects experiencing a genuine posthypnotic trance is suggestive of being in a deep trance. The criteria of this posthypnotic trance behavior are listed above. Extensive study of Erickson's original paper (1980e) on posthypnotic suggestion and experience are required for competent scoring of this item.

Summary

The current form of the Indirect Trance Assessment Scale (ITAS) is an unstandardized set of procedures for exploring the nature of altered states of consciousness. These procedures derive primarily from Milton H. Erickson's indirect forms of suggestion. While the entire development of the scale to date has been an effort to systematize and continue his investigation of hypnotic and nonhypnotic realities, the scale's very flexible rules of administration could make it applicable to any situation where altered states of mind and behavior need to be evaluated. In its present form the scale is of particular value as a learning tool for students and practitioners of hypnosis who wish to incorporate an easy and unobtrusive set of indirect hypnotic approaches into their work. It has been used in this way by the author in teaching demonstrations exploring the nature of deep trance phenomena. It is the hope of the author that workers with academic and clinical research facilities at their disposal will undertake the necessary labor of standardizing ITAS so that it can become a more valuable instrument for all professionals in the future.

ITAS References

Erickson, M. (1980a). A brief survey of hypnotism. In E. Rossi (Ed.), *The collected papers of Milton H. Erickson on hypnosis: Vol. 3. Hypnotic investigation of psychodynamic processes.* (pp. 1–12). New York: Irvington.

Erickson, M. (1980b) A special inquiry with Aldous Huxley into the nature and character of various states of consciousness. In E. Rossi (Ed.), *The collected papers of Milton H. Erickson on hypnosis: Vol. 1. The nature of hypnosis and suggestion.* (pp. 83–107). New York: Irvington.

Erickson, M. (1980c). An hypnotic technique for resistant patients: The patient, the technique, and its rationale and field experimentation. In E. Rossi (Ed.), *The collected papers of Milton H. Erickson on hypnosis: Vol. 1. The nature of hypnosis and suggestion.* (pp. 299–330). New York: Irvington.

Erickson, M. (1980d). An instance of potentially harmful misinterpretation of hypnosis. In E. Rossi (Ed.), *The collected papers of Milton H. Erickson on hypnosis: Vol. 1. The nature of hypnosis and suggestion.* (pp. 531–532). New York: Irvington.

Erickson, M. (1980e). Concerning the nature and character of posthypnotic behavior. In E. Rossi (Ed.), *The collected papers of Milton H. Erickson on hypnosis: Vol. 1. The nature of hypnosis and suggestion.* (pp. 381–411). New York: Irvington.

Erickson, M. (1980f). Deep hypnosis and its induction. In E. Rossi (Ed.), *The collected papers of Milton H. Erickson on hypnosis: Vol. 1. The nature of hypnosis and suggestion.* (pp. 139–167). New York: Irvington.

Erickson, M. (1980g). Explorations in hypnosis research. In E. Rossi (Ed.), *The collected papers of Milton H. Erickson on hypnosis: Vol. 2. Hypnotic alteration of sensory, perceptual and psychophysical processes.* (pp. 313–336). New York: Irvington.

Erickson, M. (1980h). Further experimental investigation of hypnotic and nonhypnotic realities. In E. Rossi, (Ed.), *The collected papers of Milton H. Erickson on hypnosis: Vol. 1. The nature of hypnosis and suggestion.* (pp. 18–82). New York: Irvington.

Erickson, M. (1980i). Historical note on the hand levitation and other ideomotor techniques. In E. Rossi (Ed.), *The collected papers of Milton H. Erickson on hypnosis: Vol. 1. The nature of hypnosis and suggestion.* (pp. 135–138). New York: Irvington.

Erickson, M. (1980j). Hypnotic investigation of psychosomatic phenomena: Psychosomatic interrelationships studied by experimental hypnosis. In E. Rossi (Ed.), *The collected papers of Milton H. Erickson on hypnosis: (Vol. 2.) Hypnotic alteration of sensory, perceptual and psychophysiological processes.* (pp. 145–156). New York: Irvington.

Erickson, M. (1980k). Literalness: An experimental study. In E. Rossi (Ed.), *The collected papers of Milton H. Erickson on hypnosis: (Vol. 3). Hypnotic investigation of psychodynamic processes.* (pp. 92–99). New York: Irvington.

Erickson, M. (1980l). The "surprise" and "my-friend-John" technique of hypnosis: Minimal cues and natural field experimentation. In E. Rossi (Ed.), *The collected papers of Milton H. Erickson on hypnosis: (Vol. 1.) The nature of hypnosis and suggestion.* (pp. 340–359). New York: Irvington.

Erickson, M. (1980m). Visual hallucination as a rehearsal for symptom resolution. In E. Rossi (Ed.), *The collected papers of Milton H. Erickson on hypnosis: (Vol. 4.) Innovative hypnotherapy.* (pp. 144–146). New York: Irvington.

Erickson, M., & Rossi, E. (1981) *Experiencing hypnosis: Indirect approaches to altered states.* New York: Irvington.

Erickson, M., Rossi, E., & Rossi, S. (1976). *Hypnotic realities.* New York: Irvington.

Orne, M. (1959). The nature of hypnosis: Artifact and essence. *Journal of Abnormal & Social Psychology, 58*, 277–299.

Orne, M. (1972) On the simulating subject as a quasi-control group in hypnosis research. In E. Fromm & R. Shor (Eds.), *Hypnosis: Research developments and perspectives.* Chicago: Aldine.

Rossi, E. (1983). Demonstration given at The Second International Congress on Ericksonian Approaches to Hypnosis and Psychotherapy. Phoenix, Arizona.

CONCEPTUAL
FRAMEWORKS

Key Concepts of an Atheoretical Approach to Psychotherapy

by
J. Adrian Williams, Ph.D.

The approach to psychotherapy developed by Milton H. Erickson, M.D., has been much publicized and popularized during recent years. The ingenious and uniquely effective interventions that were the hallmark of Erickson's approach have inspired a number of attempts to capture the essence of his creative intellect through theoretical conceptualizations (Bandler & Grinder, 1975; Grinder, DeLozier & Bandler, 1977; Wilk, 1982). Such attempts have generated a great deal of theory, yet have failed to deal with several fundamental facts about Erickson and his work. Perhaps the most basic problem has been a rigid insistence on casting Erickson's work into a theory-based format, replete with technical jargon. Erickson clearly, and for many years, criticized a theory-based approach as far too limited for dealing with humans and their various problems (Erickson, 1952; Erickson, 1958; Erickson, Rossi & Rossi, 1976; Erickson, personal communication, September, 1978; Erickson, personal communication, July, 1979; Erickson & Rossi, 1979; Erickson & Rossi, 1981). Further, though possessed of a tremendous working vocabulary, Erickson typically spoke and described his work in a simple, straightforward manner that eschewed theoretical constructs and technical jargon.

Fundamental to Erickson's work were several principles that he reiterated throughout his career. These principles alone do not form the framework for a theory base, yet they *can* serve to provide coherent organization and understanding for Erickson's approaches to therapy. The purpose of this paper is to briefly describe these organizing principles, offering them as an alternative to the artificial forcing of Erickson's approaches into a theory framework. Such theory gains simplicity at the expense of the richness of complexity so fundamentally a part of Erickson and his work.

The principles under consideration focus on a naturalistic approach to psychotherapy, one based on intense observation of the patients who form the subject matter of that therapy. Thus, Erickson's lack of a formal system of theoretical constructs may be understood as resulting from an emphasis on achieving clinical results rather than generating scientifically elegant theory (Williams, 1982b). Erickson's ingenious interventions were based, not on prediction from theory, but from a profound empirical understanding of human nature gained from a lifetime of careful, intense observation. Thus, one may comprehend the principles discussed in this paper not as the postulates of a theory, but as a set of principles which Erickson, with his respect for the complexity of the human experience, found to be useful organizing concepts. Therefore, though these principles are of importance, they do not necessarily bear any particular hierarchical relationship to one another (other than as dictated by the specific clinical situation under consideration). With these ideas clearly in mind, we may turn to an examination of the principles alluded to. The first of these is that activity Erickson characterized as "speaking the patient's language."

Speaking the Patient's Language

"Speaking the patient's language" was the phrase that Erickson used to describe the process by which he entered the patient's frame of reference in order to more effectively communicate significant understandings and ideas (personal communication, 9/78; personal communication, 7/79; Erickson, Rossi & Rossi, 1976; Erickson & Rossi, 1979). An integral part of any therapy is the communication and elaboration of ideas by the therapist to the patient. The patient may then take in and in some way act upon these ideas in a manner beneficial to himself. For this elaboration of ideas to occur in a way which the patient can assimilate, it is necessary for both therapist and patient to speak a common language. This obviously refers to more than both parties simply speaking English! By speaking a common language, Erickson referred to an ability to communicate in cognitive, affective, behavioral, and attributional terms that are of personal relevance to the patient. It is not necessary that the patient *agree* with what is said in this language, or even find it pleasant. For example, Erickson was quite proficient at speaking a "power language" with those individuals to whom this was an important component of experience. From the inevitable power distributions found in any relationship, Erickson's patient may have found himself in a position one up relative to Erickson, or one down (Zeig, 1980; Erickson, 1983). The case described by Haley (1973) of the young man who called himself a "dumb moron" offers an excellent illustration. Rather than attempting to immediately help the patient feel better, Erickson forcefully defined their relationship as one in which he was the doctor and the patient was just "a miserable moron" (p. 98); Erickson would tell the patient what to do, the patient had only to follow orders. The patient responded to Erickson's authoritarian directives, and subsequently effected a radical alteration in his employment, education, sexual preferences, and general lifestyle. Subjectively, the patient may or may not have found this pleasant, yet the important point is that he was familiar with relating to others from a one down position, and intuitively understood relating within those terms. Such understanding frequently proceeds from an unconscious level, thereby allowing the therapist to relate to the patient in a way that inherently makes sense to the patient at an experiential level. Thus, nothing alien need be imposed upon the patient. Rather, therapist and patient can interact within a framework determined by the patient's unconscious understandings and experiential learnings.

The ability to speak the patient's language in an effective manner is clearly predicated upon highly refined skills of observing and analyzing what that language might consist of in terms of structure and content. The ability to observe was one that Erickson developed to an advanced degree. Skillful observation forms another of the key principles Erickson stressed for understanding his approaches to therapy. We therefore will consider observational skills next.

Observational Skills

Erickson's observational skills were literally phenomenal, and have become something of a legend in the field (Haley, 1980). While all schools of psychotherapy emphasize the importance of carefully observing the patient, few therapists are so perceptive as to develop highly sensitive observational skills. The purpose of observation in the psychotherapeutic context is to acquire information useful in the treatment of the patient. Erickson routinely practiced thorough observation of a patient's physical structure, behavioral mannerisms, affective responses, voice qualities, body movements, and other such characteristics. He considered the patient's nonverbal behavior to hold special significance, interpreting many of these behaviors as unconscious level communications about the patient's problem. These factors have obvious importance both in understanding the patient's symptoms and in learning to speak the patient's language in a psychologically engaging manner. Erickson's observation of a particular patient was only one of a long series of observations of many other people. He was thus able, based on his empirical experience, to identify idiosyncratic mannerisms and characteristics that yielded a great deal of information about the unconscious patterns of the person sitting across from him. His perceptive interventions become far more understandable when one considers the superior information about the patient that Erickson had access to in comparison with therapists of lesser observational skill and experience.

One area of particular interest to Erickson was the discovery and observation of various areas of rigidity in the individual he was treating. Rigidity forms another of the main organizing principles by which Erickson approached therapy, and will be examined next.

Rigidity

Erickson's concept of rigidity involved a consideration of those areas in which the patient lacked flexibility, i.e. was stiff, unyielding, and/or was inflexibly set in his behaviors, affect, and/or cognitive processes (personal communication, 9–78). Erickson believed that rigidity in the patient's behavior, affect, internal frames of reference, attitudes, beliefs, and cognitive associations served to limit that person's ability to function in a creative and productive manner. Thus, the patient's rigidities functioned as constraints, limiting the patient to a set of patterned, stereotyped behaviors, attitudes, beliefs, etc. Erickson considered such rigidity to play a significant role in the formation and maintenance of symptomatology (Erickson & Rossi, 1979). Thus, to Erickson, a critical aspect of psychotherapy was assisting the patient in breaking out of his or her rigidities.

Erickson did not offer a distinct categorization of types of rigidity. For purposes of clarity in this article, however, patterns of patient rigidity may be divided into several component categories. Rigidities in patient behavior, for instance, may be noted to occur in several areas. These might include behaviors "personal" to the client, as well as behaviors related to an interpersonal context. Personal behaviors are those behaviors not specifically related to interpersonal interaction, although they may occur in interpersonal interaction. For example, an individual's typical behavior in cigarette smoking (how he or she lights the cigarette, which fingers hold the cigarette, etc.) is not likely to be significantly different when alone or with other people. Similarly, the manner of walking, breathing, holding the body posturally, and a multitude of other actions are not necessarily dependent on whether or not there is another person present. Interpersonal behaviors, however, refer specifically, to those behaviors engaged in during interaction with another person. Such interpersonal behaviors might include the style of a person's responses in conversation, such as listening behaviors, interrupting, the verbal emphases with which the person speaks, as well as a multitude of nonverbal reactions and behaviors (Birdwhistell, 1970; Erickson, 1983; Williams, 1982b).

Rigidities may also occur in relation to the patient's affect. The emotional responses of the patient may range along a continuum from outward, observable expression of affect to the form of internal feelings which are experienced, but not overtly expressed by the patient. For instance, the individual who experiences a rigidity of affect tends to express and/or experience his or her feelings in a constrained, stereotyped pattern (Berne, 1961; English, 1971; Erickson & Rossi, 1979). This pattern might be one of restraint, it might be one of emotional escalation, or it might be one in which only certain emotions are available for expression or internal experience by the individual.

Rigidities in patient cognition refer to inflexibilities in the patient's thinking, attitudes, beliefs, and associational structures. This form of rigidity may serve to blind the individual to the various options which are available for problem solving. Alternatively, it may make the existence of viable options of little value. For example, consider the individual who refuses badly needed medical assistance because she or he deems it a violation of strongly held religious beliefs. Medical help exists, and the person is aware of that help, but the rigidity of his or her belief precludes the acceptance of that assistance. A patient's cognitive rigidity appears to play a role in almost every psychological problem, as it seems impossible to examine any psychological condition without discovering components of the condition due to the involvement of the patient's cognitive structures and reaction (Williams, 1982b).

Erickson developed a fantastic array of techniques and methods for dealing with patient rigidity (Erickson, 1952; Erickson, 1959b; Erickson, 1964a; Erickson, 1964b; Erickson, 1964c; Erickson, 1964d; Erickson, 1964e; Erickson, 1965a; Erickson, 1965c; Erickson, 1966; Erickson, Rossi & Rossi, 1976; Erickson & Rossi, 1979; Erickson & Rossi, 1981). Though it is not possible to examine those techniques in detail here, there are some general considerations that Erickson found of value for dealing with rigidity. He devised each intervention for the particular patient with whom he was consulting, thus making each specific response to patient rigidity unique for that patient. Perhaps at the most general level, Erickson considered what he called a depotentiation of conscious sets (Erickson, Rossi & Rossi, 1976) to be an important factor in dealing with rigidity. The depotentiation of conscious sets may be defined as any method of circumventing or disrupting the rigid and learned limitations of the client's conscious mind and its habitual patterns. Once these learned limitations are circumvented or disrupted, the patient is in a position to react affectively, behaviorally, and/or cognitively in a different manner. Erickson considered this breaking of rigidity to be fundamental to any therapeutic change (Erickson & Rossi, 1979). Other methods employed by Erickson included psychological shock, surprise, confusion, cognitive overloading, structured amnesia, binds, double binds, and distraction (Erickson & Rossi, 1975; Erickson, Rossi & Rossi, 1976; Erickson & Rossi, 1979; Erickson & Rossi, 1980; Rossi, 1973). All of these methods result in a depotentiation of conscious sets, and thereby serve to inhibit the patient functioning in terms of his or her previous typical rigidity, and create an opportunity to develop new, more adaptive behavioral, affective, and cognitive experience. One of the key methods by which Erickson accomplished this was by use of what he described as the utilization approach (Erickson, 1959). This approach will be examined below.

The Utilization Approach

Many patients prove to be resistant to or uncooperative with the very psychotherapy that they seek. In many cases, these clients are evaluated as not amenable to psychotherapy, and thus receive a lesser degree of therapeutic attention than do more cooperative or more motivated clients. Erickson developed a general approach which he described as a utilization approach or utilization technique (Erickson, 1959; Erickson, Rossi & Rossi, 1976) for dealing with this type of patient. This utilization approach forms a key theme in Erickson's work, and elements of it are to be found in a great many of his reported cases (Erickson, 1935; Erickson & Kubie, 1941; Erickson, 1943; Erickson, 1948a; Erickson, 1952; Erickson, 1954a; Erickson, 1955a; Erickson, 1958a; Erickson, 1959a; Erickson, 1959b; Erickson, 1960a; Erickson, 1963a; Erickson, 1964d; Erickson, 1965a; Erickson, 1965c; Erickson, 1966; Erickson, Rossi & Rossi, 1976; Erickson & Rossi, 1979; Erickson & Rossi, 1981). The utilization approach focuses on accepting and utilizing the client's behavior and attitudes in such a manner that they are reduced or eliminated as blocks to cooperation with the therapy.

Erickson considered it important that the therapist not impose his patterns of thinking and behaving on the patient. Rather, he considered the proper application of psychotherapy to be a rearranging or expansion of the patient's existing abilities or potentials (Erickson, personal communication, 9–27–78). Although existent in any person, such abilities may often be hidden, even from the individual's own conscious awareness. They are often obscured by the patient's symptomatology or maladaptive behavioral patterns. Perhaps the clearest statement of the utilization approach is to note that the therapy should somehow employ the patient's presenting behavior, and even his or her symptomatology to effect a cure of the patient's problem (Erickson, 1983; Williams, 1982b). This point is illustrated in Erickson's comments (Erickson & Rossi, 1981) on the client who came in and proceeded to curse Erickson. Erickson described his handling of the case, explaining that the therapist's response might be to agree with the patient, and even offer several additional expressions that could make the attack more powerful and emphatic. Thus, the therapist can suggest something the patient is in agreement with, something which allows the patient to gradually accept other suggestions and ideas from the therapist. The acceptance and utilization of the patient's resistance can therefore result in a progression of the therapy.

A consideration of utilization approaches should demonstrate the critical role of the examination of each client for his or her own individual patterns of thinking, behaving, and so forth. A discussion of this type of examination with Erickson (personal communication, 9–25–78) elicited a strong statement from him regarding the viewing of patients through the concepts of a general theory of human behavior (such as psychoanalysis, learning theory, or even a synthesis of current theories). Erickson stated that to do so was a gross injustice to the individual. He commented that the therapist had to work with the unique person in front of him, making use of the behaviors that that person presented, and not presupposing things about the patient on the basis of some theory.

Components of the utilization approach have a common framework integrating careful observation with the therapist's facility in adequately speaking the patient's language. The therapist must first join the client in his or her behavioral, cognitive, and/or affective patterns, and internal experience. When the therapist has adequately done this there is an increase in rapport and a reduction in patient resistance. At this point the therapist has an enhanced ability to offer suggestions which may serve to effect a subtle direction of the patient's patterns of experience. When this procedure is effectively carried out the therapist may then use the patient's symptomatology, ongoing stream of behavior, attitudes, thoughts, feelings, etc. to effect a resolution of the symptom or presenting problem of the patient. As a *general* paradigm, this can be useful. Clearly, it requires experience and clinical acumen to successfully apply even this greatly simplified statement of Erickson's utilization approach. In identifying the general structure of the utilization approach, this is *not* to be interpreted as a mechanical cookbook for generating standardized responses to the individuals seen for treatment. Rather, it offers a rule-of--thumb rubric by which a therapist can conceptualize the patient's presenting symptoms, behavior, feelings, thoughts, attitudes, and beliefs as not only problems, but as potential tools for resolving the difficulties experienced by the patient.

Multiple Level Communication

Erickson's approaches to psychotherapy and hypnosis owed a great deal to his ability to communicate in complex and subtle ways. His interventions were often directed to the patient at many different levels, and were facilitated by his ability to simultaneously communicate many different messages (Erickson & Rossi, 1976; Williams, 1982b; Williams, 1983). This multiple level communication, which Erickson commonly employed, is a fascinating and complicated area. It was this ability to communicate on multiple levels that allowed Erickson to deal with both conscious and unconscious components of a patient's personality so readily (Erickson, personal communication, 9–27–78; Erickson & Rossi, 1976; Haley, 1973).

The techniques that Erickson employed to communicate on multiple levels were seemingly endless. He was noted for his indirect approaches to therapy and hypnosis, and the use of multiple level communications played a significant role in those indirect approaches. Yet simply to note that he employed indirect approaches is rather vague for one who wishes to learn the essentials of Erickson's psychotherapeutic methods. Several constituent parts may be identified as basic to the indirect approaches to hypnosis and psychotherapy. One of these is what Erickson described as an interspersal technique (Erickson, 1966).

The interspersal technique is conceptually rather simple. Application of the technique with finesse can become quite complex, however. The interspersal technique itself consists of placing therapeutic ideas, comments, and symbols within the context of another communication. These ideas and suggestions are embedded within a surface level conversation that serves to disguise the therapeutic communications. The interspersed suggestions are subtly directed to the patient's attention through altered voice tone and volume emphases, alterations of voice rhythm and tempo, and other such nonverbal emphases. These alterations serve to mark the special emphasis being placed on them. This emphasis is typically perceived by the patient at unconscious levels, while escaping the conscious awareness, which is distracted by the content of the more superficial discussion presented by the therapist. A classic example of this technique is found in Erickson's (1966) description of his treatment of the cancer patient, Joe. In the course of an apparently unrelated conversation about a tomato plant, Erickson was able to embed suggestions of comfort, ease, hope, and satisfaction. All of these suggestions were presented in a linguistic context appropriate to talking about the tomato plant, yet they had a more personal relevance for the patient, who was suffering extreme pain and discomfort. Erickson counted on the patient's unconscious mind to receive and utilize the deeper levels of his communication.

Another important mode of multiple level communication commonly employed by Erickson was that of psychological implication (Erickson, personal communication, 7–9–79; Erickson & Rossi, 1979; Williams, 1985). Through the use of implication one can communicate far more than would be indicated by the surface content level of a particular verbalization. Implication, by definition, involves an interaction in which multiple level communication is taking place. Erickson's use of psychological implication helps to explain how he was able to accomplish so much with "just a talk therapy." By his subtle use of implication, situations were structured in such a manner that patients and students developed ideas, plans, and actions that were experienced as originating from within themselves. As a result, changes actually generated by the therapy proceeded from the inside out, rather than vice versa. Patients were therefore in a position to experience therapy as a somewhat familiar process, since they were making use of personal resources and potentials that had existed all along, but were not necessarily being employed. Consequently, Erickson's therapy and teaching approaches were generally experienced as unobtrusive. Positive gains were experienced as resulting from personal effort and creativity, not as some achievement on the part of the therapist. This in itself is a powerful implication; if a patient or student can achieve one new, therapeutic accomplishment, it implies possibilities for other therapeutic accomplishments as well.

In general, Erickson utilized whatever was presented to him by the patient in the total interpersonal context as the basis for formulating the psychological implications he could weave into the therapy. This interaction with the patient served as a stimulus for the implications that Erickson could introduce with therapeutic intent; therapy was not developed *a priori* and then applied to the patient. Rather, Erickson had a wide variety of therapeutic approaches which he applied in an experimental fashion, given the stimulus of a particular patient and problem. Erickson's therapy was, in this sense, always experimental since he might try any number of "keys" before "opening the lock" of the patient's problem. Keeping this orientation clearly in mind, we may briefly consider some of the methods by which Erickson employed psychological implication.

A number of Erickson's techniques of psychological implication have been described in detail elsewhere (Williams, 1982b; Williams, 1985). These techniques include implication by omission, by presupposition, by implied directive, through apposition of opposites (Erickson, Rossi & Rossi, 1976), by ambiguous language, by negation, nonverbally, and by multiple meanings in interpersonal situations.

In applying verbal strategies of psychological implication, Erickson's language frequently contained intentional ambiguity. Such semantic ambiguity encourages multiple levels of interpretation. A typical outcome for such a procedure was for the patient to develop a very specific conscious understanding of what Erickson had been talking about, while processing alternate meanings of the communication at unconscious levels. An example of this use of verbal ambiguity was Erickson's assignment to a young lady to go home and draw a picture of herself in the nude (Erickson, personal communication, 9–29–78). One interpretation is that the picture drawn should represent a likeness of the patient when naked. Another, equally accurate interpretation would be that the patient should go home, remove her clothing, and then draw a picture of herself, with no reference as to what condition of dress that the actual drawing should depict. In discussing this example with Erickson (personal communication, 9–29–78), he commented that people tend to hear, consciously, such an assignment only one way, but that with the multiple interpretations possible, the patient could in fact perform the assignment with some latitude for her own individuality.

Erickson was a master of the use of implication by omission. An example of this technique was evident in his comment to a group of students or patients that he was "certain that no one will go into a trance sitting in *that* chair" (personal communication, 7–10–79). A potent indirect suggestion has been given, since only one person at a time can sit in the designated chair! This example illustrates the sort of linguistic distinction that Erickson casually and commonly employed. A detailed examination of such techniques is too lengthy, however, to include here. Suffice it to note that the careful use of language, taking full advantage of distinct meanings of words allowed Erickson to communicate exquisitely through implication.

Other methods of multiple level communication employed by Erickson involved the use of puns, plays on words, jokes, metaphors, symbols, and anecdotal approaches to therapy which combined all of these patterns. These are all potentially powerful means of communicating on multiple levels, and could easily fill volumes with adequate descriptions and indications for their application. All, however, have in common the characteristic of allowing the patient or student to learn one thing consciously, while facilitating the learning of other things concurrently at unconscious levels.

Summary

This paper has attempted to present, in an abbreviated form, key concepts utilized by Milton H. Erickson, M.D. in his approaches to psychotherapy and hypnosis. The author views the current trend to interpret Erickson's work in terms of a specific theory base as a critical error in attempts to understand his approaches. Erickson was concerned with achieving clinical results, and he viewed each patient as unique, and therefore requiring individual management. The concept of responding to patients on the basis of any particular theory of personality was abhorrent to Erickson, and he resisted attempts to simplify the clinician's work at the expense of treating individuals as if they were all derived from a common mold.

This paper has described a set of concepts that Erickson found useful in organizing his own understanding of what he was doing, and how he was to do it. Though lacking sophistication in terms of formal scientific theory, this approach offers the advantage of not changing Erickson's work in order to simplify it. Rather, it challenges the clinician to give up the security of simplistic theory, and to work instead with the reality of human behavior with all its irrationality, contradictions, and complexity.

References

Bandler, R. & Grinder, J. (1975). *Patterns of the hypnotic techniques of Milton H. Erickson, M.D., (Vol. I.),* Cupertino, California: Meta Publications.

Berne, E. (1961). *Transactional analysis in psychotherapy.* New York: Grove Press, Inc.

Birdwhistell, R. (1970). *Kinesics and context.* Philadelphia: University of Pennsylvania Press.

English, F. (1971). The substitution factor: rackets and real feelings. *Transactional Analysis Journal, 1,* 27–32.

Erickson, M. H. (1935). A study of an experimental neurosis hypnotically induced in a case of ejaculatio praecox. *British Journal of Medical Psychology, 15,* 34–50.

Erickson, M. H. (1943). A controlled experimental use of hypnotic regression in the therapy of an acquired food intolerance. *Psychosomatic Medicine, 5,* 67–70.

Erickson, M. H. (1948). Hypnotic psychotherapy. *Medical Clinics of North America,* New York, W.B. Saunders Co., 571–584.

Erickson, M. H. (1952). Deep hypnosis and its induction. In L. M. LeCron (Ed.), *Experimental hypnosis* (pp-70–114). New York: Macmillan.

Erickson, M. H. (1954). Special techniques of brief hypnotherapy. *Journal of Clinical and Experimental Hypnosis, 2*, 109–129.

Erickson, M. H. (1955). The hypnotherapy of two psychosomatic dental problems. *Journal of the American Society of Psychosomatic Dentistry, 1*, 6–10.

Erickson, M. H. (1958). Naturalistic techniques of hypnosis. *American Journal of Clinical Hypnosis, 1*, 25–29.

Erickson, M. H. (1959a). Further clinical techniques of hypnosis: utilization techniques. *American Journal of Clinical Hypnosis, 2*, 3–21.

Erickson, M. H. (1959b). A transcript of a trance induction with commentary. *American Journal of Clinical Hypnosis, 2*, 49–84.

Erickson, M. H. (1960). The utilization of patient behavior in the hypnotherapy of obesity: three case reports. *American Journal of Clinical Hypnosis, 3*, 112–116.

Erickson, M. H. (1963). Hypnotically oriented psychotherapy in organic brain damage. *American Journal of Clinical Hypnosis, 6*, 92–112.

Erickson, M. H. (1964a). The confusion technique in hypnosis. *American Journal of Clinical Hypnosis, 6*, 183–207.

Erickson, M. H. (1964b). Hypnotically oriented psychotherapy in organic brain damage: an addendum. *American Journal of Clinical Hypnosis, 6*, 361–362.

Erickson, M. H. (1964c). The "surprise" and "my friend John" techniques of hypnosis: minimal cues and natural field experimentation. *American Journal of Clinical Hypnosis, 6*, 293–307.

Erickson, M. H. (1964d). An hypnotic technique for resistant patient: the patient, the technique and its rationale and field experiments. *American Journal of Clinical Hypnosis, 7*, 8–32.

Erickson, M. H. (1964e). Pantomime techniques in hypnosis and the implications. *American Journal of Clinical Hypnosis, 7*, 64–70.

Erickson, M. H. (1965a). Hypnotherapy: the patient's right to both success and failure. *American Journal of Clinical Hypnosis, 7*, 254–257.

Erickson, M. H. (1965b). A special inquiry with Aldous Huxley into the nature and character of various states of consciousness. *American Journal of Clinical Hypnosis, 8*, 14–33.

Erickson, M. H. (1965c). The use of symptoms as an integral part of therapy. *American Journal of Clinical Hypnosis, 8*, 57–65.

Erickson, M. H. (1966). The interspersal technique of symptom correction and pain control. *American Journal of Clinical Hypnosis, 8*, 109–209.

Erickson, M. H. (1983). *Healing in hypnosis*. New York: Irvington Publishers, Inc.

Erickson, M. H. & Kubie, L.S. (1941). The successful treatment of a case of acute hysterical depression by return under hypnosis to a critical phase of childhood. *Psychoanalytic Quarterly, 10*, 593–609.

Erickson, M. H. & Rossi, E. (1975). Varieties of double bind. *American Journal of Clinical Hypnosis, 17*, 143–147.

Erickson, M. H., Rossi, E. & Rossi, S. (1976). *Hypnotic realities*. New York: Irvington Publishers, Inc.

Erickson, M. H. & Rossi, E. L. (1979). *Hypnotherapy*. New York: Irvington Publishers, Inc.

Erickson, M. H. & Rossi, E. L. (1981). *Experiencing hypnosis: Therapeutic approaches to altered states*. New York: Irvington Publishers, Inc.

Grinder, J., DeLozier, J. & Bandler, R. (1977). *Patterns of the hypnotic techniques of Milton H. Erickson, M.D., (Vol. II.)*. Cupertino, California: Meta Publications.

Haley, J. (1973). *Uncommon therapy*. New York: Norton.

Haley, J. (1980). The contribution to therapy of Milton H. Erickson, M.D. In J. Zeig (Ed.) *Ericksonian approaches to hypnosis and psychotherapy* (pp. 5–26). New York: Brunner/Mazel.

Rossi, E. L. (1973). Psychological shocks and creative moments in psychotherapy. *American Journal of Clinical Hypnosis, 16*, 9–22.

Wilk, J. (1982). Context and know-how: a model of Ericksonian psychotherapy. *The Journal of Strategic and Systemic Therapies, 1*, 2–20.

Williams, J. A. (1982a). Indirect hypnotic therapy of compulsive stealing. *Swedish Journal of Clinical Hypnosis, 9*, 41–44.

Williams, J. A. (1982b). An analysis of an atheoretical system of psychotherapy: Ericksonian approaches to psychotherapy (doctoral dissertation, University of Illinois, Urbana-Champaign). *Dissertation Abstracts International, 43*, 740A.

Williams, J. A. (1983). Ericksonian hypnotherapy of intractable shoulder pain. *American Journal of Clinical Hypnosis, 26*, 26–29.

Williams, J. A. (1985). Erickson's use of psychological implication. In J. Zeig (Ed.), *Ericksonian psychotherapy*, (Vol. 2) (pp 179–184). New York: Brunner/Mazel.

Zeig, J. (1980). *A teaching seminar with Milton H. Erickson*. New York: Brunner/Mazel, Publishers.

Rigidity and Pattern Interruption: Central Issues Underlying Milton Erickson's Approach to Psychotherapy

by
Michael R. Samko, Ph.D.

A young man wanted clear statements about Erickson's method. Erickson interrupted the discussion and took the man outside. He pointed up the street and asked what he saw. Puzzled, he replied that he saw a street. Erickson pointed to the trees that lined the street. "Do you notice anything about those trees?" The young man eventually noted that they were all leaning in an easterly direction. "That's right, all except one. That second one from the end is leaning in a westerly direction. There's always an exception (Haley, 1967, p. 549).

Interest in the therapeutic techniques of Milton Erickson has surged in the past several years. Numerous models examining Erickson's work have been developed (Bandler & Grinder, 1975; Erickson, Rossi, & Rossi, 1976; Watzlawick, Beaver, & Jackson, 1967; Lankton & Lankton, 1983). These attempts at describing and systematizing Erickson's style share several common features. Perhaps the most striking feature is the emphasis on individuality, flexibility and interaction with unconscious patterns. This focus on unconscious patterns of behavior incorporates the viewpoint that symptoms are a function of rigid patterns and thus represent a difficulty in adapting to change. Successful therapeutic intervention involves the interruption of rigid maladaptive patterns and, consequently, involves the facilitation of increased flexibility so that the client is free to acquire a new framework. Thus, rigidity can be viewed as the basic ingredient of psychopathology and facilitating flexibility can be viewed as the basic goal of psychotherapy.

The ability to perceive beyond conventional patterns of thinking underlies the very nature of the creative process. Bartlett (1958) noted that the creative moment is a gap in one's habitual pattern of awareness. Barron (1969, p. 16) reiterated a similar theme: "A creative moment occurs when a habitual patterns of associations is interrupted." Erickson (1948) described hypnotic trance as, "A special psychological state that affects a break in the patient's conscious and habitual associations so that creative learning can take place" (pp. 571–583). Erickson, Rossi and Rossi (1976) also defined a successful clinical hypnotic experience as "One in which trance alters habitual attitudes and modes of functioning so that careful formulated hypnotic suggestions can evoke and utilize other patterns of associations and potentials within the patient to implement certain therapeutic goals" (p. 20). It was further pointed out that psychological problems develop when people do not permit the naturally changing circumstances of life to interrupt the old and no longer useful patterns of associations so that new solutions and attitudes may emerge. Haley (1967) reiterated the same point by saying, "Erickson teaches a patient to deal with him and others differently. He does this largely by blocking off the ways a person typically behaves and, simultaneously provides him with new experiences which prove more successful and satisfying" (p. 132).

A sample of Erickson's style is well illustrated in a case involving a patient with serious brain damage (Haley 1967). Erickson determined the patient had a well-developed pattern of frustration and despair which could be used constructively as a motivational tool in eliciting responses leading to new learnings of self-expression. "The plan devised was complex and involved; sometimes it varied not only from day to day but within the day itself so that, outside of certain items, the patient never knew what to expect, and even what was done often did not seem to make much sense to her. As a result, the patient was kept in a striving, seeking, frustrated, struggling and emotional state in which anger, bewilderment, disgust, impatience and an intense, almost burning desire, to take charge and do things in an orderly and sensible manner became overwhelming" (p. 540).

One intervention Erickson employed in this case involved utilizing the patient's regressed level of functioning. He taught the patient a childhood rhyme which he used regularly with the gradual introduction of errors in the rhyme. These deliberate errors began to force this depressed and passive client to begin responding in a therapeutically desirable manner which involved correcting the rhymes. Erickson noted an important goal of this particular intervention involved, "Inducing an open mindedness or mental receptiveness for new, inexplicable, curiosity-evoking ideas causing the patient to look forward with hopeful anticipation and not to expend her energies in despondent despair over the past. The ever-changing and challenging activities of the present and the future occupied her mind and thus there existed a mental frame of reference conducive to recovery of lost learnings and the development of new learnings, possibly by new and alternative associative neural pathways" (p. 465).

Some interesting perspectives on Erickson's work have been offered by Watzlawick, Beaver and Jackson (1967) and others of the Mental Research Institute of Palo Alto. They have discussed how behavior patterns are maintained within the context of a larger system, like a family, and that when the rules that are operative within the system become so rigid that they do not adapt to change, pathology develops. For example, the same patterns that were biologically and emotionally vital at an earlier stage of development can become a serious handicap at a later developmental stage. Watzlawick et. al., (1967) noted that, "The therapist, as an outsider, is capable of supplying what the system itself cannot generate, mainly a change in its own rules" (p. 233). Mention is also made of "the law of requisite variety" which basically states that the element of a system with the greatest flexibility will be the most powerful element of that system.

The concept of "pattern interruption" has been extensively discussed by Grinder & Bandler (1981). Grinder & Bandler noted that when a single unit of behavior is interrupted, there is uncertainty and confusion as to what the next step in the pattern should be. An unconscious search begins to fill the gap. This process creates an opportunity for a new frame of reference and for new behaviors. Thus, pattern interruption involves finding a single unit of behavior that is composed of a sequence of well-established, rigid steps and interrupting the sequence in the middle. Erickson would typically initiate a small, seemingly irrelevant change. This change, if properly initiated, would create a momentum, leading toward a pattern change in a desired direction.

For example, Erickson described a situation in which he presented a paper as a guest speaker at a conference. When invited by his hosts to dinner, he discovered that they had developed a rigid pattern of going out to dinner once a week, eating at the same restaurant and ordering the same meal. They had done this for perhaps as many as 15 years. In attempting to influence a pattern change, Erickson ordered "snails;"

something they had never conceived of eating in that restaurant. Eventually, he enticed them into sampling his "snails" which they surprisingly enjoyed enough to order for themselves. Approximately one year later, Erickson described visiting the same host and his wife again and discovering they had not eaten in that particular restaurant since he had been with them and, in fact, had been sampling numerous other restaurants whenever they went out to eat.

Another example involved a case where Erickson was working with a couple with marital and sexual difficulties. They had not engaged in sexual intercourse for numerous years. Erickson's intervention simply involved asking the couple to switch the sides of the bed that they always slept on. He determined that the husband slept on the outside of the bed and would typically get out of bed in the middle of the night to go to the bathroom. That night, after switching sides, the husband crawled over his wife to go to the bathroom and, according to Erickson, "discovered her" and initiated lovemaking.

Numerous pattern-interruption techniques designed to depotentiate habitual frameworks have been described by Erickson and others (Haley 1967; Erickson & Rossi 1979; Grinder & Bandler, 1981). Some of these include: (1) Surprise and shock—these techniques would include the use of jokes, unorthodox behavior and Erickson's handshake induction. Erickson, Rossi & Rossi (1976) described one case where Erickson shook hands with a woman but lingered before releasing her hand. Gradually, and with seeming hesitation, he alternately applied and released pressure with his fingers on different parts of her hand. The subject was not even sure when he finally disengaged his hand. Her hand was left in a cataleptic position in midair. During this handshake, Erickson looked toward her face but focused on the wall behind her. In discussing the technique, Erickson noted the woman's disconcerted look indicative of her trance state. Erickson acknowledged that this was a confusion technique and stated that "in all my techniques, there is confusion" (pp. 84–85). The purpose is to momentarily fixate typical associations and allow the situation to be viewed or experienced differently. Confusion opens the possibility of a creative moment during which the patient's unconscious is engaged in an inner search for an answer that can reestablish equilibrium.

Another case involving surprise and shock involved a young man with intractible back pain. He and his fiance were very skeptical and hostile about the prospect of hypnosis being able to help. In session, Erickson asked the woman to stand on a carpet in the middle of the floor. He told the couple they were not going to like what he was going to do—that it would be offensive. He then gave the fellow a heavy cane and said he could "clobber" him with it at any moment Erickson was doing something wrong. Erickson, as the woman stood in the middle of the floor, used his own cane to begin to open the buttons of her blouse as if he was going to expose her breasts. He told her he would do so until she developed a deep trance state. Quite rapidly, she developed a trance and her fiance was so surprised that he dropped his cane and also developed a bit of a trance state himself. Erickson noted that he channeled the hostility and doubt about hypnosis in general into a specific rejection of what he was doing. This particular unorthodox technique certainly fixated her attention, and the shock depotentiated both her and her fiance's usual mental frameworks. This allowed Erickson to then proceed to work with her fiance in a successful manner.

Another example of the shock and surprise technique involves the case of a chronic bedwetter who wet her bed every night. In this situation, Erickson induced hypnosis and regressed the young girl. He had her imagine herself on the toilet, urinating. While she was experiencing that image, he introduced the image of a stranger who had popped his head in the door and was looking at her. Erickson asked her what she would do if that happened? Her response was that she would freeze—essentially that she would stop urinating. At that moment, Erickson used the experience of knowing she could stop urinating as a way of building a framework of further suggestions which included that she practice starting and stopping urinating on a regular basis.

(2) Reframing—interrupting a pattern by changing the meaning or perception of the usual associations. Bandler and Grinder (1982) defined reframing as, "Changing the frame in which the person perceives events in order to change the meaning" (p. 1). When the meaning changes, the person's response and behavior is also changed. An example is a case that the author worked on where a father and son were being seen in the context of family therapy. In every session, both the father and son engaged in vehement arguments. The situation was a very volatile one. During one of the sessions, the father was given the statement that I was very impressed with the degree of his anger toward his son because it seemed to reflect a very deep level of caring to experience such emotion. At that moment, the anger was turned—for both the father and son—from a response labeled as hate to a response labeled as love, thus allowing movement in a new direction.

Another example involved Erickson introducing the notion that you can have phantom good feelings, not just painful ones. In working with an amputee patient who complained of phantom limb pain, Erickson used a metaphor in which he described working with another amputee who described scratching an itch. In the metaphor he began to discuss the possibility of having phantom good feelings, such as the aforementioned ability to scratch an itch. In that sense, he introduced another possibility for experience.

(3) Double-binding and paradox—Bateson (1979) defined paradox as, "A contradiction in conclusions that were correctly argued from consistent premises" (p. 23). Lankton and Lankton, (1983) noted that "Paradoxical commands result in the suspension of normal frameworks of rule and logic and the initiation of an internal search. This search involves a trance state" (p. 66). There are three examples of double-binding and paradox. (1) The conscious-unconscious double-bind. If your unconscious wants you to enter trance, your right hand will lift; otherwise, your left hand will lift (Erickson, Rossi & Rossi, 1976, p. 67). (2) Nonsequitur double-bind which involves the use of illogic to disrupt a person's conscious set so that choice and behavior tend to be mediated on a more involuntary level. For example, "Do you want to take a bath before going to bed, or would you rather put your pajamas on in the bathroom?" (Erickson, Rossi & Rossi, 1976, p. 73).

The third example is prescribing symptoms. For example, in dealing with a patient who had gone through a number of weight-reduction programs, seen a number of therapists involving this problem and had no success, possible intervention might be to ask this person to gain some weight between now and the next session. In doing so, if the person does gain weight, they have established a new pattern of cooperation with the therapist and if they decide not to gain weight, they still are basically cooperating with the therapist as the primary reason to be there is to lose weight. Another example of paradox involves working with pain. The patient is encouraged to experience a higher degree of pain and in that way, learn to gain control of the pain.

(4) "If you can't lick them, join them." This technique involves utilizing a person's typical patterns by redirecting them to produce a different end result, as illustrated by three cases.

In the first case, Erickson encountered a patient who had been hospitalized for several years and had the well-established delusion of believing he was Jesus. Rather than directly confronting this delusion, Erickson simply asked the fellow if he was a carpenter, to which his reply was, "Yes." Erickson then told him that he needed some carpenter's help in building some cabinets in the ward. The patient, who previously was withdrawn, passive and alienated from others in the ward, was put to work and began interacting with the other patients working with him and began to improve dramatically.

A second example involved a patient who was hospitalized. The only words he muttered were the chant, "Don't hurt me, don't scare me."

Erickson's intervention involved chanting with that person and slowly introducing suggestions within the context of the chant, thereby gradually changing the patient's pattern.

The third example involves a well-known case of Erickson's in which he was working with a patient who spoke "word salad." Erickson's secretary transcribed the word salad, after which he learned the pattern and began to communicate with the patient, using word salad. The patient's response was that he was glad to meet someone, especially a psychiatrist, who made sense. At that point, therapy began to progress.

(5) Confrontation—direct or indirect confrontation of usual patterns. Erickson could be directly confrontive, even quite intimidating, in dealing with certain patterns patients seemed to have; or he could also use a lot of indirect confrontation. An example of confrontation occurred when he worked with two nurses who were lifetime friends. They had grown up together, chosen the same profession and had even had a double wedding. Independent of each other, each had consulted Erickson about the fact that they were disturbed when they discovered their respective husbands to be sexually deviant. One nurse described her husband as a deviant because he enjoyed having sex with his thighs outside of hers. The other nurse described her husband as a sexual deviant because he enjoyed having sex with his thighs inside of hers. Erickson asked both nurses to come into his office together. He had each describe to the other the particular deviancy that disturbed them. Basically, they reached the conclusion that the problem was not a matter of deviancy, but rather a matter of lack of knowledge about sexual matters.

(6) Regression—to bring to consciousness early-established patterns (memory revivification); bringing to consciousness, resources that lie within a person's personal history. An example of regression was presented earlier in the case of the brain-injured patient. Erickson typically had clients reconnect with positive experiences or resources from the past. During induction, Erickson could discuss the experience of learning the alphabet and the process of learning to read and write; thus allowing the patient to tap into some early successful learning sets that might lay a foundation for further experiences that Erickson wished to exploit.

(7) Alteration of established perceptual patterns—for example, time distortion, amnesia, hallucination and other qualities of trance. These techniques basically allow unconscious response patterns to become accessible. In a case of time distortion technique, Erickson saw a patient who, for 15 years, had compulsively visited his mother's grave every day. Upon being offered an excellent job position in another state, the patient was experiencing panic about what decision to make based upon the inability to make such daily visits if he moved. Erickson disoriented

this patient for time; then, oriented him into a time frame two weeks in the future, making the statement that two weeks had passed and he had not visited his mother's grave, yet he had remained alive and strong. The response at that moment was, "Good God! How did I stop?" Using that experience as a basis, Erickson began to work initiating further therapeutic steps, allowing the patient to feel why the issue was finally resolved and that he was able to accept the new job.

Another example is a case that the author worked on in which a client, who was very resistant to hypnosis and did not believe that he had the ability to be hypnotized, sought treatment. His particular problem was that he was unable to achieve an erection and had not been able to for a number of years. The only intervention employed was the experience of arm levitation which effected a significantly deep enough shift in his perceptual patterns. He was able to leave the office with a different frame of mind regarding the possibility for having an erection, which he was able to successfully have later on that day.

The above-noted pattern-interruption techniques highlight the central role that the concept of rigidity plays in this form of psychotherapy. Psychotherapists need to be aware of the extent to which the problems their clients have are sustained by the rigid boundaries they function within. Psychotherapists need also be aware of their own rigidities and how these rigidities might limit therapeutic progress in their clients. Erickson's concern with the issue of therapist rigidity was strongly reflected in his teaching seminars. This concern should be particularly emphasized now that Erickson's style is gradually being systematized.

Perhaps Erickson's most powerful metaphor was the manner in which he lived his own life. Erickson's many stories reflect his delight in seeing the world from a different perspective and the value that he placed on flexibility and innovation. Erickson's unique style of therapy and his attraction to hypnosis as a primary therapeutic medium is a reflection of his personality. It is with the same spirit of openness, adventure and sensitivity to rigid patterns that the therapist might best integrate Erickson's concepts.

References

Bandler, R., & Grinder, J., (1975). *Patterns of the hypnotic hechniques of Milton Erickson*, (Vol. 1). Cupertino, CA: Meta Publications.

Bandler, R., & Grinder, J., (1982). *Reframing*. Moab, Utah: Real People Press.

Barron, F., (1969). *Creative person and creative process*. New York: Holt, Rinehart and Winston.

Bartlett, F., (1958). *Thinking: An experimental and social study*. New York: Basic Books.

Bateson, G., (1979). *Mind and Nature*. New York: Dutton.

Erickson, M., Rossi, E., & Rossi, S., (1976). *Hypnotic realities*. New York: Irvington Publishers.

Erickson, M., & Rossi, E., (1979). *Hypnotherapy: An exploratory casebook*. New York: Irvington Publishers.

Erickson, M., (1948). *Hypnotic psychotherapy*. The medical clinics of North America.

Grinder, J., & Bandler, R., (1981). *Trance-Formations*. Moab, Utah: Real People Press.

Haley, J., (1967). *Advanced Techniques of hypnosis and therapy*. New York: Grune and Stratton.

Lankton, S., & Lankton, C., (1983). *The answer within: A Clinical Framework of Ericksonian Hypnotherapy*. New York: Brunner/Mazel.

Watzlawick, P., Beaver, J., & Jackson, D., (1967). *Pragmatics of human communication*. New York: W. W. Norton.

Balance: A Central Principle of the Ericksonian Approach

by
Christopher J. Beletsis, Ph.D.

This paper offers a conceptual model for understanding and applying principles of balance in communication, hypnotic induction techniques, and for the purpose of developing effective therapeutic strategies. First, general ideas regarding balance and "parts" are introduced. Second, the positive value and potentially beneficial effect of using seemingly opposite communications is discussed. Third, the development, transformation and integration of a client's opposing parts is illustrated through case examples with commentary. This paper proposes that working with these principles increases therapist flexibility, provides a guideline for further developing professional and personal integrity, and can allow him to reach the client at deeper levels than he otherwise might. The naturalistic and utilization approaches of Milton H. Erickson are emphasized throughout.

Therapists of differing theoretical approaches each have unique ways to describe the various component parts of a person. For example, Satir (1983) described a process called a "parts party," which can "help a person become aware that he is made up of many different parts, get acquainted with them, understand them, and learn to use them in an harmonious and integrated manner" (p. 258). Gestalt therapists often focus on developing and increasing contact between opposing "polarities" of the individual (Perls, 1969; Polster & Polster, 1973). The Polsters (1973) noted that:

Once contact between these parts is established, each party to the warring struggle can be experienced as a valid participant. They can then become allies in the common search for a good life, rather than uneasy opponents maintaining the split (p. 248).

Bandler and Grinder (1979) developed a formal model for working with parts called "reframing," and described it this way:

Reframing is a specific way of contacting the portion or part . . . of the person that is causing a certain behavior to occur, or that is preventing a certain other behavior from occurring. We do this so that we can find out what the secondary gain of the behavior is, and take care of that as an integral part of the process of inducing a change in that area of behavior (p. 138).

Carter (1983) developed a "Parts Model" for working with human problems. In his view, "change is based on a person developing new and more complete models of herself. This occurs generally through accepting and developing many different parts of herself and specifically through reframing certain parts that she has represented as 'bad or worthles' " (p. 28).

An implicit assumption of these different approaches to therapy is that all parts, even those regarded as hurtful, have some value for the person. An individual's "parts" can be represented by conflicting feelings, inherently contradictory goals or beliefs, and by incongruent behavior (Grinder & Bandler, 1976). To deny, suppress or stifle a specific part may lead to dis-ease (Simonton, Simonton & Creighton, 1978; Carter, 1983), and therefore a major goal of therapy may be to develop a fuller expression and integration of *all* parts of an individual. This includes the other individuals and the environment the person relates to. In working with an individual or any other system composed of interrelated "parts," it is essential to recognize the system's wholeness. Division of a whole into parts can provide clinicians with effective ways to conceptualize and transform human problems, however, these parts are interdependant and inseparable and can best be understood or defined in relation to all other parts (Capra, 1975). One part can never be completely separated or isolated from the whole without potentially negative consequences.

The above ideas about "parts" can also apply to one's ability and willingness to communicate in differing and complementary ways with the client. In communication and hypnotic induction, for example, Erickson often balanced permissive approaches with directive and authoritarian approaches; support with confrontation; confusion with clarity; association with dissociation; and, indirect with direct approaches (Haley,

1967; Rossi, 1980). Satir (1983) also seemed to recognize this point when she emphasized balance between "toughness and empathy" (p. 219). In this paper it is argued that when the clinician focuses on only one side (e.g., either confrontive or supportive communications) of a continuum of possibilities, it is an incomplete approach lacking in balance.

Likewise, when a client identifies with or focuses on only one part of himself, such as depressed, fearful, alcoholic, or dependent parts, his behavior, communication and problem solving abilities typically become very limited and rigid. As the client begins to develop complementary parts, behaviors and resources, new choices may open up. Complementary parts refer to parts which help to balance and complete each other. For example, in a dependent relationship a "letting go" part can serve to complete a "hanging on" part. Erickson recognized that when a patient offered seemingly contradictory messages (e.g., wanting to go into trance, and wanting to stay out of trance) he could and would offer communications, particularly metaphors, which accepted and supported both needs. A basic principle of this approach is to accept and support *all* parts of the person in the process of transformation.

The goal of balancing communications and parts is not to use them for equal lengths of time or to make them the same size, but rather to have them support and complete each other. The author distinguishes between an "either/or" causal epistemology and a "both/and" systemic epistemology, and discusses the Ericksonian approach in light of this distinction. Choosing one alternative tends to exclude others, thereby potentially limiting or creating an inflexibility in the approach and development. In contrast, this "both/and" approach allows great flexibility and a sense of completeness.

The importance of balance, and the continuous movement and growth towards balance, is well illustrated in nature and the environment. One's breath goes in and out, and as it does one's body moves up and down. Erickson typically made use of these often overlooked processes in his inductions; for example, when a subject breathed in and the body gently shifted up, he would speak in a slightly higher voice or move his head up in synchronization with the subject's movement. Then as the subject breathed out Erickson would lower his voice while moving his head down again. By mirroring these subtle shifts Erickson joined the subject's natural rhythm, thereby enhancing rapport and trance development.

Countless other aspects of nature exhibit similar processes. The tides of an ocean or lake move constantly in and out, back and forth, and up and down, as do the waves. As the body develops, the limbs grow to roughly the same length and size. Each of the eyes are similiar in size and capabilities and complement each other to create binocular vision.

As trees grow, the weight of the branches is equally distributed above the trunk to create the necessary balance. These are simple examples of the complex balance that exists in systems. One might imagine the consequences if this balance ceased to continue, that the tide comes in but no longer goes out, or that one arm grows much longer or larger than the other. The negative effects are readily apparent. When out of balance the goals of the system become more difficult to reach, and the life of the system may even become threatened.

Balance in Communication and Induction Techniques

Go Into Trance & Stay Out Of Trance

It is often the case that a subject wants to go into trance and yet another part of him or her is hesitant about going into trance. Erickson handled such situations by communicating in a way that accepted and supported both needs. In one example Erickson (1975) said to the subject: "Well, Monde, this time I'd like to have you take your time about going into a trance. I don't want you to go into a trance too soon. And you know how easy it is for you." Each individual has unique needs and desires, thus the degree to which the hypnotherapist must accept or acknowledge the part that wants to stay out of trance will necessarily vary. Occasionally a brief comment like the one above will suffice. However, in other cases it may be necessary to elaborate on the value of staying out of trance in order to handle the subject's particular interferences with experiencing trance.

Generally speaking, supporting the part of the subject that wants to stay out of trance will serve several purposes: it sets him or her at ease (there is no pressure to go into trance; that part is valued); it fosters a feeling of safety and trust such that when the subject does go into trance he or she tends to be more willing and able to explore that state; and finally, it creates a context in which therapeutic change can more effectively take place. One method the hypnotherapist may employ to support the part that wants to stay out of trance as well as the part that wants to enter trance is metaphor. These may include stories about other subjects who had some hesitations about entering trance, and then finally went into trance. Direct comments which value the subject's need to feel safe, or stay alert and in control can be interspersed in the stories as an additional way of supporting the "stay out of trance" part. Other more abstract or indirect stories which involve similar processes to those of going in and out of trance are also effective. These stories may involve the general themes of going in and out, up and down, or hanging on and letting go. (For a detailed discussion of the construction and use of metaphors, see Gilligan, 1986).

Two important points can be emphasized here. First, it is important that the hypnotherapist adapt his communication and behavior to the ongoing needs of the subject. When the subject gives minimal cues indicating the "stay out of trance" part, such as an overreliance on conscious processing, a preoccupation with internal dialogue, excessive tension, opening of the eyes, or other such conscious movements, then there is a need to utilize and support that part. If the subject goes into trance without difficulty then "stay out of trance" communications may interfere with the induction. Second, each individual and each part has its own unique needs and desires. Thus, some subjects who want to go into trance but have difficulty in doing so may need further education regarding hypnosis. Others may need more trust or comfort, a different context, or more conscious communication. Facilitating trance is most effective when the therapist can discern what exactly is interfering with the subject's development of trance and handle the interference gracefully while continuing the induction process.

Confusion & Non-confusion

Confusion, one of Erickson's greatest contributions to the field of hypnosis, is an effective communication technique for inducing trance by depotentiating conscious processes (Erickson & Rossi, 1979). Erickson (Haley, 1967) described several types of confusion, including: spatial confusion (e.g., up/down, left/right, here/there), temporal confusion (e.g., now/then, past/present/future, days, months, time), non-sequiturs, and plays on words (e.g., right, left, write and right). In this paper, the focus is upon the need for balancing confusing communications with clear, understandable communications.

Erickson (Haley, 1967) observed that after using confusion for a period of time there developed, "a growing need for the subject . . . to make some kind of a response to relieve his increasing tension and he readily seizes upon the first clear-cut easily comprehended communication offered to him" (p. 132). For example, upon recognizing that the subject is confused and is therefore more prepared to respond to a meaningful suggestion, the hypnotherapist might say "That's right, sit down and allow yourself to drop into a trance."

To the degree that the subject has a strong defensive conscious mind and a need to resist entering trance, the hypnotherapist can employ confusion techniques, while for subjects who experience trance easily, confusion may not be necessary. Erickson (Haley, 1967) discussed shifting between confusion and clarity, and the need for balance in the following way:

> . . . communications [confusing] given in a meaningfully emphatic manner become a medley of seemingly valid and somehow related ideas that leads the subject to try to combine them into a single totality of significance conducive to a response, literally, compelling a response. But the rapidity of the communications inhibits any true understanding, thereby precluding responses and resulting in a state of confusion and frustration. This compels a need for some clear and understandable idea. As this state develops, one offers a clearly definite easily comprehensible idea which is seized upon immediately and serves to arouse certain associations in the subject's mind. The medley is then continued and another comprehensible idea is offered, enhancing the associations of the previous clear understanding (p. 156).

Confusion is a potentially beneficial technique used to depotentiate the client's conscious interferences and resistances to experiencing trance. However, if used without integrity and without clear balancing communications, the subject may become angry, feel distrustful, and imposed upon.

Permissive & Directive Approaches

Many individuals perceive and believe that Erickson was permissive and indirect in his approach to hypnosis and psychotherapy. However, if one examines his work it is evident that, while he was frequently indirect, he also was often directive and authoritarian. One aspect of Erickson's work which remained constant throughout his career was that of utilization: a willingness and ability to use whatever the client offered as the basis of induction and therapy. The principle of utilization created a context within which Erickson's flexibility could develop.

Balancing permissive and indirect communications with authoritarian and direct communications allows the hypnotherapist flexibility in how to best meet the needs of the client and achieve the desired results. Permissive and indirect communication gives clients the greatest freedom to respond and explore in their own way and in their own time, while authoritarian and direct communication demands that clients respond in a specific manner or follow a certain sequence of relatively arbitrary instructions.

A potentially negative consequence of an overly permissive approach is that the client may continue down self-destructive pathways and thereby perpetuate limiting ways of being. Clients who are very confused or upset, or who go into trance and access deeply emotional negative experiences instead of following permissive instructions to carry out some other task may need very specific and directive instructions, usually offered in an ongoing fashion. Later, a more permissive approach can be used successfully. A second potentially negative consequence of an overly permissive approach is that the client may avoid meaningful issues in therapy and assume control of the relationship, believing the therapist doesn't know what to do.

The consequences of using an overly directive approach may include a loss of rapport and trust, an arousal of resistance, possible premature termination of therapy, and short lived, compliant changes in response to an authoritarian figure. This approach also tends to foster the client's dependence on the therapist for advice and direction, not giving one the opportunity to develop one's own inner learnings and resources (Yapko, 1983).

While the importance of balancing permissive with directive approaches is clear, there are no definitive guidelines governing this balance. The timing and degree of permissiveness or directiveness is dependent on the unique needs and responses of the individual client. To the degree that a client is resistant, indirect and permissive communications are called for; the more willing and responsive the subject the more successful direct communications will be (Zeig, 1980; Yapko, 1984). This is not intended to suggest that direct approaches are preferred; they are not. With direct approaches the subject may easily use conscious mediation, or simply comply with the wishes of the therapist. Indirect and permissive approaches bypass conscious interference because the relationship between the suggestion and the response is difficult to recognize. Therefore, the indirect approach tends to simultaneously depotentiate conscious processes and access and utilize unconscious processes (Gilligan, 1982).

These balance principles (Gilligan, 1985) are reflected throughout Erickson's work. They may lead to an increased flexibility in communication which enhances the therapist's rapport and trust with the client, as well as the ability to work with a wider variety of clients and human problems. In applying balance to therapy, the therapist accepts and supports all of the client's parts no matter how dysfunctional they may initially seem to be. If the client feels valued and supported, therapy is facilitated. This perspective is in sharp contrast to those approaches which may label parts or behaviors as "sick" or "crazy," in order to devalue them and attempt to get rid of them.

Balance in Developing a Therapeutic Strategy

In many approaches to therapy, therapists, as well as clients, focus exclusively on "getting rid of" or "controlling" problems, thereby devaluing them. Gilligan (1985) has discussed one of the problems with this approach:

> Complements become framed in an either/or relationship of opposition ("standing in the way of") or dissociation, thereby prompting attempts to develop (or identify with) one complement and control ("defeat," "overcome," "get rid of," etc.) the other. Since complements are inseparable (though distinguishable) and negation is impossible, such control strategies usually create increasingly "vicious" cycles (i.e., circles) of dissociational functioning. (p. 205)

In Erickson's approaches, he often would try to find the value of a problem and somehow turn it into an asset. At other times, he indirectly worked to establish other changes such that the problem either became unimportant or the symptom behavior was no longer necessary. To clarify these ideas, a conceptual model describing the process by which balance principles can be used to develop therapeutic strategies is presented. This is followed by several clinical examples which illustrate the application of the model to the treatment of specific human problems. (Incidental details in the case descriptions have been changed to protect the privacy of the clients).

Conceptual Model

One of the first tasks of the therapist is to identify: (1) what the client wants to experience (desired goals); (2) the presenting problem; and (3) any parts of the individual interfering with change and supporting the problematic patterns. For example, one client treated by the author (described in detail below) desired the goal of sobriety. His presenting problem was drinking alcohol excessively, and his interfering parts wanted to feel confident, be creative and handle pain (among other secondary gains), but feared he couldn't meet those needs without alcohol.

Once the above dimensions have been defined, the therapist can focus on experientially developing a full awareness in the client of each part. In a case example described below, one alcoholic client called the part of him that wanted to be sober "I want to love myself." Developing a part can be accomplished through the use of homework, role playing, symptom prescription, or developing an image of the part while in trance, including feelings, emotions, sounds, words and pictures which are associated with that part. (For a more extensive discussion of developing parts, see Carter, 1983)

While developing the presenting problem part as well as the part(s) interfering with change, it is of utmost importance that the therapist identify the client's secondary gains associated with those parts. The behavior of an alcoholic part often seems dysfunctional, however, the intention or wish of that part (e.g., to feel confident) is usually a resource well worth having. One assumption upon which this approach is based is that all behavior and communication is functional and valuable within the unique context of the individual's life situation (Bandler & Grinder, 1979; Carter, 1983; Beletsis, 1985). The particular meaning and function is, of course, unique to each individual. Identifying the value or intention of these parts begins to transform the problem into something useful, and can indicate the complementary parts which need be developed in order to create balance or completeness.

As a last step, the therapist consolidates and integrates the changes in a way that supports the integrity of the individual. This may be achieved by using hypnotic and therapeutic interventions in conjunction with homework assignments, and by contextualizing changes. Great care is taken to insure that the changes and new behaviors are accepted by all parts of the individual. The critical guideline of this model is utilization, meaning the therapist's ability to adapt his communication, behavior and therapeutic strategy to the ongoing needs of the client, rather than expecting the client to adapt to the therapy being offered.

Case Example: Poor Self Image

A good example of utilization is in Erickson's (Haley, 1973) description of a 21-year-old woman who came to him for therapy because she had never had a boyfriend but very much wanted to be married and have a family. She felt hopeless, reported that she had no friends and that Erickson's therapy was her last hope. She stated she would give therapy with Erickson three months to be successful before she would commit suicide.

In interviewing her Erickson found out that she had never dated and that she was very self-conscious about the fact that there "was a gap between her front teeth, which she covered up with her hand as she talked." Additionally, he found a starting place for her to develop social and dating skills:

> A young man at her office showed up at the drinking fountain each time she did, but even though she found him attractive and he made overtures, she ignored him and never spoke to him. . . . Erickson approached the problem with two major interventions. First he proposed that since she was going down hill any how, she might as well have one last fling (p. 71).

Erickson gave her elaborate instructions intended to develop, within her, an interest and caring in how she presented herself. This included giving directives for going shopping for clothing and for having her hair done. In the second intervention,

> Erickson gave her a task. She was to go home and in the privacy of her own bathroom practice squirting water through the gap between her front teeth until she could achieve a distance of six feet with accuracy. . . . When the girl was dressed properly, looking attractive, and skillful at squirting water through the gap in her teeth, Erickson made a suggestion to her. He proposed that when she went to work the following Monday she play a practical joke. When the young man appeared at the water fountain at the same time as she did, she was to take a mouthful of water and squirt it at him. Then she was to turn and run, but not merely run; she was to start to run towards the young man and then turn and run like hell down the corridor (pp. 71–72).

After dating for a few months they married and had a child!

Initially her looks and the gap between her teeth were severe self-image problems which she used to prevent herself from meeting men. By developing a part of her willing to care about her looks and use the gap between her teeth beneficially, her problem became a source of enjoyment and a way to meet a man. Erickson utilized her wish to commit suicide and her biggest problem as the basis of motivation and therapeutic change. This directive and balancing approach is in sharp contrast with other approaches which may have attempted to understand her reasons for not taking care of herself and not allowing herself to date.

This technique of turning a problem into an asset, or developing changes such that the problem is no longer a problem, can be viewed in light of balance principles. In the above example the woman saw only the ugliness of the gap between her teeth and used it to feel terrible about herself. Erickson helped her to see the potential beauty of that same gap.

Case Example: Hanging On & Letting Go

A 40 year old woman named Jane sought therapy from the author, reporting that she felt dissatisfied with her current relationship of four years and was generally unhappy with her life. She very much wanted to be happy again, and wanted to either change the relationship for the better or simply end it. In the beginning of the relationship in question, she felt "in love" with Joe, her boyfriend, and they did many activities together. During the following three years they progressively did fewer and fewer things together, and she began to feel depressed when she recognized that she was "in a rut."

During the first two sessions it became apparent that a dominant part of her was "hanging on" to the relationship, causing her much pain and stifling other parts and needs that she had. Several patterns associated with the "hanging on" part became evident: making all the compromises to meet Joe's needs; repressing her feelings and needs and not communicating them for fear that Joe would leave the relationship; living in *his* house with *his* furniture; not going to shows or on vacations; and, doing all the housework alone even though both worked full time jobs. In order for the two of them to do anything together, Jane had to provide the idea and all the motivation. She felt angry and resentful. The value and intention of Jane's "hanging on" part was to solve their problems, and make the relationship good, "like it was in the beginning."

There are many qualities and resources of the "hanging on" part that are worth having and are necessary to a satisfying relationship, however it is not complete by itself. The more Jane hung on to make the relationship work, the more it didn't work. This resulted in Jane feeling an increased need to hang on, and thus the attempted solution became the problem (Watzlawick, 1978). The resources and changes she desired were accessed by developing a complement to "hanging on," in this case, "letting go."

The focus of therapy was on developing and integrating a "letting go" part which could serve to complete the "hanging on" part and be better expressive of more of her needs. In Jane's case the development of her "letting go" part included going out to movies, attending concerts and shopping, education and skill building in communication, communicating her feelings and needs to Joe, being more spontaneous, and leaving Joe's things where he left them, letting him pick up after himself. Additionally, several sessions were used to help Jane resolve and let go of "hanging on" issues from her childhood.

As she began to integrate these two parts, the relationship transformed, becoming more satisfying. "Letting go" allowed expression and fulfillment of needs that had been missing, and elicited from Joe his desire to "hang on" to make the relationship work. He became interested in her activities and asked whether he could join her. Later, he began to suggest things they could do together. Each expressed both parts in an integrated fashion rather than Jane hanging on and Joe letting go.

Great care must be taken to consolidate and integrate the changes into a new self image that supports the value of all parts. The development of parts which the individual is unaccustomed to attending to interrupts one's typical way of being and provides opportunities for some new feelings. In Jane's case, attitudes and behaviors associated with "letting go" were, at first, both uncomfortable and exciting. As "letting go" integrated with "hanging on," Jane's comfort with both parts increased.

In developing complementary parts, the therapist needs to attend to the possibility of oscillations between the parts. In Jane's case this was evident in her shifting from overly hanging on to overly letting go. While it is effective to develop the "letting go" part fully, it is important to consolidate and integrate the changes in an ongoing fashion with the "hanging on" part, and in close relationship to the broader goals of making the relationship work. Balance is accomplished when both parts are used appropriately.

Hanging on and letting go are general parts or complements which may apply to working with a variety of human problems. Therefore, it is essential that the therapist keep in mind that each part has unique meanings, value and associations which are, in many ways, different from other clients with similiar problems. To the degree that these unique idiosyncrasies are utilized by the therapist, the therapy will be more meaningful to the client.

Case Example: Alcoholism & Sobriety

One client the author treated was a 36-year-old artist named Barry who considered himself an alcoholic since age 16. His life, both socially and professionally, didn't turn out the way that he had hoped, and he felt very depressed and hopeless. He desperately wanted to stay sober and make some changes and wanted help to achieve these goals. In the interview it was discovered that he drank alcohol every day, usually beginning shortly after waking up in the morning and stopping just prior to going to sleep.

The first two sessions were used to develop rapport and gather background information. Barry was already motivated to make changes. (For a detailed discussion of the treatment of alcoholism, see Beletsis, 1985.) In the third session, Barry was guided into trance in order to explore some of the changes that he wanted to make, and then to focus on one primary goal or wish. He said that he wanted to love himself. In further developing that image in trance, he later reported that he imagined himself staying sober and free from drugs, looking and feeling 20 pounds lighter all over his body, and riding a ten speed bicycle feeling the cool breeze go by his face. In addition he was eating healthily, having contact with friends that he had isolated himself from, and resolving early experiences and relationships which he felt hindered him from his currently desired changes. Two images came forth that seemed especially meaningful to Barry. The first was a feeling of breathing more fully and experiencing an "openness of my heart, like a window being open for the first time, letting all the bad air out and all the fresh air in." The second image was of having "a sun tan instead of a bar tan."

After developing (i.e., identifying and amplifying) this part which Barry called "I want to love myself," I asked during the trance if any parts of himself were hesitant to go ahead with those changes. Later he reported that, in trance, he had said to himself "what if I can't?", and felt afraid of failing and dying, unable to remain sober and make the changes he wanted. One objection he became aware of while in trance was that he believed he wouldn't be able to be creative unless he drank alcohol. He also couldn't imagine having fun and letting go without alcohol. In exploring the value of drinking and being alcoholic it also became clear that, in his experience, alcohol was necessary for him to feel confident in his work and with people, and that he needed alcohol to express his feelings, including his rage and anger as well as his love. Finally, alcohol had always been there to relieve boredom.

These complex secondary gains are viewed as resources that the alcoholic part achieves and can be valued for rather than labeled as bad or sick. The above objections to remaining sober and loving himself indicate important aspects of his experience which must be addressed in order to develop long term integrated changes. They are critical pieces of information necessary in developing a therapeutic strategy.

One might anticipate, with this client, as well as with those of severe personality disorders, that integrating changes may require some time due to multiple secondary gains, strong defenses, and fear. The guiding ideas of utilization, integration and balance principles are just as applicable in complex cases as in treatment of other problems.

The initial therapeutic strategy with Barry included having him begin to exercise, eat healthily, and practice using self hypnosis to develop his image of the "I want to love myself" part. His willingness to do these homework assignments in the following week demonstrated his motivation to participate in the therapeutic process. Later sessions included education and skill building in communication, facilitating or resolving relationships in which the communication was unclear, increasing his contact with himself (especially his emotional awareness and his willingness and ability to communicate it), reading, going to A.A. meetings, and working on being able to be creative and sober at the same time.

At each session work was done to develop and evolve the "I want to love myself" part. Work was also done to develop and appreciate his "alcoholic part" while handling objections to changing as they surfaced. Thus both complementary parts are developed and integrated. Between sessions homework was given designed to develop parts and behaviors which satisfied and completed the secondary gains of alcohol thereby supporting a sober lifestyle. For example, Barry was instructed to write about his feelings on a daily basis in order to increase his contact with himself and increase his ability to communicate with others. He was instructed to begin an exercise program and begin to better care for himself. Small changes were built upon in order to develop larger changes. As the "love himself" part developed, aspects of it became increasingly stable in his lifestyle. As the objections to changing were resolved, a sober lifestyle was supported, and resources, once only available by drinking alcohol, were developed.

The "I want to love myself" part was a complement to the "alcoholic part" which had become dominant and incomplete leading to a great deal of unhappiness. The therapeutic changes involved developing resources and behaviors, or balancing parts, which could express and complete the many aspects of life Barry was missing (e.g., self esteem, health, confidence, communication, etc.). A sixteen month follow-up indicated that Barry is still sober with no relapses. He has lost weight, exercises regularly, has a sun tan instead of a bar tan, has updated his relationship with his mother and is integrating sobriety into both his social and professional lives.

Case Example: Fear & Security

A 33-year-old professional woman named Ruth came for treatment and reported that she had fear which resulted in uncomfortable physical tension, often immobilizing her such that all she could do was lie down. Her fear was damaging her relationship with her husband to the point of leading to separation, interfering with her professional life, and causing frequent recurring nightmares. Therapy involved developing a part she called "safety and security", which, in the future, she could access by herself as needed. To develop this part, while she was in trance she was told that she could imagine situations in her life in which she felt very safe and secure, to feel the feelings and emotions that go along with those images, and to hear any reassuring things that she says to herself associated with safety and security. Having such a part available was a good balancing complement to her fear.

A second aspect of treatment was to contact and develop the fearful part of her. Ruth had always attempted to repress or get rid of this part, and so it never had been fully expressed, much less accepted as somehow valuable. While she was in trance her fear was accessed, which included all the physical sensations, thoughts, emotions and images that were associated with that fearful part. Then, while Ruth was still in trance, I offered general metaphors regarding the surprising value of the many parts of one's self that one may not understand. Finally, in trance, she was asked what her fear really wanted for her, and it was suggested that she effortlessly allow her unconscious mind to explore the possibilities and surprise her. After reorienting from trance she reported that her fear wanted her to allow herself to be loved and nurtured.

While exploring and developing the part of her that could be loved and nurtured, she realized that she had great difficulty accepting love and nurturing from others unless she was very sick. This led into resolving early childhood experiences with her parents, and some of the "self-programs" (e.g., don't trust men, be perfect, etc.) that she had uncritically accepted for years. For homework she was instructed to contact her fear part each day, communicate with it, and find out what it wanted and how it could be valuable to her. The purpose of this assignment was to include and integrate this part rather than denying or attempting to get rid of it. Subsequent follow-up indicated no further immobilizing fear and an increased ability to take care of her needs appropriately.

Conclusion

In discussing health, balance and complements, Keeney (1983) claimed:

> . . . health in human ecosystems refers to a vital balance of
> diverse forms of experience and behavior. To engage in an effort
> of maximization or minimization, rather than diversity, leads to
> the escalating sameness . . . defined as pathology . . . This for-

mulation characterizes the healthy individual as an integrated, whole unity of diverse differences. Consequently a whole, healthy integrated person is not necessarily one who can be called symptom free . . . health and pathology are sides of a cybernetic complementarity (p. 126).

In this paper, balance, as it applies to communication and therapy, has been discussed, and a conceptual model of how to utilize and integrate opposing communications and parts has been presented.

As with any model, this approach can be both useful and limiting. The examples used to illustrate this model were simple and brief; however, the same principles are equally applicable in more complex cases. One of the main points of this paper is the importance of accepting, developing and integrating both parts rather than attempting to exclude or deny one. This approach respects the client's conflicting parts and therefore his or her innate integrity.

Flexibility in communication is another area which was emphasized. Therapists can develop greater effectiveness by noting their ability to shift between opposite communications. For example, if one feels comfortable being supportive but feels unable to be confrontive this indicates an area where clients can hide, so to speak, perhaps decreasing the therapist's effectiveness. Thus, in order to develop flexibility the therapist could learn to integrate confrontation into his or her therapeutic style.

Last, the approach upon which everything hinges is that of utilization. To the degree the therapist respectfully and meaningfully accepts and uses what the client has to offer as the basis of therapy is the degree to which success is ensured.

References

Bandler, R. & Grinder, J. (1979). *Frogs into princes*. Moab, Utah: Real People Press.

Beletsis, C. J. (1985). "An Ericksonian Approach in the Treatment of Alcoholism." In J. Zeig (Ed.)., *Ericksonian psychotherapy (Vol. II) (pp 359–372)*. New York: Brunner/Mazel.

Capra, F. (1975). *The tao of physics*. New York: Bantam.

Carter, P.M. (1983). *The parts model*. Unpublished doctoral dissertation, International College, Santa Monica, CA.

Erickson, M.H. & Lustig, H. (1975). The Artistry of Milton H. Erickson, M.D., video tape. New York: Irvington.

Erickson, M.H. & Rossi, E.L. (1979). *Hypnotherapy: An exploratory casebook*. New York: Irvington.

Gilligan, S.G. (1982). "Ericksonian Approaches to Clinical Hypnosis" in J. Zeig (Ed.). *Ericksonian Approaches to hypnosis and psychotherapy*. (pp 87–103). New York: Brunner/Mazel.

Gilligan, S.G. (1985). "Generative Autonomy: Principles for an Ericksonian Hypnotherapy." In J. Zeig (Ed.), *Ericksonian psychotherapy (Vol. I)*. (pp. 196–239) New York: Brunner/Mazel.

Gilligan, S.G. (1986). *Therapeutic Trances: The cooperation principle in Ericksonian hypnotherapy*. New York: Brunner/Mazel.

Grinder, J. & Bandler, R. (1976). *The structure of magic* (Vol. II). Palo Alto: Science and Behavior Books, Inc.

Haley, J. (Ed.). (1967). *Advanced techniques of hypnosis and therapy*. New York: Grune and Stratton.

Haley, J. (1973). *Uncommon therapy*. New York: Norton.

Keeney, B.P. (1983). *Aesthetics of change*. New York: Guilford Press.

Perls, F.S. (1969). *Gestalt therapy verbatim*. Moab, Utah: Real People Press.

Polster, E. & Polster, M. (1973) *Gestalt therapy integrated*. New York: Vintage Books.

Rossi, E.L. (Ed.). (1980). *The collected papers of Milton H. Erickson on hypnosis* (Vol. IV). New York: Irvington.

Satir, V. (1983). *Satir: Step By Step*. Palo Alto: Science and Behavior Books, Inc.

Simonton, O.C., Simonton, S. & Creighton, J.L. (1978). *Getting well again*. New York: Bantam.

Watzlawick, P. (1978). *The language of change*. New York: Basic Books, Inc.

Yapko, M.D. (1983). "A Comparative Analysis of Direct and Indirect Hypnotic Communication Styles". *American journal of clinical hypnosis, 25*, 270–276.

Yapko, M.D. (1984). *Trancework: An introduction to clinical hypnosis*. New York: Irvington.

Zeig, J.K., (Ed.). (1980). *A teaching seminar with Milton H. Erickson*. New York: Brunner/Mazel.

Hypnosis as Science

by
John J. Koriath, Ph.D.

Overview

People often wonder what makes sense. At such times, as Yapko (1984) has pointed out to be typically Ericksonian, understanding seems to emerge from apparent confusion. Consider such a process. There are a number of experiences that a group of people share. By common agreement, these shared experiences are what they are because of "common sense," i.e., shared perception. Because they can be readily communicated with other members of the group, common sense experiences become conscious sense experiences. Experiences that this group as a whole does not acknowledge are common nonsense, or, as they explain to one another, conscious nonsense. Of course, individuals in this group may have their own unique experiences not shared in common and to understand them must call upon uncommon sense. Since these experiences can not be readily communicated, they make unconscious sense to the individual, while to the group they remain common and conscious nonsense. Even at the individual level there are some experiences which can not be acknowledged either by common sense or uncommon sense and so to even consider such happenings is uncommon nonsense. Such considerations are nonsense of the unconscious. Yet, when confronted with change, i.e., the demand to adapt to new experiences, individuals can draw upon what appeared to be nonsense, whether common, conscious nonsense or unconscious, uncommon nonsense and transform that potential into actual unconscious sense, uncommon sense which weaves the new event into the fabric of personal experience. Indeed, the group can utilize the insights of an individual, that person's uncommon sense, to solve problems and adapt to new situations. When the group does, of course, they are conscious that such experiences are nothing more than common sense. This process of discovering order in disorder seems to be inherent to information systems, whether biological, electronic, or human (Campbell, 1982).

At other times what makes sense appears to be much more systematic. A more objective point of view (Groves & Schlesinger, 1982) asserts that what makes sense is physical energy (of which all forms are not detectable by humans) stimulating sense organs. Sensory receptors transduce physical energy into a form usable by the brain, namely, electrical energy in the form of the action potential. Nerves code sensations by changes in number, frequency, and pattern of action potentials transmitted to the brain. Following numerous chemical and neurological transformations a neural pattern is formed in the sensory projection area of the brain. It is altogether different from the physical energy pattern experienced. The neural pattern is a symbolic representation of experience. Growing from "sensation" is "perception," a considerably more complicated arrangement of symbols. The perceptual process integrates not only sensations, but also recognition, recall, association, feelings, and motives. Perceptions, interwoven with current and long term goals, as well as a self-evaluation of personal adequacy in a given situation, finally lead to action.

The two portrayals just presented of what "makes sense" reflect what appears to be a conspicuous endeavor of human intelligence: the attempt to impose order on experience. Both portrayals sound quite different from one another because of the different methods used to organize experience as well as the differing language structures used to communicate them. Nevertheless, each is of value in understanding the process of "knowing." The first portrayal reflects a more intuitive transition of understanding than the second, yet still is grounded empirically. For example, the suggestion of Copernicus in the sixteenth century that the planets revolved around the sun was nonsense to the common sense of Ptolemic thought which had prevailed since the second century A.D. (Leshan & Margeneau, 1982). Through experience, however, it became the uncommon sense which gave birth to a heliocentric view of our solar system, a view now held as common sense. Likewise, the unconscious sense of a team of scientists made travel to the moon a conscious sensible consideration in the 1960's while at the turn of the nineteenth century it was conscious nonsense to entertain the thought. Hence, though individualistic in language and poorly defined in methodology, the subjective portrayal—order emerging from confusion—reflects one polarity of knowing.

The second portrayal presented reflects a more objective transition to understanding than the first, yet still draws on intuitive insight. This portrayal is easily recognized by that group of individuals involved in scientific research because it reflects the findings of empirical observation constrained by common methodology and language. Indeed, competent individuals could repeat the procedures of Nobel laureates Hubel and Wiesel (1977), used to observe the process of visual perception from the retina to the occiptial cortex and find similar results. Consequently, employing a common language and defined methodology, the objective portrayal—order emerging by consensus—reflects the other polarity of knowing.

Epistemology is the branch of philosophy concerned with the process of knowing, with how we "make sense" out of experience. The word is derived form the Greek *epistemos* and *logos*, meaning the study of knowing (Webster, 1973). Over the past century philosophers have been joined by two other groups whose operating assumptions rest heavily on epistemological concerns. The two other groups are research psychologists and psychotherapists. Viewing the epistemological processes of these three groups involved in interpreting human experience, both unity and diversity can be found. Unity among the groups exists in the recognition that human experience is the end product of a symbolic transformation of potential. Diversity among the groups is characterized in the methodologies and languages used to create and organize the symbolic transformation.

Philosophers build conceptual frameworks from the phenomenological flow of experience as it passes through human consciousness. The philosopher uses a language of formalism. Rigorously defined terms construct abstract concepts. The absract concepts are organized by rules of logic into complex theories. Subjective experience is assigned meaning only under exacting conditions.

Research psychologists study the structures and mechanisms which lead from stimulation of sensory receptors to perceptions of things and events. The research psychologist, in the tradition of science, identifies important variables, manipulates them, and then measures quantitative changes in those variables. On the basis of statistical analysis the researcher interprets the significance of the observed changes and what trends they may suggest. Objective experience is approached by creating situations under specific conditions and applying a defined method of analysis to the resulting data in accordance with agreements made by all researchers.

The psychotherapist, whose chief concern is to facilitate adaptive behavior and perspective for a client, is faced with a unique challenge. On one hand, the psychotherapist must attempt to empathize with the unique reality of the client. On the other hand, participation with others involved in strategic intervention demands comprehensible methods and language for communication. The challenge is to integrate the two polarities of knowing, which is the purpose of this paper.

For those who utilize hypnotic interventions, the challenge to not only maintain the flexibility of a subjective approach, but also present an objective model for reflection and evaluation may seem to be an unresolvable conflict. Rather than approaching this matter as inherently conflictual, it may viewed as a paradox. The matter can be approached much as the Japanese koan—"What is the sound of one hand clapping?" In answering the koan the paradox is resolved.

In an attempt to answer the above koan, this presentation will grow from three dimensions all focused on the goal of integrating the subjective and the objective frameworks in hypnotic interventions. The first dimension will explore methodological fallacies which have weakened research approaches to objectify human behavior. The second dimension will suggest one possible framework for hypnotic interventions which retains flexibility for the therapist, monitors integrity in the therapist/client relationship, and has a methodology and language which can be used in common to create objectivity. The third dimension will explore the nature of the subjective/objective paradox.

Methodological Fallacies

Two methodological fallacies have weakened research approaches attempting to objectify human behavior. Consequently, many feel that objective descriptions of human behavior are not particularly valuable for therapy done in the "real world." Once these fallacies have been surmounted, the approach may again be useful. The first fallacy involves the approach to the mind/body relationship. The second involves making assessments and predictions of individual behavior based on studies of groups of individuals.

The nature of the mind/body relationship has been described from widely divergent viewpoints. Under the Cartesian philosophical premise separating mind and body, the issue surfaces as one of whether perception is the result of the mind and body interacting or whether the body merely executes mental commands. This debate is rooted in psychological and physiological literature for nearly a century. William James (1892) suggested that what humans experience results from visceral and autonomic input to the brain, particularly on the emotional level. In this view, sensations develop perceptual qualities as a result of their experiential context, namely, the peripheral nervous system. Consequently, perceptions take on unique qualities associated with distinctive patterns of physiological response. More generally, experience results from body/mind interaction. For example, from this perspective, when encountering a frightening event, persons would feel afraid because they run, rather than running because they feel afraid. The perception of danger precedes the behavior of escape, and the feeling of fear results from the act of running.

Walter Cannon (1929) proposed a view which has been more dominant in shaping research. He suggested that the peripheral nervous system "passively" executes commands received from the central nervous system. A unidimensional nervous system response is postulated in which the brain controls a unified response of the body. In this view the assumption is that only quantitative changes in physiological responses differentiate experience; hence larger physiological responses are associated with more intense experiences. More generally, the body responds to the mind in unison and intense responses reflect intense experiences. From this perspective, for example, when encountering a frightening event danger is perceived, fear is experienced, and only then does the escape behavior of running occur.

The relative dominance of Cannon's view, along with methodological and technological constraints of the times, has resulted in a general reliance on observing limited behavioral traits in research and inferring the corresponding activity of those not directly observable. While such an approach may meet the systematic requirements of science, it now seems apparent that such investigations produce a much too narrow description of human behavior. Simultaneous observation of multiple characteristics is necessary. Such an approach is predicated on the position that the views of both James and Cannon represent opposite poles of the broad range of perceptual possibilities in which the human creates a specific experience.

The second fallacy that has weakened objective approaches to the study of human behavior arises from making predictions about individuals from the study of groups. Human beings are the product of genetic and developmental uniqueness. Albert Ax (1984) pointed out that if the full implications of psychobiological uniqueness are to be accepted, the limitation imposed by the search for general laws of psychophysiological interaction by group methods must also be confronted. The mainstream research viewpoint does not tend to focus on uniqueness, but rather attempts to average out uniqueness with group studies. Such studies have been successful in describing and predicting trends for large groups. Indeed, the enormous success of the insurance industry is just one example based upon such studies. It utilizes a viewpoint which ignores individual variance and searches instead for significant trends in group behavior. However, too often scientists or clinicians, not fully aware of the assumptions and justified conclusions which research methodology allows, have yielded to the temptation to conclude that if an individual is a member of a group, it can be predicted that the individual member will behave like the rest of the group. Such an inference is not methodologically sound and frequently leads to disastrous attempts to "normalize" individuals' behavior.

An example of an experimental study of the health benefit of pets may serve to illustrate the point. Mugford and M'Comisky (1975) gave twelve pensioners cage birds and twelve other pensioners plants. On the basis of responses to symptom and mood questionnaires, the group who received the birds improved compared with those who received the plants. The methodology in the study appears sound. The conclusion that, on the average, pensioners were happier in terms of mood when given pets, could be justified. But a treatment program providing all individual pensioners pet birds, because objective evidence for groups of pensioners exists, would be to succumb to the fallacy.

Framework for Objectivity

Gordon Allport (1968) proposed that clinical insight into individual behavior should be predicated on what he calls "morphogenic" study, that is, the organization of the specific individual under consideration. A methodology and language which can focus on multiple characteristics as they relate to the organization of a particular individual may be the foundation of an objective approach for strategic hypnotic interventions. As more clients find that assistance in maintaining their health is shared by a team of health practitioners in a variety of specialty fields, the need for objective descriptions in both diagnostic and intervention strategies becomes more immediate for those employing hypnosis in the context of therapy sessions. Communication among health practitioners of various disciplines depends upon objective description in order to optimize understanding of the client. The concepts and language of statistics, while familiar to many areas of research and medicine, are not widely utilized in the area of hypnosis (perhaps with the exception of the issues surrounding hypnotic susceptibility). However, they can be effective for assessing client needs and employing hypnotic interventions. An examination of statistical concepts and an example may serve to illustrate the point.

In the therapeutic setting, order can be imposed upon a clinician's observations using the tools of statistics conceptually. Central to the language of statistics are the concepts of mean, variance, and correlation, all of which extend a flexible yet insightful grasp on organizing observations of an individual's experience. These concepts are used to reduce, describe, and interpret a group of observations on a particular trait or characteristic.

Taken collectively, this group of observations is called a variable. A variable can be described in terms of central tendencies, the range and variance of expression, and the relationship of one variable to other variables. Ignoring mathematical derivation, from a conceptual point of view the mean represents the average observation of a group of observations. The mean can be thought of as a person's central tendency. Typically, such an observation would be interpreted as what is normal for that individual. From another standpoint, if a variable is thought of as a group of points making a line, the mean is the center of gravity for that line, the point at which the line is in balance. Also, the center of gravity is the point to which all other points are drawn.

As a central tendency the average derives its meaning from a range of observations for which it is the focal point. The statistical concept embracing the nature of this range is variance. Variance refers to the degree of spread in a set of observations. It implies that any single observation must be considered relative to the range of responses or behaviors from which it is a member.

Correlation is the concept which expresses the degree of relationship between two variables; that is, groups of observations or behaviors. Correlation is conceptualized as being the product of examining the two groups of observations relative to the variance of both from each other. This concept is illustrated well by its geometrical interpretation. If each of the variables is visualized as a line extending from a common origin, in this case the person being observed, then correlation between these two variables can be expressed as the angle between the two lines. Narrow angles reflect strongly related variables. Wider angles reflect a weaker relationship. A right angle reflects no relationship between the two variables.

A case example employing these concepts for the purpose of assessment and intervention involves a single woman in her fifties, referred for treatment by a friend. The client presented the complaint of weight gain following recovery from an illness. She had tried numerous diets for weight loss without success. Earlier in life she had been a nun. Choosing later to leave the order, she became a principal at a parochial school. She was challenged and fulfilled with the administrative tasks of her profession, and she lived alone. About two years prior to the author's contact with her, she had a radical mastectomy, underwent chemotherapy, and was currently considered to be in a state of remission. As a result of her illness she had been relieved of the responsibilities of being school principal and was working in the school system as an instructional aide.

The statistical concepts previously discussed provided a suitable framework for organizing both an objective description of this woman's difficulties in adapting to change and for developing a strategy for therapeutic intervention.

In the clinical context, assessment begins with the collecting of behavioral data since this woman's presenting complaint was behavioral, that is, her eating habits had made her overweight, and she was unsuccessful in following diets. It was also apparent to observers, such as the friend who suggested she seek therapy, that she seemed less than satisfied with her current lifestyle and was apparently feeling depressed. Nevertheless, the woman insisted her problem was strictly a behavioral one: she could not diet successfully.

Through casual conversation data was collected. It was organized within the conceptual framework discussed above. The woman's eating habits were patterned around three meals a day, in which she had a "normal" caloric intake, and evening snacks. The evening snacking seemed to most obviously contribute to her intake of excess calories, particularly since the snacking was engaged in while distractedly watching television.

This behavior, then, was normal for her. It was her mean or average behavior pattern; that is, the center of gravity to which her activity was drawn. Variance in this case was small. That is to say, the range of deviation from regular balanced meals and evening snacking was minimal. Her frequency of food binges, which would be defined as an extreme, was small. The frequency of skipping meals to compensate for excess eating, was also small. In other words, the distribution of her eating behaviors was very stable. It was negatively correlated with her daily activity level, because when she was involved with her responsibilities as an instructional aide or in any other social setting, her excess food consumption was minimal. When she was alone, inactive, and not otherwise stimulated she tended to overeat.

Clearly this assessment differs from a person whose variance indicates behavior swings between the extremes of gorging and starving. It also differs from the person whose average behavior does not consist of normal meals and snacking, but rather regular meals of inordinate proportion. Also, the negative correlation with activity level differs from a person whose activity level is positively correlated with overeating. For example, someone involved in a high number of social activities which focus on food and overeating would have a positive correlation between their social activity level and overeating.

The organization provided by the concepts of statistics can also adapt well to forming interventions. In the case presented above, prior to gaining weight, the woman's average evening activities were often filled with administrative planning and coordination as a school principal. Changes ensued with the onset of her illness in both activity level and eating habits. Since she had not been successful in following diets to change her eating habits, intervention was directed at changing how she made use of her time. Such a strategy accepted her difficulties with controlling her eating behavior and utilized the correlation between the two variables of eating and activity to initiate an intervention strategy.

Accepting the woman's average eating behavior implied utilizing her average activity level as a point of origin in expanding behavioral options. Expanding behavioral options in this case meant expanding the range of potential activities she could engage in during the evening. A time expansion during informal trance was employed. It began by having the woman imagine herself on a typical evening, starting with her average behavior pattern. From this starting point she was asked to experientially imagine different activities in two directions.

The two directions involved the range of potential activities around her average evening activities. Rather than only passively watching television in the evening she was asked to imagine herself involved in an activity in which she had participated in the past and had found enjoyable. She remembered having a garden. She recalled the different flower beds, especially their colors. She remembered planting, fertilizing, weeding, and watching the new growth. She vividly recalled how good it felt to take care of something and nurture its development.

In the opposite direction from her average evening activity she was asked to imagine an activity in which she had never participated because she had not had the opportunity. She imagined herself in a bowling league. She saw herself being more physically vigorous. She imagined mastering a new skill. She thought about how good it felt to enjoy camaraderie with her teammates.

By expanding her range of potential activities, she realized that she was not limited to her average, normal behavior pattern. She had the opportunity and room in her lifestyle to spread out and try other activities. Her average behavior had evolved from her time of illness, not from a conscious choice. She could deliberately become involved in the activities she had imagined in the therapy session as well as others that occurred to her later. Since these activities would provide challenge and actively occupy her, time for snacking would diminish. The strategy employed utilized a correlation of variables, allowing for this woman to lose weight without the stressful challenge of attempting another diet.

The framework created utilizing statistical concepts to organize behavioral data can accomplish three therapeutic goals. The first is a communicable assessment of behavioral problems which can be shared by the therapist with other health practitioners. The second is a structure for forming intervention strategies. The third is an approach which minimizes decision making for clients by the therapist and maximizes personal decision making by clients for themselves.

The third goal merits more consideration since it reflects a value system which is not exclusively, but certainly inclusively Ericksonian. Recurrent in the author's experience with Milton Erickson's writings and with those who share his views (Erickson, Rossi, & Rossi, 1976; Yapko, 1984; Zeig, 1982) are those values asserting the importance of keen observation, acceptance, and integrity.

The approach presented here emphasizes, as do most approaches, that the point of departure in a psychotherapeutic session is that of data collection. Though such collection may occur with varied degrees of randomness, nevertheless the data can be deliberately ordered in terms of observations of multiple characteristics. Organization of data into variables can be accomplished both for overt behavior as well as descriptions of inner experience because it is done on a within subject basis rather than in comparison of one person to a group.

The premise of acceptance of a person's current state is well served by the concept of correlation, since it allows for the utilization of a related variable not considered to be a problem by the client to facilitate change in the variable that is considered to be a problem by the client. In short, the client is not asked to attempt change in an area that is beyond their current capacity and the reason for their seeking help in the first place.

Integrity is, in part, promoted by the nature of the approach and the role in which it places the therapist. The concepts of "mean" and "variance" organize a range of possibilities for a particular characteristic of experience, the possibilities of chance. The therapist, in creating a strategic intervention is asked to present the possibilities of chance to the client. The client is left with choice, both as a role and a responsibility. "Chance," as the role of the therapist, and "choice" as the role of the client, are part of a triad. Herman Melville (1961), in his allegorical story of the matmaker in Moby Dick, presented the third point of this triad as necessity. Milton Erickson might call it the "knowing of the unconscious." Others might call it fate, while still others might call it a force of universal purpose, or evolution. Whatever the name, it refers to faith in a benign process. The faith is that deliberate choices made in the range of chance will be drawn by this third point in the triad to an existence in which conflict becomes resolved, even if only until we are faced with another demand to adapt. In this faith can be found continuity and a unity to the diverse experiences life.

The Paradox of Subjective and Objective Approaches

This paper has presented knowing as a human endeavor to impose order on experience. Different systems and rules for imposing order result in different assessments of what makes sense. While diversity exists in the methodologies and languages employed, all ways of knowing share in common the process of transforming energy of some sort into a symbolic representation of reality. This paper has focused predominantly on developing an objective description of individual experience that can be utilized in hypnotic interventions. Confined by the fetters of common rules and language, the possibility of objective experience is approached. An objective organization of experience enables better interaction and communication among groups of health practitioners.

Are the subjective and objective approaches incompatible? The objective approach restricts individual creativity and expression. The objective approach creates a structure to house a common sense. Releasing the fetters of common rules and language, the flexibility of subjective experience is attained, and the doors can then be opened to an uncommon sense.

There is a paradox here. It has been common in recent years to illustrate the nature of paradox by referring to the conundrum in modern physics which allows light to be both particle and wave. Insightful physicists are not bothered by this. Physicists study light as a manifestation of the electromagnetic spectrum. In the macrocosm they detect light with radio telescopes. In the microcosm they detect light in particle accelerators and cloud chambers. Between the macrocosm and microcosm is the "see and touch" world of every day reality. In this realm where physicists interpret their findings to make common sense, they become aware that they are both father and mother, in one parent combined, of particles and waves. More specifically, quantum mechanics, the branch of physics which describes the movement and mass of subatomic particles, states in its "uncertainty principle" that certain pairs of quantities, such as position and momentum of an electron, cannot be measured simultaneously (Boslough, 1985). This means that the electron, rather than being an objective, absolute and determinable bit of matter, is a sort of objective entity that can be thought of as spread around the atomic nucleus. The implied suggestion which resolves the paradox here is that the subatomic world, and even the world beyond the atom, has no structure independent of definition by the human intellect. Hence, what appears conflictual when viewed as separate from human thought becomes integrated in the recognition of parentage. Concepts are the scientist's creations, their children, vehicles for their research findings. Contradiction is experienced only when parenthood is denied, when a creation is separated from its creator.

A subjective approach and an objective approach are as different as particle and wave. Conscious mind and unconscious mind, common sense and uncommon sense, chance and choice, and client and therapist are as different as particle and wave. They exist as conceptual creations, bipolar opposites employed to generate order from disorder, actual from potential.

What are the implications? The subjective approach and the objective approach can become agreements on guidelines for imposing order on experience, balanced in mutual respect and appreciation for individuality, diversity, and interdependence. Conscious mind and unconscious mind can release their absolute and determinable aspects and find a range of relationship in which to exist. Common sense and uncommon sense may emerge as variables rather than constants in the equation of change which continually demands adaptation. As bipolar opposites these concepts can be utilized to generate a distribution of experiential and behavioral possibilities. They can forge the tools of the therapist described in this paper as the "caretaker of chance." They can enrich the soil for the client described in this paper as the "cultivator of choice." The resulting growth is an abundant garden of human experience.

What then "makes sense?" It appears to be the third point in this triad which has been given many names—necessity, evolution, purpose—just to recall a few. All of these names imply that this third point, resident within each person, is intelligence. Intelligence is the integrating force and source of bipolar opposites, the existential center which must be acknowledged and yet defies all attempts at description.

References

Allport, G.W. (1968). *The person in psychology*. Boston: Beacon Press.

Ax, A. (1984). Basic concepts of psychophysiology. *International journal of psychophysiology, 1*, 3–6.

Boslough, J. (1985). *Stephen Hawking's universe*. New York: William Morrow Company.

Campbell, J. (1982). *Grammatical man*. New York: Simon and Schuster.

Cannon, W. (1929). *Bodily changes in pain, hunger, fear and rage: An account of recent researches into the function of emotional excitement*. New York: Appelton.

Erickson, M.H., Rossi, E., Rossi, S. (1976). *Hypnotic realities*. New York: Irvington Publishers.

Groves, P.M. & Schlesinger, K. (1982). *Biological psychology*. Dubuque: Wm. C. Brown Company.

Hubel, D.H. and Wiesel, T.N. (1977). Functional architecture of macaque monkey visual cortex. *Proceedings of the royal society of London*. 198, 1–59.

James, W. (1892). *Psychology*. New York: Henry Holt.

Leshan, L. and Margeneau, H. (1982). *Einstein's space and Van Gogh's sky*. New York: Macmillan.

Melville, H. (1961). *Moby Dick*. New York: Signet.

Mugford, R.A. and M'Comisky, J.G. (1975). Therapeutic value of birds with old people. In R. Anderson (Ed.), *Pet animals and society*, London: Baillere and Tindall.

Webster, N. (1973). *The new collegiate dictionary*. Springfield, Ma: G. and C. Merriam
   Company.
Yapko, M.D. (1984). *Trancework*. New York: Irvington Publishers.
Zeig, J. (Ed.). (1982). *Ericksonian approaches to hypnosis and psychotherapy*. New York:
   Brunner/Mazel.

ISSUES IN TREATMENT

Self-Blame as a Consequence of Self-Improvement Programs

by
Beverlee Hockenstein, Ph.D.

Overview

A large percentage of people are involving themselves in self-improvement programs which offer an expanded vision of what is possible within the human experience. These "new visions" are intended to become the goals toward which the program's participants aspire. Old habit patterns and ways of experiencing the world may come to be viewed as inadequate, as things to be discarded, and perhaps even reacted to with scorn and attack. Once participants have learned and experienced a new way of "being," they may transform this new approach to life into the way they "should" be thinking. Using the new ideas as a frame of reference, they may have acquired a new, updated idealized way of being.

Participants in self-improvement programs eventually leave the controlled environment that has been created for them during the initiation into the new world view and attempt to apply in their daily lives the new perceptions, techniques of relating, and tools for behaving they have learned. Problems arise, however, because these new learnings are not completely integrated into the person's old belief system (Aronson, 1984). Due to this lack of integration, the individual is often unsuccessful in applying the learnings outside the program's controlled environment. In such instances, the person becomes frustrated at not being able to use the knowledge effectively and may begin to engage in the process of self-blame in response to failures. Messages offered by such programs such as "accept yourself," "be flexible," "notice your fear and do it anyway,'' and ''get it and get off it'' may, on the surface, appear to be useful for the individual's growth. However, what if the individuals don't know how to apply those messages meaningfully in particular situations? These people are then in an uncomfortable situation. The discomfort is compounded as they proceed to ''beat themselves over the head'' for not knowing how to act in the most enlightened way or for not successfully applying the program's messages. At this point they are using the tools they were taught as instruments for growth as weapons against themselves, which actually hinders their growth.

Therapies and self-improvement programs frequently talk about ways of dealing with self-blame in daily life, but it is rarely mentioned in reference to not living up to the ideals set up within the program itself. Participants need to have positive ways of relating to their failures in their efforts to live up to their newly established standards. It is vital for program leaders and therapists to be made aware of the different levels of self-blame in order to incorporate strategies for dealing with the potentially critical consequences of these programs.

An example of one client's behavior may make the pattern of self-blame clearer to the reader. Kenny was in his late forties and was a therapist who had been involved in self-improvement programs both as a participant and as a leader. He had been working with encounter groups continuously since the mid-1960's, and much of his life was devoted to learning, growing, and evolving as a person.

Kenny met a woman at a workshop and fell deeply in love with her. He was impressed with her but began acting shy and awkward around her. Noticing his behavior, he began to blame himself for being less than perfect and assertive. He said, ''After all the therapeutic work I've done and after all the workshops I've taught, I can't believe I'm doing this!'' When it was pointed out that he was being hard on himself and really wasn't doing anything wrong, he responded, ''I know. I can't believe I'm being so hard on myself. Why am I doing this? I can't believe it.'' He was blaming himself for blaming himself, piling misery upon misery, with no apparent positive alternative for his behavior.

The purpose of this paper is to: 1) bring to the reader's attention the higher logical processes involved in the self-blame engendered by self-improvement programs, and 2) present an approach which will allow the client to utilize his/her failures and the resulting self-blame as a method of more fully integrating his/her newly-acquired ideals in a self-appreciative way. To accomplish this, a model is described incorporating a redefinition of the nature, function, and dynamics of self-blame and an illustrative case study is also presented.

The Nature of Self-blame

Self-blame, for the purposes of this paper, is defined as a self-critical process in which the individual judges that something that he/she said, did, thought and/or felt was inappropriate, wrong, bad, contemptible, ineffective, etc., and then ascribes the responsibility for that behavior to him/herself. This ascribing of responsibility can positively lead to rectification of behavior or to learning for future reference or negatively to feelings of guilt, inadequacy, self-hate, and low self-esteem.

Ronnie Janoff-Bulman, a researcher at the University of Massachusetts, is one of the few who have studied the process of self-blame in any depth (Janoff-Bulman, 1979). She described two different types of self-blame: 1) behavioral self-blame, which represents "an adaptive, control-oriented response" and 2) characterological self-blame, which represents "a maladaptive, self-deprecating response" (p. 1799).

In behavioral self-blame, the person may say something like "I really messed up that interview." He or she is blaming past behaviors and his or her own effort. If the individual has the idea that he or she didn't put enough effort into succeeding in the interview, he or she has the possibility of being in control of putting more effort into his or her next interview and of being able to succeed. It seems that it is the sense of control that allows the process of self-blame to be functional in an adaptive and productive way.

In characterological self-blame, the person may say "I am the kind of person who inevitably fails at interviewing." In this kind of self-blame, the person is attacking his/her internal ability and his/her basic character. If he/she doesn't have the ability and doesn't feel he/she is the kind of person who can succeed at interviewing, then there is little sense of the possibility of changing the situation and of being able to succeed at future interviews.

> Behavioral self-blame is control-related, involves attributions to a relatively modifiable source (one's own behavior) and is associated with a belief in the future avoidability of a negative outcome. Characterological self-blame is esteem related, involves attribution to a relatively nonmodifiable source (one's character) and is associated with a belief in personal deservingness for past negative outcomes (Janoff-Bulman, 1979, p. 1798).

To discuss the self-blame that originates in self-improvement workshops, it may be useful to review the logical structure of different types of self-blame. Whitehead and Russell (1910–1913) discussed the theory of logical types in their important work *Principia Mathematica*. One of the basic axioms of their theory is that "Whatever involves *all* of a collection must not be one of the collection" (Whitehead and Russell, 1910–1913, p. 13). For example, "animal" is a class of objects including dogs, cats and horses as members. In turn, "animal" is a member of the class, "living beings." If the levels are mixed and a particular kind of animal, like "dog," is listed as part of the larger class "living beings," the resultant grouping can lead to insoluble logical paradoxes (Whitehead & Russell, 1910–1013).

Gregory Bateson, in his book *Steps to an Ecology of Mind* (1972), applied the theory of logical levels to the concept of change. He stated:

> The simplest and most familiar form of change is motion, namely a change of position. But motion itself can be subject to change, i.e., to acceleration or deceleration, and this is a change of change (or metachange) of position. Still one level higher there is change of acceleration (or of deceleration) which amounts to change of change of change (or metametachange) of position (p. 283).

Stepping out of the framework one is in and looking at that framework is the process of going to a higher logical level, with the changes made in that higher framework being changes of changes, or metachanges (Bateson, 1972).

Applied to self-improvement programs, the concept of logical levels reveals the structure of the logical conflicts and paradoxes that can result. When a person burns the toast while making breakfast and blames him/herself, this is an example of simple self-blame. Some programs teach participants to "do everything 100%" and to "be fully attentive to doing things as perfectly as possible." When participants go home and, instead of blaming themselves for burning the toast at breakfast, blame themselves for not paying complete attention to the task, they are engaging in a higher logical level of self-blame.

Some programs teach participants that they shouldn't make themselves wrong. In other words, they shouldn't blame themselves in a demeaning way. If some participants then go home and burn the toast, they might begin by blaming themselves for burning the toast. But then they can blame themselves for making themselves wrong, which is in turn a form of making themselves wrong. They are making themselves wrong for making themselves wrong. This is an example of "meta-self-blame" or self-blame for self-blame. It is an obvious mixture of logical levels and can result in considerable personal confusion and emotional pain through the disintegration of the boundaries separating logical levels.

The Function of Self-blame

Even though extreme self-blame can be harmful to a person, it is also true that self-blame is a necessary and positive part of the personality when it is functioning properly. Having an ideal and using self-blame or self-criticism to guide oneself toward that ideal can be useful as a source of feedback and self-evaluation. It can be taken for granted that people will do things that are unacceptable to themselves and/or to their society as a whole. A person must be willing to take responsibility for his/her own thoughts and actions as the first step toward making appropriate and necessary changes in behavior.

Consider the case of an executive who was responsible for organizing a meeting which had inadequate attendance. This person could say, "Very few people showed up for this meeting. It is my fault for not making sure that everyone who ought to be here got a memo in ample time. Next time I will be more conscientious and send the memos to the appropriate people at least one week before the meeting." This type of blame is an example of what Janoff-Bulman (1979) called "behavioral blame" and in this case it led to productive behavior.

Self-blame can also be used in a less productive way. The same executive, on noticing very few people at the meeting, could say, "It's my fault. I never get things right. Maybe I don't even deserve to be in this position." This characterological self-blame can lead to despair or to some other form of bad feeling. The executive is likely to stay in that despondent state because it is more difficult to have access to internal positive resources when one is overwhelmed by negative feelings. Dwelling on personal failures and imagining that one lacks ability leads to stasis and stagnation. In contrast, self-blame without overwhelmingly negative feelings can lead to noticing undesirable behavior. One can then use that information to rectify the present situation and/or to learn new behaviors for use in future situations so as to avoid repeating the same mistakes. This positively reframes the mistakes as "learning experiences."

The process of self-blame can vary in intensity. One can engage in light to severe behavioral self-blame and/or in light to severe characterological self-blame. As self-blame moves along the scale toward its more severe characterological aspect, the more likely it is to result in depression, anxiety, guilt, and other negative feelings. The person experiencing such overwhelmingly negative feelings will have less ability to find some productive internal re-evaluation of his/her behavior and will be less likely to produce a healthier response to similar situations in the future.

Self-blame's usefulness or lack thereof can be judged by how healthy and functional the responses it leads to are for the individual and for society. In the model proposed here, self-blame is regarded as part of a system of behavior. While self-blame may sometimes seem to lead to intentionally self-destructive behavior, it must be examined within the system in which it is used. In other words, self-blame may not make sense if it is studied in isolation without considering its relationship to other aspects of behavior. Seemingly incomprehensible behavior may begin to make sense and be seen as useful when it is observed in the context in which it occurs.

The Dynamics of Self-blame

In order to discuss self-blame in detail, it will be useful to develop a systematic model of its dynamics. Watzlawick et. al. (1974, p. 1) stated that "all perception and thought is relative and is operating on a basis of comparison and contrast." Self-blame is viewed as a behavior which comes about as a consequence of a comparison between the individual's ideal and his/her perceived inability to reach that goal. From this point of view, self-blame is part of a behavioral system involving comparisons.

The author's model of self-blame similarly describes an idealized vision and a lesser or imperfect vision. The idealized vision is a representation of what is often described as a person's true or potential nature. The lesser vision is that person's representation of an unacceptable, imperfect nature or way of being. In order to engage in self-blame, the individual must be comparing him/herself or his/her behavior to something else. With respect to the self-blame engendered by self-improvement programs, it is in most cases the idealized vision promoted in the program against which the comparison is made.

The idealized vision stores the introjected ideals which have been absorbed at different times during a person's life. The culture and significant people in the individual's life strongly influence which ideals will be introjected. Because of the common existence of differences between the ideals that are introjected, the idealized vision usually contains conflicting ideals (Wurmser, 1981). For example, a little girl may learn from her mother that she should be strong and independent and from her father that she should be subservient and coy. Both become introjected into her idealized vision and she may spend a good part of her life agonizing over the issue of how to behave, trying to decide which set of ideals is right or how to arrive at a comfortable blend of two seemingly contradictory styles.

Profound confusion can also result from a person's participation in several different self-improvement programs in which he/she learns conflicting ideals. For example, one group might hold out as being ideal the person who is consistently blissful, peaceful, and all-knowing while another group may have as an ideal the person who can fully experience and express all emotions. Similarly, one group may encourage participants to become disengaged from the mere material world while yet another group holds up success and materialism as the highest achievement.

These newly introjected ideals may also conflict with ideals introjected during childhood. If a woman is taught that "A good little girl doesn't get angry," and then enters a Gestalt group in which she is urged to express her anger, she may experience conflicting ideals. The new ideal of emotional expression is attractive and seems reasonable, but the values learned in childhood don't go away just because one has decided they aren't "right" anymore (Yapko, 1985).

The idealized vision holds within it the "shoulds," the goals and the dreams of an individual. The individual compares him/herself with this idealized vision in order to evaluate whether his/her character and/or behavior measure up. If there is a mismatch, self-blame can be the result. There are two elements which can be involved in the comparison. It can be made against the idealized vision, as has been discussed, or it can be made against the lesser vision, which includes the unacceptable aspects of character and behavior.

The lesser vision has its own set of introjected principles in much the same way the idealized vision does. What is unacceptable for a person to think, feel, do, or be is outlined in the lesser vision. These principles are introjected from significant authority figures and from the cultures. The lesser vision can include such qualities as stupidity, fear, anger, dishonesty, emotional sensitivity, imperfection, etc.

There is less conflict between differing concepts that are part of the lesser vision. Since the qualities in the lesser vision lead to so-called "negative" feelings and feelings of inadequacy, any conflict between qualities only leads to more negative feelings. If one's lesser vision indicates that one is supposed to be sensitive and at the same time stoic and unfeeling, the inability to meet either one of these qualities tends to lead to a generalized sense of failure and no sense of need to work out the underlying conflict. In contrast, people expend a good deal of energy trying to work out slight conflicts in the idealized vision. Perhaps because the lesser vision is an image of imperfection there is no need to perfect it. Most people use the lesser vision as a guide to what should be avoided, even though there actually may be valuable behaviors and attitudes contained in it. Thus, they fail to appreciate that the lesser vision, like the idealized vision, can be used as a way of guiding themselves toward achieving their goals and desires.

The process of making judgments about one's self-image on the basis of the comparison with the idealized and lesser visions leads a person to identify first with behavior and then character and to determine a sense of who and what one is on the basis of that evaluation. Those who identify more with the lesser vision may be more likely to engage in self-blame and have feelings of inadequacy, guilt, or shame. Identifying with the lesser vision makes it difficult to imagine the possibility that one could become the kind of person who can live according to his/her idealized vision. Those who identify more with the idealized vision will tend to deny that the lesser vision has any relevance to or existence in their personality.

In the process of self-blame the idealized and lesser visions are often held separately. They can exist as independent mental units, each with clear boundaries and a separate place in the functioning of the personality. This is a type of dissociation. In his book, *Unity and Multiplicity* (1982), John Beahrs described the process of dissociation:

> Dissociation, in the broadest sense, refers to the mechanism or combination of mechanisms by which two or more collections of mental units can be kept separate from one another—the process of creating and maintaining boundaries or vertical splits between various sectors of conscious experience. . . . State of consciousness, schema, mood, role, system, ego state and alter-personality all refer to some level of what I have simply called a mental unit. Separated by a boundary from others, each unit has characteristic features defining its identity and finite persistence of over an extended period of time. Dissociation, then, is the process of forming and maintaining the boundary of said unit (pp. 61–62).

This dissociation between the two kinds of vision can lead to the paradoxical situation of a person who sees him/herself as meeting the demands of his/her idealized vision that he/she be kind, benevolent, and compassionate, while at the same time experiencing him/herself as behaving like his/her separately-defined lesser vision by being selfish, resentful, and unkind. The usual result is a sense of inner conflict and confusion.

This inner conflict drives the individual to resolve the discrepancies between the two visions. The theory of cognitive dissonance addresses the dynamics of this process. As Michael Yapko (1984) stated:

> In the 1950's, social psychologist Leon Festinger (1957) coined the term "cognitive dissonance" to describe the tendency for

human beings to seek consistent self-knowledge. If one is faced with internal inconsistency in the form of opposing or contradictory bits of information about one's self, an uncomfortable internal state of "dissonance" arises, and the inconsistency must somehow be resolved (p. 112).

It is important for a person to achieve some internal unity, to produce some internal integration between the idealized and lesser visions. As Branden (1969, p. 174) said, "A strong sense of personal identity is the product of two things: a policy of independent thinking, and the possession of an integrated set of values." In order to effect the desired integration of idealized and lesser visions, the following conditions must be met:

1. The various elements of the idealized vision, ideals and expectations, need to be integrated.

2. The contents of the lesser vision need to be recognized as possibly having positive value rather than being rejected entirely. This involves reframing the client's view of the contents of the lesser vision, turning liabilities into assets (Watzlawick et.al., 1974).

3. There must be a functional relationship established between the idealized and lesser visions.

In establishing a connection between the idealized and lesser visions, the groundwork for a better functioning system is laid. With these methods of rechanneling, participants in self-improvement programs will have the opportunity to learn new ideals, while maintaining and building high levels of self-esteem in the process. This will take the place of condemning themselves for not matching those high ideals.

When a person believes he/she has found an ideal or set of ideals which can serve as an ultimate or all-embracing solution, "It is then logical for him to try and actualize [that] solution—in fact he would not be true to himself if he did not" (Watzlawick et. al., 1974, p. 48). This can result in behavior which Watzlawick called the "Utopian syndrome." As he said:

> Ours is an age of Utopia. All sorts of gurus offer to rush in where angels fear to tread. "The natural state of man is ecstatic wonder; we should not settle for less" states the preamble to the constitution of a Free University. A program offers, "A system of human development carefully structured to produce lucid thought, emotional balance, and physical joy and serenity. The result is total integration of mind, emotion, and body which is man's true natural condition," etc., etc. (Watzlawick et. al., 1974, p. 47)

In self-improvement programs ideals are directly or indirectly offered as "true" or "real." Some leaders may say they are not telling participants what's real. They may say, "This is just a way of talking about things" or "Don't believe me, try it for yourself." It has been the author's experience in these cases that the ideals are communicated indirectly anyway, which is actually a more powerful way of presenting them.

One of the forms the Utopian Syndrome takes is what Watzlawick et. al. (1974) called the "introjective." This is the process that can lead to self-blame in the context of self-improvement groups. He stated, "If that goal is Utopian, then the very act of setting it creates a situation in which the unattainability of the goal is not likely to be blamed on its Utopian nature, but rather on one's own ineptitude" (Watzlawick et. al., 1974, p. 48). The result of attacking oneself for supposed failure to meet introjected standards can be a deep, painful feeling of personal inadequacy. As one client said, "I've attended fifteen workshops and read over a hundred self-help books and still I'm unhappy. I must really be a failure." The result is that the pursuit of happiness and personal perfection can leave the seeker unhappy because of a profound sense of failure and even unhappier because of self-blame for being unhappy. This is an example of meta-self-blame.

Therapeutic Approach

A basic assumption that may be used in the analysis of the structure of self-blame is that all human behavior is purposeful and that individuals choose the best options available to them at each moment (Satir, 1972). These options, however, are not necessarily the most useful or successful for people in all areas of their lives. If the basic purpose of an individual's behavior is identified, it can then be rechanneled into behavior that is useful in a more healthy and fulfilling way.

In the author's practice, the following are common situations in which people blame themselves for failing to achieve their idealized behavior:

1. When they think there are some others who have achieved their idealized vision and so they blame themselves for failing to achieve that ideal also.

2. When they have briefly experienced a glimpse or taste of what it is like to live according to their idealized vision, but have been unable to maintain that behavior consistently.

3. When they experience themselves as living up to their idealized vision most of the time and blame themselves for the few times when they do not.

4. When they have an idealized vision that they have never fully experienced and don't know anyone who has achieved it, but still believe strongly that they should be living according to their ideal and are blaming themselves for failing to do so.

5. When they don't have a clear picture of what they should live up to, but know their current experience is inadequate and blame themselves for not being better.

In addition, there are two different patterns of self-blame that originate from the adoption of a new system of ideals such as those presented by some self-improvement groups:

1. That pattern developed by those who already have a strong system of self-blame who attend a self-improvement program and fit the new learnings into their pre-existing framework of self-blame, fortifying it. The author calls this the "blame frame."

2. That pattern developed by those who have not experienced a large discrepancy between their idealized and lesser visions in the past but then attend a self-improvement program where they learn they can be much more enlightened, powerful, successful, or lovable than they ever dreamed possible. The discrepancy between their experience of themselves in their lives and their new ideal then becomes much greater and they may begin to engage in self-blame to a much greater extent than they did previously.

Producing change in the pattern of self-blame is more difficult with the higher logical levels of self-blame and with meta self-blame. This is because higher logical levels become more abstract and become less subject to conscious inspection (Watzlawick et. al., 1967).

Those who are in this unpleasant situation often are not aware they are blaming themselves. They think the ideal is reality and that the ideal is therefore right and they are wrong. The first step in breaking up the process of this behavior is to become aware that one is engaging in self-blame and that it is not leading to improvement. This opens the way for examining possible alternatives for changing the situation.

Watzlawick et. al. (1974) described two different types of change: first order change and second order change. First order change is "one that occurs within a given system which itself remains unchanged." Second order change is "one whose occurrence changes the system itself" (Watzlawick et. al., 1974, p. 10). He offered the example of a person having a nightmare. In first order change the person has a nightmare accompanied by images of screaming, jumping, running away, hiding, etc. There are changes within the dream, but no changes within the sleeping pattern itself, which is the behavioral system operating at the time. In second order change the person has a nightmare and wakes up.

This is a change in the operating behavioral system from sleeping to being awake and terminating the dream. (Watzlawick et. al., 1974).

As people experience self-improvement groups, they learn new ideals that are added to their old ideals. As new ideals are introjected, the level of unacceptable behavior rises. As the image of what one should be increases in quality or intensity, the image of what one should not be becomes more intense by comparison, especially with the recognition of more behaviors to be avoided. These additions of new ideals to the idealized and lesser visions are examples of first order changes. The underlying system leading to self-blame is usually unchanged since it is applied unconsciously to the conscious ideal systems of the two visions. Thus, there is more opportunity for the person to blame him/herself. Participants have increased the possible ways they can decide that their behavior is unacceptable, but the basic system has remained unchanged.

First order change encourages the person to do more of the same, perhaps more intensely. When some attempted corrective action fails to produce the desired result and does not make the person more like the idealized vision, the usual response is to try more of the same and to continue to be ineffective while engaging in even more self-blame, such that a vicious circle is created. This "more of the same" type of response is derived from a limited awareness of the alternative behaviors possible. For example, many procrastinators deal with their problem by nagging themselves to get going. They are under inner pressure to take care of business and feel bad because they are procrastinating. This leads to more nagging and bad feelings. The bad feelings actually get in the way of finding effective solutions and lead to stasis. The solution has become part of the problem.

Second order change is needed so that the person can step out of the system of self-blame, look at it, and find a new way of relating to the system and its elements. By breaking the comparison cycle it is possible to reframe the experience and to find new ways of relating to the situation. One may decide that procrastination is really useful at times and prevents one from doing things that are useless or harmful. One may find better ways of getting things done, and so on. The important procedure is to apply some sort of second order change to break the cycle of ineffective first order changes that keep the system going.

In the same way, the ideals and techniques taught by self-improvement programs can become part of the problem if the changes are restricted to first order change. What the program leader intends as strategies to achieve new ideals may be interpreted by some participants as ideal ways of behaving in themselves rather than as tools. Also the structure of an individual's world view may lead to completely different interpretations of a leader's statements than what was intended, leading to the introjection of dysfunctional ideals into the idealized vision.

Producing meaningful change requires second order change (Watzlawick, et. al., 1974). One must step outside the system in order to understand the operation of the system and make necessary changes in the system itself. By examining the overall process of change in a program setting, one can examine the information, ideals, techniques, perceptions and experiences that are offered and examine how they affect the behavior of individual participants. In this way the correlation between intended results and actual results, i.e. input and output, can be evaluated.

Participants come to self-improvement programs to find solutions to problems in their lives. The "solutions" they learn in the program environment may inadvertently become part of their problem. They may begin to use the newly learned ideals and techniques to blame themselves for not achieving everything they think they should. This is because these solutions are only used on the level of first order change. Participants in self-improvement programs are given different ideals, but their system for achieving these ideals remains the same. They are only told, "Do the new behavior, not the old behavior."

Watzlawick et. al., (1974, pp. 90–91) commented on this kind of first order change:

> An event (*a*) is about to take place, but is undesirable. [Imagine that the undesirable behavior is blaming yourself.] Common sense suggests its prevention or avoidance by means of the reciprocal or opposite, i.e. *not-a* . . . [imagine *not-a* as being loving yourself] . . . but this would merely result in a "first-order solution." As long as the solution is sought within this dichotomy of *a* and *not-a*, the seeker is caught in an "Illusion of Alternatives" and he remains caught whether he chooses the one or the other alternative. [This is what happens when the ideals learned in the program are not fully integrated and there is a dichotomy between a person's idealized vision and lesser vision.] It is precisely this unquestioned illusion that one has to make a choice between *a* and *not-a*, that there is no other way out of the dilemma, which perpetuates the dilemma and blinds us to the solution which is available at all times, but which contradicts common sense. The formula for second-order change, on the other hand, is *"not-a* but also *not not-a"* (Watzlawick, 1974, p. 91). This is done by choosing neither self-blame nor self-love, but by stepping outside the system and going to the next higher logical level to find a way of relating

to choices without having to reject one or the other. When this is done, one is dealing with the whole class of behaviors rather than just one member.

As Watzlawick et. al. (1974, p. 91) stated, "This is the essence of second-order change."

To help induce second-order change in self-improvement program participants, they must be helped to move up to a more general level than merely considering *a* or *not-a* and to place their problem in a different frame. The process of "reframing" is what Watzlawick called the one essential element in second-order change. As described by Bandler and Grinder (1982) and by Paul Carter (1983) in his "Parts Model," it is a model for therapeutic change that takes aspects of the client's internal experience and helps him/her to describe those aspects in terms of personified "parts" of him/herself. Watzlawick et. al. (1974, p. 97) described it as follows:

> To reframe . . . means to change the conceptual and/or emotional setting or viewpoint in relation to which a situation is experienced and to place it in another frame which fits the "facts" of the same concrete situation equally well or even better, and thereby changes its entire meaning. The reframing process is a way of effecting second order change in a system. It is a way of stepping outside a system and perceiving it in a new way. "Reframing operates on the level of Meta-reality, where . . . change can take place even if the objective circumstances of a situation are quite beyond human control.

It is a process which involves "changing the frame in which a person perceives events in order to change the meaning. When the meaning changes, the person's responses and behaviors also change" (Bandler & Grinder, 1982, p. 1). This is the central technique in the author's approach to treating clients who have problems with self-blame.

In order to blame him/herself, a person must step back, evaluate his/her behavior and then blame him/herself for that behavior. To reframe the self-blaming process, the client would be directed to go inside and ask the part that is generating the self-blaming behavior to communicate in some way. This step has many functions. It indirectly asks the person to step outside of the frame of self-blame in order to examine it. The assumption that there is a part of the person "generating the behavior of self-blame" helps to create a distance between the person and the process of self-blame.

By telling the client that there is a part inside purposefully generating a behavior, a foundation is constructed for the possibility that the part might also generate different behaviors. The fact that the part is personified also supports this idea of the possibility of change since people can change things. A client may feel stuck with ideas or beliefs, but if there is a part inside that is responsible for that behavior, that part can also be responsible for generating other choices.

When the part responsible for self-blame has been contacted by picturing it, hearing it, and/or feeling it, the client is directed to ask that part what its positive intention is for him. Discovering that there is a positive intent behind seemingly undesirable behavior is a very important step in the therapeutic process for the client. In identifying a positive purpose behind the behavior, the client is beginning to separate the behavior of self-blame from his/her self-image. It is here that the client begins to shift from characterological to behavioral self-blame. Whether there is in actuality a positive intention behind the behavior or not, originally, is not the pertinent question here. In the author's opinion and experience, it is the change of perception or reframe of the behavior that is useful and effective for therapeutic results.

The client begins to explore his/her internal world and access the possibility that the self-blaming part is trying to accomplish something worthwhile. It is often with surprise and delight that the client becomes aware that the self-blaming part intends to accomplish something good. It is the author's experience with this model that, although the content of the behavior differs from client to client, the basic intention of the self-blaming part is to function as a feedback device, to provide information, motivation, and protection for the client.

Case Example

In order to illustrate the processes of reframing self-blame and reframing and integrating the lesser vision, the case study of Stephanie is presented. Stephanie was forty-three years old, working as a salesperson, going through a divorce, and caring for her son, age seven. She was unhappy with the way she was handling her divorce and was complaining about a general sense of low self-esteem. When she first sought treatment, Stephanie had difficulties with all levels of self-blame. She had gone through "est" workshops as a participant at least three times each and had assisted many more times. This had occurred over a period of six years.

Stephanie was blaming herself severely for her failures in the marriage and in the divorce process. She blamed herself for not being able to apply her "est" learnings to her relationship with her husband and for "making herself wrong" (higher level self-blame). She also blamed herself for blaming herself (meta-self-blame). Because she couldn't apply her "est" knowledge in the context of her relationship with her husband, she saw herself as a bad person who was psycho-spiritually inadequate (characterological self-blame).

She had mentioned that she was able to apply much of her "est" knowledge in her life when she was alone, but she could not apply it in the relationship with her husband. She didn't seem to give herself credit for the times she could apply her new learnings. To begin transforming her higher level and characterological self-blame, it was important to help her see that sometimes she *was* matching up to her ideal. She was asked to describe the times she was successful in applying her learnings. As she did this, she began to have a fuller personal experience of her successes by absorbing herself in the memories of those experiences. She was told, "It is very important to be aware of the contexts in which you are successful. Once you know you have the ability to do something in one context, it becomes much easier to begin using that ability in other contexts."

Stephanie could begin reframing her self-limiting idea that she was not the *kind* of person who was able to apply learnings by replacing that concept with the idea that success involves applying different behaviors she had already learned in other contexts. This served to help shift her self-blame from the characterological to the behavioral type.

Stephanie blamed herself for leaving her husband and, when asked what she wanted to get out of the session, she seemed able to think only about what she wanted for her husband. She blamed herself because she seemed able to focus only on him and not on what she wanted. She said, "I've always been taught it's not up to anyone else to change or 'get off it'—it's up to me." This statement is an example of higher level self-blame. She was told that it is perfectly all right to start where she is in order to slightly reframe the restrictive idea that she is "wrong" if she doesn't do things exactly as she was told.

Next, she was asked to describe exactly what she wanted to happen. She stated, both seriously and laughingly, that she would like it if all of a sudden her husband would turn to her and tell her how he had finally seen that this divorce was a positive experience, a real step forward for him. She wanted him to acknowledge her for having the courage to leave and to admit that he was having a wonderful relationship with his new girlfriend. She wanted to hear that he had found a job, was happy, and "that everything would be friendly and heaven on earth for everyone involved."

The author replied, "So, if your husband experiences all those things that you talked about—he gets a job. He acknowledges his relationship. He figures this divorce has been the best thing that has ever happened to him, and calls up and says, 'Thank you. Thank you for this great opportunity you've given me,'—then what would you get to experience that you're not already experiencing?"

Stephanie said, "That I'm OK."

If everything does not turn out perfectly, then Stephanie feels responsible and blames herself for other people's unhappiness. In this interaction, Stephanie's experience of being able to think only of what she wants for her husband was being paced and matched. This makes it easier and more productive to lead her later to what she wants for herself (Bandler & Grinder, 1981). Her perfectionism in its own way was quite extreme.

Stephanie was asked to describe her feelings about being around people who aren't happy. She momentarily stopped breathing, and so was asked to close her eyes and begin to breathe. She started to cry very controlled tears, and it seemed clear that being sad or unhappy was unacceptable to her. She looked and sounded much younger as she cried, and so she was directed to "go inside and make contact with the little girl inside who is so sad." She did so and saw this cute, happy little girl that everybody loved. Asked if she is the same little girl who is crying, she said, "no," with sadness and with a little disdain—"She [the girl who is crying] is ugly and skinny and no one likes her."

The good little girl represents Stephanie's idealized vision. She is a cute little entertainer who makes everyone feel good. The skinny, ugly little girl represents her lesser vision, is quite unacceptable, and is hidden away. Asked what the skinny, sad little girl wants, Stephanie started to answer, but had trouble getting her response out and began to cry even more. "It's hard for me to say. It's harder for me to ask for." Finally in a state of deep age regression and still crying she said, "I want someone to rock me."

Stephanie had made contact with her "ugly, skinny" unacceptable lesser vision and she allowed herself to identify with it and to relate to what that part of her really wants—nurturing. I asked her to go inside and find the part of her that is able to rock the sad, little girl. Initially she had trouble finding it. Most mother images that appeared in her mind would only nurture the cute, happy little girl. Finally she came up with Miss Pruitt, a warm, nurturing relative she had as a child. Miss Pruitt represented the part of her that could gladly agree to spending time, at least two hours a day nurturing the sad little girl. Stephanie was asked how the sad little girl felt about Miss Pruitt nurturing her. She said,

"Now, I can feel secure and relax." She was encouraged to spend some time by herself talking to that part of herself and watching what level of contact could begin to unfold within her as she allowed herself to consciously and unconsciously deepen her relationship and contact with that part of herself.

Toward the end of the session, Stephanie's altered state was deepened and it was suggested that she could even more fully develop the parts of herself with whom communication had been established. She could also review any learnings she had made and could allow her unconscious mind to integrate those learnings in ways and in contexts most appropriate to her.

Stephanie began to accept some of her previously unacceptable parts, or aspects of her lesser vision. As she began to do this, her characterological self-blame shifted to a form of simple behavioral feedback. After accepting one reframing of an unacceptable part of her lesser vision, Stephanie was able to generalize her learnings to other unacceptable parts of herself, looking for what that part actually wanted or what resource that part actually represented. When Stephanie became more comfortable with her own sadness, she could begin to let others have their own feelings and not feel that she had to bear the burden of guiding them out of their feelings.

Summary

By recognizing self-blame as a potentially useful part of life and learning how to employ it effectively as a source of motivation and feedback, we can enrich our lives and facilitate better social interaction. Perhaps the key to the whole matter lies in realizing that every part of ourselves, every element in our personality, can have a positive intention behind it. When we reframe our perceptions and accept the underlying positive intentions of our behavior, we can find congruent direction and ways to meet our ideal goals efficiently.

References

Aronson, E. (1984). *The social animal.* (4th ed.) New York: Freeman & Co.

Bandler, R. & Grinder, J. (1982). *Reframing: Neuro-linguistic programming and the transformation of meaning.* Moab, Utah: Real People Press.

Bandler, R. & Grinder, J. (1981) *Trance-formations.* Moab, Utah: Real People Press.

Bateson, G. (1972). *Steps to an ecology of mind.* New York: Ballantine Books.

Beahrs, J. (1982). *Unity and multiplicity: Multilevel consciousness of self in hypnosis, psychiatric disorder, and mental health.* New York: Brunner/Mazel.

Branden, N. (1969). *The psychology of self-esteem*. New York: Bantam Books.

Carter, P. (1983). *The parts model: A formula for integrity*. Unpublished doctoral dissertation; International College.

Carter, P. (1982). "Rapport and integrity for Ericksonian practitioners." (pp. 48–57) In J. Zeig, (Ed.) *Ericksonian approaches to hypnosis and psychotherapy*. New York: Brunner/Mazel.

Erickson, M., Rossi, E. & Rossi, S. (1976). *Hypnotic realities*. New York: Irvington Publishers.

Festinger, L. (1957). *A theory of cognitive dissonance*. Stanford Ca.: Stanford University Press.

Janoff-Bulman, R. (1979). "Characterological versus behavioral self-blame: Inquiries into depression and rape." *Journal of Personality and Social Psychology*, 37, 1798–1809.

Janoff-Bulman, R. & Wortman, C. (1977). "Attributions of blame and coping in the 'real world': Severe accident victims react to their lot." *Journal of Personality and Social Psychology*, 35, 351–363.

Satir, V. (1972). *Peoplemaking*. Palo Alto, Ca.: Science and Behavior Books.

Watzlawick, P. (1976). *How real is real?: Confusion, disinformation, communication*. New York: Vantage Books.

Watzlawick, P., Weakland, J. & Fisch, R. (1974). *Change: Principles of problem formation and problem resolution*. New York: W. W. Norton.

Watzlawick, P., Beavin, J. & Jackson, D. (1967). *Pragmatics of human communication*. New York: W. W. Norton.

Whitehead, A. & Russell, B. (1910–1913). *Principia mathematica* (2nd Ed.) (Vol. 3). Cambridge: Cambridge University Press.

Wurmser, L. (1981). *The mask of shame*. Baltimore, Md.: Johns Hopkins.

Yapko, M. (1984). *Trancework: An introduction to clinical hypnosis*. New York: Irvington Publishers.

Yapko, M. (1985) The Erickson hook: Values in Ericksonian approaches. In J. Zeig (Ed.) *Ericksonian psychotherapy* (Vol. I). (pp. 266–281) New York: Brunner/Mazel

TOOLS FOR FACILITATING TREATMENT

Practical Applied Diagnostic Evaluation and "Pre-work" Work

by
Neil J. Simon, M.A.

Introduction

Each clinician has unique sensitivities with which to make special observations about clients. This observational skill can be honed and then integrated with information about human functioning. In an attempt to enhance observational and diagnostic skills, the author has developed the "Applied Diagnostic Evaluation," presented in this paper.

A historical review of Milton Erickson's early years shows that while medically disabled he became highly sensitized to his own physiological workings (Haley, 1967). He later gained a medical knowledge base within which to structure and express his earlier self observations and how they might apply to others. With experience, Erickson learned to rapidly assess the individual expressions of others. Erickson described the basis for his evolving a system of observing others:

> I had a polio attack when seventeen years old and I lay in bed without a sense of body awareness . . . I spent hours trying to locate my hand, or my foot, or my toes by a sense of feeling, and I became acutely aware of what movements were. Later,

1. The author would like to acknowledge the following people for their help in the preparation of this paper:
Louise Dooley, Roy Gaunt, A.C.S.W., and Gary Victor.

when I went into medicine, I learned the nature of muscles. I
also became extremely aware of physical movement . . . people
used those little telltale movements, those adjustive movements
that are so revealing if one can notice them . . . (Haley, 1967,
p.2)

Other notable clinicians have gained similar insights and developed
their own systems for understanding people, each system basically developed through perceptive observation. Each clinician attempts to gain
an understanding of the client by observing the actions and/or reactions
of the client. The clinician then takes those observations and puts them
into an acquired system of understanding, i.e., the clinician's preferred
theoretical and practical orientation. The clinician develops a preferred
orientation to treatment based upon his or her own personality characteristics, theoretical belief system, and clinical training. Erickson, for
example, appeared to have a special sensitivity to physiological phenomena within the individual as evidenced in the above quote. Arising from
his own physical problems, he appears to have furthered this awareness
in medical school when learning how a normal person functions. Throughout this time period he appeared to train himself to observe patterns of
patients and develop brief intervention techniques to therapeutically disrupt dysfunctional patterns. Other skilled practitioners such as Watzlawick (1978). Bandler & Grinder (1975a) and Bateson (1951) have
developed systems of evaluation and observation based upon their unique
understandings of the client. Ultimately, each clinician must develop an
assessment system which involves developing the clinician's ability to
observe and understand the client. Unless this beginning phase of the
therapy is managed well, the chance of successful intervention is decreased.

The client comes to therapy with an individual personal history unlike
anyone else's. The client selects (consciously or unconsciously) what
he/she says and verbally discloses the relevant information. The verbal
and nonverbal patterns evident in the clients' self-disclosure to the clinician is what this author calls the "client presentation." Clinicians
experience the presentation of the client but may not be consciously aware
of what they are perceiving (Barlow, 1981). Certain structured observational processes can lead to a cohesive system of diagnosis whereby
each clinician can better utilize his skills and training.

The intent of this paper is to describe different observational systems
involved in the clinical process which can lead to the development of a
functional diagnosis. This information can then be organized in such a

way as to develop a pre-intervention treatment plan. Once the accuracy of the information obtained at this pre-intervention phase is confirmed, the clinician can then prepare the client for desired changes.

Diagnostics

The essence of diagnostics is the ability to observe the client's presentation, interpret that presentation within an appropriate context and then develop a working hypothesis of where intervention should be aimed. From the start, the client selects information that he/she feels is relevant and presents that information both verbally and non-verbally. The clinician begins interpreting what the client is communicating and attempts to make sense of that information by placing it in a personally meaningful order. In most instances, the client will present a problem with identifiable parameters and underlying patterns. Such identifications allow the clinician to define the problem and to develop a hypothesis regarding the problem's formation (Lezak, 1983). This hypothesis develops from an integration of academic knowledge, clinical observation, and the experience of the clinician.

Employed to its fullest potential, diagnosis is both a science and an art. The scientific domain involves objective observation and notation of significant information during the client's presentation, and application of these into known systems of operation (the various theories of psychopathology). The artistic aspects of diagnosis involve the spontaneous interplay unique to the specific clinician/patient relationship. The artistic aspect further involves the clinical ability to elicit meaningful information from the client in "natural" ways in order to get a valid framework from which to interpret information appropriately. A third aspect involves the clinician's ability to build responsiveness in the client to new information ("building expectancy") in order to prepare the client for upcoming change (Haley, 1967).

For the client and clinician, the diagnostic process is necessarily immediately interactive. Initially, the clinician can observe the client and attempt to gain a gestalt of the client through his/her verbal and nonverbal presentation i.e., appearance, demeanor, and so forth. Beyond this point, the clinician attempts to skillfully elicit information from the client, using learned patterns and principles of questioning. An example of one such principle is the process of Meta-modeling (Bandler & Grinder, 1975a, pp.40–53). This type of questioning process helps fill in or clarify the verbal description the client presents to the clinician. The clinician helps set the tone, mood, and pace of treatment. This initial phase of the intervention process is the starting point for the development of artistic rapport between client and clinician. The degree of rapport between client and clinician can influence the degree of success during the change process significantly (Bandler & Grinder, 1981).

It is generally important for the clinician to maintain objectivity during the interview in order to allow the client to present him/herself and also to create an environment which best allows for the establishment of rapport. As the client reveals him/herself, a baseline of behavior and a natural prioritization of issues and concerns are able to surface. Thus the clinician begins to learn about the range of client experiences, client values, and so forth.

There are two established methodologies for the diagnostic process (Singer, 1965). The first is ascertaining information through a structured interview process. The second involves "going with the flow" of the client and allowing him/her to present information as he/she sees fit. The structured interview process allows the clinician to gather all the required historical information to be considered in the assessment process, i.e., personal and medical history. At the same time, such structured approaches to history taking can interfere with the natural flow of what the client wants and needs to share with the clinician. Encouraging spontaneous self-disclosure allows the clinician to gather a global picture of the client and the environment in which he/she lives. This second approach allows the client to present information as he/she sees fit. While allowing for spontaneity, this approach is not necessarily conducive to detailed information gathering or "getting the whole picture." Each clinician must evaluate for him/herself which model better affords the opportunity to obtain an adequate diagnostic picture. This is what the author calls the "pre-work" strategy.

To structure "pre-work" strategies it is necessary to answer five questions. There exist several ways to gain the basic information necessary to answer these questions. Each clinician receives trainng from his/her discipline and chosen modality of treatment, but no matter what the preferred modality of the clinician (i.e., Behavioral, Gestalt, and so forth) the questions seem basically the same:

1. What is the problem?
2. How long has this been a problem?
3. What does the problem stop you from doing?
4. Why change now?
5. How do you know when you will be better?

In asking these questions of the client, the clinician attempts to ascertain the components of the problem and its conscious and unconscious roles in the client's life. The first two questions establish the client's conscious definition and awareness of duration of the problem. The last three questions explore the motivation for maintenance of the problem and desire to change.

The interaction between the client and clinician during the problem defining process creates a series of unique interactions which help structure the depth and scope of the clinical relationship. Depending upon the levels of client/clinician rapport and the client's motivation for change, the client will respond to the questions by outlining his/her perception of the experienced problem.

Misdiagnosis usually occurs for one or more of the following reasons. Many times the clinician does not understand the client's presentation from having asked the wrong questions, making invalid assumptions about given information, or from coming to the wrong conclusion from the information presented. Likewise, the client can create difficulties by not giving complete or accurate information, i.e., unconscious deletion and distortion, intentional deception, or by simply being unaware of "parts" of him/herself. In any case, the clinician may operate in a way that unintentionally excludes important factual information and makes any assumptions erroneous. Consequently, this interferes with obtaining the necessary baseline information which would allow for the construction of the "whole picture" and the development of successful brief short term strategies.

In summary, the diagnostic phase involves gaining an understanding of the client and assessing the client's presentation. The scientific evaluation involves baselining the relevant behavior(s), assessing the client's motivation for change, which leads to the interactive process of pre-work. Before a discussion of the pre-work phase begins, a discussion of dynamics of interviewing is presented. This information is the foundation for both the Practical Applied Diagnostic Techniques and the Pre-work Strategies.

Basic Reviews of Theories Related to Applied Diagnostic Techniques

The following section discusses the different principles involved in understanding an individual's presentation.

Domains of Reference:

There exist three major "domains" in which people function: cognitive, affective, and psychomotor (Bloom, Hastings, Madaus, 1971). The cognitive domain involves the thought processes and the organization of factual information. Based upon the work of Piaget (Ripple and Rockcastle, 1964), one can assess the individual's capacity and style for processing information. Piaget stated that individuals develop and grow through six phases of cognitive development. As we grow we develop a style which gives us a view of the world unique to ourselves in that phase. The style is based upon both natural neurological processes and experience in the cognitive realm (Looft, 1972). It can be helpful for the clinician to evaluate the individual's cognitive process through a structured Mental Status Examination to better ensure the probability of a successful encounter with brief intervention techniques. The evaluation includes a review of the client's functioning in the following areas:

Personality disorders and dysfunctions;

Disorders of motor aspects of behavior;

Disorders of perception, thinking, orientation and memory;

Disturbances of affect and consciousness (Taylor, 1981). Study of neurological functioning can give further insight into client functioning.

Socio-emotional interplay (the affective domain) helps the client frame "feeling" experiences. As with the cognitive domain, the personality appears formulated by natural development combined with the individual's experience of the world. Erik Erikson's Epigenetic Principle of maturation and the eight stages of growth (Erikson, 1963) provide good examples of the natural phenomena one grows through as one develops. For example, if an individual experiences a secure environment during the important early developmental years, he/she develops a belief in the safety, stability, reliability and nurturance of the world. This manifests itself in an inner certainty that tends to stay with the individual. If he/she does not develop a positive belief in the environment, he/she is likely to expect the worst and view the world pessimistically.

The socialization of the individual and the resulting way one expresses oneself in the culture varies. One's acculturation is the foundation for emotional presentation. An individual assimilates cultural material and develops an entire system of communication which affects all other domains (Watson & Lindgren, 1973).

The concept of psychological safety and tolerance for the behavior of others comes from this affective stage as well. People tend to interpret information based on their experiences and training. Foundations of perception and concepts of understanding the world are based in this domain.

The final domain—psychomotor—involves movement. Movement and motion as expressive systems usually are not studied or observed in detail due to the complexity of attempting to discriminate the individual effects of body, brain, and mind (Lipowski, 1977). Birdwhistle (1970), Feldenkrais (1981), Lowen (1971), and Laban (1971) have each studied different aspects of the process of the psychomotor domain. Each has concluded that physical motion and movement are developmental and experiential in nature. Human growth and development leave a unique trail in this domain. The effects of the environment leave a pattern of identifiable effects reflecting what the individual has experienced. The "reading" of this "map" allows the clinician to make observations about client experiences.

The effect of traumas in the cognitive and affective domain of the client are well documented and noted in the literature (Millon, 1969). This information is readily available in order to describe and help individuals in emotional pain. In the psychomotor domain, trauma also takes its toll but literature about this is harder to find. When identified and understood, the psychomotor "scars" evident in the client are both revealing and diagnostically helpful in the interpretation and interpolation of an individual's functioning. Further discussion of this point follows later.

Social Observations

As discussed above, there exist several contexts in which personal experience is influenced by culture and education. These interactional areas need to be observed and noted to get a social picture of the individual. The following is a list of suggested areas to observe during the initial interview process and monitor during the evaluation process:

1. Linguistic process—observations of the individual's words (definitions, syntax, symbolisms, phraseology, placement or misplacement, etc.).

2. Social interactive process—the dynamics of interaction based upon norms and mores and interpersonal needs.

3. Reward systems—the reward system for problem maintenance. Assessing the client's and his/her environment's need to maintain a behavior, even a dysfunctional one, in order to keep balance in a family or work system.

4. Neuro-communications—the established patterns that the individual uses to communicate from each realm. This encompasses observations and perceptions of the world (hemispheric asymmetry and hemispheric dominance), sensory based communications, and the brain/body relationship.

Body Language

Ray Birdwhistle (1970), a developer of the field of Kinesics, and others such as Scheflin (1972) pioneered the study of body language communication from a social communication standpoint. His studies correlated communications with body movement in a social context. The research indicates the complexity of nonverbal communication. Developing an understanding of the client's body movements or characteristics can yield important diagnostic information. Such observations can allow the clinician to examine congruence between verbal and conscious communication levels and unconscious actions. When an individual is communicating a belief or feeling the clinician can listen to what is being said and assess whether nonverbal analogues are in agreement with the verbal statements. This information can be used directly or indirectly to help guide the client into an awareness which helps prepare the client for desired changes.

Observations of nonverbal communications can lead to the following arenas for examination of client/clinician communication:

1. Individual territory. This territory is developed ("staked out") as one begins the communication process (Sheflin, 1972). It allows one to gauge the intimacy of the conversation, trust, and comfort within the client's space. One can also observe the client's limited proscribed sphere of movement. This information can provide insight into the client's psychosocial boundaries through movement. By making these observations, the clinician can utilize comments, questions and actions which would allow the client to feel desirous of being more intimate and interactive with the clinician (Sheflin, 1972).

2. Territorial bonding. Once staked out, a hierarchical position and power base are established in the areas of respect, as well as in the degree of intimacy (Sheflin, 1972). The client's ability to develop bonds and share territory are useful in acquiring an understanding of the inner workings of the client around relationship issues. Depending upon which tact the clinician uses to approach the client, the client will react giving insight about relationship needs, the ability to trust and the nature of requirements to function effectively as a resource to the client. These requirements indicate how the client prefers to be worked with and/or indicates the necessary therapeutic negotiations process one needs to follow in defining the relationship.

3. Convention and mutuality. The ability to develop convention and mutual vocabulary establishes the foundation of a relationship. Rapport, in part, is this establishment of mutualness, which acts as a good relationship gauge. It is during this phase that expressions of eccentricity can emerge and the beginning of "pre-work" can commence. Once the foun-

dations have been laid, the individual can be less guarded and reveal more of him/herself. As the client experiences the increase in trust and rapport, he/she gives the clinician an unspoken permission to begin work.

Other texts in the area of body language (Weeks,1966) yield further information about this non-verbal communication process. The "body-mental" efforts of an individual can be analyzed by defining the parts of the body used in body action, body function, and/or its restricted movement. One need observe both movements and countermovements within the body which happen simultaneously. Other important observations include origin of movement and the entire position of the body as a whole. These observations can give further insight and/or confirmation of suspected dynamics the client may hold in the psyche. For example, a person who flails from the hip and shoulder joints evidently has a different emotional composure than those who flail from the knees and elbows.

Other authors (North, 1972, pp. 16–21) indicate that looking at the body and its psychological functioning, of "what is" versus "what should be," gives insight into an individual's way of dealing with the external world. One can interpret, with a considerable degree of confidence, the emotional restrictions, suppressions, and repressions one feels using this type observation methodology. A clinician with training can observe intended and/or restricted movements which show alterations of natural movement patterns (Todd, 1977). The individual who shakes hands pushing your arm and hand away versus the individual who shakes your hand and pulls you toward him/her are simple examples of how the person reacts interpersonally.

The "size" of movement (normal, reduced or exaggerated) and "shape" (angular, rounded or twisted) can reveal the person's attempt to influence the communication. Shape and space of body can be useful in interpretation of the way the client attempts to position him/herself. When an individual presents him/herself, the movement and motion of the body reveal further internal information about such things as desire to control, avoid, spatial needs, and kinesthetic needs.

A final observation deals with evaluation of the "stress" or the weight under which the body moves. Motion factors such as flow of movement (weight, time and space), elements in movement (exaggeration and suppression, etc.) and the patterns and rhythms of movement help refine the understanding of the individual's internal patterns and pace. This refinement allows the clinician to develop a more effective and efficient timing strategy when preparing to intervene with the client.

Laws of Learning

Information is recorded in the brain in short term memory and then converted into long term memory if conditions are appropriate (Luria, 1980). What comes into memory is subject to our unique processing, and then is subject to the momentary frame of reference. The entire frame (event, context, comprehension) is stored in long term memory. Analysis of new data, decision making and information gathering are built upon existing frames (Restack, 1979). Therefore, it is important to review how one learns in relation to perception and referencing functions. The author has compiled ten "laws of learning" which may help the clinician develop an understanding of the learning process.

1. The Law of Primacy.

Whatever happens first is more likely to stay first in the memory (Schacter, 1982). Research indicates that the first experiences an individual has (if significant) are maintained by the individual and become an experiential/factual foundation for that individual for further building of information. For example, if one mislearns something, one has a tendency to continue recalling the mislearned information. However, when an individual relearns information, he/she eventually can integrate it, and the new information becomes the new foundation for building more information (Schacter, 1982).

2. The Law of Concentrated Attention.

Whenever attention is concentrated on an idea in a setting which is emotionally charged, extraneous information is accepted by the subconscious (Bandler & Grinder, 1981). This state of concentrated attention is an altered state of consciousness which has a tendency to reduce critical cognitive faculties. When this occurs, psychological defenses are lowered, opening the client to suggestion. This phenomenon can be shown by having a client focus attention on one subject while suggestions are given on another topic. Often the client will have amnesia of the extraneous suggestions. The more highly charged the emotional setting during a concentrated period, the stronger the memory (Schacter, 1982). These concepts tie directly into the next law.

3. The Law of Dominant Effect.

Stronger emotions tend to replace weaker ones (Dilts et. al., 1980). Individuals tend to remember emotions with the strongest effect regardless of their history. Individuals tend also to form their perspective around strong emotion. The strength of the emotion may also cause a distortion process in which things seem either better or worse. The stronger the sensory experience, the stronger the effect. If the effect is too strong, then information may not even be learned (Whatmore and Kohli, 1974).

4. The Law of Reverse Effect.

This paradox of learning is associated with the previous law in that if one tries too hard to do something, there is less chance of succeeding. When an individual "over attends," it appears to restrict or interfere with the actual ability to learn. For most people, negative associations mount and the individual builds a block against learning material (Cudney, 1975).

Dynamically, there appear to be several "life scripts" associated with this law. If a person encounters a prohibition such as being told he/she is not capable of performing an action, he/she will have difficulty overriding the prohibition and concomitantly will experiences failure (overcoming a "not set"). Often when the individual encounters such failures, an approach/avoidance conflict occurs which creates a strong emotional situation predisposing further failure. The individual "gets into a space" where he/she wants to do an activity but feels unable to or is afraid to accomplish the task. He/she may desire the "rewards" but is paralyzed by the expected failures. This ambivalent condition may eventually create one of several situations. The individual may refuse to engage in the activity in order to avoid a potential failure. Second, the individual may engage in the activity but only half heartedly go through the action to "show" he/she tried. The third scenario is when the individual intently tries, but due to the intensity of the effort loses the perspective of the task. Each of these scenarios eventually manifests as a state of ambivalence, a paralysis from not knowing how to approach the task successfully.

5. The Law of Repetition.

Whether done directly or indirectly, purposely or non-purposely, if an individual hears an acceptable suggestion repeatedly, he/she tends to incorporate that suggestion into his/her intrapsychic structure (Schacter, 1982). For example, a child is consistently given feedback indicating that he/she is a certain way (i.e., dumb, smart, good looking, etc.) he/she will most likely incorporate that percept into the intrapsychic structure. Once incorporated, he/she seeks reinforcers for that perception and functions within those parameters.

6. The Law of Proximity.

If there are two or more possible perceptions of an experience, the individual will tend to associate or reference the experience to that which is closer to his/her predisposed perception. People expect to see what they have seen before. People tend to associate similar emotional experiences, even if they are dissimilar (Demer, 1960).

7. The Law of Similarity

Elements of greater similarity are grouped together (Demer, 1960).

For several neurological reasons people perceive things in units. Unit perception helps consolidate the information we perceive into manageable pieces. One's cognitive structure creates situations whereby one tends to associate and organize information based upon what is already known rather than attempting to develop new points of reference (Schacter, 1982). If such past experiences are positive, one will tend to have a positive hue about a new experience (Bugelski, 1964). This is evidenced as a positive mind set.

8. The Law of Common Fate

Occurrences in the same field of perception are assumed to relate. Individuals tend to believe that occurrences in the same field also have a "common fate" (Mathis, Cotton & Sechrest, 1970). People tend to proximate and associate things based on past or similar experiences and expect similar historical outcomes. If an individual approaches an experience and has a negative outcome, he/she will expect a similar outcome with all future experiences in that area (Mathis, Cotton & Sechrest, 1970).

9. The Law of Continuity

Individuals tend to perceive a whole rather than its component parts (Demer, 1960). This allows the individual to complete his/her Gestalt (Perls, 1969). One tends to put pieces into a whole and reference that whole based upon known perceptions. This gives one a sense of continuity and contiguousness. If the individual is given what appear as either unrelated pieces or pieces separated by time and space, he/she will attempt to put the chain of information together in such a way as to make sense of all the information. That appears as unrelated information may also be incorporated into the same segment of memory which may lead to confusion, non-comprehension of information or chains of memory which misassociate information and create disorganized thought (Schacter, 1982).

10. The Law of Closure

Individuals tend to like simple and symmetrical formats. If incomplete events are presented, the individual tends to fill in the gap with known information or seeks an answer in order to "complete business" (Schacter, 1982). If only parts are presented, one tends to conceptualize or even perceive a whole (Demer, 1960). If something is imbalanced, one tends to balance it in representing it internally. Likewise if something is complex, one is likely to attempt simplification. All these help lead to a sense of resolution and thus allow experience to go on.

Individual Processing of Information

The above ten laws of learning can be helpful when diagnosing an individual and assessing pre-work approaches. As information (the stimulus) is taken in by the client, it is processed. The client eventually reacts to his/her interpretation of the significance of the information. This reaction is the cue for "pre-work." The clinician can assess how to best approach the client in order to clarify points, check out the quality of the information, intervene, and/or confirm or deny the perception. Once done, the clinician can ascertain how to best approach the client.

The therapy process begins with the client perceiving the stimulus of the clinician's demeanor and feedback, as well as relevant situational variables. What the basic senses perceive (hear, see, feel, smell, taste) may be altered by situational influences or past experience (Weitzenhoffer, 1968). Each of the five basic senses has its own unique method of enabling external stimuli to be internally recognized. The following mindset was developed by the author and has been useful in the training of clinicians in order to be able to recognize some important aspects of sensory input. The auditory sense listens—it reacts to and interprets such things as tone, rhythm, loudness, inflection, pitch, resonance, and quality. The visual sense looks—it views color, perspective, shape, contrast, movement, and size. The kinesthetic sensory mediums feel—they consider texture, pressure, temperature, movement, environmental conditions, and density. The gustatory sense tastes—it interprets sweetness, bitterness, saltiness, and sourness. Finally, the olfactory system roots—it searches for aroma, strength of odor, temperature, and moisture.

The individual needs to encode the information, organize it into a recognizable format, and then interpret it (Watzlawick, Beavin & Jackson, 1967). Basically, individuals understand because organization of perception is predisposed. Either information has been experienced and we have a data base of information to call upon or one gathers information and references it as a new experience. By this process one gains what is labeled "understanding" and is able to reference what was "understood" with that which is known. Once one consciously or unconsciously recognizes information (interprets), one reacts. The reaction is followed closely in time by the receiver's reaction, which then becomes a precursor for the next interchange in the communication process (Watzlawick, Beavin & Jackson, 1967).

The collation of information from the observations arising in the client/clinician interchange is important in order to accurately diagnose the client. One methodology for reviewing the clinical observations, clinician logic, and relationship between presentation and desired clinical outcome involves note taking.

Clinical Note Taking

It may become useful, and at times be critical, to have adequate notes. These notes can be used for reference during a session, for retrospective learning, or for prospective planning. Often, from a good set of notes, a clinician can recreate information to plan different strategies.

Note taking can take place in several formats. The clinician can take formal notes during the session. He/she can retrospectively record notes from memory after the session. He/she can also engage the client in a note keeping process and/or have the client actively participate by making a written summary of the session.

Appropriate note taking and utilization of the notes can lend itself to helping the clinician learn skills of observation, organization, and implementation. One can practice observing select systems and eventually develop a shorthand that codes what one has observed. By using note taking as a form of study, one can develop skills that will improve diagnostic prowess.

Compiling Diagnostic Information

As a matter of self training the author has found it useful to write out clinical findings through careful consideration of the client's presentation, including present experience, and desired outcome. The author has developed a matrix analysis for Practical Applied Diagnostic Evaluation. This tool helps the clinician focus upon the different areas of functioning and helps prepare for "pre-work."

"Pre-work" Work

This phase of work involves setting the client up to work with his/her presented material in order to help achieve his/her goals. Throughout the interactive process of evaluation there is a constant communication taking place (Kiesler, 1973). This interaction should be focused in such a way as to guide the client into a therapeutically useful position. Simply stated, one begins to create a "mind set" in interacting with the client (Rossi, 1980). Utilization of this mind set helps direct the brief interventions one uses when utilizing Ericksonian techniques.

Once the clinician has enough information to understand what the client wants, and determines whether or not it can likely be achieved, he/she can begin to focus on the creation of a mind set. The goal of the "pre-work" phase is to successfully build rapport and expectancy and to create an environment for growth. When done elegantly, it appears to the client that he/she is "just talking" to the clinician. This initial talking phase has several clinical objectives. It is an opportunity to build rapport (trust

MATRIX ANALYSIS FOR PRACTICAL APPLIED DIAGNOSTIC EVALUATIONS

REALM	PROBLEM(S)	PRESENT OUTCOMES	DESIRED OUTCOME
BEHVIORAL			
AFFECT			
PSYCHO-MOTOR			
THOUGHT-PROCESS			
SOCIAL-PROCESS			
BIOLOGICAL, NUTRITIONAL PHYSICAL			

and confidence) with the clinician. The client has the opportunity to query the clinician about training, perspectives, intentions, and so forth. This initial contact further reveals to the clinician real and unreal concerns, valid and diversional information and a potential "map" of the clients reactions (Bandler & Grinder, 1976).

Finally the clinician has the opportunity to confirm his/her hypothesis about the problem and its components. He/she can begin strategy planning and can attempt to discover where to enter the client's system in order to begin therapeutic work.

The internal strategy the clinician utilizes to engage the client in the "pre-work" process is singular to that clinician/client dyad. It comes from training, experience, and an interaction of personalities which are unique. The clinician must not "put on" during this sensitive phase where genuineness is critical. Words, phrases, syntax, movement, and all other forms of communication by the clinician must be natural and comfortable, understandable, and congruent. If the clinician attempts a strategy that is too uncomfortable, i.e., personally threatening to the client, this may deter from obtaining the desired outcome sought by the client (Erickson, Rossi & Rossi, 1976).

The outcome of the development of the internal strategy is summarized in this simple statement: "This is what I feel I can do for this client." Once that point is reached, the clinician is in a position to begin using the contract as the bridge into the next phase of treatment.

Often the actual "hands-on" entry point for treatment is the informed consent which the clinician is mandated to give the client in certain settings such as mental and physical health facilities approved by the Joint Commission of Accreditation of Hospitals (1984). Clients appear to believe that "things get serious" at this point. During this phase one is obligated to share findings and recommend a course of action. This obligation to give informed consent can be framed in such a way as to be clinically advantageous.

The emphasis during informed consent is on sharing with the client what impressions the clinician has formed, the service they will perform, and how they are going to perform it. The client can then render a decision as to whether he or she wants to participate in the clinical proceedings. Throughout this duty bound phase the Ericksonian clinician can advantageously begin laying the ground for the work of later phases.

Arguments may evolve about informed consent curtailing or prohibiting the spontaneity that is necessary when one utilizes Ericksonian techniques. Whether the arguments are accurate or not, many laws state that informed consent must be performed. Without it, the clinician increases his/her legal liabilities. With creativity, the clinician can integrate these duties into his/her work and advantageously utilize them as part of the therapeutic process. The key to meeting the requirements and at the same time maintaining the spontaneous nature of interaction must be carefully gauged by the clinician.

Once accomplished, the therapeutic relationship can formally begin. The clinician has the information necessary to help guide the client, has developed strategies and formed a mutually acceptable relationship that would allow the client the opportunity to succeed.

Conclusion

The "pre-work" phase of therapeutic intervention is often overlooked, yet it is usually this phase that involves the most work for the clinician. The "pre-work" phase involves developing the agreement for the parameters of working together, including a setting of the relationship rules. Both parties ideally become committed to facilitating change in this phase. Once completed, this phase becomes a solid framework from which one can develop and execute the strategies promoting the changes the client desires.

References

Bandler, R. & Grinder, J. (1975a). *The structure of magic (Vol. I).* Palo Alto, Ca: Science and Behavior Books.

Bandler, R. & Grinder, J. (1975b). *Patterns of the hypnotic techniques of Milton H. Erickson, M.D. (Vol. I).* Cupertino, Ca: Meta Publications.

Bandler, R. & Grinder, J. (1976). *The Structure of magic (Vol. II).* Palo Alto, Ca: Science and Behavior Books.

Bandler, R,. & Grinder, J. (1981). *Trance-Formations.* Moab, Utah: Real People Press.

Bandler, R. & Grinder, J. (1982). *Reframing.* Moab, Utah: Real People Press.

Bandura, A. (1974). *Psychological modeling.* New York: Lieber-Atherton.

Barlow, D. (Ed.) (1981). *Behaviorial assessment of adult disorders.* New York: Guilford.

Bateson, G. and Ruesch, J. (1951). *Communication: the social matrix of psychiatry.* New York: Norton.

Birdwhistle, R. (1970). *Kinesics and content.* Philadelphia: University of Pennsylvania Press.

Bloom, B., Hastings, J. & Madaus G. (1971). *Handbook on formative and semantive evaluation of student learning.* New York: McGraw-Hill.

Bugelski, B., (1964). *The psychology of learning applied to teaching.* New York: Bobbs-Merrill.

Cudney, M., (1975). *Eliminating self defeating behavior.* Kalamazoo, Mi: Life Giving Enterprizes, Inc.

Demer, W. (1960). *The psychology of perception.* New York: Holt, Reinhart and Winston.

Dilts, R., Grinder, J., Bandler, R., Bandler, L., & De Lozier, J., (1980). *Neuro-linguistic programming: (Vol. 1).* Cupertino, Ca.: Meta Publications.

Erikson, E. (1963). *Childhood and society.* New York: Norton.

Erickson, M., Rossi, E. & Rossi, S. (1976). *Hypnotic realities*. New York: Irvington.
Feldenkrais, M., (1981). *Body and mature behavior*. New York: International University Press.
Flavell, J. (1963). *The developmental psychology of Jean Piaget*. New York: D. Van-Nostrand Co.
Gordon, D., (1978). *Therapeutic metaphors*. Cupertino, Ca: Meta Publications.
Haley, J. (1963). *Strategies of psychotherapy*. New York: Grune and Stratton.
Haley, J. (Ed.) (1967). *Advanced techniques of hypnosis and therapy*. New York: Grune and Stratton.
Haley, J. (1973). *Uncommon therapy*. New York: Norton.
Haley, J. (1977). *Problem solving therapy*. San Francisco: Josey-Bass.
Hacaen, H. & Albert, M. (1978). *Human neuropsychology*. New York: John Wiley and Sons.
Joint Commission on Accreditation of Hospitals (1984). "Consolidated standards manual/85". Chicago, Ill.
Kiesler, D. (1973). *The process of psychotherapy*. Chicago: Aldine.Kornhumer, H. (Ed.). (1975). *The somatosensory system*. Stuttgart, Germany: Publishing Sciences Group, Inc.
Laban, R. (1971). *Mastery of movement*. Great Britain: Mac Donnald and Evans, Ltd.
Lazarus, H. (1981). *The practice of multimodal therapy*. New York: McGraw-Hill.
Lezak, M., (1983) *Neuropsychological assessment*. New York: Oxford.
Lipowski, Z., (1977). "The importance of body experience for psychiatry." *Comprehensive Psychiatry*: Vol. 18. No. 5. Sept/Oct 1977.
Looft, W. (Ed.) (1972). *Developmental psychology*. Illinois: Dryden Press.
Lowen, A. (1967). *The betrayal of the body*. New York: Collier Books.
Lowen, A. (1971). *Language of the body*. New York: Collier Books.
Luria, A. (1980). *Higher cortical functions in man* (2nd ed.). New York: Basic Books.
Mathis, C., Cotton, J., & Sechrest, A., (1970). *Psychological foundations of education*. New York: Academy Press.
Millon, T., (1969). *Modern psychopathology*. Philadelphia: W. B. Saunders.
North, M. (1972). *Personality assessment through movement*. Great Britain: Mac Donald and Evans, Ltd.
Perls, F. (1969). *Gestalt therapy verbatim*. Lafayette, Ca: Real People.
Restack, R. (1979). *The brain, the last frontier*. New York: Doubleday.
Ripple, R. & Rockcastle, H. (1964). *Piaget rediscovered*. New York: Cornell University Press.
Rosen, S. (1982). *My voice will go with you*. New York: Norton Co.
Rossi, E. (Ed.) (1980). *The collected works of Milton H. Erickson (Vols. I and IV)*. New York: Irvington.
Taylor, M. (1981). *Neuropsychiatric mental status exam*. New York: Medical and Scientific.
Todd, M. (1977). *The thinking body*. New York: Dance Horizions.
Schacter, D. (1982). *Stranger behind the engram*. Hillsdale, New Jersey: Lawrence Erlbaum Associates.
Scheflin, A. (1972). *Body language and social order*. New Jersey: Prentice Hall.
Singer, E. (1965). *Key concepts in psychotherapy*. New York: Random House.
Thass-Theinemann, T. (1973). *The interpretation of language (Vols. I and II)*. New York: Jason Aronson, Inc.
Watson, R. & Lindgren, H., (1973). *Psychology of the child*. New York: Wiley.
Watzlawick, P., Beavin, J. & Jackson, D. (1967). *Pragmatics of human communication*. New York: Norton.
Watzlawick, P., Weakland, J. & Fisch, R. (1974). *Change*. New York: Norton.
Watzlawick, P. (1978). *The language of change*. New York: Basic Books.
Weitzenhoffer, A., (1968). *General techniques of hypnotism*. New York: Grune and Stratton.
Weeks, K. (1966). *Kinesiology*. Philadelphia: W. B. Saunders.

Whatmore, G., & Kohli, D. (1974). *The physiopathology and treatment of functional disorders.* New York: Grune and Stratton.
Zeig, J. (Ed.). (1982). *Ericksonian approaches to hypnosis and psychotherapy.* New York: Brunner/Mazel.

Humor as a Form of Indirect Hypnotic Communication

by
Waleed A. Salameh, Ph.D.

> Richard Benjamin: "You ask me about my goals. . . . You ask me what my plans are. Well, I don't have any plans. . . . I'm not a planner, I'm a liver."
> Ali McGraw: "And I'm a pancreas."
> (Dialogue from the movie *Goodbye Columbus*, 1969)

> "Gentlemen, why don't you laugh? With the fearful strain that is upon me night and day, if I did not laugh, I should die. You need this medicine as much as I do."
> (Abraham Lincoln, in an address to cabinet members, 1865)

Stranded on the edge of meaninglessness, groping for relief, alone in the cold expanses of human fate, nothing seems to lighten a heart's heavy burdens. Suddenly, at this moment of existential melancholy, a consoling smile appears at the horizon of memory, a passionate laugh can be heard at the corridors of choice, and a generous ray of jubilant warmth bursts forth to vivify the inmost marrow. And the magical gift is unwrapped.

The topic of this chapter is the entrancing experience of humor, and how humor can be strategically used in psychotherapy to encourage exploration of new ways of being, question the validity of blindly accepted

This paper was given an award by the Milton H. Erickson Institute as the most valued presentation at the conference.

133

assumptions, and impl:nt constructive messages to help clients overcome maladaptive patterns. The chapter includes seven sections. The first section describes some of the hypnotic qualities in humor. The second section proposes a more inclusive representation of the unconscious which would recognize its liberating, mirthful identity. The third and fourth sections present specific humor techniques and clarify how some of these techniques can be incorporated within the author's Integrative Short-Term Therapy (I.S.T.T.) model. Sections five and six address the issues of igniting or developing the therapist's own humorous persona through Humor Immersion Training,™ and establishing clear distinctions between therapeutic and harmful humor. Finally, section seven summarizes the chapter's overall perspective in relationship to other therapeutic models.

I. Hypnotic Qualities in Humor

What is it about humor that can be qualified as hypnotic? Five unique characteristics of the humor experience seem to facilitate its hypnotic effect.

1. *Humor is a form of indirect communication that allows easy access to the unconscious*:

Humor can be defined as an amusing form of indirect communication which does not follow the fixed rules of ordained or expected forms of interaction (Koestler, 1965; Salameh, 1980, 1983; Watzlawick, 1978). Its playful qualities reflect a higher form of seriousness, a colorful tactical arrangement which disarms and surpasses resistance in order to attract the subject's unconscious attention. Once the resistance barriers have been penetrated, then the humorously depicted message can be assimilated and absorbed by the unconscious with full force, thus initiating movement in the direction of desired change.

2. *Humor serves as a bridge between emotional and cognitive processes*:

Humor holds a unique position as a bridge between emotional and cognitive processes in that it is lived both as an emotional state related to joy or happiness and as a cognitive state. The cognitive process is activated by the invitation to decipher the meaning of a message presented to the subject under the guise of a humorous construction. The apparent lack of cognitive meaning in an "absurd" humorous communication provides the "trojan horse," i.e., the vehicle of access with which the communication can penetrate to the level of unconscious functioning. This presumed lack of cognitive sense may trigger a stream of cognitive scanning energy directed at attempting to resolve the state of momentary cognitive dissonance induced by humor. Such energy can subsequently be tapped in order to anchor unconscious understandings in cognitive awareness, with the anchoring being followed by a beneficial state of cognitive-emotional balance leading to conflict reduction. Furthermore, the positive emotional experience afforded by humor provides a greater sense of affective freedom which can help clients in discharging other unacknowledged emotions.

3. *Humor activates clients' abilities to make use of their own resources in addressing current problems*:

Humor is a form of communication which respects clients' autonomy by allowing them to tailor personally relevant solutions from the humorous fabric presented them. Once a helpful and open-ended humorous intervention is formulated, clients can interpret the humorous message in ways that address their individual needs without feeling violated or admonished by the therapist. In this sense, humor represents an accurate map upon which clients can chart their own navigational journeys, choosing where to stop along the way, which route to take, and how long the journey will last. Technical advice can, of course, be offered by the therapist regarding the map's coordinates and how to make the sailing smooth—humor provides half of the equation, the client's personal choices provide the other half. It is both surprising and gratifying to observe clients' creativity at work, interpreting a joke or humorous parable in ways that may be personally slanted yet remain refreshingly appropriate for addressing the issue at hand.

4. *Hypnotic rhythmicity in laughter*:

The dervishes sway again and again around the same circumference, the grandfather clock ticks left and right, the pendulum swings back and forth, the echo reverberates throughout the wilderness. Laughter tends to possess similar repetitive and rhythmic qualities. It may also be contagious: a laugh on the part of one person often provokes another's laughter, and another laugh. Once the therapist begins to laugh, he or she may actually be starting a repetitive humorous cycle which, if adroitly maneuvered, can offer possibilities of hypnotic infiltration due to the distraction and reduction of conscious cognitive vigilance caused by any phenomenon involving rhythmic repetitions. The content of the message communicated before and after laughter is to be structured by the therapist depending on the defenses, symptoms, and needs of the patient.

5. *Humorous storytelling can induce a hypnotic state of being*:

Humorous quotes, parables, metaphors, anecdotes, jokes, bons mots, and other humorous scenarios represent forms of storytelling which can be hypnotically formulated to encourage therapeutic change. The use of stories for teaching purposes is a venerable tradition in all cultures. In the therapeutic context, using humorous stories is a nonthreatening way of engaging the client's unconscious without eliciting resistance. The story gradually builds fascination and intrigue, ultimately leading to a crescendo of anticipation followed by a symbolic denouement. Although the story is about someone other than the listener, listeners can naturally identify with the story's characters as they become engrossed with the narrative flow. In some instances, the listener may disidentify with or reject some of the characters in the story, but in so doing he or she is still relating to the story in a personally meaningful mode. In the psychotherapeutic utilization of humorous storytelling, the therapist may elect to: (a) formulate an already existing scenario in such a manner that it is applicable to client issues while also offering potential solutions interspersed or implied within the natural weave of the story, (b) create a new scenario for the client addressing the client's special needs, or (c) report the story as is, in toto, when it is found to contain the elements necessary for client mobilization.

Cognitively, clients are simply paying attention to the explicit details of an amusing story. Unconsciously, the story's implicit messages tend to filter and fit with their receptive correspondents on the level of unconscious processes. Humorous stories can come from various sources such as Boccacio's tales, Chaucer, the Brothers Grimm, Zen stories (Hyers, 1973), and Sufi stories (Farzan, 1973; Shah, 1970, 1971a, 1971b, 1972). Sufi stories are particularly interesting since they tend to reflect an eminently practical sense of wisdom applied to the human condition. For example, the following two Sufi stories (Farzan, 1973, pp. 44, 87) were successfully used with a man experiencing problems in controlling and constructively channeling his aggressive feelings toward the unrealistic demands of authority figures in his life.

Ask the Flies Not to Bother Me

One day King Harun al-Rashid, who wasn't very pleased with the freethinking Bohlul, said to him:

"If you can prove that I am no more powerful than other mortals, including yourself, I'll give you a hundred gold pieces. If you fail, I'll have you placed, with your beard shaven, on the back of a donkey and driven around town as an imbecile."

Bohlul replied, "I'll try, but first I would like you to order these flies not to bother me."

"But flies won't follow my orders," the King said. Then he thought for a while and dropped the subject.

Bad Poems

The emir of the town read a poem he had composed and asked for Bohlul's opinion.

"I don't like it," Bohlul replied.

The emir became angry and ordered Bohlul to be put in prison.

The following week the emir summoned Bohlul and read him another poem. "What do you think of this one?" he asked.

Bohlul got to his feet.

"Where are you going?" asked the emir.

"To the prison," answered Bohlul.

Moreover, the following are some guidelines relating to the effective framing of hypnotic and humorous stories:

1. There are four attributes that make a good story: capturing the listener's attention, compression, striking tone, and details.

2. A story produces optimum results when it is goal-directed, not too lengthy, and relevant to client issues.

3. A story may be meaningfully introduced with: "I want to tell you this interesting story I thought you might like," or "Someone told me a fascinating story I'd like to share with you," etc.

4. Time your breathing to the client's breathing throughout the story and employ other similar pacing techniques for attaining unconscious rapport (Bandker & Grinder, 1975, 1976a, 1976b; Phillips, 1981; Watzlawick, 1978; Zeig, 1980).

5. Watch the client closely as you tell the story for noticeable physical cues (blinking eyelids, changing facial expression, body posture, etc.) that indicate the client is in rapport with the story's content.

6. Whenever such specificity is desirable, the client's primary representational system or PRS (Bandler & Grinder, 1975a, 1976, 1979) can be determined before a story is told. The PRS may be determined by checking an individual's speech for predominance of visual ("I *see* your point"), auditory ("That *sounds* right"), or kinesthetic ("That *feels* good") terminology. Subsequently, the therapist can match the story's language structure to that of the client's PRS by using predominantly visual, auditory, or kinesthetic language. There is some evidence in the literature (Yapko, 1981) to the effect that identifying and matching clients' PRS language structures enhances effective rapport in hypnosis and psychotherapy.

7. Give emphasis to key terms and sentences in the story which are related to its cardinal message. Words can be emphasized by changing or pacing one's tone of voice, inflection, or cadence during certain passages. Some words can then be used to auditorily anchor certain experiences or messages within a story.

8. Synchronicity seems crucial. The story needs to be sequenced or broken down in a way that elicits specific reactions and builds progressive anticipation from one idea to the next, like eagerly going up each step of a flight of stairs to call upon a valued friend.

9. Stories are more meaningful when they are somehow related to the client's background or occupation. A client who grew up on a farm might enjoy stories about rural life. Similarly, a musician may identify with troubadour stories.

10. Design the circumstances and details of the story in affirmative terminology, using positive antonyms to describe experiences whenever possible. Negative expression tends to elicit resistance whereas affirmative language encourages a favorable integration.

Beyond the above rules of humorous story construction, further guidelines on constructing metaphors and hypnotic suggestions can be found in Bandler and Grinder (1975, 1976a, 1976b, 1979), Bettelheim (1976), Cooke and Van Vogt (1965), Erickson, Rossi and Rossi (1976), Gordon (1978), Haley (1967, 1973), Kroger (1977), Kroger and Fezler (1976), Phillips (1981), and Watzlawick (1978).

In conclusion, it can be proposed that humor is a mode of unconscious dialogue which transcends resistances and offers optimal potential for therapeutic impact if domesticated and refined by the therapist to serve specific therapeutic ends.

II. Representations of the Unconscious

Unconscious. The very word often sends shudders up the spines of the uninitiated. The concept, *the entity*, has been described in both mechanistic and religious language, debated, negated, buried, and resurrected. This section will briefly review established as well as emerging views of the unconscious, and emphasize how one's perception of the unconscious can either restrict or expand its usefulness within the context of strategic psychotherapeutic interventions.

The term *"unconscious"* was probably coined by the German philosopher Friedrich Nietzsche yet was popularized by Sigmund Freud who used it extensively in his writings (e.g., Freud, 1905). The predominant impression which emerges from Freud's work is a rather gloomy view of the unconscious, depicted as a somber underworld, a primarily sexual and aggressive entity with self-destructive inclinations. Freud's understanding of the unconscious was initially disputed by his own disciples (Jung, Adler, Rank and others) and later challenged by other psychological schools of thought. More recently, Milton Erickson offered a refreshing view of the unconscious (Bandler & Grinder, 1976a; Haley, 1967; Erickson, Rossi & Rossi, 1976; Erickson & Rossi, 1981). Erickson understood the unconscious as a wellspring of human resourcefulness and problem solving which can readily respond to therapeutic intervention if spoken to in its own language. Simply stated, Erickson's position was that therapists can tap into unconscious learnings and experiences by learning about unconscious patterns of communication. Consequently, therapist communication does not need to be solely rational or linear in the format since multilevel communication is as available to therapists to utilize as it is to their clients. Erickson's work introduced new images of the unconscious: a "rehabilitated" unconscious, an unconscious that is a predominantly constructive, even convivial force; a decipherable unconscious; an unconscious that may be a friend. In contrast to the tedious and rather slow technique of free association, Erickson developed numerous approaches of indirect communication based on hypnotic principles and aimed at accessing and restructuring unconscious processes within a relatively brief time period. Erickson's methods have been extensively described both by himself (Erickson, 1966; Erickson, Rossi & Rossi, 1976; Erickson & Rossi, 1981), and by others (Bandler & Grinder, 1976a; Gordon, 1978; Grinder, DeLozier & Bandler, 1977; Haley, 1967, 1973; Watzlawick, 1978; Zeig, 1980, 1982).

The view of the unconscious presented in this chapter essentially builds upon and further develops the Ericksonian view, with special focus on the phenomenon of humor and its therapeutic usage. Rather than viewing the unconscious solely as an underworld scavenger, the unconscious is seen as a holder of the history of inner evolution, a wise and liberating ally. It is also proposed that the unconscious is naturally humorous, engaging in humor to illustrate and accept absurdity, to celebrate the joy of life's very continuity, to help refresh and energize existence through the infinite tribulations of the human condition, to express needs and wishes, as well as to reveal simple solutions to seemingly complex problems. Of course, as Freud (1905, 1928) postulated, there may also be economy in expenditure of psychic energy and a lifting of inhibitions during the humor experience. An illustration of the unconscious' mirthful nature was recounted to the author by a pregnant client who had called her aunt in Texas to report on the difficulties of her pregnancy: the contractions, troubles in moving about, etc. After listening patiently to her niece's story, the aunt retorted: "Don't you worry about it, honey! When I was pregnant, my husband once woke me up in the middle of the night and told me he had dreamt that he was a cowboy sleeping with his horse."

As indicated by Erickson's work, one can modify one's thinking about the unconscious in the following ways:

1. Respecting the inclusiveness and adaptablility of the unconscious world: The unconscious can be likened to Noah's Ark: two of every kind on board to insure survival, cohabitation of unlikely roommates, peace in the midst of turbulence, ingenuity in the face of despair, saving graces, self-regulation and respect for different ways of being, playful integration, extraordinary resiliency under stressful conditions, continuing courageous evolution toward an unknown destination, and the benevolent presence of Noah as master of ceremonies!

2. Changing the term: Some individuals (clients, therapists, or others) react negatively to the term "unconscious" since it can evoke metaphors of blindness and an absence or exhaustion of awareness (as in "he was unconscious for two days"). Due to the prefix "un," this term can also evoke a frame of inflexible negation or opposition (as in unconstitutional, unacceptable, etc.). However, it may be misleading to imply that a mode of expressiveness lacks awareness because it happens to be codified according to a particular formation: for example, one cannot say that the sign language used by deaf-mute persons lacks awareness because one hasn't learned how to sign. Perhaps it would be more descriptive as well as more faithful to human evolutionary history to replace the term unconscious with a more neutral term like "*rootconscious*," reflecting the inclusiveness, resourcefulness, and historical components of this part of consciousness.

And the journey resumes. The history of the world is still played on the inner stage, with ever-evolving potentials, limitations, and possible modes of action in the face of the challenging chaos presented by our everyday world. The imperfection of worldly structures leaves room for the exercise of human improvement. The evolution of consciousness continues.

Table 1 presents an oversimplified summary of the perceptions of the unconscious (or *rootconscious*) in different psychological theories.

Table 1
Perceptions of the Unconscious

Theorist	Perception of the Unconscious	Metaphor
Freud	Unconscious as a primarily sexual and aggressive entity with self-destructive inclinations.	Oedipus Rex
Jung	Unconscious as a repository of archetypal identities, powerful primordial images, and spiritual symbolisms.	Kabuki Theater

Theorist	Perception of the Unconscious	Metaphor
Sartre (Existential School)	Unconscious as choices disowned. Unconscious represents the denial of conscious choice.	Statue of Liberty
Rogers (Humanistic School)	Freudian theory of the Unconscious represents human nature as evil, does not do justice to constructive human tendencies.	The Good Samaritan
Skinner (Behaviorist School)	Unconscious as a useless and scientifically unfounded concept.	For whom do the bells toll?
Ellis, Mahoney, Beck (Cognitive Behaviorism)	Unconscious as irrelevant to cognitive restructuring	Tabula Rasa
Erickson	Unconscious as a wellspring of human resourcefulness and problem solving which can readily respond to therapeutic intervention if spoken to in its own language. Therapists may enlist the unconscious' learnings and experiences when they learn to speak unconscious dialect. Therapist communication does not need to be unidimensional—multilevel communication is as available to therapists as it is to clients.	Oriental Bazaar
Salameh	Unconscious as holder of the history of inner evolution, as a gracefully inclusive and adaptive entity, a wise and liberating ally. Unconscious as naturally humorous, engaging in humor to illustrate and accept absurdity, to celebrate the joy of life's very continuity, to help refresh and energize human existence, and to reveal simple solutions to supposedly complex problems. The term *Unconscious* can be misleading since it implies blindness or lack of awareness; terms like *Root-conscious* or *Sourceconscious* may be preferable.	

III. Creative Uses of Absurdity: Paradoxical
Humorous Prescriptions as Indirect Suggestions

In Albert Camus' 1959 movie *Black Orpheus*, an intriguing scene casts a maintenance worker in a huge record-keeping office building who decides to give up on sweeping papers off the floor because no matter how many papers he sweeps there are always more meaningless papers falling from the inundated files cluttering up the office floors. A highly anxious client made the startling announcement during a therapy session that he had decided to stop worrying and start taking things one day at a time because: "Behind every worry there's a worry, and behind that worry is another worry." These two experiences illustrate important understandings which can result from a person's coming to grips with the ubiquitous absurdity of existence: the absurdity of things that don't have to be but are, of events that escape the human capacity for logical comprehension, of unexpected discoveries and chance happenings. Absurdity offers a fertile soil for humor since humor builds on parasitical realities to drive home important messages. In psychotherapy, the client's zealousness at repeatedly applying maladjustive solutions to everyday problems may at times constitute an absurdly humorous scenario. Accordingly, the judicious therapist can make creative use of the absurdity theme to design indirect suggestions which address specific therapeutic issues the client is grappling with. As Watzlawick (1978) observed, indirect suggestions derive their potency from the paradoxical inference that they hide what they reveal: "There seems to be a tacit rule of communication that what is said without being said is 'not really' said, but somehow is communicated with particular power" (p. 86). Some strategic therapists are adept at constructing indirect paradoxical suggestions based on absurdity. For example, Erickson (as cited by Watzlawick, 1978) treated a sexually unresponsive woman by instructing her, either in a trance or waking state, to imagine how she would go about defrosting her refrigerator: how she would deal with this situation, which shelf (top, middle, or bottom) to begin with, what to take out first, how would she tackle the thawing, what unexpected thoughts or memories might come up as she does this, in what order would she put things back in, and so on. Throughout the interaction, myriad minute details of the defrosting chore were elicited. In another example, Madanes (1985) reported that Haley instructed a student intern who was overly worried about making mistakes under supervision to deliberately make three mistakes during a supervised psychotherapy session: two that Haley would be able to detect and one that he would not be able to discern. Another case reported by Madanes (1985) refers to a male client who was concerned about being rejected by women. The client's therapist gave him the assignment of "practicing rejection" by standing at a certain corner in front of a boutique and spending several hours during two weekends inviting young women to have a cup of coffee with him. It was explained to the client that the women would refuse, and that he would therefore have the experience of being rejected and tolerating it. Unfortunately, so many women accepted the invitation that the client did not really have the chance to experience rejection! Frankl (1963) used his technique of "paradoxical intention" to similar ends by asking a young physician who had a fear of perspiring to deliberately decide to show people how much he could sweat whenever his sweating reappeared. Frankl reports that the patient was able to extinguish the excessive sweating by telling himself whenever he met anyone who triggered his anticipatory anxiety, "I only sweated out a quart before, but now I'm going to pour at least ten quarts!"

A common element in the interventions described above is the use of absurdly humorous prescriptions to redefine phenomenological reality. By redirecting the attentional flow regarding a given situation (through the use of confusion, distortion, deletion, and generalization devices), the normal boundaries of one's conceptualizations can be altered such that the core dilemma may be seen in a different light. Another example involves a ruminating obsessive man who was treated by asking him to plan his worrying and set a specific time for worrying on Tuesday and Thursday evenings between 7–9 p.m. The client was instructed that since he was *very organized*, he could devote a specific time for his worrying. In this way, the rest of his time would be *efficiently* spent on other *secondary* pursuits. He was to mark in advance on his *organized* calendar the exact times and items he intended to worry about for a given week so that he would not forget to worry about important things: "Remember to save all your worries for this time and this time only, and forget about it for the rest of the week. Otherwise, you would be cheating on your program." The client took the assignment to heart and started to worry at the specified times, but only at these times. This gave him ample time to engage in more productive or enjoyable activities for the rest of the week. Three weeks later, the client rquested that his "worry time" be reduced to one night per week only since he was now busy with other things. The therapist agreed to this request with some reticence. Four weeks later, the client requested that his worry time be reduced to one hour on Tuesday evenings. In pure paradoxical logic, he needed to be given permission to worry deliberately at specified times in order for him to stop worrying!

In another case, a severely disturbed anti-social client with poor impulse control was constantly leaving group psychotherapy before the group's termination. Typically, he would come to the weekly group sessions, attend group for about ten minutes, then mutter some angry comment and storm out of the room. One day at the beginning of group the therapist stated to the client in a serious tone, "I think you would probably want to sit pretty close to the door because you usually leave after a few minutes. That way you'll make it easier on yourself to leave when your time is up." The therapist pointed to a chair for the client to sit in which was actually the closest chair to the door but was also the closest to the therapist's own chair. The client laughed and said: "Well, now if I leave it'll all be your fault!" However, he stayed in group for a half hour on that day which was a record for him. Before leaving group, he excused himself and told the therapist: "I'm leaving now, but it's not because of you. I just can't stay in one place for too long." In the next group session, he came on time and stayed for the duration of the group, adequately contributing to the group process and sharing his favorite joke with group members. Over time, this client became more friendly with others, including the therapist. Whenever the group met, he always chose to sit in the chair to which he was originally assigned by the therapist, closest to the door but also closest to the therapist. His impulsivity decreased. His humor became less sarcastic. For instance, he once stated to the therapist at the end of the Thursday group session: "I'll see you on the second Thursday of next week!" Other problems related to inadequacies in social functioning remained, requiring longer treatment, yet some emotional connection was made with the client through the use of humor and paradoxical directives.

The author will now describe the use of goal-directed humorous suggestions in psychotherapy. The term "suggestion" is used here in the general sense proposed by Kroger (1977), namely, the utilization of the client's ability to respond experientially to the therapist. (Regarding the delimitation of hypnotic phenomena, the interested reader is referred to Orne, 1980, and Weitzenhoffer, 1962a, 1962b, for two interesting viewpoints on this topic.) The suggestions discussed here have a humorous quality, a specific target, are indirect in nature, and are used to convey therapeutic messages either with or without formal induction. Since these suggestions are indirect by definition and may be subject to misinterpretation, the author usually prefaces the use of any form of humorous intervention by relating the following to the client during the first therapy session:

> It is important for you to *know* that I am your ally, *totally* on your side, and that we're *cooperating*, working together to tackle your problems. My orientation is not to judge you or tell you

what to do but to help you clarify your available choices, where you are now and where you can go from here if you so decide. I *respect* the *courage* you have shown today by seeking treatment for intimate issues that are usually hard to talk about. I will do my best to *support you* and *help* you feel comfortable *throughout* our working *together*. I may sometimes use humor in working with you, not to *make light* of your problems but to point out patterns or help *identify new options*. I also encourage you to use humor because positive forms of humor can help us see things in new, refreshing ways. When I use humor at a certain point, I may ask you what I meant by using a joke or a story and *you might want* to ask me what I meant as well so that things can *make sense* as we *go along*.

Statements similar to those mentioned above can prevent many misunderstandings and create a cognitive framework within which humorous interventions will not only be welcomed but will also receive favorable consideration. In this context, it is important that clients come to feel that humor is not at their expense and that they own the solutions embedded in the humorous metaphor. Moreover, the author sometimes encourages clients' anchoring of solutions by asking, "Why are you laughing?" upon seeing the smile of recognition in response to a humorous intervention that has been made: a client's explanation of why she or he found what was said to be funny can help to "lock in" an interpretive cycle which has been fermenting throughout the therapeutic work.

Given the aforementioned structure for using therapeutic humorous suggestions, the therapist can make creative use of absurdity in developing paradoxical humorous prescriptions for clients. Table 2 offers some target-specific humorous suggestions and illustrates each with a pertinent clinical vignette.

IV. Structured Hypnotic Humorous Experiences for Integractive Short Term Therapy (I.S.T.T.)

Although humor is a product of spontaneity, its use in psychotherapy can sometimes be directed toward eliciting distinct emotional and imagery experiences related to a determined time period in the client's life or to a given phase of therapeutic work according to the psychotherapist's own theoretical framework. Since it is difficult for this author to dissociate his use of humor in psychotherapy from his overall psychotherapeutic

Table 2
Indirect Humorous Suggestions

Indirect Humorous Suggestion	Definition	Clinical Issue	Therapist Intervention
Restorative Suggestions	Replacing client's negative sense of uniqueness by a positive sense of uniqueness with the over-all goal of building self-esteem.	Client reports that she was able to overcome her negative self-ruminations and ask for a well-deserved promotion, which was actually granted by her employer.	"So good to be driving up that freeway at sunrise, bright-eyed and bushy-tailed, your favorite song on the radio, taking in the sweet smell of early morning, happy as a lark, knowing that the best is yet to come, not a care in the world."
Self-Permission Suggestions	Encouraging clients to take reasonable (and sometimes unreasonable) risks in order to explore new ways of being that can be therapeutic for them.	Rigid client prides himself on his maturity and "not engaging in childish acts," thus missing much of the excitement and happiness available to him.	"I know I can say this in strict confidence to a mature person like yourself: I believe that maturity has been overrated."
Hibernating Suggestions	Detecting a major recurring maladaptive pattern, describing it humorously, letting it hibernate, then going back to the same theme	Client denies feelings (especially his own) about various situations by keeping himself busy with work. Following a long, drawn-out divorce, he claims	"Sounds like you just haven't had time to enjoy your misery!" Patient picks up on this theme to describe his alienation

Table 2 (continued)

Indirect Humorous Suggestion	Definition	Clinical Issue	Therapist Intervention
Hibernating Suggestions (cont'd)	later on in therapy to verify that the issue is being dealt with appropriately.	that he is "too busy to think about meaningless things like my divorce."	from his feelings, and uses above statement in later sessions, "Well, again, I haven't had time to enjoy my misery this past week."
Ratification Suggestions	Expressing encouragement for new client behaviors reflecting autonomy and healthy change.	Dependent client reports, "Feeling a little better" by doing things that make her happy instead of her usual pattern of adopting only those behaviors that others usually condone.	"Feel better, feel better, that's all you think about! Some people have so much to be responsible for in this world, and all you're concerned about is feeling better."
Discarding Suggestions	Helping clients get rid of old carcasses by creating a humorous image representing the maladaptive pattern.	Client imprisons himself within his own constrictions, then complains bitterly about his self-created imbroglios.	"By the way, did I warn you about not swimming in wet cement pools anymore? To start with, it's bad for your skin. On top of that, it's not the kind of execise activity that allows you free-flowing movement."

Table 2 (continued)

Indirect Humorous Suggestions	Definition	Clinical Issue	Therapist Intervention
Win/Win or Positive Double Bind Suggestions	Framing seemingly insolvable issues in such a way that no matter which part of the frame clients choose to focus on, they can still end up with a viable alternative that is preferable to their present stuckness.	Middle-aged client reports that she has not been dating recently: "I have a UFO (ugly, fat, and old) syndrome. I feel like men don't find me attractive anymore."	"There are normally two answers to a scientific question of this kind: a blue answer and a green answer. The blue answer is that there are plenty of UFO men out there who come from that very same planet, and it's usually rather easy to recognize them. The green answer is just to leave your UFO behind, divorce E.T., and find out why it is that you are afraid of getting close to *ordinary* men. I mean, just because you don't speak the dialect. . . ."
Uncontested Contest Suggestions	Highlighting the untenableness of dysfunctional patterns by explaining them "from within," in paralogical ways.	Client chooses to punish himself for *crimes* he did not commit, ends up "inexplicably dissatisfied" while ignoring simple solutions to his problems.	"You know, a masochist is a person who likes a cold shower in the morning, so he takes a hot one."

Table 2 (continued)

Indirect Humorous Suggestion	Definition	Clinical Issue	Therapist Intervention
Sealing Suggestions	Locking-in specific client insights at the conclusion of a given interpretive cycle in therapy by providing a positive ambient environment within which the insight can be retained.	Client comments that he is beginning to realize that it is acceptable for him not to be *perfect* because being perfect means there is nothing left for a person to learn in life.	"And *they* keep throwing monkey wrenches at you! Just when you're ready to graduate from the school of life, someone thinks up a new course."

approach, the purpose of the present section is to introduce some structured hypnotic humorous experiences used within the context of the author's Integractive Short Term Therapy (or I.S.T.T.) approach.

I.S.T.T. is a short term psychotherapeutic modality developed through the amalgamation of five processes:

1. Culling the most elegantly relevant principles and therapeutic moments from the author's repertoire of training experiences, both academic and clinical.

2. Integrating these principles with insights which emerged from everyday therapeutic work with clients and from thinking about the process of psychotherapy.

3. Searching for a sound yet simple model of psychotherapy which can be clearly communicated and adapted without unnecessary abstractions. As a result of working against client legacies of confusion and misunderstanding and being exposed to mastodonic manifestations of high priest psychobabble, one comes to value the clarity, vigor, and economy which simplicity can bring to human communication. In this respect, part of the attractiveness of humor is that it appeals to the human need to communicate simply and economically.

4. A preference for short term over long term treatment modalities.

5. Wanting to include the beneficial properties of humor in psychotherapeutic work in a systematic and effective manner.

The following is a brief delineation of the I.S.T.T. approach. Firstly, four components of I.S.T.T. will be explicated: (1) the I.S.T.T. process model, (2) five working propositions, (3) eleven therapist factors, and (4) twelve intervention recommendations. Secondly, the author will propose structured hypnotic humorous experiences that may be used in conjunction with different stages of the I.S.T.T. process model.

1. *I.S.T.T. Process Model*

The I.S.T.T. process model is the cornerstone of therapeutic movement in I.S.T.T. Figure 1 depicts the model. Essentially, the process model encapsulates a universal chronology retracing the seasons of being that individuals automatically bring with them into psychotherapy, as well as the progressive stages which the therapist works through with clients in I.S.T.T. The process model consists of six elements:

(1) the archaelogical stage: the identification of past influences and learnings in a person's life including parental constellation, significant others, family upbringing, childhood and adolescence, early traumatic

Figure 1

I.S.T.T. Process Model

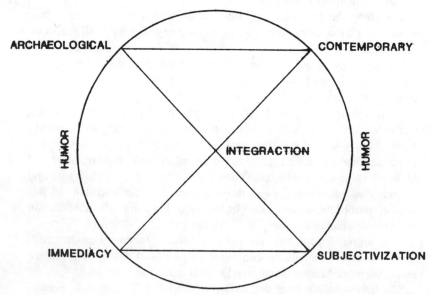

or positive episodes, educational or military experiences when applicable, and other formative patterns of early development.

(2) the contemporary stage: the "presenting problem," a person's present situation and that which has prompted him or her to seek help at this juncture.

(3) the immediacy stage: the exploration of the "here and now" relationship between therapist and client, including the client's feelings toward the therapist as well as the therapist's feelings toward the client. It can be safely assumed that the same major patterns learned by an individual at the archaelogical stage and carried into the contemporary stage will be replayed at the immediacy stage with the therapist, i.e., the client's interaction with the therapist will tend to represent a microcosm of her or his interactions with others. The therapeutic relationship then becomes a laboratory for the client to risk interpersonal openness, try out new modes of interaction and undergo a *corrective emotional experience*. The therapist's task at this point is to make clear connections between Archaelogical-Contemporary-Immediacy (or ACI) material for the patient such that the common threads underlying thought and behavior can become apparent.

(4) the subjectivization stage: this stage reflects a critical turning point in psychotherapy and includes two phases: [a] the patient, having objectively or cognitively understood the ACI connections, moves to "working through" the emotional implications of such an awareness. An integral part of the re-educational process at this juncture is the recognition that one's feelings do not go away just because one wants them to. Subsequently, the patient can learn to accept and even welcome feelings instead of fighting them or treating them as explosives: if one attaches danger to feelings, then one will deny one's right to feel. The subjectivization of personal experiences and understandings allows individuals to settle various emotional scores, do grieving if necessary, come to grips with their feelings about their parents, acknowledge the validity of their emotions, let go of lingering doubts, own their needs, and finish unfinished business. [b] the second fundamental element in subjectivization work is a progressive bridging and harmonization between the cognitive and unconscious (or rootconscious) aspects of the self. As patients begin to explore their subjective world, they can develop an appreciation of unconscious insights and resources, gradually allowing these resources to be utilized to effect productive change. If the different parts of the self can be likened to the voices in a choir, then the acknowledgement of the different voices of subjectivity can enable each voice to take its appropriate place and make its particular contribution. In this sense, giving proper voice to different parts of the self allows the individual to deliver

a fuller rendition of the choir of personhood. In a choir, each voice is important but all voices agree to cooperate in order to create the harmonious sound which expresses the choir's distinctive identity. For example, the voice of the unconscious can contribute important raw materials, historical learnings, and early constructive resources. The voice of cognition can contribute analytical machinery, structure, and focus. Accordingly, the patient may come to realize that cognitive and unconscious voices need not be counteractive in function but can rather work synergistically, along with the other voices of subjectivity, within the choir of personhood.

(5) the integraction stage: as coined by this author, the term *integraction* refers to a harmonious blend between integration and action whereby patients are able to integrate their learnings in psychotherapy to reach new personal configurations involving constructive behaviors toward self and others. A change in self-concept usually includes a change in one's perceptions of reality and concomitant actions which would naturally derive from such a perceptual-emotional shift. At this stage, patients typically test out new behaviors, take *healthy risks*, seek corroboration rather than validation from the therapist, and can eventually conclude treatment.

(6) the humor stage: encompasses the continuous use of humor throughout psychotherapy to lubricate the machinery and infuse liveliness into the therapeutic process—what tastes bland to the unconscious (or root-conscious) does not sink in, whereas flavorful and crisply succinct forms of communication tend to be easily assimilated. The therapist who uses humor and encourages a healthy humorous perspective on the client's part is indirectly inculcating a mechanism of attitudinal healing, a back-up (or back-off) system which can be expected to kick in during periods of distress to provide perspective, self-nurturance, and courage.

Throughout therapeutic work in I.S.T.T., the therapist sticks to the above model, moving with the patient through each stage and encouraging movement to the next stage. It is not necessary to begin with the archaeological stage, but it is vital that connections be made among the various stages during psychotherapy with the goal of leading up to integraction.

2. Five Working Propositions

I.S.T.T. operates according to the following five propositions regarding psychological functioning:

Proposition 1—Emotional Reincarnation. Children go to school in the family just as they go to school in the traditional educational system. Over time, a child learns certain emotional and behavior patterns from either or both parents in terms of personality style, self-perception, and how to approach relationships with others. These parental patterns are then reincarnated within the individual and acted out without conscious awareness in youth and adult life.

Proposition 2—Mirror Love. Human beings are naturally inclined to seek love and recognition from others. When children seek healthy love from their parents and do not receive it, they engage in a distortional project: they begin to imitate or mirror undesirable parental traits as the only alternative for *getting close* to a rebuffing parent. Mirror love thus provides the only possible form of identification with the parent(s) which neutralizes the risk of rejection. This distorted form of identification usually takes place when healthy identification with a mature and caring parent is not available to the child.

Proposition 3—The Heroic Project. As Becker (1973) pointed out, most individuals (even the most humble, angry, or self-deprecating) tend to think of themselves in their inner sanctum as unsung heroes. The challenge of therapy is to properly acknowledge, channel, prune, balance, and help synchronize the human bent for heroism so that it can lead to constructive outcomes.

Proposition 4—Native Endowments. It is quasi-impossible to have a life that is completely devoid of constructive or happy experiences. Most individuals already possess within their psychological repertoire many of the resources they need to change. However, these constructive resources can sometimes elude the person's cognitive reach. In I.S.T.T., individuals are assisted at recomposing past successes, positive memories, and early rewarding interactions. If these resources are experienced in a revivified way, they can then be enlisted to recharge and help reconstruct present capacities. The effective use of hypnotic and strategic approaches in therapeutic work can help facilitate such a revivification.

Proposition 5—Self-Determination. The quest for personal change ultimately converges around the theme of self-determination and how individuals choose to create their own worlds. While a person cannot be held responsible for being thrown in a certain family and having certain parents (i.e., unconditional situations), it is important for clients to realize that the perpetuation of dysfunctional patterns in adult life or the negation of authorship regarding essential decisions (i.e., conditional situations) constitute a denial of personal responsibility which will block the way to further growth. Accordingly, the resources for personal change can be mobilized when one realizes that one is the maker of reality and not just its witness. I.S.T.T. focuses on this interplay between unconditional and conditional situations, between boundedness and freedom in human experience. Patients are encouraged to own their choices as to their self-concept, their view of their own world and the world of others. Once choices are owned, they can then either be maintained or altered depending on the direction one intends to take. Furthermore, individuals are helped to make their available options explicit so they can develop informed decisions.

3. *Eleven Therapist Factors*

The personal characteristics which therapists bring into the consulting room can exert an important influence on the course and nature of psychotherapy. The research conducted by Carkhuff and his associates (Carkhuff, 1969; Carkhuff & Berenson, 1967) has identified important therapist traits which were found to differentiate effective therapists and their distinct style of therapeutic intervention. Together with other facilitative characteristics identified by this author, these traits form a group of helpful therapist factors that constitute an integral part of the I.S.T.T. approach to treatment. These traits are defined as follows:

(1) Respect—Respect involves a recognition of the client's personal worth, of the client's right to make his or her own choices, and of the client's ability to constructively change her or his knowledge, affect, beliefs, and behaviors in identified problem areas.

(2) Empathy—Empathy is the ability to accurately perceive both verbal and nonverbal expressions of the client's feelings or cognitions and to communicate this understanding to the client.

(3) Concreteness—Concrete communication corresponds with zeroing in on specific (how, what, when, where, who) feelings, experiences, and behaviors which are personally relevant to the client. The opposite of concreteness is vagueness, the indication of which is a feeling of boredom and aimlessness on the part of either the therapist or client. When the therapist is focusing on appropriate material, there is usually no feeling of vacuum in the therapeutic interaction.

(4) Confrontation—The therapist uses confrontation to point out discrepancies wherever they may occur. Commonly, discrepancies exist between verbal versus nonverbal behavior, insight versus action, stated versus actual knowledge, beliefs versus behavior, ideal versus real self, illusion versus reality, client's labeling of his or her experience versus the therapist's perception of this experience, client's verbalization of failure and inadequacy in situations where actual strength and adaptation were shown, and client's verbalization of successful coping in situations where actual dysfunction and maladaptation were shown. Confrontation is optimally helpful when it is simultaneously balanced with statements of affirmation (the expression of constructive, likable aspects of the client). In this way, individuals can digest and productively react to relevant confrontation of maladaptive patterns without feeling devastated in their personal worth. Furthermore, confrontation should not be con-

fused with rudeness, explosiveness, or the expression of dogmatic views. When used appropriately by the therapist, confrontation can provide a model of assertive communication for clients.

(5) Genuineness—Genuineness refers to being authentic beyond role or technique in interaction with the client and expressing accurate information regarding feelings and reactions toward him or her.

(6) Humor—The therapist uses non-sarcastic humor to devitalize clients' maladaptive patterns, convey insight in economical format, encourage creative problem solving, and establish successful rapport with clients. Table 3 presents a five-point *Humor Rating Scale* constructed by the author (Salameh, 1983) to help rate therapists' use of humor in psychotherapy. Level 1 on the *Humor Rating Scale* refers to destructive humor, level 2 to harmful humor, level 3 to minimally helpful humor response, level 4 to very helpful humor responses, and level 5 to outstandingly helpful humor responses. An illustrative clinical vignette is included for each of the five levels of therapist humor.

(7) Warmth—Showing appreciation, encouragement, and concern for the client can be manifested in verbal and nonverbal therapist behavior. Warmth is also expressed by helping clients feel comfortable in working with the therapist.

(8) Self-disclosure—Self-disclosure, when appropriate, consists in relating relevant examples or incidents from the therapist's own history which are directly pertinent to the client's issues. Such information is communicated for the purpose of denoting common human reactions to universal developmental and social experiences, thus illustrating specific items to be learned and facilitating client self-exploration. Self-disclosure does not provide a license for therapist testimonials or deviations away from client issues.

(9) Interpersonal patience—Ideally, the therapist carefully and patiently listens, allowing clients time to convey their concerns and alternatives on their own, in their own words. In addition, the therapist avoids imposing premature therapeutic interpretations, discrediting client expressions, or offering immediate solutions that may run the risk of seemingly oversimplifying the client's problems.

(10) Articulate use of language—Having at one's disposition a solid vocabulary permits the therapist to put to therapeutic use concise as well as allegorical forms of language without stumbling in search of appropriate words. Since language is a major tool of psychotherapy, the therapist who lacks sound verbal skills is at a decided disadvantage. Such a disadvantage can lead to the possibility of confusion or lack of precision in communication resulting from inarticulate verbalizations, misnomers, unfortunate connotations, use of "loaded" terms, and other linguistic

Table 3
Humor Rating Scale

Level of Therapist Humor	Clinical Vignette
Level 1 Destructive Humor Therapist humor is sarcastic and vindictive, eliciting client feelings of hurt and distrust. Therapist abuses humor to callously vent his/her own anger toward clients or the world and is consequently insensitive to and unconcerned with the impact of his/her humor on clients. Therapist humor may judge or stereotype clients; its caustic quality denigrates clients' sense of personal worth, leaving them with a typical "bitter aftertaste" reaction. Since the therapist's use of humor is destructive and retaliatory in nature, it tends to significantly impede client self-exploration and divert the therapeutic process.	Therapist to client who reports feelings of inadequacy related to a negative self-image: "Well, you obviously have much to be modest about; your face could sink a fleet, and on top of it you have the I.Q. of a tree. On the other hand, being stupid could help you qualify for disability payments."
Level 2 Harmful Humor Therapist humor does not manifest the blatant client disrespect found at level 1, but is still not attuned to clients' needs. Therapist mixes the irrelevant use of humor with its abuse, at times introducing humor when it is unapplicable to the issues at hand. The therapist may follow up his/her abuse of humor with a "redemptive communication" that essentially acknowledges the inappropriateness of the previous abusive comment and attempts to make verbal or non-verbal amends for it. Overall, therapist humor is harmful and incapable of facilitating therapeutic process since it is indiscriminate and invalidated either by missed timing or by the attempt to redeem derisive comments.	Client states that he is confused about his goals in life and unable to understand himself. Therapist replies, "Here you go off on a fishing pole again! It's almost like your mind is full of wallpaper." Client, with a nervous titter: "So I guess I should be perfect! Asking confusing questions can lead me astray, right!" Therapist, now self-conscious: "Well, uh, I'm like that too sometimes. Sometimes I can't think straight." Therapist goes on to explain about his own periods of confusion, indirectly apologizing. Attention is gradually shifted away from the client's experiencing.
Level 3 Minimally Helpful Humor Response Therapist humor *does not* question the essential worth of individuals and is adequately attuned to clients' needs. Therapist uses humor for and not against clients as a means of reflecting their dilemmas in a concerned yet humorous manner.	

Therapist humor promotes a positive therapist-client interaction, yet remains mostly a reaction to clients' communication rather than an active or preferred therapist-initiated mode of communication.

Level 4 Very Helpful Humor Response

Therapist humor is substantially attuned to clients' needs and to helping them identify new options. Therapist humor may expose or amplify specific maladaptive behaviors yet simultaneously conveys a respect for clients' personhood. It facilitates clients' self-exploration while inciting them to recognize and alter dysfunctional patterns. The educational, comfortable, and enjoyable nature of therapist humor stimulates a positive and candid patient-therapist relationship. Nevertheless, therapist humor still lacks some of the intensity, timing, and graphic language characteristic of level 5 humor responses.

Obsessive client constantly rejects interpretations with the statement: "No, that's not my bag." Therapist: "So, what's your bag, or rather, what's your briefcase?"

Level 5 Outstandingly Helpful Humor Response

Therapist humor conveys a profound understanding of clients, is characterized by spontaneity and excellent timing, and challenges clients to live to their fullest potential. Therapist humor reflects his or her emotional and cognitive freedom used to facilitate clients' emotional arousal and cognitive restructuring. It generates significant self-exploration and accelerates the process of client change by defining problems, condensing and symbolizing therapeutic process material, identifying new goals, and promoting constructive alternatives. The creative nature of therapist humor can elicit decisive existential insights and encourages clients to develop their own humor along with other attitudinal changes.

During a group therapy session, a manipulative client is recounting to the group his repeated failings at achieving honest non-manipulative communication with others. Although he tries, others don't seem to believe or respond to his "authentic" self-revelations. Therapist: "You know your situation reminds me of a corrida scene with the bull and toreador. We don't know whether you're the bull for whose slaughter we should feel sorry or the toreador whose courage we ought to admire." Another group member: "But he's really not the bull, he sets other people up as being bulls." Client, laughing: "So I end up being the toreador. I give my coup de grace and demand my Ole!" Group members, in unison: "Ole!"

Note: This author's observational data indicate that physical responses to levels 1 and 2 humor are usually characterized by a preponderance of giggling, tittering, forced laughter, or short anxious laughs. Levels 3, 4, and 5 humor usually elicits predominantly diaphragmatic or abdominal gut-level laughter.

misconstructions. Articulate use of language also includes the therapist's ability to adapt his or her language to the client's language style.

(11) Ethical/legal responsibilities—The effective therapist possesses thorough knowledge of the ethical and legal aspects of conducting psychotherapy and can translate this knowledge into practice in interactions with clients.

4. *Twelve Intervention Recommendations*

The last component of the I.S.T.T. system to be summarized in this section is the therapist's intervention strategy. The following twelve intervention recommendations will convey the thrust of the therapist's intervention strategy in I.S.T.T.:

(1) Select the therapeutic focus area(s) and explicitly define problems to be addressed early in treatment. Stick to the therapeutic focus throughout treatment until therapeutic foci are replaced with new constructive foci which the patient can carry out on her or his own.

(2) Establish as quickly as possible a positive working alliance with the patient. Communicate support for the patient's active participation in the therapeutic process.

(3) Attend to immediacy/process issues in the initial phase of treatment for indications of important patient behavior patterns, resistances, conflict areas, communication style, reactions to the therapist, as well as personal limitations and strengths. It is particularly important at the outset of therapy not to import knowledge into the session but to use session-generated material in order to develop working hypotheses or bring important patterns into the client's awareness. Psychological process is not unlike the human pulse: it is always there, it can be taken at various arteries, if it is missed at one point it can always be accurately detected at another, and it reflects the person's overall health condition.

(4) Make Archaeological-Contemporary-Immediacy (ACI) connections once historical data has been gathered, relating past patterns to present functioning. Depending on the patient's needs, resistance level, and defensive formations, ACI connections can be conveyed both directly and indirectly at different junctures in therapeutic work. ACI connections can be made directly by pointing out recurring themes and the general structure of patient defenses and coping mechanisms around these themes. Indirectly, ACI themes can be expressed by using anecdotes, humor, as well as other modes of hypnotic and metaphorical communication.

(5) Encourage Subjectivization by helping the patient express the unexpressed emotional correspondents attached to specific experiences in the ACI constellation. In addition, help the patient acknowledge and constructively utilize the voices of subjectivity, including unconscious (or rootconscious) resources and insights.

(6) Move to Integraction with proper consideration given to the patient's pace and personal absorption levels. Assist the patient in detecting alternatives, developing autonomy, and shortening the distance between insight and action. Keep in view that the acid test of therapy is whether the patient effects actual changes in everyday behavior toward self and others. Assign homework when indicated such as practical readings related to the patient's issues, expressing feelings to significant others by way of unaddressed letters, and other specific activities that provide a propitious context within which the patient can discover pertinent alternatives.

(7) Help the patient differentiate between primary and secondary goals and realign his or her actions accordingly.

(8) Provide continuous support throughout treatment to give the patient a *corrective emotional experience*, thus conveying a successful (but by no means exclusive) model of mature relationships with others.

(9) Enlist the help of the patient's resources. Identify and highlight previous constructive experiences, positive interactions, and past or current successful coping mechanisms. Use hypnosis, guided imagery, rehearsals, and related approaches to help patients recuperate and reactivate personal resources in addressing present or future challenges.

(10) Use humor in treatment as applicable, encouraging patients' development of a personal sense of humor. Introduce him or her to humorous interactions by using self-directed or situational humor, then moving to unobtrusive other-directed humor when the therapeutic ambience becomes more relaxed. Underscore the use of humor as an attitudinal healing resource.

(11) Take time for an evaluation session at midpoint in treatment to review progress and specifically discuss what has been accomplished so far as well as what work remains to be done.

(12) At termination, ask the patient to review the overall progress made, therapeutic gains, and future direction. Emphasize preventive aspects and continuing self-help activities. Arrange for follow-up and leave the door open for the patient to re-establish contact should it be desired.

5. *Structured Hypnotic Humorous Experiences in I.S.T.T.*

Given the above therapeutic horizon, we can now address the question of how structured hypnotic humorous experiences can enter at specific stages of treatment within the I.S.T.T. process model. These experiences are utilized in an adjunctive manner and may be introduced in psychotherapy for one or more of the following reasons:

• to strengthen and support adaptive functioning
• to give a boost to the self by reviewing positive experiences
• to elicit the patient's productive resources

- to make "change" behavior an offshoot of early, recent, or session-generated constructive experiences
- to build mutual rapport
- to further the patient's sense of mastery and self-confidence
- to neutralize dysphoric rumination and shift motivation toward a peaceful or energetic mood
- to support the internalization of a healthy and gratifying internal representational world with appropriately defined boundaries and identifications
- to enhance autonomy and self-control
- to encourage the integration of insight and emotional change, with subsequent maturation and effective growth
- to provide explicit alternatives for self-restoration
- to teach relaxation and stress reduction
- to give patients the license to experience themselves in gratifying ways which are neither solemn nor gloomy

The following are some of the structured humorous experiences used for each stage of the I.S.T.T. process model (see Figure 1).

(1) *Archaeological Stage*. Two experiences were found to be helpful in working with archaeological stage material: the "Happy Times Elicitation" and the "Tragi-Comic Reconciliation" techniques. These and the other experiences presented below for subsequent stages are usually prefaced with a mild relaxation induction which sets a comfortable tone to the communication. Numerous relaxation suggestions are available to the operator in the literature; the one frequently used by this author is as follows:

> You are sitting in this chair, in this room. . . . And your eyes are closed. . . . And your arms are on the armrest. . . . And your feet are on the carpeted floor. And you are breathing in . . . and out, in-n-n and ou——t [time breathing to patient's own inhalation and exhalation].
>
> And you are relaxing more . . . and more, mo——re and mo——re.
>
> And just as I next say the word *now*, you are *now* allowing yourself the comfort of breathing deeply, slowly, freely [5 seconds], and relaxing more and more, relax——ing *every* muscle, *every* organ, *every* tendon, *every* cell, *every* nerve, *every* vein, *every* pore, *every* bodily function—*all* relaxed more and more merely by taking in a long, slow breath through your nose and letting it ease out through your mouth. Relaxed physically and mentally, consciously and automatically, naturally, rest-*fully*, relaxed [5 seconds].

Once the relaxation response has developed, it is then immediately followed with the suggestions for the "Happy Times Elicitation" process.
A. Happy Times Elicitation:

And as you *now* notice how comfortable and relaxed *you feel*, how effortlessly and smoothly your functions flow, you may *find* it *easier and easier* to give yourself permission for even deeper, earlier relaxation experiences just waiting to be relived down the roads of memory. And why not savor the enjoyment of drifting slow—ly, at your own pace, to a happy time and place, to memories so refreshing that you would enjoy reliving them once more at this very moment. And I wonder if in your mind's eye you *can imagine, imagine* watching on a big movie screen a humorous slice of your life, a special fun memory which you cherish, which makes you laugh every time you remember it. Now appearing on the screen of your imagination is this special, enjoyable, fun memory, a memory that can be from your childhood or your adolescence [or your adult life or recent past—depending on patient's age and the issues being worked on]. Now let the image form, take your time, let the whole memory come on your screen. Retrace the place, the time of day, the feelings attached to this experience . . . all now coming into focus on the screen. Now you can picture the event as concretely as possible [5 seconds] . . . the activities taking place, the appearance of the surroundings, how old you are, what you are wearing, what you or others said [5 seconds]. You can presently recapture exactly what happened with all the funny details [5 seconds] and you can spontaneously relive and enjoy all the happy feelings, the refreshing feelings you are experiencing again *at this moment*. Let go . . . *now* . . . and simply have fun being with this unique experience. You may want to take *ti——me*, take *your ti——me* enjoying this experience because you know that it is totally *yours* . . . You know that this beautiful memory is completely yours now and will be yours to keep and relish. And as you discover that this experience is here for you *right* now, you also know that it is here to stay and will always be available for you to bring up at any time when you want to feel restored and replenished with happy humor. And somehow life seems . . . *to you* more buoyant, more zestful, more lighthearted, full of cheerfulness and joy. Now take this time to give yourself additional suggestions about how you can have more humor and happiness in your life, give yourself suggestions that are in your very best interest [10 seconds]. And you know that you can *trust* your inner awareness to bring all this information to bear whenever you need it. I am now going to count to 3. At the count of 3, you will open your eyes and you will return to this room, to today. You will feel awake all over, upbeat, better than before, totally relaxed, and more joyful and cheerful than you have felt for a long time, with happy feelings . . . harmonious thoughts . . . energetic alertness. 1, 2, 3.

Upon disengaging, the therapist may adopt either of two approaches to help the client in processing the above experiences or any of the other experiences presented below. In one approach, the client is asked how he or she currently feels and what exactly happened including what the actual memory was, the comic details, and so forth. For some clients, the recounting of the memory to the therapist can serve as an anchoring and a validation of the subjective humorous state which encourages its continuation in everyday reality. In the second approach, the therapist makes little or no commentary regarding the induction, thus allowing the client to decode the experience in a personally relevant manner. The therapist can flexibly use his or her clinical judgement to determine which of these two approaches would be most effective in productively addressing client issues, depending on each client's individual needs, interactive style, degree of resistance, and defense mechanisms.

B. Tragi-Comic Reconciliation

In this intervention, humor is used to facilitate the substitution of anxiety-provoking or depressing childhood experiences with humorous experiences. The humorous experiences can help reconcile the tragic aspects of an event with its absurd dimensions. Such a reconciliation may be beneficial in the sense that absurdity can be construed as incompatible with a depressed or anxious mindset. Subsequently, tragi-comic reconciliation can promote mastery in coping with adverse conditions, assist in bearing the emotional brunt of a tragic occurrence in a person's life, and facilitate a transformation of detrimental tragic energies into constructive energies. However, care should be taken in this context to not ignore or minimize the importance of the client's feelings about a negative experience since the goal of tragi-comic reconciliation is not to dismiss the existence or importance of depressing occurrences but rather to integrate them within a larger perspective. Tragi-comic reconciliation techniques have equivalents in other cultures such as the tradition of the Irish wake and similar cultural rituals associated with death or loss.

Tragi-Comic Reconciliation can be implemented in two ways:

(1) The relaxation state described above is evoked, followed by the Happy Times Elicitation. At the end of the Happy Times Elicitation, the client is asked to bring up on the screen in the "mind's eye" a negative childhood experience (i.e., an experience that provokes painful, sad or angry emotions). The client is asked to remember this tragic experience in detail and with all the feelings associated with it just as was done in reliving the Happy Times Elicitation. Once the emotional components of the tragic experience have been expressed, the following instructions may be given:

> I now want you to slowly bring back up on the movie screen the happy experience you had just relived some moments ago [10 seconds]. Bring it *back up* . . . bit by bit [5 seconds]. Notice how the humorous, happy, cheerful feelings associated with this humorous experience are *gradually coming back to you. Feel the comfort* of knowing that you can *experience* relief from pain or worry simply by bringing your cherished humorous *experience* back up on your screen any time you wish, any time you *want* to use this ally, this constructive resource, to help you deal successfully with past or present hurt [5 seconds]. Now let's practice to make sure that you can use this system whenever you want to. I am going to give you a simple technique for bringing up your constructive humorous experience. Now slowly bring back your tragic experience on the screen [15 seconds]. When you can see it clearly on the screen, I want you to shut your eyelids closed very tightly, open them up as wide as you can, then close them again in normal fashion. [Verify eye movements.] When you close your eyelids the second time, your humorous experience will automatically appear on the screen and you will experience relief, inner contentment, lightheartededness, and joy [10 seconds]—simply by shutting your eyelids closed very tightly, opening them up as wide as you can, and closing them back in normal fashion to relive on your imaginary screen, in your imagination, the humorous experience you now recognize and appreciate *so readily*. You will remember this system and use it as you want to wherever you are, whenever you're upset, sad, or unhappy. [The client is always brought out by reciting the last lines of the Happy Times Elicitation.]

Upon awakening, the client can be asked how he or she feels, what happened during the induction, and what the actual tragic experience was in all its details.

(2) In another variation of the Tragi-Comic Reconciliation technique, the relaxation state is elicited, followed by a full reliving of the tragic experience on the screen, after which the following instructions are given:

> Now I wonder what it would be like if you changed the ending of this scenario, if you imagined a different ending to this situation, a humorous, absurd, incongruous, funny ending. Go ahead . . . change the situation in any way . . . *you want to . . . make it funny* . . . You can change the actions or words of those present including you, the setting, the activities taking place, or the feelings of those involved in this situation . . . *any change* that would add *a humorous twist* to this situation on the screen in your mind's eye [20 seconds]. Notice how your reactions can change [verify for physical signs of humor—smiling, relaxed facial expression, etc.], how you can *feel better* by bringing humor into an unhappy situation with an absurd funny twist. So that from now on it will be *up to you* to spontaneously use this simple system to your very best advantage wherever you are, whenever negative thoughts or situations become overwhelming and cause you unnecessary distress.

Upon awakening, the client is asked about what was changed, how the scenario was twisted, etc. Furthermore, the instructions can be tape-recorded and later replayed by the client as a homework assignment to practice relaxation, stress reduction, reconstruction of happy memories, or tragi-comic reconciliation.

In many instances, clients have reported using the above techniques to constructively deal with negative ruminations, to handle interpersonal conflict situations in an appropriate manner, to control impulsive tendencies, or to gain perspective on previously unfinished business.

(2)*Contemporary Stage*. Three structured experiences can be used when working with issues related to a client's present life situation:

A. The Happy Times Elicitation and Tragi-Comic Reconciliation instructions can be transposed to the context of present events by asking the client to recollect a recent happy experience or a current tragic experience that needs to be reconciled, then applying the other sections of these procedures as previously indicated.

B. The client can be given as a homework assignment the "exercise for evoking serenity" developed by Assagioli (1965). This short and uncomplicated exercise basically consists of concentrating on the desirability of serenity, then directly evoking it by imagining oneself in a serene frame of mind in circumstances which one would usually find irritating.

C. Ejection of Negative Thoughts

This technique is used with persons who suffer from ongoing negative ruminations which are continuously disseminated on the inner intercom system, causing distress, depression, anger, or hopelessness. The purpose of this procedure is to uproot these negative thought patterns and replace them with more positive, even humorous, messages. The procedure begins with the relaxation suggestion described above followed with:

> And as you *now* notice how comfortable and relaxed . . . *you feel* . . . how effortlessly and smoothly your functions flow, you *can* become more *keenly aware* of your inner processes . . . and what takes place *within you* that may influence your feelings and your behavior [5 seconds]. And you can *imagine* that *inside* of you, inside your head, is a cassette tape-recorder which can play *different* tapes with *different* stories, different recordings about your life. Take your time to picture this tape-recorder inside your head [5 seconds]. Now imagine *two* cassette tapes stacked right next to the tape-recorder [5 seconds]. Each tape has a different recording on it. You put in the first tape and start playing it . . . You *start hearing* the familiar voice of your mother/father [or stepfather, etc.—change word depending on who instilled the negative identification pattern in each case]. You *can now hear* her/him making disparaging comments about you, putting you down, humiliating you, repeating typically false things about you which she/he has said many times before [10 seconds]. Now her/his voice fades away [5 seconds]. The tape is still playing. . . . Now you are hearing another voice. . . . it's the voice of [a person who exerts a negative influence on the patient's present functioning]. You can *hear* him/her discrediting you, again judging you and condemning you as he/she usually does [10 seconds]. Now his/her voice fades away [5 seconds]. The tape is still playing. . . . Now you are hearing a voice that is most familiar to you, *your own voice*. . . . *You can hear your own voice playing* on the tape inside your head. . . . *You can hear* your voice saying gloomy negative things about you; *your voice* is repeating your own negative comments about yourself, terms or phrases you frequently harass yourself with. . . . thoughts you harp on . . . things you rehash in your mind time and again during the day. . . . And as you hear your voice repeating these negative statements you can immediately recognize them because you've created them yourself, you know exactly what they are [15 seconds]. You can

recognize all the negative comments on this tape because you've heard them repeated in your head again and again, and every time you've heard these *now* self-perpetrated comments they've made you feel unhappy. So *now* is the *time* to eject this tape from your inner tape-recorder once and for all, since presently you don't *need* it any more. And all it would take on your part to eject the tape is one single hand movement . . . just to *put your right forefinger* in your belly-button and *push to eject this negative tape* [verify for action]. Put your right forefinger in your belly-button and push to eject all remnants of negativity and unhelpful self-criticism, eject fruitless negative statements that end up making you feel depressed and hopeless, push to eject *any* negative thoughts or feelings that make you unhappy [20 seconds]. Now that your mind is free from negative thoughts and ruminations, like a *clear, clear blue sky* after the morning rain . . . you can presently take the second cassette tape next to the tape-recorder, the cassette you haven't played yet, and put it in your tape recorder to hear what it contains. . . . You *start hearing* pleasant voices, happy voices, the voices of people who care . . . about you. First you hear the voice of a caring member of your family, a family member you feel especially close to, making positive comments about you, comments of praise and pride in who you are. You can clearly hear him/her repeating the *positive* comments he/she has made about you over the years in his/her own pleasant . . . calming . . . voice, a voice you always like to hear . . . saying good things about you . . . things you cherish . . . remembering . . . things that make you feel so happy inside [15 seconds]. Now his/her voice fades away [5 seconds]. The tape is still playing. . . . Now you are hearing another supportive voice from the past. . . . it's the voice of your favorite teacher . . . he/she is enthusiastically praising your performance in a certain subject or the way you handled a certain situation . . . his/her *pleasing* voice and his/her supportive comments bring back to life this unique moment of achievement, a moment you are still . . . *now* very proud of [15 seconds]. . . .

The tape *keeps* playing. . . . Now the recorded voice changes into that of your friend [a person who is supportive of and exerts a positive influence in the patient's present life context]. You can hear him/her telling you friendly comments, comments you remember and appreciate because they reflect the lasting bond of friendship between you and your friend [15 seconds]. . . . This soothing, enjoyable tape keeps playing . . . and now you are hearing your own voice again. You *can hear your own voice* making *approving* statements about you . . . your voice is listing attributes and qualities you like about yourself, commenting about things you have a knack for, your special talents, gifts, abilities and accomplishments, some of which only you may be aware of as a source of personal satisfaction [15 seconds]. And as this comforting tape keeps rolling, you *can* experience the feelings of inner serenity, cheerfulness, and joy . . . the pleasantness of feeling competent, upbeat, and ready to tackle the world with whatever challenges it may bring forth [5 seconds] and all these good feelings are available to you, all yours . . . at your disposal . . . simply by *remembe—ring* to put your right forefinger on your belly-button and push to eject negative self-statements from the past and present. It is quite an interesting aspect of inner awareness . . . *You now know* . . . how negative self-evaluations can be ejected with a single automatic right forefinger movement. . . . You will from now on remember that the positive tape is permanently recorded and always available for your use any time you need to play it on your private tape recorder in your head. And you can feel comforted in knowing that you can trust your inner awareness to bring all this information to bear whenever you need it. [Then end by reciting last lines of Happy Times Elicitation.]

When the client awakens, he or she can be encouraged to share the details of his or her experience. The aforecited technique is often time-consuming but it can be effective in engineering a healthier and constructively-oriented internal environment while simultaneously helping to wash away the cobwebs of exaggerated self-doubt and endless negative ruminations. Furthermore, due to its highly auditory loading, this technique might be optimally suitable for use with clients whose primary representational system (or PRS) is determined by the therapist to be auditory in nature (Bandler & Grinder, 1975, 1976a, 1979; Yapko, 1981).

(3) *Immediacy Stage.* The following two experiences can be used at the immediacy stage to develop a "here and now" cheerful and relaxed mindset on the patient's part. Both experiences make use of a trade secret that some stand-up comedians employ in elaborating their routines: "K" and "P" sounds are funny and tend to elicit a laughter response when utilized in different words or sentences (Horn, 1982).

A. Tropical Market Scene

This scene uses "K" and "P" sounds together with vivacious colors to elicit a relaxed and positive stage of mind. As with the other experiences presented above, it is most effective when preceded by the relaxation induction specified earlier and concluded with the last lines of the "Happy Times Elicitation."

In your mind's eye, I wonder if you can imagine that you are taking a vacation on a tropical island. It is a nice sunny day and you happen to have some time today to explore this lovely island. You decide to go to the fruit market and see for yourself what fruits and vegetables are sold there. Now you picture yourself right there at the market. . . . take your time, let the image form [5 seconds]. You can *now* hear the islanders calling out, announcing the price and quality of their fruits as they bargain with customers over prices in a dialect which sounds funny to you because you don't understand what they're saying. . . . You are amused by the lively pace of the conversations and the new interesting sounds in the words you hear. You are *now* walking down a long street on each side of which stand local fruit merchants selling the fruits of their native land . . . Some of them have luxuriously colored parrots perched on their stands or on their shoulders. *Now* you see all kinds of fresh, interesting fruits and vegetables, and you are even tempted to touch the fruits and smell their savory aroma as you walk down the street. First you see big yellow pineapples, huge luscious yellow papayas, and round brown coconuts. . . . You keep walking and enjoying just the sight, smell and touch of these succulent tropical fruits. Next you see beautiful ripe orange mangoes. . . . You pick up a fleshy mango and smell its sweet aroma. You hear a refreshing music playing and can recognize the energizing beat of drums resonating in the background. As you walk down the crowded market street, you see more delicious fruits and vegetables . . . prime yellow pears, green and purple grapes, purple plums, big green watermelons, yellow and green bananas, yellow and red peaches, yellow lemons, green limes, purple and white rutabegas, brown turnips, spinach greens, red strawberries, plump pink grapefruits, orange passion fruit, sweet potatoes, bright red apples. . . . You pick up a round juicy apple and sink your teeth into it . . . hear the apple skin crunch under your teeth and savor its flavor-*full taste* on your tongue. . . . It's *such* a lovely, sunny day. . . . A gentle sea breeze caresses you as you fill your lungs [time words to patient's breathing] with the ambrosial aromas of the tropical market mixed with the balmy smell of the sea. . . . You feel privileged to be here today, at this special moment, enjoying this cornucopia . . . this inexhaustible abundance of sights, smells, and sounds. You're happy to be alive, you accept and cherish life as it offers itself to you in its infinite diversity. . . . You feel *so* relaxed, cheerful and upbeat.

B. A Trip to Australia

(Some passages in this narrative have been excerpted from Blunden, 1963). This experience again makes use of "K" and "P" sounds as well as luxurious colors in an exotic setting to induce a comfortable state of relaxation. It may be more appropriate for intellectual clients who like reading:

It is a warm Sunday afternoon. You are relaxing in your favorite chair and reading a color-*fully illustrated* travel book about the land, the customs, the animal and plant life of Australia. And you read about various places in Australia which have amusing native aboriginal names . . . Paramatta, Koondaloo, Wonwon-dah, Wagga Wagga, Wooloomooloo. . . . Now you are reading about the interesting varieties of vegetation and trees found in Australia . . . the eucalyptus trees which blossom into heavy tasseled flowers colored in crimson, scarlet, vermilion, orange-red, lemon-yellow, and white . . . the coral tree, and the flame tree with its bright flame-colored flowers. You can virtually smell the unique scents of the Australian forest, the fine her-baceous fragrance, the light sweet candy scents . . . never over-powering, yet fleeting and evanescent. As you become more engrossed in reading about this fascinating country you can al-most imagine yourself there enjoying the sights with your very own eyes . . . And now you are reading about the marine life of the Australian coral reefs and their exotic colorful fish . . . orange-spotted leatherjackets, beautiful small blue and green fish like the ones you see in aquariums, great lazy green turtles lying on the underwater sandbanks. . . . Next you are reading about the animals of Australia . . . the jolly kangaroo, the charming furry little koala bear . . . You are captivated by the engaging, relaxing aspects of your reading as your imagi-nation roams further and further in your explorations of this unique land. . . . Now you are reading about the birds of Aus-tralia, of which your book provides beautiful colored illustra-tions. . . . as you flip the pages you see different kinds of parrots, cockatoos, and red, brilliant green, yellow and blue parakeets . . . You read about a peculiar bird with a big beak called kookaburra or laughing jack. You are reading that the kookaburra's nickname alludes to its peculiar habit of sitting in the branches of trees in the morning and evening hours and pouring out *peals* and *peals* of lively laughter [5 seconds]. You now put your book aside, feeling relaxed and entertained by your reading, not a care in the world, with pleasant sensations and happy thoughts. You feel *free, buoyant, uninhibited*, enjoying your ability to experience new worlds and new ways of being [5 seconds]. Through your window, you watch the sun *slowly* set in the clear blue horizon.

C. Another important element for indirectly encouraging client humor at the immediacy stage is the inclusion of humorous objects in the therapeutic environment. For instance, some of the humorous objects in the author's therapy office include: a concave mirror that deforms the body in unexpected and often hilarious ways which clients are invited to use, a large glass cup on which all the "Peanuts" cartoon characters are depicted in a laughing mood, a statuette of a laughing zen monk, and humorous books on the bookcase shelves. The purpose of such objects is to create a therapeutic milieu that emits an unwritten invitation, a spontaneous message to clients that humor is healthy and acceptable within the context of psychotherapeutic work. Once clients sense that their humor is welcome in psychotherapy, they may feel free to venture new humorous responses or bring forward their own humorous style. The therapist can then support healthy humor and discourage sarcasm or other harmful abuses of humor as indicated in each client's specific situation.

(4) *The Subjectivization Stage.* A major goal of the subjectivization stage in I.S.T.T. is to encourage the patient's restructuring of his or her internal environment in such a manner that new or modified patterns of emotional responsiveness can emerge. The following experience can encourage a new mode of emotional responsiveness regarding humor:

A Visit With Jolly Santa Claus:
As your physical and mental functions continue to flow smoothly and naturally, as you continue to experience a wave of relaxation going through your entire body, you now *begin* to feel yourself shifting to a happy, humorous, positive mood . . . getting in touch with the part of you that knows how to be happy [5 seconds]. And in your mind's eye, you can *now picture yourself* sitting on a park bench under the shadow of a

tall pine tree in a beautiful park. Take your time, let the images form [5 seconds]. From where you are sitting, you can view all the trees, the shrubbery and neatly mowed green lawns that make this park such a calming, serene place to be. It is a warm, pleasant, sunny day. Smell the pine trees and flowers, hear the birds singing, the wind in the trees, the sounds of nature . . . see the shadows that the trees cast on the grass, feel your back merge with the firm back of the bench . . . allow yourself to enjoy the *peace-fullness* and soothing calm of the scenery around you [10 seconds]. Now you see a smiling jolly old man with a white beard walking towards you. He is dressed in green and red and his face is beaming as he approaches you. As he gets closer, you suddenly recognize his features. It's *Santa Claus*, whom you have seen many times before in your life in so many places, since the time you were a child. Santa Claus now comes and sits right next to you on the park bench, *smiling* and *laughing* goodheartedly, encouraging you to join in his cheer [5 seconds]. You admire Santa's cheerfulness and everpresent *zest-fullness*. You want to tell Santa Claus about some of the fears you have about being humorous, some of the blocks that prevent you from being as cheerful as he. Go ahead and tell Santa about whatever fears or apprehensions you may have that can prevent you from letting go and enjoying happy humor [10 seconds]. Now you are asking him about how you can be more humorous and serene, how you can be more *lighthearted* [5 seconds]. Santa listens to you *very carefully* . . . he wants to answer your questions. Now Santa reaches in his big leather bag and hands you a green envelope. You open the envelope and inside it you see a note to you. As you *now* read the note you can see that it contains *three suggestions* about how you can be more humorous. Go ahead and read the three suggestions, take your time [20 seconds]. As you finish reading the note, you look and see Santa smiling and nodding his head approvingly [5 seconds]. Now Santa bids you farewell and slowly walks away. Now alone in the park, you re-read the note from Santa . . . and you just know that you can trust your inner awareness to remember and put to use your three suggestions about being more humorous . . . because you *real-ize* that these suggestions are in your very best interest and will bring more happiness into your life.

The patient is then brought out and may be asked to describe how he or she is feeling, what actually happened in the park, and what the three suggestions were.

(5) *The Integraction Stage*. At this stage, it is important that the therapist attempt to ignite a certain awareness on the part of the patient, beyond all techniques, that misery is optional in many respects and that one can be happier if one chooses to structure one's life to welcome happiness. If certain attachments make a person unhappy, the person can decide to let go of these attachments. And even when one is stuck with lemons, one can still make lemonade! The therapist can accordingly facilitate a humorous client attitude by encouraging clients to make sense of issues in a humorous way. This does *not* imply that the person would give up seriousness, but rather that he or she *can* give up solemnity. The attitude of the *therapist* is, of course, crucial since an inflexible and solemn therapist would probably be unable to convey a humorous attitude to his or her clients, a factor which leads to the topic of the next section.

V. Entering Humorland: Humor Immersion Training™

The French philosopher Voltaire, an early proponent of the organic gardening movement, suggested that "We must cultivate our garden." One cannot prescribe humor for clients unless one can accept humor in one's own life. It often seems difficult for therapists to enter into the world of humor for many reasons: Some therapists may reject humor because they associate it with overt aggression or because of past negative experiences in being the victim of sarcasm. Others may feel that using humor discredits clients or may even discredit the therapist's own "professional" stance. Moreover, conventional clinical training does not usually encourage a humorous perspective since one must often work against a background of the grim view of life presented by many clients who harbor a pessimistic outlook. While it may be understandable why clients are pessimistic, it is often *not* understandable why therapists cannot raise their "humor quotient" as they struggle with the stress of working with distressed individuals. In this sense, humor is sometimes the best gift one can offer clients and oneself in order to move from a negative view to a constructive one where problems are solvable. Consequently, *Humor Immersion Training*™ was developed by the author and is currently offered as a workshop training experience for therapists, clients, and other individuals who are interested in exercising their humor muscles. In *Humor Immersion Training*, workshop participants can boost their humorous abilities through the exposure to mini-lectures on the psychological and physiological benefits of humor as well as through the practice of specific humorous experiences, techniques, exercises, games, and role-plays.

The following are some of the humorous training methods used in *Humor Immersion Training* to help individuals begin to open up to the humorous perspective:

1. Practice overstatement, incongruity, and understatement. Most humorous material can be subsumed under three general categories of humor creation:

A. Overstatement: making mountains out of molehills, taking an accurate fact and exaggerating it to absurdity. Examples: (1) "I don't mean to exaggerate the degree of discipline in your family. There are more disciplined contexts. Devil's Island, for example. The Wax Museum, the changing of the guards at Buckingham Palace, an interview with the Queen Mother." (2) "Are you aware that having lunch with men friends when you are a married woman can constitute grounds for excommunication?" You can practice overstatement (as well as the other humorous techniques presented herein) by deleting the punchline in the above examples (Devil's Island, the Wax Museum . . . , excommunication) and filling in your own punchlines or adding new punchlines to the ones offered above.

B. Incongruity: putting together two non-sequiturs, i.e., two events or experiences that are apparently unrelated but for which you can find an unexpected underlying humorous "fit." The ensuing joke was developed by using this system: The two non:sequiturs are: (a) the recent debate over capital punishment in our legal system, and (b) the religious belief in reincarnation in India. The joke (a + b): "A lawyer is trying to defend a capital punishment case in India. He appeals to the judge: 'Your honor, I believe that my client deserves another chance. I submit that his sentence be reduced from death without reincarnation to death *with* reincarnation!' " Other examples: (1) "If you want to be a hypocrite, you might as well be honest about it." (2) "You seem to be a glutton for punishment." (3) "It sounds like you haven't had any time to enjoy your misery."

C. Understatement: the opposite of overstatement, consists in shrinking giants down to pygmies, and sizing down important happenings to benign proportions. Examples: (1) "Depression is a low tolerance for euphoria." (2) "Death is nature's way of telling you to slow down." (3) "Getting a divorce could ruin your whole day."

Beyond the above techniques, Table 4 (Salameh, 1983) defines twelve therapeutic humor techniques and illustrates each with a clinical vignette.

2. Developing a sense of humor can be facilitated when one exposes oneself to humorous experiences via:

Table 4
Therapeutic Humor Techniques

Therapeutic Humor Technique	Definition	Clinical Vignette
Surprise	Using unexpected occurrences to transmit therapeutic messages.	Drilling noise outside office. Patient is talking about his domineering wife. Therapist: "Your wife is talking to you *now*!"
Exaggeration	Obvious overstatement or understatements regarding size, proportions, numbers, feelings, facts, actions.	To patient who romanticizes his depression while refusing to consider alternatives: "I could help you, but I guess that wouldn't do any good anyway. You know we all die eventually."
Absurdity	That which is foolish, nonsensical, insane, irrationally disordered. That which *is* without having any logical reason to be.	A young businessman is spending inordinately long hours at the office and on business trips. He reports that his wife has complained about his increasing lack of interest in their sexual relationship. Therapist responds: "It sounds like the best way for you to get more invested in your sex life is to make it tax deductible!"
The Human Condition	Refers to problems of living that most human beings encounter, viewed from a humorous perspective to stress their commonality.	Therapist to a perfectionist patient who worries that he is not being "totally honest" in communicating *all* his feelings to others: "As the holy books have indicated, it is difficult for mankind to be honest at all times. But if you want to be a phony, you should be honest about it."
Incongruity	Linking two or more usually incompatible ideas, feelings, situations, objects, etc.	Oppositional female patient reacts to therapist interpretation by stating that she "has already entertained that possibility." Therapist responds: "You've entertained it, but you didn't go to bed with it."

Confrontation / Affirmation Humor	Confronts patients' maladaptive and self-defeating behaviors while simultaneously affirming their personal worth as individuals. Assumes that patient confrontation is best digested by patients when coupled with affirmation.	A patient in group therapy is confronted by other group members regarding his compulsive nose-blowing behavior. He passionately defends his need to "Breathe clearly." Therapist responds: "You know, we can all see that you've got a lot of intensity, but you don't have to blow it out your nose!"
Word Play	Using puns, double entendres, bons mots, song lines, and well-known quotes or sayings from popular culture to convey therapeutic messages.	Therapist to patient who keeps depriving himself of what he really wants: "You know what Oscar [Wilde] said, 'I can resist anything but temptation.' " To another man who prevents himself from enjoying life or other people because he refuses to take small acceptable risks: "Mae West did say, 'When I choose between two evils, I always like to take the one I've never tried before.' "
Metaphorical Mirth	The use of metaphorical constructions, analogies, fairy tales and allegories for therapeutic story-telling to help patients assimilate new insights or understand old patterns.	Patient is talking about how his interpersonal communication is becoming less confused as he really listens to others and gives relevant feedback. Therapist: "It's like that lion you see at the zoo who always growls at you but you don't know what he means. And one day you go to the zoo and he smiles and says, 'Hi there, I've been fixin' to talk to you.' And you talk to each other and become pen-pals."
Impersonation	Humorously imitating the typical verbal response or maladaptive style of patients and of significant others they may bring up in therapy.	Patient repeats a characteristic "Fssss" sound with his tongue whenever he experiences sadness or other "vulnerable" emotions, so as to block the expression of such feelings. Therapist imitates this "Fssss" sound when patient displays it. Patient gradually shifts from suppression to acknowledgement of his feelings.

Relativizing	Contextualizing events within a larger perspective such that they lose their halo of absoluteness. Relativizing gives the message that: "Nothing is as serious as we fear it to be, nor as futile as we hope it to be" (Jankelevitch, 1964).	Patient recounts his painful struggle with his "weight problem," even though his physician informed him he is only 3-5 pounds overweight. Therapist: "Well, I notice you've lost some weight behind the ears since last week."
The Tragi-Comic Twist	A delicate humor technique requiring almost surgical precision that consists of a transformation of patients' detrimental tragic energies into constructive comical energies. It begins with a well-timed implicit or explicit juxtaposition of the tragic and comic poles of a given phenomenon followed by a reconciliation of the two poles in a humoristic synthesis that triggers laughter.	Patient who has chosen depression and crying as a behavioral mode of response to any environmental stressor is crying during session about feeling rejected and tense. Therapist responds: "I guess you're trying to relax now." Patient's crying turns into frantic laughter as he replies: "That's one thing I do really well, I know how to cry." Therapist: "Maybe you can relax about crying." More laughter. Therapist asks patient why he is laughing. Patient: "I suppose there are other ways of releasing tension besides crying." The entire session then focuses on the above issue.
Bodily Humor	Using the entire body or specific muscle groups in physical activity aimed at imitating or creating nonverbal reflections of typical maladaptive mannerisms in order to encourage their extinction.	Patient exhibits a typical rotational hand movement to express disillusionment with others' behavior when it does not meet his "requirements." Therapist uses this same hand movement in therapy whenever patient is expressing disillusionment with therapist's behavior not meeting his expectations.

A. Humorous books. Examples of books the author finds particularly humorous: *The Groucho Marx Letters* (Manor Books, 1975), *Titters,* a collection of women's humor, edited by Deanne Stillman and Anne Beatts (Collier Books, 1976), *How to Make Yourself Miserable* (by Dan Greenberg and Marcia Jacobs; Random House, 1966), *Side Effects* (by Woody Allen; Random House, 1975).

B. Humorous Records. Examples: "Eddie Murphy, Comedian" (Columbia Records 1983), records by George Carlin, Lily Tomlin, Bill Cosby, Bob Hope. Also, listening regularly to the smiling, sunny music of Frankie Laine.

C. Humorous magazines and publications. Examples: (1) *Journal of Polymorphous Perversity* (Wry-Bred Press, 20 Waterside Plaza, Suite 24H., New York, NY 10010), (2) *Journal of Irreproducible Results,* (3) *New Yorker* magazine, (4) *Laughing Matters* (Edited by Joel Godman, Ed.D., Sagamore Institute, Saratoga Springs, NY).

D. Comic performers can be seen in action at standup comedy clubs ("The Comedy Store" and "The Improvisation" clubs in Southern California, "The Holy City Zoo" in San Francisco, "Catch a Rising Star" and "Caroline's" in New York City, and others). Such performances can literally be a moving experience.

E. A concerted effort can be undertaken to locate quality comic movies, plays, and television shows.

3. Draw cartoons (without worrying about their artistic value) about situations, persons, or events which you found to be particularly humorous. Create humorous collages.

4. Take an art or photography catalog (or even your own family photo album) and make up humorous captions for each picture.

5. When you come home every evening, try to remember at least one funny event that happened during the day. Write it down and share it with friends and family.

6. Practice "intentional dyslexia" by creating new words that cannot be found in dictionaries.

7. Ask your friends to tell you their favorite jokes and tell them yours.

8. Find some time to be alone, sitting in your most comfortable position, relaxed, and breathing soundly. Close your eyes and bring up a past or recent humorous experience. Visualize the event as concretely as possible, and allow yourself to fully re-live and enjoy it in all its details and with all the feelings you experienced at that moment. Make a date with yourself to repeat this experience on a regular basis by bringing up the same event, constructing a cassette tape of the experience, or picturing other humorous events you have lived (all of us have had happy, humorous experiences, but we are sometimes more prone to remember negative

happenings). Cassette tapes of the Structured Humorous Experiences delineated in Section IV can also be ordered directly from the author.

9. List five facts or life situations you come in frequent contact with which you find to be absurdly humorous. Examples: (a) Why can't public telephones return change? or (b) Why do some envelopes have a caption on the top right corner saying, "Place stamp here?"

10. List all the fears or objections you have to being humorous in general or in specific situations. Read them again and determine if they are valid objections. Share them with others and ask for their feedback. Remember that undue fears sometimes cripple creativity.

11. Make written notes of all the humorous car stickers you notice as you drive every day. Examples: "Plumbers do it with a flush," "Teachers do it with class," "Fishermen have all the angles," "Quilters do it warmly." Start your own " . . . do it with . . . " sequence.

12. Think of a problem that has been bothering you for some time. Think of one sentence which you could use to define your problem in a humorous vein and write it down.

13. Don't be afraid to share with others the spontaneous humorous associations or scenarios that cross the freeways of your mind. Of course it is to be expected that some of what you find humorous may not be humorous to others because different individuals have predilections for different humorous genres. Example: My spontaneous Transactional Analysis Scenario for what I just wrote is: "It is okay for some people to feel that some other people's humor is not okay."

14. With your friends, start a Humor Support Group of people who meet to share jokes and success stories on the constructive applications of nondestructive humor used with oneself or with others. The group may also enjoy doing various humorous exercises. Examples: imitating animal sounds or experimenting with improvisational comedy sketches.

15. Start the day with a zing. As soon as you get up in the morning, make a habit of calling up a good friend and exchanging humorous repartee with him or her. This will get you perked up and humorously ready for the day. You can also call any of your friends during the day (especially those who are unhappy and need to laugh) and leave humorous messages on their answering machines. Examples: imitating various dialects or funny advertisements, remembering private jokes, sharing new jokes, etc.

16. Make funny lists to exaggerate, stretch, and spoof some of your own nagging problems, unfavorable patterns, disadvantageous behaviors, fears or anxieties which you seem unable to shake off. You may find that writing such comical lists is not only a lot of fun but can also help you deflate and gain perspective on hitherto insurmountable or disquieting

concerns. And who knows, you may find out about things you always wanted to know but were afraid to ask. Examples: "Ten things I must remember to do to fail my exams," "Twelve recommendations that would virtually squelch my chances of ever getting a promotion," "Five things I must remember to do to spoil my relationships with others," "Ten favorite anxieties I can't live without," "Twelve worries I want to indulge in worrying about from now until death do us part," "Five myths I want to keep believing about myself so I can enjoy depression," "Seven myths and seven realities about my fear of success," "Three reasons why undue guilt is good for me."

17. Take the *Humorous Sentence Completion Blank* (see Table 5) developed by this author.

VI. And After the Clouds Clear: Limitations and Ethical Considerations in Using Indirect Humorous Approaches

The purpose of this section is to examine some of the limitations and ethical dimensions related to the therapeutic uses of humor. First, it is important to clearly differentiate between therapeutic and destructive humor. What has been discussed throughout the various sections of this chapter is a wholesome, therapeutic form of humor which covers a wide range of psychological states: joy, happiness, lightheartedness, cheerfulness, joie de vivre, gusto, zest, contentment, gaiety, bliss, conviviality, celebration, and other associated experiences. Such forms of humor would by definition exclude sarcasm, scorn, mockery and other abuses of humor commonly known as "putdowns" which can usually be detected by the "bitter aftertaste" reaction they trigger when used toward self or others. Table 6 summarizes some of the differences between therapeutic and harmful humor.

Subsequently, an important component of *Humor Immersion Training* consists in training participants (through various role-play situations depicting non-therapeutic versus therapeutic humorous interventions) to clearly differentiate between the therapeutic use of humor and its harmful abuse. In this respect, is it important to indicate that therapeutic humor is gentle and respectful, even when it confronts clients' defenses. It is not fueled by anger but rather by joy and by an authentic commitment to help clients change in healthy ways. Therapeutic humor is also well-timed, taking into account clients' sensitivities as well as their specific needs at the moment when a humorous intervention is considered. Moreover, the judicious therapist is aware of when *not* to use humor, depending on the therapeutic material and the level of absorption and emotional

Table 5
Humorous Sentence Completion Blank
by Waleed A. Salameh, Ph.D.

NAME   SEX   AGE   MARITAL STATUS
PLACE   DATE

Instructions: Please complete the sentences below with the first spontaneous response that occurs to you. Since this is *not* a scholastic performance test, there are no right or wrong responses. The only requirement is that you make complete sentences and that your responses reflect your spontaneous reaction to each item below. Please wait for the signal to begin.

1. Although I realize roosters cannot lay eggs, I

2. While I know I cannot count all the raindrops, I

3. Although it is vain to build castles in Spain, I

4. Given that winter follows fall and summer follows spring, I still

5. Squirrels store their nuts, and I

6. When the lights are on but nobody is home, I

7. While it is apparent that chickens do not have lips, I

8. It is widely known that tickling provokes pleasant vibrations, yet I

9. Bankers do it with interest, and I do it

10. Martial artists do it for kicks, and I

11. Although others make hay while the sun shines, I still

12. Every dog has his day, and every frog

13. When I am as happy as a lark, I

14. While research has proven that real men don't eat quiche, I

15. Athletes go for the gold, and I

16. Due to the fact that I remember some people's names, I

17. The early bird gets the worm, and I

18. When I wake up in the morning, I insist

19. Although I acknowledge that a stitch in time saves nine,
    I

20. Some dress for success, yet I

21. When all else fails, my saving grace

22. If misery is optional, then joy

23. Since I stopped going to the circus as often as I used
    to, I

24. If Virginia is for lovers, New York for muggers, and
    Los Angeles for uncertains, then

25. If I could be either John Wayne, Mae West, Elvis Presley, Tarzan, or Lily
    Tomlin, I

26. When I'm singing in the rain, I

27. The most important difference between pirates and
    buccaneers is

28. When my mother calls to inquire about my last visit to
    the zoo, I

29. When I think about counting all the hairs in some
    people's beards, I

30. Although I abhor swimming in wet cement, I

31. All good things must come to an end, yet at this moment
    my heart

state of the client. The *Humor Rating Scale* (see Table 3) can again be useful in this context. By using the *Humor Rating Scale* to rate role-played, live, or video-taped therapeutic interactions, therapists can have a reference point by which to assess whether their present level of humorous intervention is harmful or helpful and can also rate their degree of improvement in using humor therapeutically following *Humor Immersion Training*. Fry and Salameh (in progress) introduce current perspectives on the clinical uses of humor in psychotherapy with different client populations using several theoretical orientations.

VII. Summary

Within the last two decades, a new generation of clinicians has entered the psychotherapeutic arena. This new generation of strategic psycho-

Table 6
Therapeutic Versus Harmful Humor

Therapeutic Humor	Harmful Humor
Concerned with impact of humorous feedback on others.	Unconcerned with impact of comments on others.
Has an educational, corrective message.	May exacerbate existing problems.
Promotes the onset of a cognitive-emotional equilibrium.	Prevents the onset of cognitive-emotional equilibrium.
May question or amplify specific maladaptive *behaviors* but does not question the essential work of all human beings.	Questions sense of personal worth, such as in racist jokes.
Implies self- and other-awareness.	Implies self- and other blindness.
Has a gentle, healing, constructive quality.	Has a callous, "bitter aftertaste," detrimental quality.
Acts as an interpersonal lubricant; constitutes an interpersonal asset.	Tends to retard and confound interpersonal communication; constitutes an interpersonal liability.
Based on acceptance.	Based on rejection.
Centered around clients' needs and their welfare.	Reflects the perpetuation of personal, dysfunctional patterns.
Strengthens, brightens, and alleviates.	Restricts, stigmatizes, and retaliates.
Aims to reveal and unblock alternatives.	Aims to obscure and block alternatives.

therapists has differentiated itself from the first generation of clinicians that preceded it along four major dimensions of psychotherapeutic work: (1) Long term versus short term treatment: strategic therapists refuse to accept the traditional assumption that the durability of therapeutic results over time is commensurate with the length of treatment. In effect, the existing research on the comparative effectiveness of various psychotherapeutic approaches (Garfield, 1981; Garfield & Bergon, 1978; Luborsky, Singer & Luborsky, 1975; Sloane et al., 1975) seems to indicate that most psychotherapies tend to produce comparable results, usually substantiating moderately positive effects in the direction of reduction of major symptoms and improvements in social and occupational adjustment. Moreover, the consumers of psychotherapeutic services are increasingly requesting shorter and cost-effective forms of treatment with an emphasis on therapist accountability for the services provided (Garfield, 1981). These trends are congruent with the short term treatment perspective adopted by strategic therapists as they continue to develop a variety of short term psychotherapeutic interventions that can be said to have at least equal potency, resiliency, and constructive outcome for patients as do traditional psychotherapies. (2) Uniformity versus fluidity of approaches: in contrast to the earlier monolithic conceptions of therapeutic work whereby one treatment method was slightly adjusted to working with all patients, strategic therapists tend to tailor unique patient interventions that can specifically address the individualized needs of each patient (Erickson & Rossi, 1981; Haley, 1967, 1973; Phillips, 1981; Watzlawick, 1978; Zeig, 1980, 1982). This adaptability to the patient's internal milieu can thus take into account the patient's resistances, sensitivities, and strengths in order to develop treatment modalities that are personally relevant and applicable to the patient's situation. (3) Therapist unresponsiveness versus existential presence: In examining the deleterious effects of the unresponsiveness artefact in psychotherapy, Greben (1981) described the unresponsive therapist as follows:

> He does not answer when answering would be more helpful. He does not speak his mind or express his ideas when the patient would gain much more were he to do so. In trying to be "neutral" or "objective," too often he becomes a shadow of a person, projecting distance and coolness where closeness and warmth are essential. . . . Because such a person is not only serious about therapy, but is very serious about himself, it is difficult for us not to respond inwardly with humor at his expense, because in fact he cuts a pompous or even farcical figure. Such a therapist is wooden not only in his relations with his patient, he is wooden in much of his life. In a business or social context he resorts to critical even supercilious deliberateness, when reaction and spontaneity would be appropriate. He says "uh-huh" when much more is expected. He is slow to speak, and careful not to reveal himself and his ideas. . . . It feels to the observer as though this person's responses have been put in low gear. (pp. 245–246)

Greben (1981) points out that unresponsiveness has undesirable side effects for therapists, their patients, their families and friends, as well as for the public's perceptions of therapists as unusual and odd. He suggests that the teachers of psychotherapy become more responsive to their own students, encouraging natural and open modes of interaction. In comparison to the traditional view that therapists should project a "neutral" image which often evolves into a sterile unresponsiveness to patient needs, Milton Erickson's therapeutic and teaching style (Haley, 1967, 1973; Zeig, 1980, 1982) reflected a genuinely responsive attitude toward students and patients coupled with gentleness and non-judgemental encouragement.

In a similar vein, the humorous perspective proposed in this chapter postulates that the therapist's appropriate use of humor conveys acceptance of the human condition and its imperfections, helps patients develop realistic perceptions of themselves and of their therapists, facilitates rapport and frees the patient to appreciate spontaneity and joy, deactivates maladaptive patterns, infuses therapeutic interactions with energy and hopefulness, and can model flexibility for patients (Salameh, 1983). The overall thrust of such a perspective is to move away from stifling solemnity or other unncessary expressions of unresponsiveness in order to generate a therapeutic momentum that is both human and effectively conducive to patient progress. Consequently, what is meant by the term "existential presence" used above is a modus operandi whereby the therapist is fully available to the patient in a compassionate, interactive, humorous, and responsive way, strategically mobilizing therapeutic process to effect productive change. (4) Segmented versus unrestricted patient accessibility: a fourth dimension on which strategic and short term therapists differ from the first generation of therapists is that they give vital emphasis to the issue of enlisting patient resources in the service of therapeutic change. If the therapist's unresponsiveness can constrict his or her accessibility to the patient on one side of the therapeutic equation, then on the other side of the same equation the segmented use of patients' resources can curtail their contribution to their own cure. In strategic work, the patient ceases to be a passive recipient of therapist insights. Essentially, patients are invited to assume a co-active role in that they participate with the therapist at accessing their conscious and unconscious resources and bringing these resources to bear on their present condition. Patient participation in therapeutic work can take many forms: carrying out assignments as suggested by the therapist, reading practical information related to a particular therapeutic concern, rehearsing new responses for addition to the behavioral repertoire, checking the applicability of therapeutic learnings in everyday life, partaking in role-plays and guided imagery processes during the therapeutic session, transferring the special abilities or skills one may already display in a given sphere of functioning to the therapeutic sphere where these skills can be mustered in dealing with treatment issues, partaking in specific educational or social experiences to learn new coping skills. Another important tool for inner transformation, of which Erickson made skillful use, is the utilization of hypnotic modalities to tap unconscious (or rootconscious) resources that may help in facilitating change. Consequently, the judicious and focused application of multilevel communication techniques has the beneficial effect of increasing patient participation in psychotherapy while simultaneously empowering the patient as a primary agent in his or her treatment.

And behind any comprehensive discussion of hypnotic and strategic approaches looms the figure of Milton Erickson. Erickson's own life provided a telling illustration of his clinical perspective. His personal ecology reflected a most elegant expression of human adaptation: against a terrain of limitations (two painful bouts with polio, partial colorblindness and some tone deafness), he planted the seeds of structure (devising unique strategic approaches for each patient, arranging conducive contexts and propitious meetings for students) which he irrigated with the fertile waters of the unconscious (using the wealth of unconscious experiences to develop useful alternatives). The vibrant message of his life was that personal blueprints can change when individuals appreciate and actualize the inner richness they already possess. The fruits of Erickson's labors endure in the hearts of those whose lives he touched, in his clinical legacy, and in the ongoing work of his students.

In conclusion, it is evident that the use of humorous approaches in psychotherapy is not sufficient for achieving constructive therapeutic results since humor is only one element in the successful synthesis of factors which make a therapeutic experience effective. What seems to be needed in conjunction with humor is a sound theoretical frame of reference, a certain emotional maturity, and a cluster of therapist characteristics similar to those described in Section IV. It is under such conditions that humor can have an optimally beneficial effect. Beyond the above considerations, there seems to be a general leitmotif associated with the technology of therapeutic humor presented in this chapter: tilting cognitions to provide fresh perspectives (i.e., reframing), collapsing barriers and differences to allow for creation of new realities and relationships, and inoculating a supple tenacity in the face of what can be called the swarming absurdity of human existence. As we awaken to the exceptional existential power derived from experiencing every day with a humorous outlook (or a humorous ''in-look''), we can begin to recognize that humor is an act of courage in a world fraught with alienation and violence. In this sense, humor can be seen as a radiant meditation, a higher form of seriousness which goes to the headwaters of the human condition and makes them potable.

The addiction of gloom and rigid solemnity can, in some instances, be likened to alcoholic or drug addiction with respect to the shrinking of the individual's personal world to predictable dysfunctional patterns which he or she insists on repeating coupled with a complete elimination of possible alternatives without the slightest consideration as to their applicability. An ideal humorous therapist would address an individual suffering from morosity in these terms: "Don't palliate, change. If you can make yourself stuck, then you can make youself unstuck—every time some door slams somewhere a window opens. Unload your unnecessary burdens at the nearest Burden Recycling Center. Find out what is important for you: choice is better than chance. First finish your unfinished business. Then go for your goals, even if it means looking ridiculous; the alternative is a swampland called stagnation. Do unto others as they (in their healthier moments) would have you do unto them. When material resources get scarce, remember that humankind is the ultimate resource. And you might as well learn to laugh."

D. H. Lawrence said it even better: "The living self has one purpose only: to come into its own fullness of being, as a tree comes into full blossom, or a bird into spring beauty, or a tiger into lustre."

References

Assagioli, R. (1971). *Psychosynthesis: A manual of principles and techniques*. New York: Viking Press.

Bandler, R., & Grinder, J. (1975). *The structure of magic (Vol. 1)*. Palo Alto, CA: Science and Behavior Books.

Bandler, R., & Grinder, J. (1976a). *Patterns of the hypnotic techniques of Milton H. Erickson, M.D.* (Vol. 1). Cupertino, CA: Meta Publications.

Bandler, R., & Grinder, J. (1976b). *The structure of magic (Vol. 2)*. Palo Alto, CA: Science and Behavior Books.

Bandler, R., & Grinder, J. (1979). *Frogs into princes*. Moab, UT: Real People Press.

Becker, E. (1973). *The denial of death*. New York: MacMillan.

Bettelheim, Bruno. (1976). *The uses of enchantment*. New York: Alfred A. Knopf.

Blunden, G. (1963). *The land and people of Australia* (rev. ed.). Philadelphia: J. B. Lippincott.

Carkhuff, R. R., & Berenson, B. G. (1967). *Beyond counseling and psychotherapy*. New York: Holt, Rinehart & Winston.

Carkhuff, R. R. (1969). *Helping and human relations: A primer for lay and professional helpers* (Vols. 1 & 2). New York: Holt, Rinehart & Winston.

Cooke, C. E., & Van Vogt, A. E. (1965). *The hypnotism handbook* (2nd ed.). Alhambra, CA: Borden Publishing Co.

Erickson, M. H. (1964). The confusion technique in hypnosis. *American Journal of Clinical Hypnosis, 6*, 183–207.

Erickson, M. H. (1966). The interspersal technique for symptom correction and pain control. *American Journal of Clinical Hypnosis, 3*, 198–209.

Erickson, M. H., Rossi, E. L., & Rossi, S. I. (1976). *Hypnotic realities: The induction of clinical hypnosis and forms of indirect suggestion.* New York: Irvington.

Erickson, M. H., & Rossi, E. L. (1981). *Experiencing hypnosis: Therapeutic approaches to altered states.* New York: Irvington.

Farzan, M. (1973). *Another way of laughter: A collection of Sufi humor.* New York: E. P. Dutton.

Frankl, V. (1963). *Man's search for meaning.* New York: Pocket Books.

Freud, S. (1928). Humor. *International Journal of Psychoanalysis, 9*, 1–6.

Freud, S. (1963). *Jokes and their relation to the unconscious.* New York: Norton. (Original work published 1905)

Fry, W. F., & Salameh, W. A. (Eds.). *Handbook of humor and therapy.* Book in progress.

Garfield, S. (1981). Psychotherapy: A 40-year appraisal. *American Psychologist, 36*, 174–183.

Garfield, S., & Bergon, A. E. (Eds.) (1978). *Handbook of Psychotherapy and behavior change* (2nd ed.). New York: Wiley.

Gordon, D. (1978). *Therapeutic metaphors.* Cupertino, CA: Meta Publications.

Greben, S. E. (1981). Unresponsiveness: The demon artefact of psychotherapy. *American Journal of Psychotherapy, 35*(2), 244–250.

Grinder, J., DeLozier, J., & Bandler, R. (1977). *Patterns of the hypnotic techniques of Milton H. Erickson, M.D.* (Vol. 2) Cupertino, CA: Meta Publications.

Haley, J. (Ed.). (1967). *Advanced techniques of hypnosis and therapy: Selected papers of Milton H. Erickson, M.D.* New York: W. W. Norton.

Haley, J. (1973). *Uncommon therapy: The psychiatric techniques of Milton H. Erickson, M.D.* New York: W. W. Norton.

Horn, J. C. (1982, July). Minding your P's and K's. *Psychology Today,* p. 75.

Hyers, C. (1973). *Zen and the comic spirit.* Philadelphia: Westminster Press.

Jankelevitch, V. (1984). *L'ironie.* Paris: Flammarion.

Koestler, A. (1965). *The act of creation.* London: Hutchinson.

Kroger, W. S. (1977). *Clinical and experimental hypnosis in medicine, dentistry, and psychology.* (2nd ed.) Philadelphia: J. B. Lippincott.

Kroger, W. S., & Fezler, W. D. (1976). *Hypnosis and behavior modification: Imagery conditioning.* Philadelphia: J. B. Lippincott.

Luborsky, L., Singer, B., & Luborsky, L. (19755). Comparative studies of psychotherapies: Is it true that "everyone has won and all must have prices?" *Archives of General Psychiatry, 32*, 995 1007.

Madanes, C. (1985). Finding a humorous alternative. In J. Zeig (Ed.), *Ericksonian Psychotherapy* (Vol. II). (pp. 24–44). New York: Brunner/Mazel.

Orne, M. T. (1980). On the construct of hypnosis. How its definition affects research and its clinical application. In G. D. Burrows & L. Dennerstein (Eds.), *Handbook of hypnosis and psychosomatic medicine.* New York: Elsevier North:Holland.

Phillips, A. (1981). *Transformational psychotherapy: An approach to creative hypnotic communication.* New York: Elsevier North-Holland.

Salameh, W. A. (1980). Personality of the comedian: The theory of tragi-comic reconciliation. Unpublished doctoral dissertation, University of Montreal.

Salameh, W. A. (1983). Humor in psychotherapy: Past outlooks, present status, and future frontiers. In P. E. McGhee & J. H. Goldstein (Eds.), *Handbook of humor research: Applied studies Vol. 2,* (pp. 61–88). New York: Springer-Verlag.

Shah, I. (1970). *Tales of the dervishes.* New York: E. P. Dutton.

Shah, I. (1971a). *Wisdom of the idiots.* New York: E. P. Dutton.

Shah, I. (1971b). *The pleasantries of the incredible Mulla Nasrudin.* New York: E. P. Dutton.

Shah, I. (1972). *The exploits of the incomparable Mulla Nasrudin.* New York: E. P. Dutton.

Sloane, R. B., Staples, F. R., Cristol, A. H., Yorkston, N. J., & Whipple, K. (1975). *Psychotherapy versus behavior therapy.* Cambridge, MA: Harvard University Press.

Watzlawick, P. (1978). *The language of change*. New York: Basic Books.
Weitzenhoffer, A. M. (1962a). The nature of hypnosis: Part I. *American Journal of Clinical Hypnosis, 5*, 295–321.
Weitzenhoffer, A. M. (1962b). The nature of hypnosis: Part II. *American Journal of Clinical Hypnosis, 6*, 40–72.
Yapko, M. D. (1981). The effect of matching primary representational system predicates on hypnotic relaxation. *American Journal of Clinical Hypnosis, 23*, 169–175.
Zeig, J. K. (Ed.) (1980). *A teaching seminar with Milton H. Erickson*. New York: Brunner/Mazel.
Zeig, J. K. (Ed.) (1982). *Ericksonian approaches to hypnosis and psychotherapy*. New York: Brunner/Mazel.

THERAPY WITH
SPECIFIC POPULATIONS

Overview: The Nature of Stepfamilies

by
Neil G. Ribner, Ph.D.

As the twentieth century has progressed, the nature of the family in America has undergone a radical transformation. No longer is there such a thing as a "typical" family, and it is becoming more and more rare for people to remain with one spouse throughout their lifetime. Divorce and remarriage are now more the rule than the exception, with estimates of 40-50% of first marriages ending in divorce (Glick & Norton, 1976). While remarriage after the death of a spouse is still common, 80% of divorced individuals also remarry, and 60% of these remarriages involve children under the age of 18 (Visher & Visher, 1979). Many adults, of course, live together without being married, so that many more children than the census data reports are living with or visiting a new "parent figure."

The pattern of family formation that is thus becoming increasingly more common is the stepfamily (Visher & Visher, 1979). A stepfamily can be defined as a family in which there is an adult couple living together with one or both adults having a child (or children) from a previous relationship. This includes families in which the adults are married or living together, and in which the children live in the household with one biological parent and his/her new partner. The definition may be expanded to also include visits with the new couple. In some instances, both partners bring children to the new household, while in others only one or the other adult does so. More common today, especially when younger people divorce and remarry, is the "yours, mine, and ours" family, where each spouse brings children from a prior relationship and the couple then have children together (Visher & Visher, 1979).

In the early 1980's, it was estimated that there were 35 million adult stepparents in the United States, with 1300 new stepfamilies being formed *every day* (Visher & Visher, 1982). In some states where the divorce rate is higher, such as California, a conservative estimate is that 1 in 4 children under the age of 18 is in a stepfamily (Furstenberg, 1979). Projections are that by 1990 there will be more single-parent and stepparent families in the United States than nuclear families (Visher & Visher, 1982).

A common myth is that stepfamilies are easier to form than were nuclear families. After all, theoretically the adults are wiser and more mature, having gone through the trials and tribulations of family life once before and having learned from the experience. Wrong! In fact, over 40% of *remarriages* end in divorce within 4 years, in large part due to the complexities of stepfamily formation (Becker, Landes, & Michael, 1977). Imagine the despair at having lost the nuclear family, and now being threatened with the loss of the stepfamily.

This data makes it vitally important for the counselor or psychologist to understand the nature of stepfamilies so as to be better prepared to assist such clients in their development. The following discussion will highlight some of the intrinsic differences between nuclear and stepfamilies, and progress into the therapeutic implications of stepfamily dynamics and guidelines for therapeutic intervention.

Life Cycles of the Nuclear, and Stepfamily

Until recently, the attention of researchers interested in psychological development has been focused on the individual (Freud, 1905; Freud, A., 1965; Levinson et al., 1974, 1978; Gould, 1972, 1978). Erikson (1968) provided, perhaps, the most comprehensive theory of development. According to Erikson's epigenetic principle, the interaction of biological maturation and environmental support must occur at the proper rate and sequence in order for the individual to achieve psychological health.

From a systems perspective, the family can be thought of as having a life cycle which unfolds along with the individual life cycle (Sager et al., 1983). The family, like the individual, has tasks which it must meet successfully at certain critical points in its development. Each developmental phase requires that the family learn new techniques of adaptation which allow for the continued growth of the family as a unit as well as provide for meeting the needs of individual family members. Haley (1973) suggested that a symptom in an *individual* is a signal that the *family* is having difficulty in mastering the tasks inherent in their stage of development. That is, when the natural evolution of the family is disrupted, and the family does not adapt to the disruption in a healthy way, one or more individuals in the family may experience psychological difficulties.

The attention of the family therapist can thus go beyond the individual and include the system as well. When discussing the nuclear family, the concepts of individual and family life cycles are generally clear. But can the therapist apply the same principles of family development to the stepfamily? Anyone who has been in or worked extensively with step-families would likely caution a therapist to do so, since the life cycle and developmental tasks of the stepfamily differ considerably from that of the nuclear family.

Solomon (1973) proposed the following stages in the life cycle of nuclear families, described here with accompanying tasks:

1) *The Marriage*: separation from families of origin, work and career choices, commitment to one partner, development of new relationships.
2) *Birth of Children*: inclusion of new member(s) of family, re-negotiation of spousal relationship, development of new roles as parents.
3) *Individuation of Family Members*: renegotiating power and boundaries, dealing with problems of school and adolescence, generational issues, development of higher earning power.
4) *Departure of Children*: consolidation of family, re-establishment of spousal relationship, development of new relationships with adult children.
5) *Integration of Loss*: "empty nest," finding new interests in life, retirement, death.

With the formation of the stepfamily, a new life cycle is created. At this point both the individual and, to some extent, nuclear family life cycles continue, while the stepfamily life cycle begins. Sager et al. (1983) noted that, "The task for the clinician is to be aware of the many simultaneous tracks on which the systems and their members are likely to be operating and to ascertain if needs are being met well enough in the different systems (p. 39)."

Ransom, Schlesinger, and Derdeyn (1979) described three steps in the formation of a stepfamily.

I. *Entering the New Relationship:* It has been said that "step-families are born of loss" (Visher & Visher, 1979). The reality is that *everybody* in a stepfamily has experienced a loss, and the healthy formation of the stepfamily requires the resolution of the loss. The initial stage of the stepfamily life cycle also requires a recommitment to the new marriage and family.

II. *Conceptualizing and Planning the New Marriage and Family:* Unlike the nuclear family, there is no period in the stepfamily without children (stepfamilies are a "Package Deal"). All members of the stepfamily bring with them values and ideas about how families "should be," as well as myths about how new families are formed. Loyalty conflicts develop and must be handled appropriately, and innumerable logistical details surrounding money, visitation, and roles must be worked out.

III. *Remarriage and Reconstitution of the Family:* It is often at the time of the remarriage rather than at the time of the divorce that problems develop, because it is at this point that the fantasy of the intact family must be relinquished and a new model of a family be accepted. New boundaries must be negotiated making room for new family members. Control and power issues between ex-spouses must be resolved so as to not triangulate children.

As with intact families, crises in the stepfamily that bring them to a therapist are tied to the tasks corresponding to the stepfamily's phase of development. One example is the Seller family, which included Ed (age 38), Trish (age 32), Eddie (age 7, Ed's son from his first marriage), and Cindy (age 5, Trish's daughter from her first marriage). Ed and Trish had lived together for 6 months when Eddie was 5 and Cindy 3½. Both had been divorced about one year at the time they moved in with each other. After six months, Trish began to have doubts about their relationship, and she and Cindy moved out. Although they lived in separate apartments, Trish took care of both children and prepared dinner for Ed most nights. After dinner, Ed and Eddie would return home to sleep. Occasionally, Cindy and Trish would spend the weekend with Ed and Eddie, and Eddie would spend about one weekend each month with his biological mother.

The Seller family had been referred for counseling by Eddie's teacher, who reported that in the first grade Eddie was disruptive, wouldn't pay attention, daydreamed in class, and was being sent to the principal's office almost daily. At the intake, Ed and Eddie showed up. Ed explained that he and Trish were not yet married, but were planning to be in the next six months, "if everything worked out well." Evidently, as time elapsed after Trish moved out, she began spending more and more time at Ed's, and after four months had moved back in. She had not, however, given up her own apartment, and on occasion spent the night there.

It was at the time of Trish's moving back into Ed's apartment that Eddie began having problems in school. According to Ed, and confirmed in a later interview with Trish, Eddie and Trish did not get along as well as the adults hoped they would. Trish had reached a point of resenting Eddie, feeling that she was trying to establish a relationship with him but got nothing in return, stating "I'm tired of giving, and not even getting a hello from Eddie when he comes home from school." Ed was in the middle of the two, trying to get Trish to be more patient with Eddie while losing patience with him himself. Fears of Trish's moving out permanently were in the back of his mind, so much so that he would not encourage her to get close to Eddie for fear this would backfire. Likewise, Ed was reluctant to involve Trish in counseling, rationalizing that Eddie had had problems in kindergarten and that he (Ed) and Trish were not yet married and might never be if Eddie's behavior didn't improve.

Developmentally, Eddie had never fully grieved the loss of his mother, and Trish's constant moving in and out of his life only rekindled the threat of abandonment once more. Ed denied this, pointing out that Eddie was always closer to him than to his (Eddie's) mom, and that Eddie didn't seem to miss his mom at all. It soon became apparent that in his strong denial, Ed, too, had not emotionally divorced his first wife, wanting to "chalk that one up to experience" and start fresh. Additionally, Ed and Trish had expectations about how the new family would operate, but never discussed these openly, each fearing that bringing up their concerns and doubts would indicate a lack of trust of the other. Eddie, in the meanwhile, was hearing one set of rules from Trish, another from Ed, and still a third from his mother. Feeling confused, threatened by the loss of another family, pushed out of his special place with his dad by both Trish and Cindy, Eddie "acted out" and got lots of negative attention at school.

According to Ransom et. al.'s (1979) theory, the difficulties which the Sellers were experiencing can be tied to the stage of "entering the new relationship." Before Ed and Eddie would be ready to fully commit themselves to the new family, they would need to work through the loss of their first family.

Structural Characteristics of Stepfamilies

Even in the healthiest of stepfamilies, there is a structure inherent in the nature of the stepfamily that may cause problems. For a complete discussion, the reader is referred to Visher and Visher (1979). In summary, potentially destructive characteristics that are unique to stepfamily structures include:

1. *There is a biological parent elsewhere.* This fact may lead to power struggles, triangulation of children, and comparisons of the biological parent to the stepparent.

2. *The biological parent/child bond predates the couple relationship.* The stepparent may feel like an outsider, while the biological parent must balance his or her loyalty for the child with feelings for the new spouse.

3. *The child lives in two households.* Different rules of the household do create confusion and anger, and the child who visits one household may feel like an outsider. The nature of household boundaries is important.

4. *The two households have value and lifestyle differences.* Power plays, discipline problems, and step-sibling rivalries are common.

5. *Financial and legal arrangements must be made.* Questions of alimony, child-support, property, and wills must be negotiated.

6. *The role of the stepparent is ill defined.* Both within the stepfamily and in interactions with the rest of the world, the stepparent's role(s) in the stepchild's life must be worked out.

7. *Step relationships are constantly being tested.* In the nuclear family, patterns of relationships within the family evolve and can be counted on to be consistent. In the stepfamily, nothing can be assumed as "given" since all relationships are in a state of flux, at least initially.

Necessary Tasks in the Achievement of Stepfamily Integration

Visher & Visher (1979), pioneers in the stepfamily movement in the United States, listed the following tasks as crucial to the formation of a healthy stepfamily:

1. *Mourning the Losses.* Since incomplete mourning of past relationships can interfere with efforts to create relationships, the loss of the nuclear family must be dealt with. Deviant behavior in children (as in the above case example) and depressive behavior in adults may be symptoms of a failure to acknowledge this hurt. Like the stages in grief following the death of a loved one, so may go the stages of giving up one's dreams and fantasies of what a family is like.

2. *Development of New Traditions.* Since everyone in a stepfamily has experienced ways of living in a family, each has ideas about how families work. In a stepfamily, though, there are no longer any givens, because what was right for the Jones family or right for the Smith family may

no longer be right for the Smith-Jones stepfamily. New traditions must be worked out through open negotiation.

3. *Forming New Relationships*. The strength of the spousal dyad in maintaining smooth family functioning is well documented. In the stepfamily, however, the couple's honeymoon takes place in the middle of a crowd. The spouses must nourish their relationship in the face of loyalty conflicts and an increasing number of demands. Also, relationships that people neither asked for nor wanted are thrust upon them, and the myth of "instant love" is rampant. While stepchildren and stepparents do not ever have to love each other, they do have to learn to live with each other.

4. *Re-negotiating Relationships with Non-custodial Parent*. The phenomenon of triangulation in dysfunctional intact families is common in stepfamilies, with a child being a messenger between his or her biological parents. Loyalty conflicts in children of divorce are strong, especially if one of the parents has not remarried. The task for the adults is to leave the children out of their conflicts, and to accept each other's parenting.

5. *Arranging for Satisfactory Movement Between Households*. Children can adapt to different households as long as the expectations of each are clear. Boundaries must be firm enough to aid clarity while being flexible enough to allow the child to move in and out.

Brief Therapy with Stepfamilies

Because of their unique culture, stepfamilies present challenges to the therapist that are different than those of intact families. Typically, when an intact family presents itself for treatment, they have achieved a state of homeostasis at the expense of one or more members of the family (Haley, 1973). Over the years the family has been together, the system has organized itself around a set of rules that have enabled it to survive. These rules have generally developed covertly, and prescribe patterns of interaction that occur in repetitive sequences. Over the course of the family's development, and through developmental as well as idiosyncratic crises, the homeostatic mechanisms must both keep the family functioning as a unit as well as allow for growth and change. The rules, with concurrently prescribed roles and sequences, are the glue that hold the family together (Jackson, 1965).

In the stepfamily, particularly in the first 2-4 years of its development, there is not enough glue to hold the family together yet. Some family members, particularly the adults, may believe that their ability to love another is proof that their prior relationships have been resolved. Yet, time has not yet allowed for the working through of losses and the breaking of old bonds, as well as the formation of new ones. The new spouses themselves have a head start; they have chosen each other, gotten to know one another, and (hopefully) have discussed the formation of the new family. But when the children are brought into the picture, which of course is a given in stepfamilies, all bets are off!

The above discussion underscores a crucial issue in working with stepfamilies; that is, that stepfamilies *are* different from intact families. As noted, family members themselves may operate on the assumption that "a family is a family, is a family," and unknowingly create numerous problems for themselves as a result. At conferences and workshops, stepfamily members are often heard exclaiming, "Too bad I didn't know this back then! I would have reacted much differently."

Psychotherapists often presume dynamics of stepfamilies to be identical to those of intact families. Treating the stepfamily as they would the intact family, practitioners may do more harm than good. Although the issues raised by stepfamilies may be similar to those raised by intact families, they may differ due to the inherent structure of stepfamilies, as noted above. Also, while the techniques of therapy with stepfamilies have a basic similarity to techniques used with intact families, they differ on dimensions such as the nature of the symptoms, the goals of treatment, and practical matters such as timing and spacing of sessions, whom to include, etc. While nothing replaces a sound theoretical and practical knowledge of family dynamics and family therapy, it is critical for the practitioner who works with stepfamilies to expand his/her expertise.

In treating stepfamilies, it seems best to view them from a systems perspective. That is, although one person (e.g., an angry adolescent) or one dyad (e.g., stepparent-stepchild) may be identified as "the problem," it is most helpful to view the troubled member or pair as reflecting a faulty whole, and to work toward helping the family as a whole establish patterns of interaction that support both individual and family growth. This perspective does not necessarily mean the family will always be seen together in treatment, but rather that the focus of the treatment is on the troubled system as a whole.

Many family systems approaches revolve around the concept of "entropy" (Beavers, 1977). This implies that the therapist increasingly destroys the dysfunctional order until the system arrives at a more functional state of equilibrium. In the stepfamily, however, caution is needed since in destroying the existing order, there is no backup order to maintain the family unit. This leads one to consider a strategic approach as ideal for stepfamily therapy.

Family systems work with stepfamilies lends itself to a brief, strategic approach. Reasons for this include the following:

1. The stepfamily is likely to experience conflicts in the early stages of its development. At this point, the family structure is so tenuous, and the family members so suspicious, as to make an attack on the structure inappropriate. Whereas the intact family has well practiced rules and interactive patterns to fall back on, the stepfamily does not. Too much of a shapeup by the therapist may result in the breakup of the stepfamily.

2. Because the stepfamily does not have a lengthy history together as a unit, behaviors of family members must be seen as attempts to adjust and create a functional whole rather than as symptomatic of "deeper" issues. What the stepfamily often needs is education—a new perspective. A lengthy, uncovering type of therapy is thus generally inappropriate, while an approach focusing on observable behavior in the present can be much more useful.

3. Like all systems, the stepfamily is continually evolving. In contrast to intact families, however, the evolution is taking place on many simultaneous life-cycle tracks, some of which may conflict with each other. For example, the new couple may be in a honeymoon phase of their relationship, while simultaneously needing to provide a nurturing environment for his prepubescent biological son, while also dealing with the individuation of her adolescent daughter. Unless the life-cycle needs of all members in the stepfamily are satisfied, the likelihood of the family staying together is minimal. Although clearly a therapist should not get caught in a myth of "instant cure," the stepfamily may need some evidence early on in treatment that there is reason for optimism.

4. All human beings have cognitive maps through which they filter behaviors in an attempt to understand the world (Beck et al., 1979). Individual members of stepfamilies have different, sometimes radically different, beliefs about families based on each individual's prior experiences in families. Retention of old maps keeps the family stuck and does not allow for creation of a new family structure. Brief therapy facilitates the formation of new realities, and opens the stepfamily up to establish new patterns of behavior.

5. When problems develop in the stepfamily, there is a tendency to blame someone in the family. Although this often happens in intact families as well, the difference is that this becomes much more complex in the stepfamily because of attributions concerning the breakup of the first family as well as loyalty conflicts in the new family.

For example, in the Hill family, stepmother Joan was convinced that 15-year-old stepson Craig was the source of the problem in the family. Since her marriage to Craig's father, Jeff, Joan had had a difficult time getting Craig to do any chores, to come home on time, or to treat her with respect. She was constantly met with versions of "I don't have to listen to you; you're not my mother!" Jeff was caught between the two, at times blaming Craig, but at times feeling guilty about the divorce and wanting Joan to be more understanding of what Craig was going through. A linear epistemology adopted by a therapist in a case like the Hills' might perpetuate rather than reduce the conflict. Seeing Craig as "passive-aggressive," or Joan as "critical and unsympathetic" may miss the crucial issues. It also sets up the therapist to make value judgements, which in parallel process may be part of the problem the family experiences. Particularly, then, with stepfamilies, adoption of a circular model of causality is important.

6. The stepfamily seeking treatment often can be compared to a suicidal patient—if something doesn't change *quickly*, their very existence is threatened. Everyone in the stepfamily has been through a crisis before, one which ended in the "death" of the original family unit. "If things aren't going to work out," family members will say, "we'd rather know now and avoid all the pain we went through before." Feelings of hopelessness may pervade the sessions. A therapist, then, must respond actively and firmly; certainly not out of his/her own panic, but rather out of a well-supported sense that change is possible, restoring hope to the family.

7. In therapeutic sessions with stepfamilies, particularly when former spouses are present, emotions are at a peak. The therapist must be comfortable with being in charge, being both active and directive.

8. Because of the large number of people in a stepchild's family, including absent parents and their new spouses, four sets of grandparents, etc., the possibility of bringing the entire family together for family therapy may be nonexistent. The therapist, therefore, must be able to do "family therapy" with subgroups of the family. That is, while the goals remain behavioral and ultimately involve structural change of the entire family, the therapist may have to accomplish this through seeing individuals or family subgroups.

9. Crucial to the understanding of problems in stepfamilies is

the concept of "myths." The myths which people bring to the new family result in structure and patterns of behavior that are not only preventing adequate family formation but may, in themselves, be a major problem. In other words, "the attempted solution is the problem" (Watzlawick et al., 1974).

There is no way for a stepfamily to avoid a period of confusion. The period of time in which two adults form a union, and the time in which this union organizes itself around parenting, and the time in which children learn and assimilate rules, are not available to the stepfamily. There is no time without children, without house rules, without expectations, without subsystems. Right from the start the family must develop new rules and patterns that allow the growth of the unit while not stifling the growth of the individuals. Thus, a period of time is needed for the family to experience these growing pains, and to work out solutions to these normal crises in its development. Experience shows that 1½-2 years is about the average time for this to occur (Visher & Visher, 1979). However, when stepfamilies have not established a coherent, functional unit after this time, a therapist must wonder: what got in the way? How did the family prevent itself from resolving the crises? Often, the problem can be traced back to the myths of "instant family," "love me, love my kids," "we'll never be a 'real' family," and so on. When stepfamilies base their solutions to normal developmental crises on these myths, the resultant patterns of interaction themselves become dysfunctional. Two common losing strategies have been discussed by Goldner (in Messinger, 1982). The first is based on a myth of "instant family," the second based on a myth of "we're not a 'real' family." In the first case, Goldner said, the family becomes *pseudomutual*, "with happy parents foisting their fantasies on their appropriately angry and ambivalent children (p. 200)." In the second, loyalty conflicts lead to *symmetrical* escalations, resulting in "two single-parent families living under one roof (p. 199)." In either case, and others which fall between these extremes, it is the solution that has become the problem. For the therapist, the key tactic involves interrupting these dysfunctional patterns, challenging the myths upon which these are based, and directing the family toward the development of healthy interactions.

Assumptions of Brief Therapy as They Apply to Stepfamilies[1]

1. Problems develop when an ordinary difficulty or developmental crisis is treated as a problem by the family; or when this difficulty or crisis is treated as no problem at all. As examples in the stepfamily, when a child's pouting at the time of the remarriage is treated as a sign of disrespect, or when the child's anger or sadness is ignored because the two new spouses are too much in love to be bothered, problems develop.

2. Once a difficulty is treated as a problem or vice versa, the continuation of the problem results from the creation of a vicious cycle in which the attempted solution (or denial) of the problem exacerbates the problem. For example, if a stepchild is forced to treat the stepparent as a natural parent, the child may resist either passively (pouting) or actively (acting out). When this occurs, if the new spouses insist even more strongly that the child obey the stepparent, call the stepparent "Mom" or "Dad," hug and kiss the stepparent, or the like, the child may act out further. Thus the positive feedback loop is created.

3. Problems persist only if they are maintained by current interactions. If A leads to B, which leads to more A which leads to more B, and so on, A will persist only if and when B persists, and vice versa. Thus, observable interactions in the present are the data base of treatment.

For example, the Meadows family came into treatment when the father, Al, became so frustrated with his 14-year-old, biological son, Chris, that he was ready to send the boy to live with his mother. Six months prior to the initial appointment, Al had married Linda, and he and Chris moved in with Linda and her 13-year-old biological son, Tom. A presenting problem of the Meadows family was the ongoing conflict between the stepsiblings. After meeting several times with the parents, and twice with each boy, the therapist hypothesized the following: 1. Al and Linda were attempting to replace Chris's mother with Linda; 2. the myth of "instant family" was operative, in which neither Al nor Linda could understand why two boys so close in age wouldn't feel positive about living together; 3. Tom had been the "man of the house" since his parents divorce four years ago; 4. loyalty conflicts prevented both adults from establishing the couple as the authority in the family.

These factors would result in an interactional sequence such as the following: Al wanted Linda to exert some authority over both boys, as he had hoped his first wife would do in relation to Chris. When Linda

[1]Taken from material presented by Robert Green, Ph.D. in March 1983 workshop on "Stepfamily Therapy," San Diego.

attempted to do so, Chris would shout variations of a "You're not my mother" theme. To this, Tom, who had been protecting mom for years, would shout back at Chris, and often the two boys would come to blows. Linda would pull Tom aside and lecture him about trying to get along better with Chris. Al would encourage Chris to be "nice" to his "new mother." However, since Linda usually felt helpless after such an interchange, Tom usually felt more resolute in defending her, and angrier with Chris for attacking her. Likewise, Chris felt put upon by Al's demands, and wanted Tom and Linda out of his life.

The therapist's job in such a sequence is to change the problem—maintaining interaction. In the above case, the therapist insisted that when Chris shouted at Linda, that Al protect his wife rather than Tom protecting her, and that if Tom defended Linda, she was to thank him while reassuring him that her new husband would protect her now. This allowed the boys to see and treat each other for whom they were, rather than as representatives of the adults.

4. Regardless of the nature, origin, or duration of the problem, it is maintained by the attempted solution. Changing the problem-maintaining interaction will result in resolution of the "problem." In the example cited in number 1 above, if the new spouses change the behavior which they based on the myth of the instant family, the "problem" of the child's pouting will disappear (if, in fact, the therapist's assessment of the problem-maintaining interaction is correct).

5. Long standing problems are repeated attempts at "more of the same." That is, the poor solution to the difficulty is attempted repetitively. In the same example, if the stepchild has pouted for a long time, most likely this behavior has been continually followed by the biological father pushing his son even harder to treat stepmom as a "real" mom.

Therapeutic Techniques

As in all strategic therapy, the therapist's task in working with a stepfamily is to design an intervention strategy that interferes with the problem-maintaining behavior (Watzlawick et al., 1974). This may involve the reframing of situations, which can then allow for and encourage new behavior that is more consistent with a new definition of reality. Behavioral directives may also be utilized, which can illustrate a point or change a behavioral sequence, or both.

Much of the heart of therapeutic work with stepfamilies is educational. In order to decide whether a behavior is really a problem, and should be continued to be treated as such, the family must be educated by the therapist as to stepfamily norms. Like other interventions, educative comments by the therapist must be framed in a way that makes them acceptable to and easily integrated by the clients. By paying attention to the positions the family members take, the therapist can gain useful clues to help him or her decide how to present information.

For example, although the therapist knows that members of a remarried family don't *have to* love each other, simply stating this to the family may encounter resistance and possible discounting of the therapist as an ally. The new spouses *want* everyone to love each other as, they may insist, they (the spouses) already do. The therapist might utilize this "I love everyone" position by explaining to the spouses that "as people who are very loving yourselves, I'm sure you know that love must grow and cannot be forced. Perhaps the best way you can show your love for your children is to give them the time and space they need to make up their own minds. They have been disappointed and hurt before by a parent figure whom they loved, so they may be now and possibly forever reluctant to let themselves love a new parent. Your understanding in this is a wonderful expression of your love for them."

Relabeling situations as normal occurrences in stepfamilies can also help break unrealistic myths. Reframing stepsibling fighting as "their way of getting to know one another's limits," or labeling arguments about the "right way" to spend holidays as the family members attempt to establish new traditions can help unblock the new family development.

Interventions

It is beyond the scope of this paper to discuss general principles and procedures of case planning. The reader is referred to texts such as *The Tactics of Change* by Fisch, Weakland, and Segal (1982) for such a discussion. Rather, several examples of reframing and giving directives to stepfamilies will be presented below.

Forced Blending. When Roberta got remarried, she insisted that her 5-year-old son Josh call his stepfather "Daddy." The family was told that forcing two people to be close to one another usually prevents true closeness from ever happening. Several examples from the parents own lives of trying hard to love someone were discussed as examples of this. Stepfather and Josh were given the task of together coming up with a new name for stepdad, which only Josh would use.

Loyalty Conflicts. (a) Sue felt hurt and rejected that her 6 year old daughter, Tracy, was calling her stepmother "Mommy." The therapist complimented Sue on her obvious skills as a parent. Since Tracy's ability to form intimate relationships was not damaged by the divorce, Sue must have done an outstanding job in raising such a well adjusted child.

(b) Mark felt caught in a battle between his biological children and his new wife, Nan. He loved Nan and wanted to see her happy, but he also loved his children, and didn't want to hurt them even more than they had already been hurt by appearing to take Nan's side. The therapist agreed that the children had been hurt, but went on to point out that a major source of hurt was the conflict between Mark and his ex-wife. Thus, the new spouses presenting a unified front would, in the long run, be essential in helping the children *avoid* future hurt. The therapist proceeded to compliment the children for being so protective of their father, and further encouraged the symptomatic behavior (Haley, 1973) by saying: "Since you've seen how relationships between a man and a woman can fail, it is a very loving thing you're doing for your father by testing out the strength of his new relationship before he gets too involved. If I were you, I wouldn't just continue to give your father and stepmother a difficult time, I would try even harder to break them up. Certainly if they can't stand the pressures that a kid puts on them, they won't be able to stand the pressures of the world!"

Acting-Out Children. Children often act out the conflict between their parents. In a stepfamily, the children may have three sets of parents: biological mother and father, biological mother and stepfather, and biological father and stepmother. The potential for acting out is thus multiplied.

A typical pattern is for a child to be the "go-between" of biological mother and biological father. One or both adults may pump the child for information or give the child messages to relay to the ex-spouse. As a consequence of being placed in the middle of two feuding adults, the child acts out. This, in turn, gives each parent more support for being critical of the way the ex-spouse is raising the child. The feedback loop is thus complete.

In treatment a parent might be told that their child's behavior is actually a poor reflection on *them*, not the ex-spouse: "Since you are the more reasonable and competent parent, you are the one who is expected to be able to control your child. Being annoyed with your ex-spouse, or curious about them, or whatever, gives your child the idea that your ex-spouse is still very powerful in your life, thus making you seem less competent." The parent might be instructed to change tactics by not mentioning the ex-spouse to the child. If the parent is disbelieving, they can be directed to be even angrier and more curious about the ex-spouse to see if the child acts out further.

Discipline: A parent often remarries with the hope or expectation that the new spouse will discipline the children. Because it takes 1½-2 years of positive interaction with a child before an adult is valued enough to matter (Visher & Visher, 1979), it is best that the biological parent do the majority of disciplining for that period of time. Stepparents may see this as a sign of their own weakness, and believe that only through stricter discipline will the stepchild obey.

In a case example, Barbara was told that her attempts to discipline her stepdaughter, Mary Ellen, were making her look like the wicked witch, just as did Mary Ellen's mother (in the reverse case, Barbara's behavior would be reframed as a shock to Mary Ellen, since her mother was so passive). She was further told that her disciplining was very confusing to Mary Ellen, since it was too early in the remarriage for Mary Ellen to know whom she should listen to. This created loyalty conflicts and the notion, albeit unfounded and probably unconscious, that Mary Ellen was losing her father. The therapist explained that Mary Ellen's father needed to reassure her of his caring by being the main person to set limits on her. She further explained that the new spouses needed to be unified as to their methods of discipline, so that Mary Ellen wouldn't fear the breakup of the new family; that Dad and Barbara discuss with each other the rules of the house, and present these to Mary Ellen together. Also, Barbara was told that Mary Ellen's action were a test of Barbara's commitment to her, so that Barbara needed to spend time doing fun things with the child "to reassure her that you're here for her."

Conclusion

Because of the nature of this paper, the reader may come away with a highly negative and pessimistic view of stepfamilies. Yet, in reality stepfamilies may provide a child with a fuller, richer view of family life, with the opportunity to learn from four or more adults, and with the opportunity to learn to deal productively with family crises. It behooves us as practitioners to familiarize ourselves with the growing phenomenon of stepfamilies, so that in practice we, too, can break away from outdated stereotypes and help create new traditions.

REFERENCES

Beavers, W. R. (1977). *Psychotherapy and growth: Family systems perspective*. New York: Brunner/Mazel.

Beck, A. T., Rush, A. J., Shaw, B. F., & Emergy G. (1979). *Cognitive therapy of depression*. New York: Guilford.

Becker, G. S., Landes, E. M., & Michael, R. T. (1977). An economic analysis of marital instability. *Journal of Political Economy, 85*, 1141–1187.

Erikson, E. H. (1968). *Identity: Youth and crisis*. New York: W. W. Norton.

Fisch, R., Weakland, J., & Segal, L. (1982). *The tactics of change*. San Francisco: Jossey-Bass.

Freud, A. (1965). *Normality and pathology in childhood: Assessments of development*. New York International Universities Press.

Freud, S. (1905). *Three essays on the theory of sexuality*. New York: Basic Books. (Reprinted, 1962).

Furstenberg, F. (1979, March). *Remarriage and intergenerational relations*. Paper presented at the Assembly of Behavioral and Social Sciences, National Academy of Sciences, Annapolis, Maryland.

Glick, P. C., & Norton, A. J. (1976, October). *Number, timing and duration of marriages and divorce in the U.S., June, 1975*. Current Population Reports, Washington, D.C.

Gould, R. L. (1972). The phases of adult life: A study in developmental psychology. *American Journal of Psychiatry, 129*(5), 521–531.

Gould, R. L. (1978). *Transformations: Growth and change in adult life*. New York: Touchstone Edition, Simon and Schuster.

Haley, J. (1973). *Uncommon therapy: The psychiatric techniques of Milton H. Erickson, M.D.* New York: Norton.

Jackson, D. D. (1965). Family rules: Marital quid pro quo. *Archives of General Psychiatry, 12*, 589–594.

Levinson, D. J., with Darrow, C. N., Klein, E. B., Levinson, M. H. & McKee, B. (1978). *The seasons of a man's life*. New York: Ballantine Books.

Levinson, D. J., Darrow, C. N., Klein, E. B., Levinson, M. H., & McKee, B. (1974). The psychosocial development of men in early adulthood and mid-life transition. In D. R. Ricks, A. Thomas, & M. Roff (Eds.), *Life history research in psychopathology*, (Vol. 3.) Minneapolis: University of Minnesota Press

Messinger, L. (1982). *Therapy with remarriage families*. Rockville, MD: Aspen Systems Corp.

Ransom, J. W., Schlesinger, S., & Derdeyn, A. (1979, January). A stepfamily in formation. *American Journal of Orthospsychiatry, 49*, 36–43.

Sager, C. J., Brown, H. S., Crohn, M., Engel, T., Rodstein, E., & Walker, L. (1983). *Treating the remarried family*. New York: Brunner/Mazel.

Solomon, M. (1973). A developmental conceptual premise for family therapy. *Family Process, 12*, 179–188.

Visher, E. G., & Visher, J. S. (1982). Stepfamilies in the 1980's. In L. Messinger (Ed.), *Therapy with remarriage families*. Rockville, MD: Aspen.

Visher, E. B., & Visher, J. S. (1979). *Stepfamilies: A guide to working with stepparents and stepchildren*. New York: Brunner/Mazel.

Watzlawick, P., Weakland, J. H., & Fisch, R. (1974). *Change: Principles of problem formation and problem resolution*. New York: Norton.

Hypnosis and Ericksonian Interventions with Children in the Elementary School

by
Timothy J. Wolf, Ph.D.

Milton Erickson provided a model of using hypnosis as a special type of interaction between people, as a way in which one person communicates with another (Haley, 1973). In the elementary school setting, educators have a unique opportunity to use their hypnotic training to enhance the communication of concepts and values to children. Children are generally very responsive to the influence of their teachers and counselors; and there is an everpresent opportunity to consciously and unconsciously influence positively the learning environment of the child. Using hypnotic and strategic abilities can improve teachers' and counselors' observational and motivational skills, and can also enhance skills in using words, intonations, and body movements in communication with children. Hypnotic and strategic approaches can broaden the range of experience of the school child, enhance flexibility on several levels, and encourage a sense of autonomy which can lead to better mental health and learning. What follows in this chapter are some of the rationales and examples of adapting these strategies to the private elementary school setting in which the author works.

The elementary school environment can provide unique opportunities for short-term hypnotic and strategic interventions for the school counselor, teacher, and other consulting professionals. Some of these interventions are necessitated by a changing school system. Fiscal constraints necessitating excessive caseloads require optimal use of the counselor's time. Short-term intervention strategies may accomplish counseling goals in relatively short periods while at the same time addressing those goals previously deemed unsuitable for intervention through school situations. Using hypnotic patterns as part of a comprehensive approach to the school counseling program emphasizing preventative mental health can ultimately translate into a more healthy school environment and smaller caseloads.

Short-term hypnotic strategies are empowered by the school environment's inevitable influence on the child's development, and are further enhanced by the generally acknowledged elevated susceptibility of children to hypnosis (Baumann, 1982). Unlike the private office or agency setting, the school allows the counselor to apply his or her strategies in a setting already promoting ongoing change in a child's development. The school can provide an environment where positive mental health interventions for students can be instituted with a special emphasis on "wellness" rather than remediation. The counselor and teacher trained in the effective use of hypnotic communications can direct change in many areas of the child's educational development.

In considering the above elementary school model, two areas of intervention will be examined in this chapter. The first is group hypnotic interventions as part of a comprehensive "wellness" approach. The second addresses individual strategies of problem resolution.

Elementary students of all ages are given instruction in methods of self-hypnosis in the classroom group setting. Initially, this is done by the counselor and is later offered by the teacher. Sixth, seventh, and eighth graders typically use techniques of self-hypnosis for anxiety reduction associated with personal adjustment difficulties, test anxiety, or sleeplessness. Some of these students use self-hypnosis to improve study habits, reporting that this allows them to accomplish more work in less time. These students also benefit from positive hypnotic suggestions designed to facilitate positive self-esteem and the exploration of alternative behaviors in difficult situations. Counselors can set examples of positive suggestions for teachers who may later utilize these statements. An example appropriate for use in the seventh grade follows:

> As you feel relaxed and comfortable you will focus on your dreams about growing into adolescense and adulthood. As you are more comfortable, your goals for achieving and reaching your dreams will become clearer. You will begin to accept the healthy changes in your body, looking forward to feeling good about your physique. Your relaxed mind looks forward to the

rewards of learning new and different and exciting concepts and ideas. You feel ready to tackle difficulties in growing with new solutions and ideas.

These suggestions allow adolescents to begin to explore their adjustment to adulthood with a self-management tool facilitating positive change. Through self-hypnosis and teacher and counselor guided suggestions, they learn to see hypnosis as a positive technique to enhance self-understanding. The introduction to hypnosis also alerts them to the myths promoted by stage hypnosis and the media (Yapko, 1984).

For students ranging from kindergarten through fifth grade, the education in self-hypnosis often takes the form of guided imagery or "fantasy trips." Students are taught to use their imaginations to take them on trips to enjoyable, remembered or imagined places. They generally seem more open to such experiences than do the older students, and often remark how much they enjoy following the guided trance processes. The importance of this trance education is reinforced by research which emphasizes that make-believe and fantasy should be encouraged as means for enhancing students' cognitive skills (Singer, 1973; Pulaski, 1979). Make-believe and daydreaming are cognitive skills enhancing flexibility in problem solving and in learning to delay the need for immediate gratification. Both of these are important skills for healthy personality development in children (Singer, 1973). In addition, the stimulation of fantasy through hypnosis may be of special help in better developing the positive inner resources in the restless student who is often characterized as overactive or hyperactive (Singer, 1973).

As part of the school's training program, teachers receive formal instruction in self-hypnosis and in techniques for applying hypnotic imagery and relaxation exercises in the classroom. Teachers are taught strategies such as "encouraging resistance," "providing worse alternatives," "emphasizing the positive," communicating in metaphors, and giving paradoxical communications (Haley, 1973). In an example of "emphasizing the positive," one sixth grade teacher ends disruption in his class by verbally rewarding one non-disruptive child after another until the entire class is quiet. Another teacher encouraged resistance in one of her students in order to promote participation in class discussions. She accomplished this by encouraging the student's lack of eye contact and slumped head-on-desk posture. In a series of small steps, she gave communications which allowed the student to lift his head but not make eye contact, then to make eye contact but not speak. Eventually, the student was drawn into fully participating with the class. A student afraid of a class oral report reluctantly submitted to read her paper for a small group of students rather than face the "worst alternative" of performing before the entire school at assembly. Teachers using techniques such as these have reported decreases in restlessness and enhanced creativity in their students.

The second focus of short-term strategic intervention in the school is on individual conflict resolution. Often the strategies are covert, thus avoiding the trauma of being singled out for treatment. Ericksonian techniques can be of assistance to the counselor in dealing with traditional school problems. For example, Baumann (1982) suggested the following double-bind strategy for children having difficulties with their homework:

> I'd like you to think about the fact that everyone needs recreation, it is important for all of us, and I would like you to make your plans for homework now with the idea in mind that you are leaving time for recreation (p. 312).

The double-bind created by Baumann's statement creates new alternatives for the child avoiding his or her homework. The counselor or teacher can direct a student to do the things he or she typically does voluntarily, and at the same time communicate an expectation of change.

For the oppositional student who refuses to do homework, the teacher or counselor can encourage the resistance. For example, one bright but passive-aggressive seventh grader who was failing most of his classes first began to do his homework when he found out how much work his parents and teachers would have to do if he produced pages of homework.

A problem that is unique to the school setting is the fear of school or "school phobia." Although enlightened teachers are often sensitive to and trained in remediating these fears, some troubled individuals eventually come to the counselor's attention. In the case of one fourth grader, the first few hours of the new school year brought more than the usual anxiety and tears. He had involuntarily left his previous class and friends because his parents could no longer financially afford his previous school. Metaphor and double-bind strategies were chosen as interventions. After acknowledging his predicament and feelings, the author told him a story about his own childhood refusal to go back to school. The session continued by discussing his friends at length. At this point, the boy was left alone for about one-half hour with this parting suggestion: "When I come back, you can choose to return to your new friends during recess or join them in class when recess is over. I'll let you decide." When the author intentionally came back later than expected, he had chosen to join his classmates after recess. At the end of the day, he was smiling; he continued to adjust well to school work throughout the year.

In the above example of a brief metaphor and double-bind intervention, the student's anger and fears were recognized and accepted, as was his need for friends. Metaphor was used to diffuse resistance by providing a non-threatening and analogous situation with which the student could spontaneously identify. The use of a metaphor to seed possibilities and match his reality followed by time alone to process its significance allowed the student to take greater control over his feelings and beliefs. The double-bind suggestion insured his choosing to assimilate into his new school environment.

For some younger children, the author's play room provides the necessary toys and games for therapeutic play. These toys and games divert the child's attention when necessary and can promote "trance play" for the therapist's intervention. "Trance play" is used instead of play therapy to emphasize a new approach developed by the author. In "trance play," the emphasis is on the induction of trance and the communication of the possibility of behavioral change via the medium of play. This approach contrasts the traditional play therapy emphasis on creating insight for the child. For the younger school phobic child, for example, a short session with a model school house, and "teacher" and "student" doll figures can quickly change behavior. The technique is analagous to the use of metaphor with the older student. Since the younger child often responds well to play as a developmental model of change, when he or she resists "A" (e.g., school), the counselor can introduce "B" (e.g., the play school situation). The child can discover the connection between "A" and "B" in a non-threatening play situation and eventually generalize the responses appropriately to the classroom. The counselor can modify the traditional form of play therapy to induce trance, promote suggestibility, and produce behavioral change.

Problems only indirectly related to school often come to the counselor's attention. Hypnotic interventions may be well suited to address these issues. In one case, a fifth grade girl reluctantly came into the office at the request of her mother. In a phone conversation with her mother, the student had been described as unhappy in school, increasingly absent because of illness, and having difficulties with sleep. During the session, the student volunteered a description of frightening recurring nightmares in which the walls kept "moving in on me." Suggesting to her that she close her sleepy eyes and imagine herself falling asleep, she quickly slipped into trance. At this time the author had her recall the nightmare in a new framework, one in which she successfully moved back the walls with a motion of her hands and arms. While the author repeatedly suggested pushing back the walls, she practiced her technique. When she returned one week later, she emphatically stated she saw no need to continue treatment sessions because she no longer had a problem. She began attending school regularly, reported sleeping soundly, and appeared increasingly happier with school. In this case, mastery of her dreams began a "snowballing effect" of mastery of other problems. This was accomplished in a short time and without traditional diagnosis and assessment. Within an Ericksonian strategy framework, the important changes in the student's life took place outside of the counselor's office after she had been given a strategy to begin her change.

One of the concerns which often arises is that of administrative and parental support of such methodology in the schools. Prevailing myths of the dangers of hypnosis continue to influence school policy (Yapko, 1984, p. 5). The questions which arise in regard to the use of hyponsis in the schools must be skillfully addressed by the counselor. The effectiveness of the counselor will certainly be challenged at this point. Although obtaining support for counseling programs which incorporate hypnotic strategies may encounter difficulties, little opposition will continue if parents, teachers, and administrators participate in educational programs exploring the myths and realities of hypnosis and become convinced of its benefits. Certainly the future will be different when these students take their places as adults and parents having seen hypnosis as a natural extension of the process through which they learn.

Milton Erickson was a pioneer in educating professionals and the general public about the myths, realities, and strategies of hypnosis. His career spanned an era through which hypnosis moved from suspicion and contempt to gradual and increasing acceptance and support. The task of completing this education of the public is left to many of those who learned from Milton Erickson. Counselors and teachers in schools have a unique opportunity to address this task in a special arena. Ultimately, the most important strategy of all may be to educate the children who will finally take our places.

References

Baumann, F. (1982). Hypnotherapy with children and adolescents: Some Ericksonian ideas. (pp 310–314). In J. Zeig (Ed). *Ericksonian approaches to hypnosis and psychotherapy*. New York: Brunner/Mazel.

Haley, J. (1973). *Uncommon therapy*. New York: Norton.

Pulaski, M. (1979). Play symbolism in cognitive development. In Schaefer, C. (Ed.) *Therapeutic use of child's play*. New York: Aronson.

Singer, J. L. (1973). *The child's world of make believe: Experimental studies of imaginative play*. New York: Academic Press.

Yapko, M. (1984). *Trancework: An introduction to clinical hypnosis*. New York: Irvington.

Depression: Diagnostic Frameworks and Therapeutic Strategies

by
Michael D. Yapko, Ph.D.

Overview

Depression has been called "the common cold of psychopathology" (Seligman, 1973). Clinically considered a mood disorder, depression is a universal experience, one that virtually all people experience at one time or another in their lifetime. While the specific parameters of a given individual's depression will be discussed later, it is worth noting at the outset that while all people experience depression to some degree at some time in their lives, each person necessarily experiences depression in their own unique way. The single common denominator of these various forms of depression is the subjective pain associated with it. Depression is virtually always an unpleasant experience for the afflicted individual, motivating many of its sufferers to seek clinical intervention with the hope of obtaining relief from its many related symptoms.

Statistically, at any given moment about 15% of Americans are thought to suffer from depression severe enough to be considered clinically significant (Secunda, Friedman and Schuyler, 1973). While this large number is in itself distressing to clinicians, it literally represents only the tip of the iceberg.

Because depression distorts one's perceptions, skewing them in a negative direction, many depressed individuals hold self-limiting beliefs that

The author would like to gratefully acknowledge Linda Griebel for her assistance in the preparation of this manuscript.

the problem is not depressed thinking or feeling. Rather, the world is viewed as a truly negative place and the individual is simply being "realistic." When such negative thoughts, feelings, and behaviors are viewed as expressions of an objective perspective and not reflective of an emotional disorder, the probability of seeking help is marginal at best. The depressed patterns of thought, behavior and feeling all too often preclude seeking help, for the belief is "nothing can help, for things are the way they are."

It is well established in clinical research that quite often, and far more frequently than most clinicians recognize, the depressed individual engages in a variety of behaviors meant to help manage the discomfort associated with the depression (Suinn, 1984). Problematic patterns such as alcohol and drug abuse, excessive overeating, excessive spending, hypersexual behavior, somatization, relationship problems, work problems, as well as many other problem behaviors may all be manifestations of an underlying depression. If the depression is not diagnosed by the individual, his or her social contacts, or by clinicians (particularly physicians performing routine examinations) who come into contact with the depressed person, the symptomatic behavior alone may be the target of an intervention with a significant probability of leaving the depression intact.

For clinicians in general, but particularly those with an interest in working with depressed individuals hypnotically and strategically in a brief therapy mode, it is crucial to appreciate the higher incidence of depression than most statistics suggest. While depression is often unrecognized as a primary disorder when other problematic feelings, thoughts, or behaviors are present, a fundamental goal of this chapter is to highlight the nearly everpresent nature of depression in the overwhelming majority of clinical disorders. In other words, even when depression is not the primary presenting complaint, a clinician can and must assess any level of depression that may be associated with the complaint in order to formulate as complete a treatment plan as possible. *Some* elements of depression can safely be assumed to be present from the simple observation that an individual seeking treatment for a problem, *any* problem, feels negatively about him or herself, at least relative to the presenting problem. Furthermore, the individual feels unable to resolve the problem effectively independently, particularly after repeated attempts to resolve the problem autonomously have met with failure. No one feels good about his or her problems. Negative self-evaluation and a personal sense of helplessness are basic components of the experience of depression (Beck, 1983; Seligman, 1983). Intervening in a presented problem without addressing the dynamics of depression associated with the problem, directly or indirectly, increases the probability of an incomplete intervention with greater potential of a relapse of symptoms later (Yapko, 1984a).

Parameters of Depression and Scope of this Chapter

Thus far the term "depression" has been used as a general term describing a mood disorder. Depression can be described along several different but related continuums. Describing the depression in terms of these continuums is a necessary first step toward developing an understanding of the client's ongoing experience for the purposes of gaining rapport with the individual as well as determining at what general level an intervention must be aimed. Particularly in working hypnotically with the depressed client, in order to formulate effective suggestions, defining the parameters of the experience of depression helps convert the static nominalization of "depression" into a dynamic, changeable experience (Bandler & Grinder, 1975).

In this chapter, the discussion centers around the disorder known as "major depression," described in the *Diagnostic and Statistical Manual*, 3rd edition, or DSM III (American Psychiatric Association, 1980). The assumption is that of a unipolar affective disorder, that is, there is no known history of the client having had a manic episode.

The continuums that are generally used to describe the parameters of depression include considerations of duration, severity, and origin (Suinn, 1984). The continuum of duration encompases how "acute" vs. "chronic" the depressive experience is for the client. If the depression is a relatively acute experience for the individual, it may be intensely painful but not be integrated into the person's ongoing personality and lifestyle. By contrast, long term or chronic depression affects the personality and lifestyle of the person, restricting their range of thoughts, feelings, and behaviors over time. A depressed client's problems may have originated in an acute situation, but became chronic when the situation was reacted to with the formation of generalizations (i.e., subjective world view assumptions) involving defeatist thoughts, feelings, and behaviors (Seligman, 1975).

The continuum addressing "severity" is characterized as having "mild" at one extreme and "severe" at the other. The experience of depression is not a static one, and the depressed individual can fluctuate widely on the continuum over time. Generally, the more severe the depression, the less competent the person becomes in handling their day to day affairs. The associated symptoms dominate the clinical picture.

On the other hand, someone mildly depressed can continue to function well at high levels of responsibility for the duration of their lifetime, and would be characterized as a "chronic, mildly depressed" individual. For example, many high achievers fit into this particular category, accomplishing noteworthy things yet maintaining the lowered self-esteem, anxiety, and other problems typically associated with depression. Pride in the accomplishment is short-lived, and the person focuses on "what next?"

The third continuum relates to the suspected origin of the depression, and conceptualizes depression as having either an internal or external etiology. Internally generated depression is termed "endogenous" depression, and is thought to have biological origins, i.e., genetic or biochemical causes (Suinn, 1984). Depression associated with external causes is termed "reactive" depression, encompassing psychosocial dimensions of experience. The individual learning history, psychosocial environment, contextual cues, and other such dimensions are the suspect variables in reactive forms of depression.

The implications for the treatment of depression rest heavily on the parameters described above. Generally, chronic depression is more difficult to treat than is acute, mild depression is more responsive to treatment than is severe, and endogenous is more difficult to diagnose reliably and treat effectively than is reactive. Particularly on the "endogenous/reactive" dimension of depression are there the greatest differences in interventions. The "nature-nurture" controversy surfaces in this arena, and because endogenous depression is by definition typically considered a biological condition, medical-physical interventions are most widely applied (e.g., ECT, medications, etc.). In such cases, the client is generally regarded as a poor candidate for psychotherapy (Kolb & Brodie, 1982).

The Diagnosis of Depression and Its Influence on Subjective Experience

Discussed earlier were the recognitions that depression is almost inevitably a part of the client's experience when seeking therapy, and that depressive symptoms can easily be camouflaged by more readily apparent symptomatic coping attempts on the part of the client. Operating on the assumption that some degree of depression is present in the client's experience can allow the clinician to more readily observe its effects in order to determine how primary or secondary its role is relative to the presenting complaint(s). Consequently, the clinician can more efficiently organize and conduct an intervention that takes more of the client's needs into account. It seems likely that a therapy aimed at resolving central complaints (when the central complaint is not depression) without addressing the secondary depressive component(s) runs a greater risk of solving a problem but not imparting a skill of problem-solving that the client can later apply independently (Yapko, 1983).

In this section on diagnosis, several frameworks will be provided for recognizing many common dimensions of depression a clinician is likely to encounter. One is the description contained in DSM-III (APA, 1980). A second framework is one more easily adapted to the spontaneous assessment of an individual in that it is a more highly individualized system and is more closely related to the formation of an intervention for a specific individual. This assessment is considered rooted in Ericksonian approaches to hypnosis and psychotherapy (Zeig, personal communication, 1984; Lankton & Lankton, 1983). A third system is a "multiple-level" assessment plan, one also meant to identify parameters of a specific individual's unique experience of depression while simultaneously offering insight into where intervention may be aimed.

The three systems are by no means mutually exclusive, rather each merges with the other providing substantiating information for the clinician's impressions and plans for intervention.

DSM-III Diagnosis of Depression

The DSM-III (APA, 1980) describes depression as an affective disorder which is diagnosed according to the following criteria:

> Dysphoric mood or loss of interest or pleasure in all or almost all usual activities and pastimes . . . (with) at least four of the following symptoms . . . present nearly every day for a period of at least two weeks: 1) poor appetite or significant weight loss or increased appetite or significant weight gain; 2) insomnia or hypersomnia, 3) psychomotor agitation or retardation, 4) loss of interest or pleasure in usual activities, or decrease in sexual drive not limited to a period when delusional or hallucinating, 5) loss of energy; fatigue, 6) feelings of worthlessness, self-reproach, or excessive or inappropriate guilt, 7) complaints or evidence of diminished ability to think or concentrate, 8) recurrent thoughts of death, suicidal ideation, wishes to be dead or suicide attempts. (pp. 213-4)

Ericksonian Diagnostic System

More sensitive to characteristics of the client's unique experience of depression is the Ericksonian diagnostic system described in part by Zeig (personal communication, 1984), Lankton and Lankton (1983), and further developed and elaborated upon here. These diagnostic criteria of the individual's experience often imply general treatment strategies as well, and when they do these implications will be so addressed.

Zeig (personal communication, 1984) described the following diagnostic criteria as a basis for formulating an approach to intervention:

1. Response style
2. Thinking style
3. Concentration style
4. Primary representational system
5. Developmental considerations
6. Family position
7. Internal or external focus
8. Processing style

Added to these categories are the following criteria relevant to the idiosyncratic nature of the client's experience:

9. Master or victim of experience
10. Age and value programming characteristics
11. Past, present, or future orientation
12. High or low emotional reactivity

Each of these criteria is briefly discussed in the remainder of this section.

1. *Response Style:* This refers to the client's relative degree of willingness or lack of willingness to follow directives of the clinician. If the client is compliant, the clinician can afford a more direct approach, while a client who communicates in either a more self-directed pattern or a polar response style will require a more indirect approach (Zeig, 1984; Yapko, 1983, 1984a).

2. *Thinking Style:* A person's thinking style may be described on two continuums: "abstract-concrete" and "global-linear." Noting a client's spontaneous language patterns can lead a clinician to develop an awareness of how capable of abstraction the individual is. This piece of information will be significant in the intervention phase, for the more concrete the client, the less likely he or she is to generalize learnings beyond the immediate problem-solving context without assistance from the clinician. Noting the word choice of the client as well as how he or she relates to previous personal experiences (i.e., whether connected in a sophisticated stream of living or disconnected bits and pieces of seem-

ingly random experiences) can give the clinician insight into this dimension of client experience. On the "linear-global" continuum, the client's thinking style can be assessed as to whether the individual thinks in a linear, sequential, ordered manner, or whether many thoughts and feelings are jumbled in the person's consciousness leading to a "shotgun" approach to problem-solving. Simply the client's style for presentation of symptoms can be a good indicator of the thinking style. For example, does the client say "I'd like to resolve this and then work on that," or does the client say "I want to resolve this, this, this, and this?" For the depressed person in particular, the global style is more common; the client typically has numerous complaints existing simultaneously on multiple levels, and is depressed with the overwhelming amount of problems to be faced. Most, if not all, of current interventions for depression emphasize breaking the problem into smaller, manageable pieces to be addressed one at a time in a linear fashion.

3. *Concentration Style:* A person's concentration style may be described as existing along a continuum with "focused" at one end and "diffuse" at the other. These are, of course, relative terms meant to suggest degrees of focus or diffusion. In the course of spontaneous interaction, is the client able to follow the flow of discussion? Is he or she able to tune out extranous variables or is there a significant level of distractability? A person's concentration style is immediately relevant to the person's level of hypnotic responsiveness. Thus, in determining the likelihood of effective use of formal patterns of hypnosis, the concentration style must be assessed. When the concentration style is a diffuse one, as is generally the case with depressed individuals who find it difficult to concentrate, the clinician can initially use simpler hypnotic patterns in order to facilitate the building of hypnotic responsiveness. In a relatively short period of time, the client can begin to build the more focused attentional style associated with trance. This can provide a certain measure of relief as the client has the experience of one of the more troublesome symptoms of depression subsiding.

4. *Primary Representational System* (PRS). Developing an awareness for the client's preferred sensory modality for acquiring, storing, and retrieving information can allow the clinician to respond to the client in the language of that sensory medium (Bandler & Grinder, 1975, 1979). This enhances rapport and thereby increases the likelihood of therapeutic influence on the client's experience (Yapko, 1981). Noting the sensory-based predicates in a client's spontaneous speech patterns can allow the clinician to identify the PRS and thus utilize that information in the structuring of the intervention. With the depressed person in particular, the PRS relative to the symptoms is, by the definition of depression, a

kinesthetic one. The client's depressed *feelings* occupy his or her awareness. Addressing the feelings, directly or indirectly, will allow for the
building of trust and rapport, while leading the client into a greater
awareness for another level of experience may be the thrust of an intervention.

5. *Developmental Experiences and World View Consequences.* Erickson was aware of the impact of one's environment on one's development,
and sought information from his patients as to whether they were reared
in an urban or rural environment (Zeig, 1980a; Yapko, 1985). This
information can provide an indication as to the type of values, experiences, and world view one has. Such "urban vs. rural" consideration
seems less relevant in today's society, and might best be replaced by
comparing the characteristics of those raised in urban versus suburban
environments. Values associated with personal space, the meaning of
time, the value of money, and a respect for institutions, are all formed
to a large extent on the basis of one's developmental experiences with
family, school, church, and other socializing institutions. The quality of
experiences one is exposed to can differ dramatically from person to
person on the basis of such developmental differences. Statistics suggest
that depression is more prevalent in urban environments (Mahoney,
1980).

6. *Family Position.* Research has provided some evidence that birth
order may have significant impact on one's personality development
(Gibson, 1983). For example, it is not uncommon that the oldest sibling
is made partially responsible for day-to-day care of younger siblings.
Learning the responsibilities associated with being a "caretaker" in the
family can lead one to develop a highly responsible atittude toward others.
In the depressed individual, this sense of responsibility can be distorted
to the point of the individual assuming responsibility for things that one
objectively *cannot* be responsible for, or to the point of accepting no
responsibility for things one is genuinely responsible for. The issue of
responsibility is a prominent one in depressed individuals (and is discussed in greater detail later), but is used here as an example of one
characteristic that may arise in association with family position.

7. *Internal or external focus.* Some people are remarkably sensitive
to their own internal experience, with a high level of awareness for their
motives, feelings, and needs. Such people might be described as having
a strong internal focus. When consciousness is directed inwardly, there
is naturally less opportunity for awareness of external events. When
someone is internally absorbed episodically, he or she may be accused
of being insensitive to others, i.e., "off in their own little world." Others,
by contrast, have a high degree of awareness for others, for subtle changes

in the environment, and for other external events. Similarly, when one is preoccupied with meeting external demands, it is often at the price of noticing internal responses. Assessing the degree of insight and involvement with others will assist the clinician in forming an impression of the client on this continuum. The implications of this diagnostic category for the etiology and treatment of emotional disorders may be quite profound. For example, stress related disorders typically arise because the individual is so absorbed in a project (external), he or she does not notice the accompanying negative stress until it surfaces dramatically as a symptom of some sort. Therapy then takes the general form of learning to recognize internal cues indicating stress, i.e., building more of an internal focus in order to determine appropriate points to apply stress management techniques. In the depressed individual, the focus is an intensely internal one, absorbing the individual in their subjective discomfort. Most interventions for depression, deliberately or otherwise, suggest a means for "getting out of one's self" and involved elsewhere. For example, simple interventions that yield positive results include having the depressed individual volunteer time in a hospital or some similar institution, joining in recreational activities, entering group therapy, and other such "getting out of one's self" activities. Hypnotic and strategic interventions can be used to facilitate the process of better balancing internal and external focus in the client.

8. *Processing style.* There is an inevitable gap that exists between the universe as it objectively exists and the way it is represented internally by someone. Due to 1) the inherent limitations that exist in the human body and mind's capacities, 2) the limitations of what can be learned as a member of society based on the limits of that society's knowledge, and 3) the limits of one's own personal range of experiences, a subjective world view is formed that will necessarily differ markedly from objective reality (Bandler & Grinder, 1975). In order to form the world view, or world model from which one perceives the range of choices in living, one must necessarily represent the world internally in a manageable way, reducing the infinite range of possible experiences to a meaningful level. Bandler and Grinder described the "modeling mechanisms" (1975) as the principal mechanisms each person utilizes to reduce the world to subjectively manageable levels. These mechanisms are "deletion," "distortion," and "generalization," and each involves either amplifying or diminishing certain aspects of experience in order to maintain one's concept of reality. Zeig (personal communication, 1984) described the effects of the modeling mechanisms as the individual's "processing style," and described the processing style of the individual in terms of tendencies to "enhance" or "reduce" experience. In other words, the

individual responding to a particular context will tend to either embellish and magnify components or will diminish or minimize contextual components. Metaphorically, some people tend to "make mountains out of molehills," while others tend to "make molehills out of mountains." Some are prone to exaggeration, others to understatement.

In the case of the depressed individual, the processing style is a relatively consistent one relative to the nature of the information being processed. When the situation offers positive possibilities (e.g., praise, opportunities, encouragement, etc.), the depressed individual typically minimizes their value and impact. When the situation offers negative feedback (e.g., criticism, obstacles to progress, discouragement, etc.), the depressed individual typically exaggerates their value and impact. Small delays, less than enthusiastic responses, small hurdles involving protocol, and other such naturally occurring barriers to be overcome typically represent insurmountable obstacles to the depressed individual through the exaggeration process.

Some depressed individuals intuitively seem to recognize their own tendency to exaggerate the negative and minimize the positive about themselves. Judging this negatively, they may make an effort to compenate for it with overt expressions to others or to themselves of exaggerated positive self-descriptions. However, these are not internalized, and so remain more of an attempt to convince oneself than a true recognition of competence or worthiness.

Implications of the depressed processing style for recognizing the natural mechanism of distortion at work is a basic requirement of therapy with the depressed individual. This allows him or her to recognize the distortion process at work in the formation of conclusions about day-to-day interactions. As the distortions become regularly challenged, the generalizations regarding self-worth and one's relationship with others or with life in general can be contradicted and ultimately modified.

As the individual learns to represent experience more accurately (i.e., with less embellishment or minimization), perhaps by taking into account others' perspectives or being encouraged to self-generate numerous alternate views, he or she can learn to consider a variety of views before continuing on in the old pattern of settling on an unrealistic negative or positive interpretation of events. The emotional content of such distorted interpretations tends to skew perception further, reinforcing the processing style that maintains depression.

9. *Master or victim of experience.* The issue of responsibility for one's experience has been the subject of countless debates in numerous arenas. How one interprets the events of one's life is affected by whether one views oneself as active or reactive in the experience under consideration.

Some people accept the notion that much of what one experiences is under one's control and thus is the product of conscious or unconscious choices. Others believe that they have little or no control over what they experience and must always be in a secondary, reactive position. Ultimately, how much one is a "victim" or "master" of experience is determined by the context one is in—no one can be totally masterful *everywhere;* situations in which one is totally ignorant can be enslaving, and no one can know everything. The degree of control one has in a situation is partially context determined. For the depressed individual, and for the person who experiences troublesome symptoms apparently beyond control, there is a significant element of "victim" accompanying the complaints. The client feels utterly helpless to do anything useful, and desperately turns to the clinician to make the problem go away. Even if the person is masterful elsewhere in life, the "victim" identity is present in relation to the problem at hand. Martin Seligman's "Learned Helplessness" model (Seligman, 1973, 1975, 1983) is a highly sophisticated one in its ability to describe this "victim" dimension of the depressed individual. The issue at hand for the clinician is to assess how much of a "victim" the person seeking help really is, i.e., how much of the depressive content is context determined and objectively uncontrollable, and how much is subjective and controllable? Furthermore, is this client chronically a victim throughout many or all aspects of his or her life, or is the client generally quite masterful but just a victim relative to the presenting problem? This assessment is pivotal in the intervention stage when the clinician must make use of the client's level of direct involvement in the therapy. For example, a "die-hard" victim is far less likely to carry out therapeutic homework assignments designed to teach mastery skills simply because being masterful is too inconsistent with his or her "victim" self-image (Yapko, 1984a). This is when the clinician typically experiences the rejecting "Yes, but. . . ." objections from the client who has been given alternatives and tasks designed to be helpful. Shifting the depressed individual from a desperate victim role into one of exerting mastery over experience is a dominant theme in the successful treatment of depression.

10. *Age and value programming characteristics.* The value system one inevitably acquires during the socialization process is a composite of numerous inputs and is critical in the development of one's subjective concept of reality. Massey (1979) described the value acquisition process in terms of cultural norms at different periods of recent American social history. In a general but surprisingly accurate way, Massey described the values one holds as the things one accepts as right or wrong, good or bad, normal or not normal, and as having been determined in large part

by the values dominant in the society as the individual was growing up ("value programming"). Massey claimed that 90% of one's values are established by age 10, plus or minus 2 years, and that values only change when one experiences an event that is emotionally powerful enough to reach the deepest levels of an individual. Such an experience is termed a "Significant Emotional Event," or "SEE" by Massey. Therapy may be viewed as the artificial and deliberate creation of a SEE (Yapko, 1985), which can only be accomplished by first developing an awareness for the value system underlying the problematic pattern. Once the values associated with the problem are identified, they may either be used as catalysts in the treatment process, or may be used as targets for therapeutic intervention. These processes are described in detail in "The Erickson Hook: Values in Ericksonian Approaches" (Yapko, 1985).

In the depressed individual, there may be values held that create or complicate the depressed condition. For example, valuing "perfection" may lead one to evolve obsessive traits that inevitably leave one dissatisfied since nothing is perfect. In another example, valuing the commitment of marriage may lead one to stay in an emotionally unhealthy relationship which will likely serve as a basis for depression. The examples of a deeply held value that limits one's options in hurtful ways are too numerous to describe here, but assessing the value system of the client is essential in the formation of an appropriate treatment plan.

11. *Past, present, or future orientation*. Each person relates to the construct of "time" in their own way. Depending on the person's value system, range of experience, and degree of emotional investment, an individual may be more oriented to one time frame than another. For example, some people "live in the past," evidenced by preoccupation with past experiences at the expense of present and future involvements. Such people seem to prefer the way things were, talking incessantly about past history when things were so much better ("the good old days"), and are generally less interested in and able to relate meaningfully to current and future trends. Other individuals are so "now" oriented that their impulses become the basis for much of their behavior, with little regard for future consequences or previous traditions. Still others are so future oriented as to have only future goals in mind, i.e., the house to be bought, the career to be built, the travels to be done, and so forth, all to the point of taking little or no time to "stop and smell the roses along the way."

Each of the above descriptions are general characterizations, for no one can "live" in any one orientation exclusively without serious disruption to their sense of reality. The issue here concerns to what degree the individual is oriented to one dimension of time to the point of maintaining the dysfunctional system. With the problem of depression in particular, an individual might be oriented to any of the time dimensions to his or her detriment. Typically, however, the degree of depression experienced seems to be correlated highly with the degree of past orientation.

Relative to time, the depressed individual is likely to have had a past personal history of significant losses, aversive and uncontrollable external events (Seligman, 1973, 1975, 1983), non-supportive family members with pathological communication patterns, and other pathogenic variables. The intensity of the individual's emotional pain becomes the focal point of the person's experience, and is an emotional burden the individual attempts to manage. The effect on the present is to diminish or eliminate awareness for relief-providing alternatives, and stabilizes a negative expectation for the future that can easily become a self-fulfilling prophecy. In short, the past is the depressed individual's frame of reference from which present and future experiences are negatively distorted. It is precisely this past orientation that leads to the most difficult aspects of working with depressed individuals. With a negative frame of reference based on a highly emotionally charged (and therefore powerful) past history of learning, the depressed individual may come to believe that their current experience of pain is all that there is in life, and that things cannot or will not get better. This erroneous belief more than any other is the single underlying rationale for committing suicide. When the person looks to the future and anticipates only more pain, suicide seems a reasonable alternative. A clinician telling a severely depressed individual that "things will get better" and to "look ahead" is providing suggestions that are too inconsistent with the depressed person's frame of reference, and are typically rejected as meaningless on that basis (Yapko, 1984a). A more emotionally-charged approach to building better but realistic future expectations is indicated in such instances.

Clearly, the depressed individual shows responsiveness to each of the dimensions of time. The present is responded to with an acute awareness of the internal discomfort and environmental conditions that are experienced as hurtful but uncontrollable. The future is responded to with expectations of "more of the same," or conversely, with unrealistic positive expectations that "when 'X' happens, then I'll be O.K." 'X' refers to some accomplishment or some significant event. For example, many depressives will move from one geographical location to another to try to find relief, only to find that they have simply moved their depression from one place to another based on an incorrect assumption that it was the environment that was causing the depression. Others may think that a different job, a college degree, a new lover, or some other external change will cause a reduction in depressive symptoms. Such changes are most seriously considered with a distorted future orientation that precludes insight into the genuine dynamics of the depressive experience.

The relationship between depression and past orientation is a strong one, with implicit strategies for intervention involving shifts to more adaptive present and future orientations. These will be discussed in the later section on treatment alternatives.

12. *High or low emotional reactivity.* American society places a large emphasis on rationality. For many, this value of logic becomes internalized to the point of the individual becoming what Virginia Satir (1972) called the "human computer", an individual whose emotional reactions are buried beneath layers of logic, effectively distancing him or her from threatening feelings of almost any type. Therefore, there is a great variability of reactivity in people ranging from emotionally expressive and unfeeling to overy expressive and even hyperemotional. For the clinician, it is most useful to know the degree to which an individual is emotionally reactive, for the level of reactivity is closely related to the individual's self-esteem, value system, and further indicates where resistances to intervention are likely to surface.

The term "emotional reactivity" is being used to describe how aware the client is of his or her affective reactions to experience, how responsive the client is to those affective reactions, and how expressive of those affective reactions the individual is. Clearly, self-esteem is closely related, for if one must inhibit or deny the presence of feelings, then one is uncomfortable with a significant portion of one's self. Consequently, a clinician who has the goal of "helping you get in touch with your feelings" will be likely to encounter resistance since the feelings are a source of discomfort and are defended against.

In the depressed individual, emotional reactivity is typically high on one dimension, and typically low on others. There is high reactivity in the sense that the person is very aware of the emotional pain of the depression. However, the depressed person's range of emotions is so narrowed by the depression that feelings of love, closeness, interest, humor, and other positive feelings are all but absent from the person's awareness. Consequently, there is little or no sense of humor, playfulness, romance, sexual interest, or other such positive feelings. Self-esteem is low, and the low level of reactivity creates what often seems like a wall of apathy between clinician and client. In reality, the client is not apathetic, but resticts involvement for a variety of reasons.

Stirring up and making available to the depressed client the positive feelings that have been buried broadens the range of possibilities open to the person. Drawing out feelings in a nonthreatening way and guiding them into appropriate contexts is desirable in hypnotic interventions. Concurrently, diffusing negative feelings and building more of a balanced reactivity to both positive and negative feelings instead of only negative ones is essential.

The Multiple-Level Diagnostic System

A third system of assessing the characteristics of the depressed individual concerns the "multiple level" nature of depression. It has been recognized that depression, like all experiences, occurs on multiple levels. One such model of depression has been called the "SCAB" model (Miller, 1984; Beck, 1967, 1973, 1983). SCAB is an acronym for the Somatic, Cognitive, Affective, and Behavioral levels of depressive symptoms. The various symptoms associated with depression described by the DSM-III (APA, 1980) can be categorized according to the SCAB model for the purpose of evaluating which levels of the depression are most prominent in the overall clinical picture.

The somatic level includes such symptoms as sleep disturbance, appetite disturbance, diminishment of sexual drive, lethargy, and various somatic complaints that may seem vague and have no apparent organic etiology.

The cognitive level includes such symptoms as negative self-evaluation, negative expectations, inability to concentrate, confusion, pessimism, and suicidal ideation.

The affective level of depression encompasses the feelings of dejection, diminished sense of humor, irritability, lack of self-worth, guilt, ambivalence, anxiety, and sadness.

The behavioral dimension of depression includes excessive crying, suicide attempts, social withdrawal, and hypo or hyperactivity.

Given that the client is experiencing the depression on multiple, interrelated levels, it can be helpful in the treatment planning phase of intervention to know on which level(s) treatment may be most effectively aimed (ultimately, of course, the goal is to address all the levels of the problem). It is well known that of all the dimensions of experience available to one's consciousness, only a small portion can be in one's awareness at a given moment in time (Zeig, 1980a). It is significant, therefore, to notice from the client's spontaneous linguistic patterns which dimension of the depression is most prominent in his or her awareness. Such awareness on the part of the clinician can lead to a greater likelihood of being able to effectively "pace" or match the client's experience

(Bandler & Grinder, 1979) and thereby establish a greater rapport. Furthermore, it allows one to choose whether to aim the intervention at the level of the problem most in the person's awareness, or whether to aim the intervention elsewhere. For example, a depressed client might present the following description of experience:

> . . . I'm tired all the time. I don't know what's wrong with
> me lately. . . . Maybe I'm just getting older or something; all
> I know is I'm not sleeping well at night, I'm eating enough to
> feed an army, and I just don't want to be bothered by anybody
> or anything. . . . It's even affecting my sex life, I mean lately
> I don't even want my wife to get near me, and yet I know I still
> care for her. . . . Oh, I just don't know what's wrong with me,
> all I know is, I better do something to change before I drive
> myself and everyone around me crazy. . . .

In this sample, the client presents a series of symptom descriptions, each reflecting an awareness for a disturbance on the somatic level. Similar in theory to the concept of a "primary representational system" (PRS), the issue here concerns what level of experience is in the person's consciousness, and by implication, which levels are not. When the clinician has become aware of which level of the depression is most prominent in the person's awareness, he or she has a choice of whether to approach the symptoms directly on that level, or whether to approach the client on other levels deemed partially or entirely out of the individual's awareness. The basic generalizations guiding the choice of indirect or direct approaches apply here: The greater the perceived resistance on the part of the client, the greater the need for indirection (Zeig, 1980a; Yapko, 1983, 1984a). In other words, if the client is a compliant, responsive one, who is clear about his or her goals, and has the available resources for change, then indirection is not particularly necessary. If the client is unlikely to respond to direct approaches, then indirect approaches have a greater likelihood of succeeding. Specifically, if the client has a high degree of awareness for the somatic difficulties associated with depression, and direct approaches seem unlikely to be effective, then treatment should be aimed at the level that seems to be least available to the person's consciousness, whether it be the behavioral, affective, or cognitive. As Zeig (1980a) pointed out, the level of the problem most in the person's awareness will likely have the least defensiveness associated with it. The clinician can build a momentum of success with the client as he or she begins treatment on a less involved level and can then guide treatment progressively closer to the problem.

The SCAB model delineates four levels of the problem of depression. It is possible to delineate many more when one accounts for all of the elements of experience that are integrated into one overall experience. These other levels can include relational, contextual, symbolic, social, and attitudinal (Zeig, 1980b). Mapping out the client's symptoms according to these various levels can provide the clinician a variety of choice points regarding where to begin treatment and how to address all of the levels in the interventions used.

Summary

The diagnostic phase of the therapeutic interaction is critical in the overall formulation of an effective treatment strategy. When spontaneous assessment is preferred to structured psychological tests, or is used to supplement such tests, the above diagnostic criteria can be most useful. Such spontaneous assessment allows for a more naturalistic approach to the building of the therapeutic relationship, focuses the clinician more on the recognition of the client as a unique individual with his or her idiosyncratic experience of the problem of depression, and allows for the recognition much earlier on in the therapeutic process of what elements of the client's experience have stabilizing and destabilizing effects on the depression itself. This allows for swifter intervention, certainly a goal in the use of hypnotic and strategic interventions.

Uncovering Psychodynamics as a Precursor to Intervention

The diagnostic strategies described in the previous section focus on particular dimensions of the client's experience involving the nature of the symptoms and patterns of personality. Such information is critical in the formation of a treatment plan and clinical demeanor. In this section, common psychodynamics underlying depression are briefly explored, building a framework for the later emphasis on the creation of treatment strategies intended to therapeutically address these dynamics in whole or in part.

Uncovering and addressing the dynamics underlying depression (or *any* problem, for that matter) involves a series of decisions by the clinician regarding procedure. First, the clinician must decide whether to approach uncovering the dynamics through analysis of "here-and-now" symptomatic manifestations, or whether "focusing on the past" by emphasizing a conscious analysis of previous history is in order. Second, the clinician must decide how much information-gathering is sufficient in order to reach a conclusion about where and how the client has created and maintained the self-limiting generalizations associated with the depression. For example, how many contexts does the clinician need to explore with the client before he or she recognizes a generalized pattern of relating? Too few samples of experience can lead one to hastily make incorrect conclusions, while too many can lead one to miss opportunities to make interventions because of the need for further information. Obviously, how much information one needs is an entirely individual decision.

Once the clinician has the confidence that he or she has identified the patterns maintaining the depressive condition, the third decision involves whether a sharing of the interpretations will be therapeutic or anti-therapeutic. This issue directly involves the clinician deciding whether providing an interpretation designed to promote "insight" in the client is the best of approaches, or whether the use of techniques designed to facilitate change in the absence of insight is indicated. Each approach is useful, but one will be more likely to succeed depending on the needs of the particular client (Yapko, 1984a).

Described in the remainder of this chapter are several of the major psychodynamic models of depression used to conceptualize the origin and structure of the disorder. They are presented here in exaggeratedly simplified form in order to facilitate an awareness for how such dynamics can be addressed therapeutically, since many of the techniques described in the next section are based on the insights these models offer. Familiarity with other, less common models of depression can lead to the creation of hypnotic and strategic patterns addressing depressive dynamics more fully.

The "Learned Helplessness" Model

Even the most "here-and-now" therapists acknowledge the influence of past experience on current patterns. In the case of depression, the typical client presents as someone with a cynical, pessimistic view of self and others. Directives from the clinician to actively take self-help steps are typically met with the "Yes, but. . ." refusals. Opportunities to take obvious self-help steps in daily living are passively allowed to slip by. The effect is that of a client who is "helpless." How does such a pattern evolve? In part, the answer comes from the valuable research of Martin Seligman (1974, 1975, 1983), who named his model of depression "Learned Helplessness." Seligman described a series of experiments in which research subjects, both animal and human, were exposed to negative, uncontrollable external events. Simply, subjects were traumatized in ways that could not be controlled by them. Once the conclusion (generalization) had been formed that "I am going to get hurt no matter what I do," subjects abandoned any efforts to help themselves. Later, when exposed to negative external events that were, in fact, controllable, the previously learned generalizations guided reactions. In other words, *even when the subject could take steps to avoid the negative events, the subject did not because previous experience proved such effort was wasted.* A consistent result was depression, paralleling the features of reactive depression. There was no discrimination made between how the controllable context was different than the uncontrollable one. The uniform reaction was passive helplessness. Furthermore, and a point highly relevant to the practice of psychotherapy with depressed individuals, once the depressed, helpless demeanor was adopted, repeated trials emphasizing awareness of the controllability of the negative events showed a startling impairment in the ability of subjects to learn "control" in the place of "no control." In a later revision of his work (Abramson, Seligman, & Teasdale, 1978), Seligman made a distinction between "universal helplessness" and "personal helplessness." Universal helplessness is experienced when a negative event is uncontrollable by *anyone*, regardless of level of competence. Personal helplessness exists when the individual is helpless, but others in the same situation would not be. Clearly the attribution process, i.e., how and where the person fixes the blame for his or her situation, plays a role in the process. Personal helplessness is considerably more likely to lead to depression via self-blame, negative self-evaluation, and so forth. Ultimately, in this paradigm, how intensely depression will be experienced depends on how uncontrollable the outcome seems to be and how important the outcome is to the individual. The established "helpless" mental set apparently acts as a filter to delete or distort more positive input. This homeostatic self-defeating mechanism is one that must be addressed therapeutically in order for depression to lift. Developing control over seemingly uncontrollable daily experience is the basis for the mastery that minimizes one's experience of depression. Such mastery involves one's self-esteem, one's ability to plan and reach goals, one's ability to initiate and allow for personal changes, and countless other abilities to meet life's demands well. Developing control over one's experience is a foundation for many of the approaches described later.

The "Cognitive Distortions" Model

The limitations of the human mind and body, the society of which each person is a part, and of one's own range of personal experiences are limitations that necessitate the development of a subjective reality (Bandler & Grinder, 1975; Watzlawick, 1976). The beliefs that one holds as true, both consciously and unconsciously, dictate the range of options one perceives as available. Such beliefs dictate perceptions (i.e., interpretations of experience) which, in turn, dictate the actions and reactions of one's lifestyle. These, in turn, dictate the quantity and quality of feedback one gets, which leads one to reinforce or modify one's approach. Conclusions or generalizations are routinely and necessarily formed about experience, a neutral process that helps or hurts an individual depending on the context in which it arises. In the case of depression, Beck (1973, 1979, 1983) focused on the cognitive generalizations that apparently foster depression. Beck recognized the often irrational and negatively distorted conclusions that depressed individuals reach about their daily experiences, and built his successful treatment approaches on the need to modify such distorted thought processes. From the observation that one's feelings arise, at least in part, from one's thoughts, the cognitive theory of depression assumes that when negative beliefs are transformed (through therapy) into positive ones, positive feelings will follow. Beck (1973, 1979, 1983) and Burns (1980), another cognitive clinician, described in detail the many categories and contexts in which such distorted thinking is evident. Beck, like Seligman, also acknowledged the inherent difficulties of therapeutically altering depressive generalizations, since the calibrated cycle (i.e., closed-loop logic) of the person's thoughts allows them to maintain their beliefs even in the face of objective contradictory evidence.

Addressing the cognitive level of experience is unavoidable in treating depressed individuals. The question for the clinician familiar with patterns of hypnosis and strategic therapy concerns whether treatment is more likely to succeed operating exclusively on conscious cognitive levels, or whether the client's depressive mind set (dysfunctional thought patterns) can be better addressed through work on other levels of experience outside the conscious limitations of the client. A point made earlier bears repeating: directing therapy at the level of experience least in awareness generates the least resistance. Starting elsewhere and allowing for a progression of successes builds a momentum of wellness. Directly contradicting a client's sense of reality, no matter how dysfunctional, must be tenaciously defended against by him or her (evidenced as resistance) since one's sense of reality is all one has. There is no frame of reference to replace it until there are therapeutic experiences that can be brought into focus. This is the purpose for using hypnotic and strategic approaches.

The "Anger-Turned-Inward" Model

Freud's conceptualization of depression was that it involved an introjection of hostility fixated at the earliest stages of development (Davison

& Neale, 1982). Simply, unexpressed anger turned back on one's self in an intrapunitive way was thought to cause depression. While research has since provided evidence that there is a correlation between anger and depression, it is not a simple "cause-effect" relationship. The recognition that frustration generally precedes aggression (Aronson, 1984) can be useful in conceptualizing how anger arises and how it is dealt with by the depressed individual.

When one is frustrated, i.e., blocked from accomplishing situational resolution or getting something deemed important, the typical consequence is anger. If the individual is not inhibited by internal (e.g., values, self-judgments) or external (e.g., contextual) variables precluding the expression of anger, then he or she may openly express the anger. If the person is inhibited by internal or external conditions, then the anger is likely to either be displaced onto a safe target ("scapegoating") or is internalized as a defect of self. The latter is a common feature of depressed individuals. Feeling badly with no relief in sight is fuel for the fire of depression. Anger with one's self for being "weak" (a conclusion supported by the American slowly-changing value that a "strong" person doesn't have emotional problems) and anger with others for numerous reasons (such as not sharing in the misery or for not being sympathetic or understanding enough) is a critical element in forming the "helpless" and other cognitive distortions and other self-limiting patterns.

Uncovering what the depressed individual might be frustrated or angry about, and what self-limiting means the person is employing to deny or otherwise ineffectively deal with feelings are important steps in formulating a plan to deal effectively with an emotion so basic to human composition as anger.

Other Models

The above models describe or allude to feelings of helplessness and anger, perceptions of uncontrollable negative events, irrational beliefs, and cultural values about emotionality. Other models involve related constructs as the dynamics of depression. These include maternal separation and social isolation (Harlow & Suomi, 1974); hemispheric processing problems (Spiegel & Spiegel, 1978); reaction to loss and the lack of meaning or purpose in one's life (Frankl, 1963); giving up one's sense of will (Kleinmuntz, 1980; Suinn, 1984); and what the author has termed "instrumental depression" that arises to be used manipulatively for personal gain. Related to a behavioral construct, the depressed person uses their depression specifically to get sympathy and attention, or some other secondary gain, and is reinforced for doing so. Consider the obviously depressed person sitting alone in the corner at a party, who draws the attention of a well-meaning "helper." Depression can be used as an instrument, a means to an end. A last model is a socialization model, one that takes into account the cultural values that support depressive episodes. Women are diagnosed as depressed almost twice as frequently as men (Sarason & Sarason, 1980; Davison & Neale, 1982). What elements of societal norms encourage this uneven distribution? Is it because women are generally socialized to be emotionally expressive and men not? Are womens' lives more stressful? Is it the cultural emphasis on males being the "strong silent type" like our archetypal heroes? Such variables of socialization are suspect in the high incidence of depression in general and the discrepancies of diagnosis according to gender in particular.

Summary

How one conceptualizes the dynamics present in a depressed individual will obviously determine the course of treatment one directs. This section has described some basic concepts about some of the patterns the author has found to be most prevalent in depressed persons. Decisions on whether to address the dynamic directly or indirectly, early on or later in treatment, consciously or unconsciously, cognitively or at some other level, and with or without insight of the client are decisions that must methodically be made before making interventions. Treatment may then be aimed at facilitating mastery, resolving feelings of anger, clarifying cognitive distortions, building relationship skills, finding meaning in life, handling relationships nonmanipulatively, and breaking out of limiting prescribed social roles, and other such dynamics that may cause or maintain depression.

Depression: Therapeutic Strategies

Goals of Treatment

In reviewing the diagnostic criteria and descriptive models related to depression, the goals of treatment may become clear. Certainly one of the hallmarks of Ericksonian approaches in general is the emphasis on attaining significant clinical results (Bandler & Grinder, 1979; Lankton & Lankton, 1983). Having a direction with specific therapeutic goals in mind in working with the depressed individual serves a number of worthwhile purposes. Goal-directedness: 1) defines the relationship as a genuinely therapeutic one, 2) brings meaning and purpose to the client's efforts, 3) demands the building of a positive future orientation, itself a therapeutic intervention for a depressed individual, and it 4) models the possibility that one can define a goal, define a progressive series of steps necessary to accomplish the goal, and actively pursue resolution. This is a pattern far from helpless and is thus inherently therapeutic.

Assuming a directive stance in applying the therapeutic interventions described here presupposes a willingness of the clinician to initiate the events of treatment (Haley, 1973). This responsibility is considerable, particularly at first, before treatment results have begun to generalize to the point where the client can fully assume a position of being responsible for him or herself. The responsibility for treatment outcomes is ideally one shared between clinician and client (Yapko, 1984b), but it is generally true that at different stages of treatment and depending on the nature of the client's problems the pendulum of responsibility can swing in either direction, creating a transient imbalance. In the case of the depressed individual, for example, expecting him or her to be fully responsible from the start of treatment may be an unrealistic expectation since problems with attributions of responsibility are a central feature of depression. Simply stated, the clinician's role is likely to be a more active one in hypnotic and strategic treatment of the depressed individual than if one were working in other modalities. The careful assessment of client patterns of experience and underlying dynamics are the early manifestations of this responsibility. Assessing the optimal sequence of interventions, including those presented here, is the overriding responsibility in planning treatment. Presenting an intervention before (or after) the client is fully ready to absorb its implications is a mistiming that may cause the client to miss the therapeutic point. Timing the presentation of interventions according to the stage of resolution the client is in is a significant part of applying these patterns meaningfully.

With an awareness of typical personality patterns and dynamics associated with depression, it is apparent that there are many dimensions of the disorder that may be addressed in treatment. It is literally impossible to address every aspect of depression with an intervention, and so the interventions presented here will be focused on resolving some of the more common dysfunctional patterns underlying depression. These include self limiting perceptions relating to issues of personal responsibility, blame, and perceived locus of control.

While family therapy can be effectively utilized in the treatment of depression, in many situations such approaches may be impractical. For this reason, the patterns in this paper are generally discussed in the context of individual psychotherapy. Strategies involving the formal use of hypnosis are discussed in the section on "hypnotic approaches," while strategies using hypnosis informally in conjunction with other directive approaches are described in the section on "strategic approaches."

Approaches Utilizing Hypnosis

Hypnotic approaches may be used symptomatically or dynamically (Yapko, 1984a). Dynamic approaches, i.e., those that address both the symptom and underlying causes, are generally more intensive and are thus more likely to accomplish a fuller resolution of client problems, but more superficial approaches can be used with some success in the treatment of depression.

Depression, at the intrapersonal level, is an inwardly focused and subjectively uncomfortable experience, and often the client is only painfully aware of what seems to be a useless set of symptoms. Depression is not the inactive state it may superficially seem to be to the casual observer. It is a state of ongoing internal agitation and discomfort, involving anxiety and perseveration of negative feelings and thoughts. Hypnosis aimed at symptom removal can serve as a "pattern interruption" intervention, and can also serve as an opportunity for "reframing" (Erickson & Rossi, 1979).

Non-Dynamic Approaches

1. Pattern Interruption. Pattern interruption through hypnosis may be accomplished simply through attainment of relaxation via the induction and general suggestions for relief. Given the generalized anxiety and negatively skewed cognitive distortions of the depressed condition, even the simplest of inductions and therapeutic suggestions can have a beneficial effect.

The negative patterns are interrupted by facilitating relaxation and focusing the individual on positive possibilities. The implicit messages to the depressed individual are that a change in experience is possible, that he or she has the ability to relax, think positively, and access positive resources from within (thus interrupting the pattern of negative self-perception that often precludes a recognition of positive personal resources).

Pattern interruption through relaxation and positive input can disrupt the anxiety spiral and allow for the building of self-management skills with self-hypnosis (Lankton & Lankton, 1983), a self-relaxation and self-management process. The effect can be to allow for better sleep and a return to other more normal vegetative functions. Less internal discomfort can alleviate the depressed person's reliance on self-abusive coping patterns involving excessive alcohol, tranquilizers, food, and the like. Discovering one's ability to relax and feel good naturally can have a profound impact on *any* individual, and this is especially true of individuals experiencing depression.

2. Reframing. Reframing through hypnosis may address the client's attitude about his or her experience of depression. Typically, the client views the depression as utterly useless: when viewed in this way, the individual blames him or herself for having the problem, and for having no ability to control it. This naturally compounds the depression. Herein lies the opportunity for reframing. To reframe seemingly useless depression as a "warning signal that paves the way for an opportunity to change" allows the client to attach positive meaning to a negative experience, altering the person's experience. In fact, depression *is* a warning signal that something is out of balance in the person's world.

Depression may signal a need to redefine a relationship, rethink a decision, alter a thought, feeling or behavior pattern, or change in other ways. Depression is also a natural and healthy outlet for grief and other significant stresses. Reframing depression as a natural and even potentially positive experience can diminish or even eliminate self-blame for the condition. Suggestions for symptom relief and positive lifestyle changes round out the symptomatic approaches.

3. Symptom Substitution. Symptom substitution is a third possible pattern of intervention when applying hypnosis for symptom relief. In circumstances where the depression is secondary to serious physical illness (e.g., terminal cancer) and the prognosis is negative, or in circumstances where the depressed individual is somehow unavailable for or unlikely to benefit from more intensive treatment, symptom substitution as a deliberate strategy may be employed. Often the depressed individual somaticizes the symptoms of depression; somatic complaints are more concrete, have more clearly identifiable parameters, and are generally inter- and intrapersonally more acceptable (Suinn, 1984).

Symptom substitution as a strategy may involve the controlled transformation of the emotional pain of depression into an acceptable physical pain, i.e., one that is mild, tolerable, and not disabling. Such a strategy of symptom substitution was described by Erickson (1954a). Somatic complaints where depression is the underlying feature are spontaneous and uncontrolled manifestations of this same process. The key to using this strategy lies in the controlled nature of choosing the site of symptom substitution, thus providing recognition at *some* level of an ability to control the symptom.

Dynamic Approaches

Applying patterns of hypnosis to address the underlying dynamics of the individual's depression is a more demanding and comprehensive means of treatment. A number of hypnotic strategies may be utilized in the course of such treatment, involving various configurations of age regression, age progression, amnesia, catalepsy, dissociation, positive and negative hallucinations, hypermnesia, ideodynamic responses, sensory alteration, and time distortion.

1. Age Regression. Regression is a most common vehicle for intervening therapeutically. It seems apparent that learned patterns provide the framework for the depression. Age regression strategies may involve the accessing of positive resources from the past to incorporate into current and future contexts, a pattern well described elsewhere (Lankton & Lankton, 1983; Bandler & Grinder, 1979, 1981).

Age regression may further involve guiding the client experientially through revivification (Yapko, 1984a) to relive past episodes in which negative generalizations (i.e., Beck et als.' (1979) cognitive distortions) were made. In general, the purpose of the technique is to alter the internal representation of the experience, i.e., the way the memory was incorporated as well as the conclusions drawn from it. In other words, the memory is "reworked" in order to reach new, more adaptive conclusions. The "reworking" may come about from any or all of the following: uncovering repressed memories, providing emotional release, shifting the person's focus from one dimension of the memory to another, helping the person organize present or desired personal resources to use effectively in past experiences, (e.g., controlling an uncontrollable event), and using techniques of cognitive restructuring (Beck et al., 1979; Beck, 1983) amplified in power due to the presence of the trance state. Once the memory has been reworked or reframed in this type of "critical incident process" (Yapko, 1984a) where significant events are re-experienced and therapeutically resolved, the new positive feelings and thoughts related to the memory and to the related dimensions of self-image can be "brought back" and integrated with current modes of functioning.

Another dynamic process involving age regression that is effective and versatile is the technique of "changing personal history," (Bandler & Grinder, 1981) involving some patterns similar to those of the "critical incident process" just described. Changing personal history involves guiding the hypnotized client back to earliest memory and providing a structured set of life experiences that unfold over time to "live and learn from." The kinds of experiences to be structured for the individual are those that can provide positive generalizations about one's self and one's life.

The client is encouraged to experience the suggested scenarios fully, and to use all the dimensions of each scenario to its fullest, most positive extent (Lankton & Lankton, 1983). Through a disorientation for time passage, the client can have months or years of experience in a single trance session. Thus, the person can have moving experiences of having the parent that was lost in youth, having significant interactions with others that enhance a strong, positive self-esteem, and so forth.

In order to fully allow for the positive learnings to generalize from the trance experiences to the rest of the individual's life, multiple sessions of changing personal history may be used in conjunction with ample utilization of post-hypnotic suggestions concerning ways "these positive memories can be the framework for which current and future choices can be made, for all people use their past learnings to guide their choices." Such a truism allows the suggestion to be more easily incorporated. Amnesia may be selectively utilized to repress specific details of the instilled memories while allowing the positive generalizations derived from them to assume an active role in guiding the person's ongoing experience (Erickson & Rossi, 1979).

2. Age Progression. Age progression can be used dynamically in the utilization of hypnotic approaches for depression. A conceptually simple goal is to provide a means for building positive expectations for the future. The hypnotized client is encouraged to experience positive future consequences arising from changes and decisions being made currently. Concurrently, the client can be dissociated from the effects of negative past experiences, making future choices on the basis of current awareness, not negative history.

As with the regression processes, the client is encouraged to fully experience the scenarios and reap the benefits of having taken active and effective steps in his or her own behalf. Thus, generalizations that only the passage of time would make available to the client can be obtained through trance sessions involving age progression, allowing the client to experience a higher degree of confidence that current efforts are worthwhile.

The benefit is not simply the enjoyment of a higher level of confidence, but includes the willingness to actively progress; after all, negative expectation has an immobilizing effect—"Why bother if it's not going to do any good?" Age progression provides an experiential reference point for the belief that making necessary changes *will* do some good.

A second age progression strategy involves orienting the client to the negative consequences of continuing current patterns, i.e., experiencing the effects of remaining ambivalent or immobilized regarding self-help decisions. Considering the degree of ambivalence in the depressed individual, hypnotically facilitating a concrete experience of the negative patterns can provide the client with the momentum needed in order to make positive decisions. Age progression can move distant expectations into the realm of immediate experience. The effect is not unlike Haley's "encouraging the worse alternative" strategy (1973).

A third treatment strategy utilizing age progression is Erickson's "pseudo-orientation in time" (Erickson, 1954b). Through use of dissociation and amnesia, the client is guided experientially into a future context to be experienced as present reality wherein he or she can assess the quality of life, reflect on the changes successfully undergone recently to improve the quality of life, and describe what the stimuli for those changes were. Essentially, the client is providing information regarding the learnings necessary to effect meaningful change and how to facilitate them. The clinician may use this information skillfully to guide the client into scenarios where such learnings may be acquired.

Dissociative patterns of hypnosis are part of the above processes, but a more pure form of dissociation may be effective in addressing dimensions of depression. For example, in the case of one depressed client, suggestions were offered to acknowledge her split feelings and split awarenesses, regarding her situation. It was suggested that she acknowledge a part of her that is characterized as "negative" and simultaneously acknowledge a part of her that is characterized as "positive." Each part could be thought of as occupying its own place within her, each with its own unique set of characteristics.

Suggestions were given to concretize these parts, giving them each a place within her on the basis of how accessible she wanted that part to be regardless of past patterns. Positively motivated, she chose to have her dominant side be positive and her nondominant side be negative. She was encouraged to internally dissociate one side from the other, and listen to (i.e., auditorily hallucinate) each side's interpretation of events before reacting.

Suggestions were given about the ability to selectively choose positive or negative interpretations based on what would be most adaptive for the situation and what would be most subjectively pleasing. Experiences were provided hypnotically to deepen the awareness of the positive side's potential influence. Positive interpretations of experience had never had "a voice in matters" before, and as the client became able to respond to her positive side appropriately, her experience of depression lifted. The pattern is structurally similar to the distorted focus on the exclusively negative aspects of experience typical of depression, but the focus is now shifted to positive dimensions of experience to create a more balanced approach to life (since no one's life is good or bad *all* the time).

3. Therapeutic Metaphors. A final hypnotic approach that may be used to facilitate recovery from depression involves the use of therapeutic metaphors. Metaphors delivered to the client in trance are able to address the multiple levels of client experience in potentially useful ways. Zeig (1980a) described the practical capacities of metaphors in diagnosis, establishing rapport, making and illustrating a point, suggesting solutions, getting clients to recognize themselves, seeding ideas and increasing motivation, decreasing resistance, and so forth. Lankton & Lankton (1983) elaborated upon the widespread applicability of metaphors, and provided comprehensive guidelines for their construction and delivery. Gordon (1978) and Rosen (1982) also described considerations for the skilled use of metaphors in the treatment process.

Metaphors in the treatment of depression must be carefully designed and delivered keeping in mind the clients' unique world views and range of personal experience. Metaphors often involve the use of other people (past clients, family members, and others significant in one's range of personal experiences) with whom the client can identify and learn from. Metaphors that simply describe other individuals with similar problems who achieved positive results may indirectly suggest the possibility of recovery from depression. These metaphorical suggestions may not be accepted, however, if the client's frame of reference is one of personal helplessness, i.e., "others may succeed but I know *I* can't." Metaphorical intervention such as the use of case histories help therapists keep in mind the powerful nature of one's world view in its ability to maintain current patterns, even dysfunctional ones.

When metaphors take into account clients' principal sources of resistance, they can build positive expectancy and seed ideas about specific changes. These, in turn, can be reinforced with post-hypnotic suggestions. Metaphors to build expectancy can be used in the earliest stages of treatment to simply match the person's experience of helplessness and hopelessness. Introducing positive possibilities may be done at this time, but only selectively. Metaphors that involve past experiences of the client in which he or she was able to succeed under difficult or uncertain conditions are generally quite useful.

Converging ideas in a non-metaphoric manner may place too much emphasis on the positive possibilities a client "should" consider and may lead a client to suspect that the clinician does not fully appreciate the intensity of his or her pain. This error is most obvious in interventions such as the one characterized in the following exchange.

Client: I'm so depressed. I don't know why, but nothing seems to matter anymore.

Clinician: Well, what do you have to be depressed about? You have a good life. You have a loving husband who cares for you, three beautiful, healthy kids that are doing well, you have a nice home, nice cars, your health which is most important of all, and. . . .

The above example of contradicting the client's reality predictably will have no impact on the client's depression, and may even compound it by causing the individual to blame him or herself for having the audacity to be depressed when everything should be going well. Metaphors that do adequately accept the client's reality are likely to have therapeutic impact. Thus, using the same example as above, a useful metaphor might begin with:

. . . I worked with another client once who was so unhappy with her life, and she didn't know why . . . on the surface, everything seemed alright in her life . . . she had a nice family, nice possessions, a nice life . . . but she knew that there was something deeper that needed to be addressed . . . and she wasn't sure just what it was . . . not yet . . . but she did know that people can change . . . and that she was someone who could change . . . even though she didn't know how . . . just yet . . . and she was so unsure at first . . . and she had every right to be . . . and her feelings were so uncomfortable to her . . . it seems no one's depression is more uncomfortable than one's own. . . .

In this example, the emphasis is on building rapport through the matching of realities and only brief mention in the form of a truism is made regarding the possibility of change, seeding the idea to be returned to at a later time.

When the relationship with the client is progressing to the point of shifting from matching realities to facilitating new perspectives (Bandler & Grinder, 1979), therapeutic metaphors may be utilized that emphasize the reframing of experience in positive ways, asserting control or abandoning futile attempts to control, accepting or rejecting responsibility and blame, and developing a more flexible and adaptive way of dealing with the experiences of one's life. Metaphors that Erickson used to illustrate the principle of "take charge of your life" are found in Rosen (1982), and other metaphors more generally addressing changes related directly or indirectly to depression can be found in Haley (1973), Lankton & Lankton (1983), and Erickson & Rossi (1979).

Other metaphors may involve descriptions of the various psychosocial models of depression (e.g., Seligman's "learned helplessness" [1973, 1974, 1975, 1983]) and the interesting research leading to their formulations, as well as nonfiction examples (from past clients or elsewhere) of contexts in which these variables are evident. Examples of effective resolution of these variables can be offered. Metaphors may also be derived from the client's own personal history, reviewing and emphasizing past experiences of transforming ignorance to knowledge, weakness to strength, fear to confidence, and so forth. The early learning sets that Erickson used (Zeig, 1980a) in his teachings were representative of this type of approach, emphasizing one's ability to learn from experience and outgrow old limitations. The implicit message is, "You have all the necessary resources to change." Metaphors are a skillful way of making such resources available to the client, an especially important goal for the client experiencing depression.

Hypnotherapeutic Approaches

The utilization of hypnotic patterns in the treatment of depression seems a most fitting style of intervention. The constricted sense of reality typically present in the depressed client is more accessible to the clinician's interventions in the trance state (Watzlawick, 1978). Hypnosis affords the clinician the opportunity to deal with the client on multiple levels simultaneously (Zeig, 1980a; Yapko, 1984a); in the case of depression, this multiple level style of intervention is especially important.

As a final point of interest, Erickson (1980) described another possible use of hypnosis related to depression:

> . . . should it be desired to make a study of the effects of a state of affective depression upon behavior in general, hypnotic subjects can be placed in a state of profound depression which will serve to govern their conduct in any number of ways. At the same time this depression can be removed and direct contrast made between depressed behavior and normal behavior . . . (p. 10)

From this statement, it is apparent that Erickson recognized the subjective nature of depression, as well as the responsiveness of depressed individuals to the utilization of hypnosis. The hypnotic patterns described in this section are practical approaches derived from these recognitions.

Strategic Approaches

Strategic approaches to the treatment of depression may include the use of behavioral directives. Such directives actively engage the client in an experience that becomes a context for learning something deemed fundamental to recovery. Simply stated, the client is guided into a situation where a high probability exists that he or she will experientially discover a personal resource or valuable concept that will facilitate recovery from depression. (Post-hypnotic suggestions to build an association between a learning and a specific context can better assure such outcomes).

The emphasis in creating effective strategies is on the client's *experiential* discovery of the significant learning. It is often not enough to simply have the client in a "normal" waking state imagine the experience (thereby restricting the experience to a primarily cognitive level and possibly increasing "intellectualization"). The world is experienced on two levels: the *empirical* (sensory-based) and the *symbolic* (the way sensory experience is organized, stored and communicated). Verbal psychotherapies operate primarily on the symbolic level, yet it is the empirical level that is the target of therapeutic intervention.

By employing strategic interventions that bring salient features of the depression (i.e., depressive thoughts, feelings, or behaviors) into play, but in a way that somehow demands they be altered, it is possible to surpass the usual limits of one's subjective experience. These types of strategic intervention are perhaps best used to rapidly and effectively resolve the impasses that so often arise in the push for therapeutic progress.

Strategic interventions can take a variety of forms, including symptom prescriptions, ordeal therapies, behavioral prescriptions or "homework assignments," double-binds, the utilization of resistance, and other patterns the clinician actively promotes. These patterns are described in detail elsewhere (see Haley, 1973, 1984; Watzlawick, 1978; Zeig, 1980a, 1982; Lankton & Lankton, 1983).

Discussed earlier in this paper was the recognition that although there are numerous ways to conceptualize or characterize depression, three interrelated core dynamics are apparent. They are: 1) a distorted sense of personal responsibility; 2) a distorted pattern of blame related to on-going experience; and 3) a distorted sense of control. How someone manages these three constructs has an exceptionally profound impact on the range of choices available to the individual. The personality, subjective reality, and all that is encompassed by these two terms are overwhelmingly determined by how one perceive's one's own experience. Thus, these three variables can serve as the framework for creating and utilizing strategic interventions. In the sections that follow, each variable and other important variables related to it will be discussed. For the sake of relevance and clarity, strategic interventions that address these variables will be presented throughout.

Personal Responsibility

The distorted sense of personal responsibility that is common among depressed individuals is evident in the tendency (however mild or extreme) to assume either too little or too much responsibility for ongoing experience. The depressed client who consistently views him or herself as a victim of others' sensitivity (i.e., lack of consideration for his or her needs and wants, however covert they may be) is clearly not sufficiently responsible for the events taking place in the relationship. Typically, the person's self-esteem is so poor that he or she is afraid to express feelings, make realistic demands (i.e., set limits), or even disagree with another person out of fear the other person will leave.

In such instances, the client is under-responsible by not being a full half of the relationship. Self-negation is the core in what has been aptly described by Satir (1972) as the "placater" personality style. In such cases, behavioral prescriptions may be effectively used, providing the clinician senses an undercurrent of frustration, anger, and resistance to placating within the client (i.e., passive-aggressiveness, a common feature of depression). If no such undercurrent is perceived, and no rebellion is likely to occur, the use of such prescriptions is not generally indicated.

Behavioral prescriptions may be used to amplify the tendencies of the under-responsible individual to the point where he or she can simply no longer continue on in such an obviously self-defeating way. Ideally, the client will rebel by responsibly asserting his or her individual rights. For example, in the case of the depressed person who self-critically exclaims, "I have no right to feel this way . . . ," the clinician might demand that the client with a sense of inadequate justification *justify everything he or she does* by giving the prescription that the client give at least three rationales for all activities engaged in (e.g., why I wear these clothes, why I drove home this way, why I chose these foods for lunch, and so forth). This prescription is intended to facilitate the more self-determined recognition that "The mere fact that I feel this way is justification enough." Such self-determination and self-acceptance can enhance the depressed individual's impoverished self-esteem.

A second behavioral prescription may be focused on another dimension of this same pattern: the need for approval. The client may be directed to *ask for permission* to do whatever he or she would like to do (e.g., would it be alright if I went to the bathroom now? Can I get myself a drink of water? Is it alright that I wear these clothes?). This prescription is intended to promote the recognition that "I can do as I wish." Thus, the cycle of self-sacrifice to get other's approval can give way to a pattern of self-approval.

A third behavioral prescription may also be used to address a dynamic that is commonly underlying the tendency to be under-responsible: the fear of making a mistake and visibly being responsible for it. Prescribing that the client *deliberately plan and execute a specified number of mistakes each day* can have the effect of teaching the client that making mistakes is not horrendously unnatural nor is it necessarily catastrophic. Watzlawick (1978, pp. 136-7) described this very intervention in one of his case presentations. Frankl (Davison & Neale, 1982) further described patterns of "paradoxical intention" that are structurally similar.

In each of the above behavioral prescriptions, the client is instructed to carry out a behavior that is a distilled and exaggerated form of a dysfunctional pattern evident in his or her lifestyle. The goal in assigning such behaviors is to mobilize a rejecting attitude against irresponsibly denying oneself in order to gain another's approval. Mobilizing resistance in this way can help build self-esteem, increase recognition of personal choice, establish the validity of one's own preferences, and decrease dependency on others' reactions as the guiding force for one's actions. Assertiveness-training exercises are useful for similar reasons.

In the case of the *over-responsible* individual, the person has created the dysfunctional illusion of responsibility for all the things that go on around him or her. It is unfortunate that the issue of over-responsibility is often fostered in awareness groups that promote the idea that "whatever goes on around you is a reflection of you; you created all of your circumstances." Since this is true only in part, behavioral prescriptions may be used to drive home the point that one cannot be responsible for *everything*. For example, a client may be instructed to clip out newspaper or magazine articles of tragedies (e.g., earthquakes, floods, plane crashes) and give at least three rationales for *how he or she directly or indirectly caused that to happen.*

Over time, the recognition can be encouraged that there are some things one would like to control, but cannot. This seems easy to understand, yet even mental health professionals are notoriously bad at avoiding over-responsibility in relation to their clients, resulting in a high rate of depression, suicide, and substance abuse within the profession (Laliotis & Grayson, 1985). One can easily understand how difficult resolving this issue must be for the layperson when even professionals are unclear about it. Setting the client up to experientially discover the limits of his or her responsibility can be very therapeutic.

Resolving the ambiguity about what one is and is not responsible for is a vital part of the overall treatment of depression. Certainly, a key symptom of depression associated with this issue of responsibility is the excessive guilt suffered by depressed individuals. Does guilt not presuppose responsibility? In a significant number of instances, the depressed client will miss opportunities to help him or herself because of the over-responsibility associated with guilt.

An example of this is a 26-year-old woman who consulted the author for treatment of depression. She knew what she wanted and needed to do to help herself, but could not because of paralyzing guilt. She wanted to move out of her parents' home and live independently, but she was afraid "it will kill my parents."

In another instance of over-responsibility, a woman seen by the author presented the complaint of depression manifesting itself in instances where she saw others' misfortunes. She would literally burst into tears if she saw a motorist on the side of the road with a flat tire, so diffuse were her personal boundaries.

In both examples, the clients were personalizing responsibility for situations or people they *could* not be responsible for. Feeling responsible for the actions, thoughts, and feelings of another person is a precursor to guilt, causes excessive stress, and has the indirect effect of encouraging others to not be responsible for themselves (which is what continues the common pattern of an over-responsible person in a relationship with an under-responsible person). The consequences include dependency, poor self-esteem, negative expectations, anger, and other depressive symptoms.

A behavioral prescription that may be employed in addressing the social level of depression relative to responsibility is to direct the partners in a close relationship to conduct an extensive "trust walk." This approach can be useful when responsibility is unevenly distributed between the partners. Person A is blindfolded and led around by person B who is totally responsible for A's guidance, a condition that gets very tiresome very quickly. Continuing on past the point of fatigue with the exercise creates a powerful and easily referenced memory of the burden of over-responsibility as well as the burden of under-responsibility. Both parties may play both roles, the role opposite their role in the relationship, or the role that parallels their role in the relationship. There is something valuable to be learned from each vantage point.

Patterns of Blame

Zeig (personal communication, 1984) described one dimension of client patterns worthy of assessment as "intrapunitive vs. extrapunitive," referring to one's tendency to blame and punish oneself vs. others. All people necessarily make attributions of responsibility for their subjective experiences, attributing the event's etiology first to an internal or external cause, and then to a more specific source of responsibility for that event.

When one assumes little or no responsibility for one's own thoughts, actions, or behaviors, one becomes extrapunitive, i.e., blames others for one's own circumstances. Recognition of responsibility for one's own choices is marginal in such instances. When one assumes too much responsibility, the tendency is to become intrapunitive, i.e., blaming oneself for one's inability to make everything alright, regardless of whether or not the power objectively exists to do so.

Attribution of blame for one's circumstances is a variable that takes different forms in the instance of depression. Certainly the concept of "learned helplessness" (specifically "personal helplessness") is relevant here, an instance where one blames uncontrollable external events for one's depressed condition. The model of depression involving "anger turned inward" also addresses the issue of blame, from the perspective of blaming oneself for the frustrations and inequities of life.

Behavioral prescriptions involving dynamics of blame may be used to shift the burden of responsibility for an event to where it belongs. For example, with one inappropriately self-blaming member of a couple seeking treatment, the author instructed the wife to make a list of 10 significant negative historical events occurring prior to her birth. She was told to attempt to convince her husband that she was to blame for these events (such as Lincoln's assassination), and to be as convincing as possible in her admission of guilt. The effect was dramatic. So easily could the woman be to blame for ongoing events that she shocked herself with how guilty she could feel about events occurring long before her birth!

In a related prescription reversing the pattern, the client may be asked to make a list of personal accomplishments, and then deny having anything to do with any of them. In a variation of this pattern, the client can be instructed to carry out assigned behaviors, and then immediately offer excuses for the outcome of those behaviors (i.e., "well, the lighting was bad, and I hadn't had lunch, and I had a hangnail, and mom always liked my brother better, and . . ."). In the use of such seemingly lighthearted interventions, the issue of ascribing blame comes to the fore and a "placater" or "blamer" (Satir, 1972) may for the first time get a glimpse of him or herself long enough to interrupt the pattern.

In a symptom prescription strategy, the other-blaming client may be told to blame others—constantly. Rather than risking whatever social life the individual might have, the client is instructed to "blame out loud" for specified periods of time when others are not around. For example, when driving alone, the client may be told to loudly "curse everything and everyone for not doing things the right way." The client is encouraged to blame others for being so stupid as to drive a different make and color car, or for being young or old, or for putting a building in a particular spot, and on and on. Maintaining the hostile, blaming demeanor soon gets very tiresome.

In another example of a symptom prescription of sorts, a 57-year-old seriously depressed woman who had just suffered the loss of her husband of 35 years presented herself to the author for treatment. Since his death, she had not left her home, terrified to emerge as an independent adult. She had been married to the "perfect husband who took care of me completely." She had never had to fill her own car with gas, had never had to make a bank deposit, never had to do many of the errands most people do routinely. Her over-responsible husband's death left her totally unable to manage her own life independently—he had, in effect, killed her with kindness.

In an early stage of treatment, the client was encouraged to express her resentment about his death and to bitterly blame him for dying. Quite emotionally, she did so. Somewhere in the midst of her hurling blame at him, it dawned on her that "it probably wasn't his idea to die . . ." Encouraging the blame allowed her to stop the blaming and begin working on her acquiring the skills necessary to live life competently.

Self-blame is not unlike the self-sacrifice of martyrdom that can clearly have a manipulative quality in its implicit message that "I'll be the scapegoat so you don't have to bear the burden of guilt . . . and what will you do for me?" When such a pattern is observed by the clinician, prescribing episodes of martyrdom can be utilized. Placing the client's body in a position of someone on a crucifix while moaning, "After all I've done for you, how can you do this to me?" with relevant personal examples can afford one a lighter glimpse at a serious pattern.

A prescription in which family members are instructed to continually blame the self-blaming client for whatever happens (e.g., rain, unemployment figures, a damaged wheat crop) can mobilize that person's resistance and lead him or her to assert blamelessness. Such assertion is a necessary step in recognizing the limits of one's responsibility; such lines are so often blurred when depression is present. In an example of this type of pattern, an attorney in his mid-40s who was quite successful despite a chronic, moderate depression was made the "scapegoat" for the family. He was all too experienced with being blamed for things, based on his having very critical, rejecting parents. This was a pattern his family continued to carry out. Absurd blaming statements heaped on him by his family were to be met only with the reply, "Please forive me."

After a few days of experiencing this prescription that everyone initially found amusing, the client became enraged and firmly declared his inability to experience any more blame for anyone unless he either first acknowledged the blame as properly his or else was approached in a more neutral "Let's talk about it" sort of manner. This was the start of a considerably more functional way of managing the issue of blame and all the related self-esteem factors.

A common reframing method that addresses the issue of blame is the often-quoted philosophy commonly related to Ericksonian approaches: the client is always making the best choices he or she has, given the range of available resources (Bandler & Grinder, 1979; Lankton, 1980). An "error" becomes "the best choice available."

An ordeal that deliberately involves self-punishment in one form or another whenever blame is inappropriately ascribed may be a useful intervention. For example, Haley (1984) described a depressed man who was told to either find a job within a week or shave off his highly prized mustache. Blame for prior lack of ambition to work was an issue bypassed when the ordeal succeeded. Demanding that clients perform tasks that are more arduous than letting go of their symptoms can be a viable therapeutic strategy. In such instances, dealing directly with the blame for the situation is unnecessary in order to obtain a therapeutic result. However, caution is advised in the use of such ordeal strategies, for although the presenting problem may be ingeniously resolved, the client may not learn how to generalize appropriate management of blame to other contexts (Yapko, 1983).

The Locus of Control

The author has repeatedly observed in his depressed clients a confusion relative to the issue of "control." Specifically, the depressed individual is lacking clarity in his or her ability to determine what is and what is not within the range of meaningful influence (Phares, 1984; Seligman, 1973, 1974, 1975). Consequently, either the person attempts to exert control over events that are objectively uncontrollable (e.g., a traffic jam at rush hour), or the individual makes no apparent attempt to control events that are objectively controllable (e.g., seeking new employment when the current work situation is somehow detrimental). When the issue of control is one that is muddled for the client, interventions may be designed to promote a refined awareness for the distinctions between controllable and uncontrollable events. With such an awareness, the client can be prevented from assuming a position of "personal helplessness" both by recognizing a wider variety of conditions of "universal helplessness" and by empowering him- or herself to effectively deal with situations perceived as controllable.

In many instances, depression is a reaction to discovering the uncontrollable nature of something important to the person. In one woman the author treated, the presenting complaint of depression was in large part a reaction to her son's refusal to attend medical school, so set on his being a physician was she. Clearly, she was attempting to control her son, whom she could not control, since he was making competent decisions on his own. Therapy involved developing acceptance for his ability to decide what his own life should be about, and began with the reframing: "How wonderful a mother you must have been in raising him to have him turn out so clear about who he is and what he wants." She had not yet seen it that way, and this guiding perspective made the rest of our work considerably easier.

Behavioral prescriptions may be used to amplify the distorted nature of the depressed individual's thought that "I should be able to control this" when it exists in reference to something perceived by the clinician as objectively uncontrollable. When the issue of control has been discussed to whatever extent is desirable with a given individual, the client may be directed to attempt to deliberately exert control over something already recognized as universally uncontrollable, such as the weather, the outcome of a sporting event, or some other such event. The client can be encouraged to use whatever methods he or she chooses (desperate pleas, etc.) to influence the outcome, acting "as if" it could make a difference. Such a role-play has had the effect with many clients of bringing true feelings of frustration and anger to the surface that had lain dormant, providing the opportunity for therapeutic resolution.

In a related assignment, the client may be directed to carefully observe the techniques of skilled manipulators who attempt to influence the thoughts, feelings and behaviors of others. The television evangelist has been a favorite example used by the author. The typical, forcefully stated presuppositions of moral righteousness mixed with techniques of manipulation involving fear and guilt are used to attempt to gain control of the lives of others. By actively and critically viewing the evangelist's use of negative manipulation tactics, the client may externalize (i.e., see as if outside oneself) his or her similar patterns and thus dissociate from them.

Simply stated, the internal emotional havoc related to depression that arises from trying to control uncontrollable events comes from the focus on one's anger, guilt, emotional distance, disappointment, and other feelings that are typically other-directed. The above example of the depressed mother is a typical example of intense anger and disappointment being focused on her son, who, if he had been a less secure young man, might have felt guilty for his mother's reaction and then complied with her wishes.

"Instrumental depression" is a term coined by the author to describe episodes of depression where its manipulative value is a key feature of its onset. In this case, the mother was encouraged to actively view the evangelists and their techniques for getting compliance with no regard for the emotional price (in guilt and fear) paid by those who comply. This "get me what I want at any cost" pattern violates the most basic of assumptions about personal integrity associated with Ericksonian approaches. Respecting another person's choice, even if contrary to one's own, is considered mandatory. The net effect on the woman, in combination with the reframing described earlier, was to promote a comfortable recognition that people can be allowed to make their own best choices for themselves. Presupposing that one is better able to judge what is good for someone than that individual is able to do for him or herself is a pattern highly likely to lead to power struggles one cannot win.

To make the point even more overt, the therapist may direct the client to choose an unimportant issue to "crusade" about for a specified amount of time. The rejecting or indifferent attitudes encountered relative to even an unimportant issue can teach the client experientially how attempting to control others' thoughts, feelings and actions is wasted energy.

Each of the strategies described thus far is intended to drive home the point that one cannot control others, and that the sooner one learns that, the sooner one will end the spiral involving anger, frustration, and depression. Further intervention can be focused on helping the client to generalize the recognition of the uncontrollable nature of people to the uncontrollable nature of other specific events.

The other side of this issue concerns the problem of not controlling things that *are* controllable. The "learned helplessness" model of Seligman (1973, 1975, 1978) suggests a gradual behavioral shaping strategy in dealing with depressed individuals evidencing this dynamic. Designing a series of tasks that can be successfully accomplished can build a positive momentum toward establishing the generalization that one can set a goal and actively progress toward its accomplishment.

Symptom prescriptions may be effectively used to facilitate an awareness for the controllability of seemingly uncontrollable experiences. For example, prescribing the symptom of depression by establishing a scheduled "depression time" can allow the client to deliberately and masterfully create the experience instead of being its passive victim. Similarly, prescribing that the client "be passive," "be whiney," "be negative," and so forth for specified and inconvenient periods of time can mobilize a considerable resistance to having those experiences.

Prescribing helplessness, in particular, can mobilize the "I'm *not* helpless" discovery. For example, the client can be encouraged to ask for direction to do things and go places already well known to him or her.

The effect can be to mobilize the feeling of "Why should I wait for directions to do what I know I can do?" Encouraging the client to passively wait for things to be done for him or her can also mobilize the frustration of waiting for others and point the way to an independent solution. In one behavioral prescription, for example, a client was instructed to wait for others to open all doors for her, including her doors at home (even though she lived alone!). If, after two minutes, no one helped her, only then could she open it for herself. She had progressively stronger reactions during the many two-minute periods of passive waiting that followed, and when the negative reaction to passivity became very intense after several days, she developed a strong awareness of ways she had been passive to a fault. This awareness became an excellent resource for later sessions that emphasized taking greater control over one's experience.

Any strategy that turns the depressing paralysis of ambivalence in a positive direction will also facilitate the recognition of one's ability to make decisions on one's own behalf. Ambivalence is conceptualized by the author as an overt manifestation of not controlling the controllable. The "approach-avoidance" conflict describes ambivalence in part, but clinical experience leads the author to believe that the client is *not* so genuinely mixed in feeling as much as he or she is fearful of committing to a course of action. The client knows what he or she wants, but does not sense the power or the right to have it.

Erickson's strategy of "encouraging the worse alternative" (Haley, 1973) is a good one to get movement in an otherwise motionless client's decision-making process. By encouraging the alternative least desirable to the client unable or unwilling to make a decision, the client's resistance to that directive encourages movement in the direction of the other, better alternative. Use of metaphors that illustrate the "He who hesitates is lost" truism (e.g., stories of missed opportunities arising from indecision) can also encourage making the transition from passive to active in one's own behalf.

Recreational approaches that encourage the depressed client to do enjoyable things are behavioral prescriptions that can lead the client to discover important insights. Such recreational therapy approaches make the point that "if you don't do things you enjoy doing, how can you expect to ever feel good?" Furthermore, the client discovers a self-controlled and reliable way to "get outside of oneself" (out of the depressive internal focus), a shift which can have great therapeutic value. Giving the behavioral assignment to list 20 or 30 enjoyable recreational activities can help the client organize a concrete list to refer to for things to do during periods of depression when anhedonia and apathy are otherwise likely to set in. Recreational activities mobilize positive energy, demand involvement, relieve stress, and give one mastery over one's own time. The key to addressing "helplessness" is to gently force the client to contradict his or her depressive generalizations, and to provide new positive stimuli in order to build greater recognition of the ever present range of personal choices one can make in one's own best interest.

Contraindications

Due to the serious nature of depression, particularly the potential for suicide, the various hypnotic and strategic interventions described in this chapter must be chosen and utilized with careful attention to the individual client's nature. Many of the patterns presented here have been intended to mobilize the resistance of a client against his or her own depression-maintaining patterns or to the demands of the clinician. Such patterns presuppose the existence of such resistance in the individual. However, clinicians *cannot* assume the presence of such resistance. Depending on the individual, the resistance may be too weak, or too deeply buried beneath depressive patterns to be effectively mobilized. In many instances, extensive supportive psychotherapy is indicated before such interventions as those described here may be effectively used. If the timing of these interventions is misjudged, these interventions can actually be anti-therapeutic. For example, in a hospital setting the author observed a psychotherapist attempt a provocative "aggression training" therapy on a depressed patient. In such an approach, the concept of depression as "anger-turned-inward" is the framework for the intervention, and the intervention attempts to so anger a patient that he or she will turn the anger outward again, and blow up angrily, with a therapeutic effect.

In this case, the clinician demanded that the patient scrub the hallway with a toothbrush. After several hours of the patient's scrubbing on hands and knees, the clinician returned and began to defiantly and deliberately scuff the scrubbed floor with his heels. Instead of the patient getting angry, he simply sighed and further withdrew. The intervention obviously was inappropriate for that patient, a destructive miscalculation on the part of the therapist. If there is any doubt as to the likelihood of an intervention being appropriate for a depressed client, then it is more conservative and respectful to not use such interventions.

Summary

As the stresses of peoples' more and more complicated lives continue to increase, it is predictable that episodes of depression will increase as well. Depression distorts perceptions and so negatively skews the direction of one's life that it may be the most insidious of all disorders. The threat of suicide is everpresent in working with depressed clients. Suicide has been called "the permanent solution to temporary problems;" the threat of suicide, as well as the deep pain of depression, necessitates the development of a wide variety of interventions varying in directiveness and in involvement of the multiple levels of the problem. When deemed appropriate after careful consideration, patterns of hypnosis and strategic psychotherapy can be most effective in facilitating escape from the chains of depression.

References

Abramson, L., Seligman, M., & Teasdale, J. (1978). Learned helplessness in humans: Critique and reformulation. *Journal of Abnormal Psychology, 87,* 49-74.

Alexander, L. (1982). Erickson's approach to hypnotic psychotherapy of depression. In J. Zeig (Ed.), *Ericksonian approaches to hypnosis and psychotherapy* (pp. 219-227). New York: Brunner/Mazel.

American Psychiatric Association. (1980). *Diagnostic and statistical manual of mental disorders* (3rd ed.). Washington, DC: A.P.A.

Aronson, E. (1984). *The Social Animal* (4th ed.). New York: Freeman.

Bandler, R. & Grinder, J. (1975). *The structure of magic* (Vol. 1). Palo Alto, CA: Science and Behavior Books.

Bandler, R. & Grinder, J. (1979). *Frogs into princes.* Moab, UT: Real People Press.

Beck, A. (1967). *Depression.* New York: Harper & Row.

Beck, A. (1973). *The diagnosis and management of depression.* Philadelphia: University of Pennsylvania Press.

Beck, A., Rush, J., Shaw, B., & Emery, G. (1979). *Cognitive therapy of depression.* New York: Guilford Press.

Beck, A. (1983). Negative cognitions. In E. Levitt, B. Lubin & J. Brooks (Eds.), *Depression: concepts, controversies, and some new facts* (2nd ed.) (pp. 86-92). Hillsdale, NJ: Erlbaum.

Burns, D. (1980). *Feeling good: The new mood therapy.* New York: Morrow.

Davison, G. & Neale, J. (1982). *Abnormal psychology* (3rd ed.). New York: Wiley.

Erickson, M. (1954a). Special techniques of brief hypnotherapy. *Journal of Clinical and Experimental Hypnosis, 2,* 109-129.

Erickson, M. (1954b). Pseudo-orientation in time as a hypnotherapeutic procedure. *Journal of Clinical and Experimental Hypnosis, 2,* 261-283.

Erickson, M. & Rossi, E. (1979). *Hypnotherapy: An exploratory casebook.* New York: Irvington.

Erickson, M. (1980). The appliciations of hypnosis to psychiatry. In E. Rossi (Ed.). *The collected papers of Milton H. Erickson on hypnosis* (Vol. IV) (pp. 3-13). New York: Irvington.

Frankl, V. (1963). *Man's search for meaning.* New York: Washington Square Press.

Gibson, J. (1983). *Living: Human development through the lifespan.* Reading, MA: Addison-Wesley.

Gordon, D. (1978). *Therapeutic metaphors.* Cupertino, CA: Meta Publications.

Grinder, J. & Bandler, R. (1981). *Trance-formations.* Moab, UT: Real People Press.

Haley, J. (1973). *Uncommon therapy.* New York: Norton.

Haley, J. (1984). *Ordeal therapy.* San Francisco: Jossey-Bass.

Harlow, H. & Suomi, S. (1974). Induced depression in monkeys. *Behavioral Biology, 12,* 273-296.

Kleinmuntz, B. (1980). *Essentials of abnormal psychology* (2nd ed.). San Francisco: Harper & Row.

Kolb, L. & Brodie, H. (1982). *Modern clinical psychiatry* (10th ed.). Philadelphia: W. B. Saunders.

Laliotis, D. & Grayson, J. (1985). Psychologist heal thyself. *American Psychologist, 40,* 84-96.

Lankton, S. (1980). *Practical magic.* Cupertino, CA: Meta Publications.

Lankton, S. & Lankton, C. (1983). *The answer within: A clinical framework of Ericksonian hypnotherapy.* New York: Brunner/Mazel.

Mahoney, M. (1980). *Abnormal psychology: Perspectives on human variance.* San Francisco: Harper & Row.

Miller, H. (1984). Depression: A specific cognitive pattern. In W. Webster (Ed.), *Clinical hypnosis: A multidisciplinary approach* (2nd ed.) (pp. 421-458). Philadelphia: Lippincott.

Phares, E. (1984). *Introduction to personality.* Columbus, OH: Charles Merrill.

Rosen, S. (1982). *My voice will go with you: The teaching tales of Milton H. Erickson.* New York: Norton.

Sarason, I., & Sarason, B. (1980). *Abnormal psychology* (3rd ed.). Englewood Cliffs, NJ: Prentice-Hall.

Satir, V. (1972). *Peoplemaking.* Palo Alto, CA: Science & Behavior Books.

Secunda, S., Friedman, R., & Schuyler, D. (1973). *The depressive disorders: Special report, 1973.* (DHEW Publication No. HSM-73-9157). Washington, DC: U.S. Government Printing Office.

Seligman, M. (1973). Fall into helplessness. *Psychology Today,* June, 7, 43-48.

Seligman, M. (1974). Depression and learned helplessness. In R. Friedman & M. Katz (Eds.), *The psychology of depression: Contemporary theory and research.* Washington, DC: Winston.

Seligman, M. (1975). *Helplessness: On depression, development, and death.* San Francisco: Freeman.

Seligman, M. (1983). Learned helplessness. In E. Levitt, B. Lubin, & J. Brooks (Eds.), *Depression: concepts, controversies, and some new facts* (2nd ed.) (pp. 64-72). Hillsdale, NJ: Erlbaum.

Spiegel, H. & Spiegel, D. (1978). *Trance and treatment: Clinical uses of hypnosis.* New York: Basic Books.

Suinn, R. (1984). *Fundamentals of abnormal psychology.* Chicago: Nelson-Hall Inc.

Watzlawick, P. (1976). *How real is real?* New York: Vintage Books.

Watzlawick, P. (1978). *The language of change.* New York: Basic Books.

Yapko, M. (1981). The effect of matching primary representational system predicates on hypnotic relaxation. *American Journal of Clinical Hypnosis, 23,* 169-175.

Yapko, M. (1983). A comparative analysis of direct and indirect hypnotic communication styles. *American Journal of Clinical Hypnosis, 23,* 270-276.

Yapko, M. (1984a). *Trancework: An introduction to clinical hypnosis.* New York: Irvington.

Yapko, M. (1984b). Implications of the Ericksonian and Neuro-Linguistic Programming approaches for responsibility of therapeutic outcomes. *American Journal of Clinical Hypnosis, 27,* 137-143.

Yapko, M. (1985). The Erickson hook: Values in Ericksonian approaches. In J. Zeig (Ed.), *Ericksonian psychotherapy* (Vol. I) (pp. 266-281). New York: Brunner/Mazel.

Zeig, J. (Ed.). (1980a). *A teaching seminar with Milton H. Erickson.* New York: Brunner/Mazel.

Zeig, J. (1980b). Symptom prescription techniques: Clinical applications using elements of communication. *American Journal of Clinical Hypnosis, 23,* 23-33.

Zeig, J. (Ed.). (1982). *Ericksonian approaches to hypnosis and psychotherapy.* New York: Brunner/Mazel.

Zeig, J. (Ed.). (1985). *Ericksonian psychotherapy* (2 Vols.). New York: Brunner/Mazel.

SPECIAL APPLICATIONS

Moshe Feldenkrais's Verbal Approach to Somatic Education: Parallels to Milton Erickson's Use of Language

by
Mark Reese, M.A.

> "Suit the action to the word, the word to the action, with this special observance, that you o'erstep not the modesty of nature."
>
> —Shakespeare's *Hamlet*, III,ii.

Introduction

Moshe Feldenkrais's ideas and methods contain a deep and subtle intelligence about nonverbal behavior, learning and communication that may enrich the work of Ericksonian therapists. Although Erickson worked primarily in the symbolic domain of image and language, and Feldenkrais worked primarily in the physical domain of touch and movement, there arc remarkable similarities between these two masters. They shared a common awareness of movement and a common philosophy about learning, unconscious processes, and the uniqueness of each individual. Furthermore, they independently developed many similar techniques. Through reciprocal study and collaboration between practitioners of Ericksonian and Feldenkrais methods, it is the author's belief that new and unexpected, more integrated and effective somatopsychic methods will be developed.

This chapter will begin with a brief overview of the life and work of Feldenkrais and the historical and philosophical parallels that exist between Feldenkrais and Erickson (Reese, 1985). Then the general orientation of Feldenkrais's verbal approach will be described, emphasizing certain parallels with Erickson, followed by a delineation of a number of specific strategies. The chapter concludes with a discussion of practical applications of Feldenkrais's verbal methods.

Moshe Feldenkrais: His Life

Moshe Feldenkrais was born in Russia in 1904 and emigrated to Palestine at the age of 13. As a young man, he was a construction worker, a tutor of problem students and an excellent athlete who played soccer and taught himself and others jujitsu (Feldenkrais, 1931). He had an early interest in hypnosis and translated Emile Coue's book on autosuggestion into Hebrew (1977b).

In the 1930's, in Paris, Feldenkrais earned his doctorate in physics at the Sorbonne and became the assistant to Joliot-Curie. Also, while in Paris, he became a second degree black belt in judo, and began to teach and write books on judo (Feldenkrais, 1941, 1944, 1952).

In 1940, escaping the Nazis, Feldenkrais fled to England where he became an antisubmarine research scientist for the allies and a teacher of judo and self-defense techniques. When an old soccer-related knee injury became aggravated from working on slippery submarine decks, Feldenkrais began a process of reeducating his movement habits. Confined to his bed, he experimented with tiny movements for hours, days and months on end, refining his kinesthetic awareness until he could feel subtle subconscious, neuromuscular connections between all the parts of himself. Through his self-education Feldenkrais learned how to walk efficiently and painlessly and originated the unique work he would later do with others.

After working for years in relative anonymity, by the late 1970's Feldenkrais became internationally known and respected for his work in the fields of rehabilitation and athletic and performing arts training (Rosenfeld, 1981). In 1978, Feldenkrais had the opportunity to meet Erickson, a man he deeply admired and who, he felt, in his work had done "the same thing" as he himself had done. Feldenkrais died in July of 1984 in Tel-Aviv, Israel.

Moshe Feldenkrais: His Work

Feldenkrais (1949, 1972, 1977a, 1981a) developed two interrelated, somatically-based educational methods. The first method, Awareness through Movement, or "ATM," is a verbal technique often used for groups (Feldenkrais, 1972). The other method, Functional Integration, or "FI," is a nonverbal, hands-on technique used with individuals desiring or requiring more individualized attention (Feldenkrais, 1977a, 1981a). Both methods address the needs of people who wish to improve their quality of life and functioning through body movement awareness and skill. They are designed to improve efficiency of movement, posture and breathing, reduce muscular tension, further flexibility and coordination, enhance neuromuscular functioning, and increase people's learning skills in general.

Some people may attend ATM classes to overcome discomforts or movement limitations; athletes, dancers, musicians and others may attend to learn movement excellence. A typical ATM lesson lasts about an hour and consists of verbally directed movements and cues for sensory attention organized around a functional theme. ATM lessons are based upon Feldenkrais's understanding of childhood learning and motor development, and the structure and function of the human body and brain. Feldenkrais taught many movements drawn from early childhood, such as rolling over and crawling, and based many lessons on the ways children naturally move. Furthermore, he sought to utilize the process of childhood's "organic learning" (Feldenkrais, 1981a) in his movement sequences and approaches, so that students would learn from their own sensory motor experience, and not from external models or dictates. An avid student of neuroscience, Feldenkrais (1981a) originated concrete ways of utilizing biological insights about neuromuscular activity and learning. In a period lasting over forty years, Feldenkrais devised thousands of lessons that include thorough explorations of virtually every joint and muscle group in the body, and a wide panorama of human movement possibilities. The major part of this chapter will describe how Feldenkrais's use of language in ATM parallels Erickson's hypnotherapeutic approaches.

The nonverbal method of FI is based upon the same principles and goals as ATM, but it involves the practitioner physically touching and moving the student in order to augment the student's internal kinesthetic feedback. Because FI is gentle and nonverbal, it is eminently suitable for working with infants and small children with developmental problems, and people with neuromuscular or musculoskeletal difficulties whose movement limitations are too great for group work. Through touch, the practitioner helps the student to assemble, at a mostly unconscious level, a new neuromuscular image of movement, which then becomes the basis of altered movement patterns in daily life.

A Parallel Philosophy of Learning

Like Feldenkrais, Erickson, too, learned to become precisely self-aware of his muscular efforts and movement while overcoming a physical trauma. After being stricken with polio at the age of 17, Erickson spent the next ten years relearning to walk (Haley, 1967, p. 2). And like Feldenkrais, Erickson was able to apply his subtle awareness of movement in his work with others. Based upon their learning to go beyond their apparent physical limitations, Feldenkrais and Erickson gained a confidence in other peoples' ability to learn to move beyond limitations.

Their philosophy of learning is basically positive and growth-oriented. Learning itself is seen as a powerful therapeutic and self-actualizing force. Learning new abilities can lead to such positive transformations that symptoms can spontaneously disappear, even without specific treatment. This can occur because learning builds a self-confidence which potentially can be carried over to every facet of a person's life.

For Feldenkrais and Erickson, learning is a sensorimotor process involving the entire body, and behind their work lays an assumption of somatopsychic unity. They transcended the pervasive mind/body dichotomy, and thus saw human beings and the human learning process as holistic. For Feldenkrais and Erickson, learning comes from doing—from movement—and this made their teaching methods profoundly experiential.

For both of these masters, learning is greatly indebted to the unconscious functioning of the nervous system. The nervous system has the life experience of the individual available to it, as well as the biological wisdom gained through the process of evolution. Thus, for Feldenkrais and Erickson, "the unconscious" was not the Freudian kettle of difficult-to-manage instinctual impulses, but a life-sustaining activity which supports our ability to think, feel, sense, act—and learn. For this reason, they often worked to reduce the interference of overly conscious controls, in favor of utilizing deeper processes of self-direction (Feldenkrais, 1949; Zeig, 1980).

A Parallel Method

Unlike most forms of movement instruction, such as exercise classes or dance training, where movements are visually demonstrated, Feldenkrais's ATM lessons relied exclusively upon an auditory means of communication. Feldenkrais employed a very sophisticated use of language in order to convey physical movements together with appropriate images and sensory and psychological cues. His language contained many "Ericksonian" hypnotic forms of communication used to effect learning at the deepest level of the self. These include 1) hypnotic suggestions, 2) neuro-utilizations, 3) indirect techniques, 4) pattern interruptions, 5) pacing and leading, and 6) relanguaging. These verbal approaches are described in this section in general terms.

1) *Hypnotic suggestions.* Feldenkrais's ATM lessons often consisted of slow, gentle, and sometimes minute movements. These were hypnotically paced in order to induce a deep absorption in internal experience not unlike the absorption of trance. His language included many direct, indirect, and embedded "suggestions," each intended to promote the sensory qualities of comfort, ease, and lightness of movement. To instill "awareness through movement," Feldenkrais encouraged an attitude of self-acceptance and non-goal-oriented attention to normally unconscious internal feelings and aspects of musculoskeletal organization. In the next section it will be described how he discouraged, even subverted, the use of conscious will and used various means to empower the "inner self" or "nervous system" to take increasing control. Hence, his characteristic admonition: "Don't you decide how to do the movement; let your nervous system decide. It has had millions of years of experience and therefore knows more than you do" (1981b).

2) *Neuro-utilizations.* The activation of unconscious processes is reinforced by what the author has termed, *neuro-utilizations,* of phenomena inherent in the nervous system. For example, many lessons contain motor-regressive infantile movements, such as the sucking reflex, tonic neck and eyes reflexes, and patterns of crawling. While inhibiting overriding patterns of habitual and conscious controls, the lessons utilize subconscious features of neuromuscular coordination to improve movement flexibility and efficiency. The experience of relaxing conscious controls and thus achieving nearly effortless movement directed by the nervous system helps people rebalance the proportional roles of conscious and unconscious regulation in everyday life. As Feldenkrais (1949) described, the basic organization of functions such as posture, breathing, movement, and sexual response should be left to "self-regulating nervous coordination," whereas the "conscious control is paramount integrating all the functions fitting the immediate circumstances" (p. 94).

"Utilization" is, of course, a leitmotif of Erickson's as well as Feldenkrais's work (Erickson & Rossi, 1979). In the section on specific strategies there will be presented examples of how Feldenkrais, like Erickson, utilized whatever neuromuscular behavior the student presented in the learning process.

3) *Indirect techniques.* Elements of Feldenkrais's "organic learning"

(Feldenkrais, 1981a) closely parallel Erickson's "indirect" techniques (Erickson & Rossi, 1979). Feldenkrais explained that his lessons were based upon the logic of nature as it is exemplified in the nonlinear, yet highly orderly, "organic learning" and development of children (Feldenkrais, 1981a, pp. 116-117). His lessons have little in common with the culturally promulgated academic mode of learning. The movements comprising the ATM lesson do not resemble the movement that is being learned; they represent "ingredients" or "constituent elements" of the final outcome (Feldenkrais, 1981a, p. 93). Feldenkrais's ability to extract these functional elements from a global learning process and to present them in a coherent, nonlinear fashion is, perhaps, the greatest example of his genius. In the course of a lesson, these movements, sensations, images, and spatiotemporal awarenesses gradually, and inexorably, coalesce in the nervous system into new neuromuscular gestalts. Conscious understanding is usually absent, not knowing what is being done nor why, until the new learning has taken place. At that time, conscious recognition and understanding may be helpful to consolidate the new learning. Consequently, many lessons have surprise endings like the *"Aha!"* experience of an exceptionally meaningful insight, not unlike the experience of an infant rolling over for the first time.

Feldenkrais used other methods that may be called indirect, such as story telling and metaphor, examples of which will be presented in the next section.

4) *Pattern interruptions*. Feldenkrais discovered how to activate the intelligence of the nervous system through "differentiated" and "nonhabitual" movements, similar to the unusual behaviors and "pattern interruptions" Erickson created in order to facilitate unconscious processes and shake people out of their limiting patterns (Feldenkrais, 1972; Haley, 1967). Learning to move the eyes and the head in separate directions is an example of differentiated movement. Reversing one's habitual way of interlacing the fingers exemplifies a nonhabitual movement. These pattern shifts reflect the plasticity of the learning behavior of small children. They disengage the individual from customary mind/body sets and foster new learning.

The next section will describe other pattern interrupting techniques including the use of paradoxical instructions, double binds, and confusion.

5) *Pacing and leading*. In FI Feldenkrais's hands adapted themselves to the contours of the student's neuromuscular responses (Reese, 1985) so that he and the student seemingly became as one, a "single ensemble" (Feldenkrais, 1981a, pp. 3-4). In ATM, which began as an outgrowth of FI, the effective "pacing and leading" (Bandler & Grinder, 1975) of

the student's experience creates the kinesthetic linkage ("rapport") between practitioner and student. In order to best accomplish this individualized learning in a group situation, Feldenkrais gave carefully worded, open-ended and often ambiguous instructions that were intended to pace and lead each student so that "we can all do our own learning in our own way" (Zeig, 1980, p. 224).

Although the instructions in an ATM lesson must be specific enough to ensure the lesson's effectiveness, it is essential that the student be free to do something which is comfortably within the limits of his or her physical abilities or habit. For this reason, rather than asking students to put their head on their knees, Feldenkrais would have them bring the head and knees *toward each other only as far as is easy*. This process-oriented language made it possible for Feldenkrais to create an intimate rapport with his students and to utilize all of the students' responses in the group, both individually and collectively, in order to further their learning (Feldenkrais, 1981b).

6) *Relanguaging*. Feldenkrais believed that a change in one's way of moving required a change in one's thinking and therefore *relanguaged* his students' problems in a way that facilitated learning, not unlike Erickson's "reframing" of problems (Feldenkrais, 1981a; Lankton & Lankton, 1983).

Underlying all of these forms of communication was Feldenkrais's belief in the freedom of individuals to make their own choices. Like Erickson (Zeig, 1980), Feldenkrais believed that people should make their own choices, and that his primary goal was enabling people to live the way they wanted to. Feldenkrais felt that the most effective route to freedom of choice is self-awareness, because self-awareness increases the number of options available. Typically, he would ask students to try a movement one way, and then another, and another, so they could learn to sense differences and know what feels best. Feldenkrais did not play an authoritative role. He said that he was not interested in *teaching*; what mattered was the student's *learning* (1981b). For this reason, Feldenkrais never demonstrated movements, nor did he say what was "right" or "wrong." His students were encouraged to find their own way. His goal was to foster the ability of his pupils to make their own choices and "fulfill their own unavowed dreams" (Feldenkrais, 1982).

In summary, Feldenkrais's language ran the gamut of Erickson's hypnotic forms of communication: direct and indirect suggestions, embedded suggestions, paradoxes, double binds, pacing and leading, confusion techniques, pattern interruptions, regression, story telling, and metaphor. In the next section there are presented a number of concrete examples of these verbal strategies.

Illustrations of Verbal Strategies

The following examples of Feldenkrais's verbal strategies are intended to illustrate some of the range and style of his approaches to somatic education; they are not intended to serve as a comprehensive catalogue.

The Pelvic Clock

Although Feldenkrais is known to have developed thousands of different lessons, he returned to some of them again and again, teaching variation upon variation. "The Pelvic Clock" (Feldenkrais, 1972) is one of these lessons. A "classic" lesson, it is at once effective and illustrative of many of the approaches previously discussed.

The movements consist of flexion and extension and rotation of the pelvis, performed in various positions, including sitting, lying on the back, leaning on the elbows, standing and kneeling. The feet are maintained in a fixed position, joined sole to sole or standing on the floor. The pelvis rests on an imaginary "clock," an easily related-to device through which a frame of reference is created for indicating the position of the pelvis and its directions of movement.

Shift in Levels

> Draw your abdomen in. Therefore the body will round up and the head lower. And now straighten your back and push your abdomen forward, full, as if pushing the air into the abdomen, and therefore the small of the back will erect itself and probably go a little bit forward. Now draw the stomach in again, and round the back, and then push forward, with your abdomen full, extended . . . and *keep on doing that, slowly, gently, without any special strain, not too much, just to feel that you understand what you are doing.* (Feldenkrais, 1976)

After Feldenkrais introduced the first movement, he made a shift in levels between the *movement* and the *awareness of movement*. Learning a movement, per se, is not the aim of the lesson, the intent is to use the movement as a vehicle to learning something applicable to any movement situation: a quality of action and experience.

Later in the lesson, after Feldenkrais has introduced the imaginary clock, he continued:

> At 12:00 *the spine is erect, the stomach full, the belly rounded,* and *the small of the back is straightened,* and *the back muscles work to erect your spine.* . . .

Note how Feldenkrais uses a different syntax in this passage compared to the first. Instead of the *command*, "straighten your back," he makes the *observation*, "at 12:00 the spine is erect." The shift from instruction to description and inquiry is characteristic of most Feldenkrais lessons. Once he has clarified *what* movement is to be done, the emphasis shifts to the metalevel of *how* it is being performed. Learning is engendered not through moving, but through awareness of the *process* of moving.

The syntactical shift elicits a change of attitude in the student from one of making the movement happen through conscious effort to a less willful mode of watching and feeling the movement as it happens. After many repetitions, the movement takes on a "quasi-automatic" quality, and the student is in a trance-like state of heightened awareness. By perceiving subtle details about the movement's muscular organization, the student is able to eliminate unnecessary efforts. Economy of effort improves movement quality and frees the individual from habitual limitations.

Pacing and Leading

Continuing from the transcript (Feldenkrais, 1976):

> and the head is high . . . and, then, 6:00, the whole strain is gone, the knees drawn together, the spine rounded, the head leaning a bit forward. . . . So, keep on, 12:00, 6:00, 12:00, 6:00, paying attention to the knees . . . to the pressure in the back . . . to how the head is drawn in between the shoulders at 6:00, and is pushed out, the neck and throat becoming longer, out of the shoulders, above the shoulders, the head higher above the shoulders.

Utilizing Bandler & Grinder's (1975) terminology for Erickson's approach, it is apparent that Feldenkrais's descriptive statements about the movement "pace" the student's kinesthetic experience. For example:

> ". . . the pressure in the back. . . ."
> ". . . the head drawn in between the shoulders at 6:00. . . ."
> ". . . at 12:00 the spine is erect, the stomach full, the belly rounded. . . ."

Pacing establishes rapport with the student by linking up with his or her ongoing kinesthetic experience. As Bandler & Grinder (1975) and Erickson & Rossi (1976) have pointed out, this is a very effective technique for trance induction.

In the passage cited above, Feldenkrais moves from "pacing" to "leading" when, describing the movement to 12:00, he says the head—

is pushed out, the neck and throat becoming longer, out of the shoulders, above the shoulders, the head higher above the shoulders. . . .

This language serves to exaggerate what the student has already become aware of doing: straightening the cervical curve when the pelvis rolls forward to 12:00. However, instead of making a directive statement, such as "hold the head high above the shoulders," Feldenkrais's suggestion to lengthen the spine flows almost imperceptibly from his descriptive language about an ongoing process. This instructional technique, whereby Feldenkrais led his students in subtle increments to experience increasing grace and excellence of movement, is characteristic of all of Feldenkrais's lessons. In this way, Feldenkrais mirrored the natural process of the nervous system in learning through awareness, through sensory and motor feedback. Wherever possible, Feldenkrais eschewed the direct command because he wanted to "o'erstep not the modesty of nature" (Harbage, 1969, p. 952).

Direct Suggestions

Later in the lesson, when the movement involves tilting the pelvis to the right and left, Feldenkrais said:

> Pay attention now, whether the knee, the right knee, and the right thigh is as close to the floor as the left, or more, or less, . . . and *by becoming aware of that difference you will find that you spontaneously, almost without wishing, correct the back* so that the weaker part works a little bit harder and the too-strong part works a little bit less, so that both knees approach the floor approximately the same way.

Telling the student that "by becoming aware of that difference you will find that you spontaneously, almost without wishing, correct the back," is congruent with the behavior of the nervous system. The information provided by doing a movement slowly and gently, with awareness but without the *intent to achieve* anything, allows the nervous system to "spontaneously," i.e., unconsciously, self-correct the movement in the direction of least effort and with symmetrical usage of the back muscles. How different this approach is from the emphasis upon *effortful* stretching and strengthening exercises existing in most physical education and therapeutics!

Embedded Suggestions

After introducing the circular movement around the "clock," Feldenkrais said:

Very, very slowly, go on, rotating, tilting your pelvis in such a way that the pressure point goes in a circle round the clock, from hour to hour, as uniformly, and as simply and as circularly as you can make it . . . 12:00, round and round and round . . . at which hours do you feel that the movement is not *satisfactory*, it's not *round* enough, it's not *smooth* enough, not *easy* enough, and as soon as you detect that, you will find that on the next arrival at the same hour, it will be better. (Feldenkrais, 1976)

The reader may notice the direct suggestion similar to that in the earlier example, "As soon as you detect that, you will find that on the next arrival at the same hour, it will be better." Also, notice the rhythmical, hypnotic pacing of the language, "12:00, round and around and round." Experiencing Feldenkrais, one hears his reassuring voice and steady tempo helping to establish the movement's rhythm and quality.

In the above passage, Feldenkrais used his voice to emphasize the words, "satisfactory," "round," "smooth," and "easy," thereby "embedding" the suggestions that the movement become satisfactory, round, smooth, and easy. In order to depotentiate the negative attitude that the movement may not, in fact, be experienced as completely satisfactory by the student, he ingeniously utilized the negative construction, "not satisfactory," "not smooth," etc., thus assuming the role of the internal critic. The intonational emphasis unconsciously elicits further improvement in the movement.

Imagery

It is worth mentioning that Feldenkrais often uses images, such as the "clock" to enhance sensory motor learning. For Feldenkrais, optimal learning requires use of the entire self (1981b). Listening to instructions and performing the movements involve both the sensorimotor and auditory systems of the brain; the "clock" adds the visual system. More advanced variations of the lesson elicit heightened precision, ease, and skill through more extensive interplay between visualization and movement.

Differentiation

During other advanced variations, Feldenkrais introduced increased "differentiation" of movement, such as that involved in having the pelvis and head roll on the floor in opposite directions to each other, and still later, moving the eyes in circles opposite to the head and pelvis. The concept of differentiation is drawn from nature. For example, embryonic development follows an increasing process of differentiation; undifferentiated cells differentiate into germ layers, and then into tissue and organ systems. Analogously, one observes in child development the gradual differentiation of movement of the extremities from global actions involving the entire body. The fine motor skills of the hands and mouth require still greater levels of differentiation. It is easy to think of other examples of differentiation at the level of the personality or society. Feldenkrais's approach to learning emphasizes both facets of biological development: differentiation and integration. These principles will be discussed further in the later example of an embryonic movement.

Nonhabitual Movements

As was mentioned before, Feldenkrais utilized nonhabitual movements to disengage people from their usual patterns, such as interlacing the fingers in a nonhabitual fashion. Similarly, doing the "pelvic clock" uses the muscles around the hip joints in a nonhabitual manner, contrary to their normal use in walking.

Muscles are usually attached to either side of a joint to two bones, one on the proximal side of the joint (nearer to the center of the body) and one on the distal side (nearer to the periphery). In most movements, the proximal side is relatively stationary while the distal side undergoes the maximum displacement. For example, when moving our arms, the movement of the chest and neck is minimal even though many of the arm muscles attach to the arm, neck, and chest, pulling equally on both the proximal and distal segments. Similarly, when walking, the legs move much more than the pelvis. In the pelvic clock, one moves all the major muscles of the thigh, but the legs (the distal parts) are stationary while the pelvis (the proximal part) is in motion. This movement can be very effective for reorganizing and increasing the efficiency of one's pelvis, legs, and back because it elicits a novel neural pattern through altering the image of ourselves in action (Pribram, 1971).

An Embryonic Movement

The following excerpt from a Feldenkrais workshop transcript contains many patterns of communication similar to Erickson's. The reader may notice many of the verbal strategies that have been previously described, including various kinds of suggestions, pacing and leading, and level shifts. In this lesson, the students were positioned on their stomachs on the floor while performing various movements related to the early childhood function of crawling. At one point in the lesson, Feldenkrais asked the students to begin bending the fingers on the right hand "as if you're going to make a fist," and then Feldenkrais continued:

> undo it, as if you stopped thinking of the fist. . . . That is the
> easiest movement we can do. It's almost like moving the eye-

lid. . . . Close and open, as slowly, as comfortably, and as little as is necessary for you to feel that you're actually flexing and stretching. . . . We can do everything to our own comfort. . . . You'll find that in order to do a thing comfortably, elegantly, and aesthetically right . . . we must do it with a minimum of exertion, with the feeling of lightness, the feeling, the sensation of lightness, of lightness of the movement. . . . You will see that the lightness exists only when you flex it a little bit more and open it, but not completely. . . . In order to make the hand completely flexed and completely open, you have to make a real effort, enough effort, but to flex it a little bit more and flex it a little bit less . . . gives you a sensation that is easy, light. . . . Now, being easy, light, will you please continue that move-ment . . . easy, light . . . so that the feeling of easy, light, is connected actually . . . it will be . . . whether you want it or not . . . you can't do it otherwise. . . . Your entire motor cor-tex, the entire nervous system is now pervaded with that feeling, light, and you should know the hand in our motor cortex oc-cupies, next to the lips, the largest area . . . so very slowly, there will be a feeling of lightness permeating the entire mus-culature . . . the entire self . . . making it . . . keep on doing it . . . and while you do that, while you feel it's really light . . . you'll find out the whole arm gets light, and slowly you will feel the neck and shoulder blade . . . over that . . . getting soft and nice and actually prepared to act with-out preparing itself. . . . In other words, it's getting ready for action, and you will see when we get that, how quickly, how nicely, we will all be moving, doing the same thing independ-ently, whether you have arthritis, whether you had an operation or not, you will still move infinitely better than you started. . . . Don't stop moving the right hand, flexing and . . . slowly, slowly . . . see a remarkable sort of thing . . . if you keep on doing that movement, it will actually teach you . . . slowly, keep on moving the fingers gently . . . and on top of that move-ment, lift your right shoulder and you will see that the gentleness of the movement, the skill of the movement permeates our entire being, and therefore you will see that other things we do improve without doing them. You don't have to exercise in order to improve . . . you only have to be your own self. (1981b)

The grasping movement in this lesson is an infantile reflex, but it is also what embryologist Erich Blechschmidt (1977) termed, an embryonic "growth action." Feldenkrais had read and appreciated Blechschmidt's observation that, in embryonic development, function both precedes and is formative of structure. Blechschmidt maintained that the grasping movement forms the hand and, in the same way, the action of sucking forms the mouth. Similarly, later in childhood, movement and weight-bearing help to shape the bones. Indeed, throughout life, *learning* structurally reorganizes neural circuits. From this perspective, Blechschmidt and Feldenkrais regard function, or movement, as fundamental to life (Feldenkrais, 1981a). Thus, for Feldenkrais, the idea of *movement* meant more than something one *does*; it creates what one *is*. A change in function is decisive for the amelioration of most difficulties, and sensory motor learning is the basis of functional change.

The enactment of the grasping movement can foster significant changes in a person's self image by inducing a deep somatopsychic regression, thus reminding the organism of a more unitary level of functioning. Whereas healthy functioning requires a high degree of integration of the neuro-muscular-skeletal system, most somatic difficulties exhibit a fragmented mode of functioning in which body segments, and often parts of the personality as well, operate in a dissociated manner from one another. The reawakening of primitive patterns neuromotorically "regresses" an individual to a time before functioning may have been impaired as a result of accident, disease, faulty learning, or degeneration. Furthermore, such reawakening can reinstate the more integrated quality of functioning characteristic of our early life, when the entire body/self was integrally cooperating in every action.

Part of the power of the hand-grasping movement is due to the inordinately large area accorded the hand in the sensorimotor *homunculus* of the cerebral cortex. This factor facilitates the spreading of the mood of the movement throughout the entire brain. Feldenkrais utilizes the "easy, light" feeling established in the hand to promote ease and lightness of movement when lifting the shoulder and to create a pervasive feeling of well-being. Ideally, what one learns through the hand movement is generalized and carried over into the whole of one's life.

> You will see that the gentleness of the movement, the skill of the movement permeates our entire being and therefore you will see that other things we do improve without doing them. (Feldenkrais, 1981b)

Additional Verbal Strategies

Double Binds

Feldenkrais sometimes created double binds for his students. For example, while students were performing a particular movement, he once said:

> Don't breathe. . . . Don't hold your breath either. . . . Just don't breathe. . . . Don't breathe in any way that you know to be breathing. . . . Don't hold your breath. . . . Don't make efforts. . . . Don't breathe with your chest. . . . Don't breathe with your abdomen. . . . Don't do any of the things that you know. . . . Just don't breathe, that's all. . . . (Feldenkrais, 1981c)

These instructions surely interrupt the students' habitual breathing patterns and also obstruct the students' conscious ideas about correct breathing and any deliberate attempt they may be making to regulate their respiration. The student cannot escape from this double bind by any rational, conscious, or familiar means. The nervous system is provoked into generating an unexpected alternative, a pattern of breathing directed by the inner self.

Paradoxical Instructions

Feldenkrais claimed that he was "a funny sort of teacher who [didn't] teach, but the students learn" (Feldenkrais, 1981b). Here is an example of his "not teaching:"

The students were doing movements on their hands and knees (Feldenkrais, 1981c). Feldenkrais directed them to lift the right knee off the floor without shifting the weight onto the left hip. Although this movement is impossible, the students in this professional training group were used to Feldenkrais asking them to do the seemingly impossible, only to discover that it was just a question of thinking in a new way. This time, however, the impossibility was real and deliberate. The students struggled for many minutes, learning all the ways one could *not* lift the right knee without shifting the weight to the left. By not teaching the fact that they had to shift the weight to the left in order to lift the right knee, the students were able to learn this in a way they would never forget.

A Confusion Strategy

In another lesson (Feldenkrais, 1980) while students were learning to roll from their back to their side and vice versa, Feldenkrais began to verbally develop the image of thinking of the body as "tall" in one phase of the movement and "short" in another phase. Then, while continuing to work with the movement, he asked the students to think of themselves as "small and tall, tall and small, at the same time." This could well be an example of what Erickson called the "confusion technique" (Haley,

1967, chapter 8). However confusing or paradoxical the instruction is, the nervous system is able to decipher the meaning at a level beyond words.

Story Telling: Indirect Suggestions

In this same lesson, Feldenkrais told a story from his judo days. He described in detail how his teacher masterfully performed a judo throw by bending very low to the ground and then using the full power of erecting himself to complete the throw. Although this story was never related directly to the movement of rolling, it indirectly cast light on the functional significance of "getting small and tall" and helped to generalize the students' sensory motor learning to other situations.

Visualization

Feldenkrais often had students perform movements on only one side of the body, leaving them to perform the movement on the other side in their imagination. Feldenkrais's use of visualization may be construed as analogous to Erickson's use of "ideomotor processes" (Erickson & Rossi, 1979, p. 23) for trance induction. Feldenkrais found that movement performed in the imagination is even more effective than physical movement for improving movement quality, but that some physical experience of the specific movement is necessary to provide the sensory information that is organized in visualization. Feldenkrais emphasized that visualization was no more a "mental" procedure than a "physical" one. Both mind and body are inextricably involved in the processes of visualization and active movement.

Utilizations

On one occasion, Feldenkrais was working with a man who had a left-sided hemiplegia resulting from a stroke. Feldenkrais had the man use his right arm and hand to mimic the spastic way he held his left arm. This resulted in the man's having to compare in detail the difference in feeling and organization of the two sides. He had undoubtedly previously tried and failed to emulate the good side with his bad side. By reversing the process and utilizing the man's better side, Feldenkrais was able to initiate a greater flow of information and learning from the healthy to the injured side.

In another situation, Feldenkrais worked with a small boy with cerebral palsy whose knees pressed spastically together as he walked. He worked on the boy with his hands until his knees were "slightly separated, no longer locked in place." Then:

> Feldenkrais makes a fist, places it in the new space between the knees. "Now, Ephraim," he says. "Please, can you press your knees against my fist." Then: "Come on, you can do better

than that! Close your knees on my fist as hard as you can.'' He keeps it up, and Ephraim, no longer relaxed, is now straining mightily with the weak muscles on the inside of his thighs, an unaccustomed workout. Soon, "listening" carefully with his fist, Feldenkrais is satisfied that the time is right.

"All right, Ephraim," he says, "you don't have to close your knees any more. You can open them now." With clear relief, Ephraim relaxes, and opens his knees—all the way.

"See how much easier it is to have your knees open? To close them requires work. To keep them open, you don't have to do anything at all." The boy moves his legs in and out, in apparent disbelief, then bursts into a peal of delighted laughter.

When he stands up again, his heels touch the floor. When he leaves, he still needs the walker for support. But his knees no longer rub together. (Rosenfeld, 1981)

In this session, Feldenkrais did not "contradict the nervous system" (Feldenkrais, personal communication, April, 1979) by trying to stretch his knees apart but utilized instead the boy's spastic pattern of holding his knees together. By exaggerating his "symptom," Ephraim was able to learn to make an involuntary movement voluntary.

Relanguaging

The author is introducing the term "relanguaging" to describe the linguistic and philosophical shifts Feldenkrais evoked in his work with people, analogous to Erickson's "reframing" of patients' problems in ways more conducive to improvement and change (Lankton & Lankton, 1983).

People commonly view their specific somatic problems as separate entities, removed from the somatopsychic self. This stems from the inherited cultural notion that the body is a mechanical assemblage of parts at best only partially connected to the mind-identified person. In standard medical practice, clinical diagnosis is used to detect and isolate the cause of a person's difficulty and to treat and, if possible, eradicate it. The cause is typically isolated in a malfunctioning *part* of the body or isolated in the system's scarcity or over-abundance of a particular biochemical substance.

Feldenkrais sought to resituate people's problems through active participation in a learning process. He demonstrated that people usually have the means to become aware of how they can make themselves feel better, or worse. With this awareness, individuals have the freedom to choose the behavior that is most congenial to their comfort and well-being. The beginning of this learning process often entails a change in thinking. The following are several instances where Feldenkrais *relanguaged* a problem in order to set the person on the road to learning.

A few years ago, in a large public workshop in San Francisco (Feldenkrais, 1981b), a woman asked Feldenkrais for an exercise for her Achilles tendonitis. Feldenkrais replied, "If you have a tendonitis, neither I nor you can do anything for you. Because, you see, the tendonitis is you." Feldenkrais *relanguaged* her sense of *having* a tendonitis, to seeing the tendonitis as an expression of herself.

Feldenkrais explained that "specific" exercises are aimed at improving isolated parts of the body, and this ignores how the human system functions as a whole. In fact, it turned out that the woman's tendonitis had resulted from her having ignored her total being while she vigorously walked up and down hills for three months as a specific exercise for her heart. Feldenkrais emphasized that if one wants to improve the foot, or any other part of the self, one should improve the organization of the entire self.

Specific, problem-oriented exercises can actually maintain problems by reinforcing a fixed belief and way of thinking about them. For example, individuals who spend years receiving treatments and doing endless exercises to correct curvature of the spine are often unsuccessful in alleviating their discomforts. Having defined their condition as a specific structural problem, their minds remain closed to alternative interpretations and avenues of improvement. These people may not have realized that perfect spinal alignment is not necessary for painfree, functional movement.

Thus, Feldenkrais *relanguaged* "structural" problems in "functional" terms. When a person came to him with a problem, Feldenkrais would not ask for a description of the problem. Instead he would ask his students what they would like to be able to do that they felt unable to do at the present time. When a woman who was diagnosed as having MS came to Feldenkrais, he told her, "I don't deal with disease. I can, however, help you to do the things you remember being able to do." When people would reiterate the elaborate, and oftentimes conflicting, technical diagnoses they had received in the past, Feldenkrais sought to *relanguage* their problems into sensory terms, thus liberating their physicality from the mystification of technical jargon.

Understanding function necessitates a holism. In functional thinking, the *relationships* between parts are primary, not the parts themselves. When a student complained of pain in a specific part of the body, Feldenkrais would *relanguage* the problem in the context of learning to improve the quality of a particular movement. The location of a pain or discomfort may be a poor source of information about what is functionally amiss. Pain, or tension, is "located" in the nervous system's patterns of activity; it is not located in a particular body part, though we may feel it "there." Tensions generally refer to *learned patterns* of faulty muscular usage. By learning a new, healthier organization of the body, one can spontaneously eliminate many pains and tensions. When one is functionally integrated, movement is accomplished with a minimum of muscular exertion and wear and tear on all the musculo-skeletal components.

While giving his last professional training course in 1981 in Amherst, Massachusetts, Feldenkrais related this wonderful example of *relanguaging* structure into the realm of function, and conscious will into the realm of unconscious learning.

An elderly woman sent Feldenkrais a letter stating that her neurologist had diagnosed her condition as ataxia (a lack of balance and coordination in walking). The doctor had explained that her nervous system was not sending the correct messages to her muscles. She was, therefore, asking Dr. Feldenkrais to teach her nervous system to send the "right" messages. When the woman came for her lesson, Feldenkrais sat down next to her, brought out her letter, and said:

> Before I can correct your problem, I need to correct your letter. Not only does your neurologist not know which messages to send to which muscles, and in which order, but G-d doesn't even know. There are just too many impulses to keep track of, and G-d, I'm sure, lost track of them a long time ago. You don't want to be kept busy worrying all the time about which impulses to send where. The point of a healthy nervous system is not to know you have one!

Feldenkrais then explained that what the woman really wanted was to be able to do those things she had once enjoyed doing, and that he would be very happy to help her learn how to do that. With pen in hand, Feldenkrais and the woman corrected her letter until the woman was able to ask Feldenkrais for what she really wanted—to learn to move more freely and live a more satisfying life.

One's way of functioning is influenced by habits often acquired without conscious choice over a lifetime. Feldenkrais (1980) said that change doesn't require *unlearning* a bad habit. One ought not want to be rid of *anything*, since all of our learning may serve us some day, perhaps when we least expect it. And, all of our habits, good or bad, are part of us, and no one really wants to lose his or her identity. These are the same "resources" that Ericksonian practitioners may utilize in the course of treatment.

Instead of trying to rid people of their problems, Feldenkrais was interested in increasing the number of options available, as he did with a woman who complained of pain in her knees. This woman was very overweight, and her obesity clearly exacerbated her trouble, but she had tried innumerable diets without success. So, Feldenkrais told her:

> I won't suggest another diet, since none of them worked before, and there's no reason to think another one will. So, I just want to suggest a change in your eating habits. What you eat, and how much, is your business. But try this: Whatever you eat, leave one bite on the plate. If you drink a bowl of soup, don't finish the last spoonful. If you eat a piece of meat, leave a little bit on the plate. (demonstration lesson, August, 1978)

This suggestion could succeed where all the previous diets had failed because this did not take anything away from the woman. By leaving only one bite of food, she was learning a new pattern of eating. In a subtle way, Feldenkrais helped to heighten the woman's sense of control over her eating and her life, thereby increasing her self-respect.

Some Applications

Based upon the author's professional experience as a Feldenkrais practitioner, Feldenkrais's verbal strategies can be successfully applied in a number of diverse fields, including athletics, dance and the performing arts, pain control, rehabilitation, special education, and hypnotherapy.

Athletics. Feldenkrais (1972) was a pioneer in the use of visualization techniques now widely acknowledged to be effective for enhancing sports performance (Bry, 1978). The standard visualization procedures employed by coaches and athletes in most sports, however, do not utilize as systematic a training approach as does Feldenkrais's methodology. Working from slow, simple movements to gradually more complex ones, the Feldenkrais practitioner is able to systematically train kinesthetic visualization. Also, the Feldenkrais emphasis on the integration of the entire body in each movement provides an important complement to the routine athletic program which is based only upon stretching and strengthening of specific muscle groups. Feldenkrais's methods have been used to enhance running (Holmes, 1976), skiing (Heggie, 1980), horsemanship (Bretag, 1982), and other sports.

Performing Arts Training. Numerous theater and dance companies and music conservatories incorporate some Feldenkrais instruction (Linklater,

1972; Myers, 1980; Bersin & Reese, 1984). In 1980, on a grant from the Canadian government, the author gave a 10-day workshop, "Somatic Trance Theater," for actors in Montreal, based upon Feldenkrais and Ericksonian approaches. In the workshop, Feldenkrais lessons helped the actors perfect the physical instrument of their bodies and develop a somatically based attention (Reese, 1979). Participants also made an interesting experiment with a trance-based acting technique using Feldenkrais methods.

Pain control. The author has found Feldenkrais's methods to be highly effective in reducing the level of pain experienced by people suffering from problems affecting the nervous, muscular, and skeletal systems. Pain is often associated with a particular, inefficient habitual neuromuscular pattern (Rywerant, 1981). Through Feldenkrais's indirect techniques, conscious fears and protective reactions can be bypassed while learning improved movement organization. The Feldenkrais approach simultaneously elicits changes in the individual's self-image, attitude, attention, and behavior.

Rehabilitation. Feldenkrais's integrated somatopsychic methodology contrasts with the artificial division of physical and psychological disciplines governing most therapeutic approaches that exist today. Through using this integrated approach, the author has repeatedly found success in his work with children who have cerebral palsy, people who have had strokes, and accident victims.

Special education. The author has successfully used the Feldenkrais approach to improve learning skills in mentally retarded and dyslexic children.

Hypnotherapy. Feldenkrais methods can be seen as innovative forms of hypnotic education and therapy, and also can be fruitfully integrated with other hypnotic approaches. ATM may be effective in producing trance states with certain individuals who are normally resistant because of the profound state of relaxation, absorption, and somatic equilibrium produced by its slow, gentle movements and sensorial focus.

Conclusion

In each of the domains just described, there are very exciting possibilities for collaboration between Feldenkrais and Ericksonian practitioners. If the author has successfully demonstrated that the verbal strategies Moshe Feldenkrais employed in his somatic educational approach closely parallel Milton Erickson's hypnotherapeutic use of language, then there is much fertile ground for collaboration and reciprocal study between practitioners of the two disciplines.

References

Bandler, R., & Grinder, J. (1975). *Patterns of the hypnotic techniques of Milton H. Erickson, M.D.* (Vol. I). Cupertino, CA: Meta Publications.

Bersin, D. and Reese, M. (1984). *The reduction of muscular effort: The key to music learning and performance efficiency.* Manuscript submitted for publication.

Blechschmidt, E. (1977). *The beginnings of human life.* New York: Springer-Verlag.

Bretag, S. (1982). T.E.A.M. work clinic. *The western horseman.* September.

Bry, A. (1978). *Visualization.* New York: Barnes & Noble.

Erickson, M. & Rossi, E. (1979). *Hypnotherapy.* New York: Irvington Publishers.

Feldenkrais, M. (1931). *Self-Defense* (Hebrew). Toelet Publishers (out of print).

Feldenkrais, M. (1941). *Judo: The art of defense and attack.* London: Frederick Warne & Co.

Feldenkrais, M. (1944). *Practical unarmed combat.* London: Frederick Warne & Co. (out of print).

Feldenkrais, M. (1952). *Higher judo.* London: Frederick Warne & Co.

Feldenkrais, M. (1949). *Body and mature behavior.* New York: International Universities Press.

Feldenkrais, M. (1972). *Awareness through movement.* New York: Harper & Row.

Feldenkrais, M. (1976). *Ten lessons of awareness through movement* (audio-tapes). Editorial Correspondents, 230 Park Ave., Suite 460, New York, NY 10169.

Feldenkrais, M. (1977a). *The case of Nora.* New York: Harper & Row. (Out of print, but available through the Feldenkrais Guild Office, P. O. Box 11145, San Francisco, CA 94101.)

Feldenkrais, M. (1977b). *Autosuggestion* (Hebrew). Tel-Aviv: Aleph Publishers. (Original work published 1930).

Feldenkrais, M. (1980). Lesson given at a professional training program, Amherst, MA (video-tape). Feldenkrais Foundation, New York, NY.

Feldenkrais, M. (1981a). *The elusive obvious.* Cupertino, CA: Meta Publications.

Feldenkrais, M. (1981b) *San Francisco "Quest" workshop* (audio-tapes). ATM Recordings, 1429 Montague St. NW, Washington, DC 20011.

Feldenkrais, M. (1981c). Lesson given at a professional training program, Amherst, MA (video-tape). Feldenkrais Foundation, New York, NY.

Feldenkrais, M. (1982). Self-fulfillment through organic learning. *Journal of Holistic Health,* Vol. 7.

Haley, J. (Ed.) (1967). *Advanced techniques of hypnosis and therapy.* New York: Grune & Stratton.

Harbage, A. (Ed.). (1969). *William Shakespeare: The complete works.* Baltimore: Penguin Books.

Heggie, J. (1980). Awareness through movement and skiing. *Somatics,* Vol. 2, No. 4.

Holmes, B. (1976). Moshe's healing touch. *Runner's world,* April.

Lankton, S. R. & Lankton, C. H. (1983). *The answer within: A clinical framework of Ericksonian hypnotherapy.* New York: Brunner/Mazel.

Linklater, K. (1972). The body training of Moshe Feldenkrais. *Drama review,* March.

Myers, M. (1980). Moshe Feldenkrais's awareness through movement. *Dance magazine,* May.

Pribram, K. (1971). *Languages of the brain.* Englewood Cliffs, NJ: Prentice-Hall.

Reese, M. (1979, July). *Feldenkrais and the actor.* Paper presented at the American Theater Association Conference, New York, NY.

Reese, M. (1985). Moshe Feldenkrais's work with movement: a parallel approach to Milton Erickson's hypnotherapy. In J. K. Zeig (ed.) *Ericksonian psychotherapy* (Vol. 1). New York: Brunner/Mazel.

Rosenfeld, A. (1981). Teaching the body how to program the brain is Moshe's 'miracle.' *Smithsonian Magazine,* January.

Rywerant, Y. (1981). The problem of pain produced by faulty functioning. *Somatics*, Vol. 3, No. 2, Spring/Summer.

Zeig, J. K. (Ed.). (1980). *A teaching seminar with Milton H. Erickson, M.D.* New York: Brunner/Mazel.

Zeig, J. K. (Ed.). (1982). *Ericksonian approaches to hypnosis and psychotherapy.* New York: Brunner/Mazel.

Strategic Supervision

by
Fritz Klein, M.D. & Sally Cutler Huntington, M.A.

Techniques for changing behavior and creating the optimal climate for growth are two important factors in therapy. When the junior author began supervision with the senior author in 1983, it was recognized that there may be a more effective way to supervise a trainee than in the traditional case report method. The senior author, Fritz Klein, M.D., is a psychiatrist trained in strategic therapy, Ericksonian hypnosis, behavior modification, and Neuro-linguistic Programming. The junior author, Sally Huntington, M.A., is a licensed marriage and family therapist currently in training for licensure as a clinical psychologist.

When supervision sessions began, it was decided that instead of the usual method of Sally presenting Fritz with her cases each week, Fritz would use patterns of strategic intervention during the course of supervision. In this way, the educational process could be experienced at deeper levels than might otherwise be accomplished by simply using didactic instruction, i.e.; "show" instead of "tell." By using strategic intervention with Sally, it was thought that she could learn more quickly and thoroughly.

There are many things that a therapist in training has to learn besides the theory and techniques he/she has already mastered in school and in actual limited practice. A supervisor introduces the trainee to new techniques and their application in the sessions with the trainee's clients. In other words, one can understand the theoretical by practicing and mastering the experiential.

A primary goal of the supervisor is to establish and maximize the self confidence of the trainee therapist. Self confidence as a therapist has to be nurtured and developed in the trainee. This is achieved by complimenting appropriately the trainee's actual skills he/she displays and had already learned. In addition, it may be necessary for the supervisor to increase the trainee's self confidence as a human being.

There are many practical issues that the supervisor can help the trainee with. Among these are the areas that are not taught in school, such as business decisions regarding office space, handling of fees, charges for breaking appointments, bookkeeping and setting up partnerships.

Issues that were possibly taught in school but had not yet taken root have also been found to be prevalent in a new therapist. Among these are the importance of making a verbal contract and knowing how to close it with the patient, creating rapport with the patient, taking time out for oneself, knowing when is the correct time to close a session, and goal setting.

This chapter describes some of the strategies used over the duration of supervision, giving examples for each. Of course, the names and situations have been changed to insure confidentiality of the clients whose cases are described. Some specific interventions were stressed by using them more frequently than others.(1)

Goal Setting

Supervision began in October 1983, with the following exchange.

Fritz: Sally, what is it that you would like to get from supervision?

Sally: I would like to learn from your experience.

Fritz: More specifically, how could you learn from my experience? How can I best teach you?

Sally: Well, when I have a case that is difficult or that I am stumped on, I would like you to offer options I might have overlooked or am unaware of, or different approaches . . . or even role play them with me.

Fritz: What we have just done is the first intervention that takes place with people coming in for therapy. The setting of goals defines why they are there and what they want from therapy, a most important first step (Bandler & Grinder, 1976).

Sally: I suppose that at this time it would be a good idea to assess if their goals are also realistic?

Fritz: Exactly. In addition, you remain focused on their needs or agenda. When these goals are reached, either new ones that have been set up on the way can be worked on or therapy, in fact, is finished. They have accomplished what they have come in to do.

Goal setting is usually one of the initial focusing points as well as an

---

(1)Transcripts used in this chapter are reproduced mostly from the notes taken from the sessions by the senior author. Some conversations were recalled from memory. Direct quotes as well as parts of cases reported were edited in order to ensure a proper flow of this chapter. Dialogue was used at times for the purpose of "showing" rather than "telling."

on-going process present throughout therapy and supervision. The goals need to be clarified not only as to expectations but also assessed as to whether they are realistic. If this is not done, the therapeutic process is either delayed or come to an impasse. It is an on-going concern since goals in fact do change. By being kept in the forefront, therapy remains purposeful. In this way, both parties in supervision as well as in therapy know when goals are being reached. It also permits reevaluation if the goals are not approached in what appears to be an adequate amount of time. The approach to goal setting is a direct approach, as modeled by Fritz' dialogue, no matter what the theoretical background of the clinician may be. Why the client is there, what he/she wants and/or expects from the situation must be clarified to insure appropriateness of the setting for any kind of therapeutic resolution.

Neuro-linguistic Programming and the Concept of Representational Systems

Sally began therapy with a new patient named Mark. She reported what his goals were, along with his presenting complaints, the history of his complaint, and the salient factors in his life history. She gave a detailed summary so that Fritz was able to clearly understand what Mark's problems were and which contributing factors seemed to maintain the symptoms. However, Sally complained that at the end of the initial session with Mark, she did not feel there was as good a rapport with him as she would have liked. There was nothing specific in her awareness to suggest this, but the feeling was there. She was aware of identifying Mark's clear and reachable goals, and so concluded that that was not the basis for the less than desired level of rapport between them.

One of Sally's patterns became apparent to Fritz when he noticed that Sally's eyes would go down to the right whenever she became internally absorbed with remembering things. Another observable pattern in Sally was her frequent use of kinesthetic words when describing her reactions. From the senior author's experience with the Neuro-linguistic Programming model (Bandler & Grinder 1976, 1979), he hypothesized that Sally's feeling of lack of rapport might have to do with her primary representational system being kinesthetic and Mark having a different representational system. Conflicting systems may cause a lack of rapport.

Fritz could not know what Mark's main representational system was without listening to his words and watching his eye movements. He decided to bring this unconscious aspect of communication into the junior author's consciousness. He began using kinesthetic words to let Sally know that he really "felt" her discomfort at not being able to get "closer" with Mark. He asked her if she could "grasp" what had to be done in order to get Mark to "feel" this closeness. Fritz explained how the therapist "moves" to the client's world and uses the client's frame of reference in order to better establish rapport.

By Fritz putting great and exaggeraged stress on the kinesthetic words, Sally was better able to understand what Fritz was driving at. She realized that she had not paid attention to Mark's primary representational system reflected in his language and accessing cues. In retrospect, she was sure that she had kept asking him questions rooted in her own primary representational system with such questions as "How do you 'feel' about that," and "What would you have to do to 'lift' yourself out of that mess?"

Sally began to review in her mind what words Mark used. She remembered specifically him telling her that "his world was 'gray'."

Sally realized that though she had had some training in Neuro-lingustic Programming, she had obviously not effectively integrated her knowledge. She had not established rapport with Mark through the use of using his primary representational system (PRS). In this case, Mark's PRS was most probably visual.

Sally "carried the ball" after she "saw" what had to be done. Subsequently, she reported back that within the first ten minutes of the following session with Mark, she had a "clearer picture" of his problems and made it "clear" to Mark that Sally would be able to "light" the way and 'brighten' his life. She had successfully entered into his model of the world and had established meaningful rapport by tailoring her communication to Mark's preferred system of relating.

Establishing rapport (i.e., the conscious feelings of comfort, sympathy, and trust) is the alliance both supervision and therapy is based on. There are many approaches to establishing this. Understanding the concept of representational systems of Neuro-linguistic Programming is yet another "tool" to assist the therapist in obtaining a desired level of rapport.

Hypnosis

Sally: Fritz, I don't think I'm really being as much help to John and Joyce as I'd like to be. I have seen them for three months with little apparent progress.

Fritz: In what way are you not helping? Be more specific.

Sally: I don't know where I am going with them.

Fritz: Do they know what goals they have, and if so, are they getting nearer to achieving them?

Sally: Yes, with respect to the goals. In fact the goals have changed from Joyce's individual needs for intimacy to mutual unmet needs in the relationship which were specifically defined in terms of the frequency of sexual intimacy. So, yes, they are getting closer to these newly defined goals, and both of them are being more intimate with each other, both sexually and non-sexually.

Fritz: So what's the problem?

Sally: It's just that I don't feel like I am doing much of anything in my interventions.

Fritz: Why don't we work on this problem under hypnosis. (Fritz felt that the problem may be more with Sally's personal discomfort than with her conduct of the therapy itself.)

Lack of self-confidence may be the most common and yet difficult dynamic that the beginning therapist experiences. Having confidence to do therapy ultimately centers on the therapists own self-esteem. Often, a major portion of supervision is focused on building a supervisee's self-confidence through in-depth personal training, building on former successes and enhancing self esteem in general.

Fritz initiated a formal hypnosis induction and then asked Sally to silently review in her mind the problem and the goals of these patients, and her interventions.

Emphasis was placed on Sally trusting her unconscious to facilitate her progress and be confident in her emerging ability as a therapist. Fritz then reinforced her feeling of competency by reminding her of the successful outcomes of previous patients. While in trance Fritz then reinforced this feeling using embedded commands and future pacing as specifically applied to this case.

Upon disengaging from the hypnotic trance, Sally reported objectively, "I really am doing fine with the case. I think it may have been my own lack of self-confidence that I was confused about."

She later reported that she felt better both about that case and about her ability as a therapist. Questioning self-esteem, self confidence, and feeling insecure about one's ability arises in both supervision and therapy. This is an issue that is best addressed early and repeatedly since it is a common and natural phenomenon; often a person does not feel confident when beginning any new task or learning.

Reframing

Sally arrived to a supervision session in a state of emotional upset for having completely forgotten an appointment with a client. She wanted to know the best way to handle this "awful" lapse on her part.

Fritz reframed the incident by smiling and telling Sally that he was delighted that she had forgotten an appointment because it offered a golden opportunity for both herself and her client. She could use this missing of an appointment as a learning tool to show the client that the therapist is human and makes mistakes. Not only can the therapist admit to mistakes without defensive excuses or apologies, but he or she can also responsibly accept the consequences of them. This allows the client the right to his or her feelings about the situation (Kopp, 1977).

In this case, Sally accepted the client's feelings of disappointment and anger over the missed appointment by listening to them without excessive apologies and rebuttal.

Reframing worked both for the junior therapist as well as for the client. Fritz changed Sally's viewpoint into another frame that equally fit the facts of the same concrete situation. This changed the entire meaning for Sally (Watzlawick, Weakland & Fisch, 1974). Sally, in turn, responded to her client with the changed viewpoint, thereby reframing the situation for the client. Not only did the client learn from a mistake that Sally made, but Sally learned the value of reframing by experiencing how her low feelings could change by making her error an opportunity and using it as a tool for growth.

Metaphor

At one supervision session, Sally arrived ten minutes late. She explained that she was having difficulty keeping a fifty minute hour, and would continually run over the time limit. Fritz decided that a therapeutic metaphor was in order. He told Sally that he used to run overtime and would frequently find that by the end of the day he was running late, sometimes by as much as half an hour. He decribed an incident from ten years earlier, one involving a patient of his who had called at the last minute to say that his flight was delayed by bad weather and that he would have to miss his appointment. Since Fritz was running late anyway, he felt relieved that instead of being late and feeling pressured by the clock, he would now have over half an hour of leisure time in the middle of the day. He decided to make use of this free time by relaxing. He made himself a cup of coffee, ate an apple, listened to music, and let himself completely relax. What he learned, as he relaxed, was that if he better spaced his appointments he could experience the same relaxation and be much more alert, ready for, and attentive to his patients.

Fritz used this therapeutic metaphor as an instructional aid, avoiding a possible authoritarian position. By this, he was able to suggest a solution in a non-threatening manner (Kopp, 1971; Zeig, 1980).

Additionally, since Fritz knew Sally's goals to be realistic, appropriate, and capable of change, the actual changes over her scheduling were all within her control (Gordon, 1978).

Although nothing more was said on the subject, Fritz noticed that in the following months Sally had begun to schedule extra time for herself during the working day and had begun to adhere to her desired fifty minute hour.

Amplifying a Deviation

Fritz: Do you have a case for today?

Sally: Yes, I'd like to talk about why my client, Mary, remains stuck in wanting to understand her non-assertive behavior with other people, particularly her husband.

Fritz: Why do you want to know?

Sally: Because by talking about it, perhaps I can better understand the dynamics of her non-assertiveness so we can work on it more effectively in our sessions.

Fritz began to describe Mary's behavior in terms of some possible psycho-sexual causes. "We know of her background with her dominating father, with her concommitant fear of her aggressive impulses. She also has not worked out her relationship with her brother. Then, as you remember, she dreamt about snakes and the whole question of penis envy and rape entered into her relationships with men in general."

After listening to Fritz, Sally understood that in this case the "cause" of the behavior was not going to be reliably identified nor would it be instrumental in her changing. It was agreed that some change of Mary's non-assertive behavior would be necessary. Fritz suggested the change could be an extremely small one, and that a small change might lead to an amplification of other positive behaviors. Ultimately, this could allow her entire system to change in relationship to her husband. It was left up to Sally as to what change she would encourage Mary to attempt.

The following week, Sally reported that Mary had agreed to become assertive in one detail relative to her husband. Mary would tell her husband that she would like him to take out the garbage in order to better balance domestic responsibilities since she did all of the cooking and cleaning.

Sally was delighted to report three weeks later that not only was Mary's husband regularly taking the garbage out, but she was able to assertively ask that he be more active in helping with the children's homework. Further, she asked that he also begin to be on time for their regular Friday night bridge lessons. Her assertive requests were responded to positively, and eased much of the tension between them by better balancing their roles and expectations.

In amplifying small deviations from her previous patterns of behavior, assertive behavior has had an expansive ripple effect. No matter how small the deviation is from the fixed pattern of behavior, it is a step in the right direction. Once a change has begun it often is amplified all on its own (Haley, 1973).

Utilization of Resistance

Shirley, one of Sally's clients, lived with a roommate who was "messy." Shirley was especially bothered by her roommate not putting things back in the refrigerator after their use in the place they belonged. About once a week Shirley would angrily blow up and then clean the "mess" herself.

Sally described Shirley as extremely orderly. Everything had to be neat and she cleaned and polished the house frequently. Rather than trying to change Shirley's patterns by allowing some "mess" and not worrying so much over every "infraction" her roommate committed, Fritz and Sally decided to use her neatness as a way of getting her to not have fights with her roommate.

She was instructed to clean and rearrange the refrigerator to her satisfaction every evening even if it was not messy. Shirley's extreme preoccupation with cleanliness could be used for her benefit. The therapist would "go" with her patterns of neatness which she would feel at one with. By cleaning the refrigerator herself she avoided having fights with her roommate, a decided benefit and advantage in their relationship.

This was proven true a couple of weeks later when Sally reported that Shirley's relationship with her roommate had improved and that they had not fought in over two weeks, an all-time record. Also, Shirley had cut down her cleaning of the refrigerator to two or three times a week.

This aspect of using a resistance was employed by Erickson in therapy. He compared it to trying to change the course of a river. If someone tries to block it, the river will merely go over and around him. But if he accepts the force of the river and diverts it in a new direction, the river will cut a new channel (Haley, 1973). We had used Shirley's extreme cleanliness by channeling it and in the process helped her in her relationship with her roommate.

Prescribing a Worse Alternative

Sally: Fritz, I am so frustrated with Jenny. She complains that she is not motivated to write her term paper. She knows she had to do it, but finds time for everything else, like watching T.V., watering plants, etc. . . . instead of writing the paper. We have explored the consquences of not completing the paper along with other aspects of the possible significance of this behavior. Yet, we return to the same issue without change.

Fritz: That's not unusual. I'm thinking here about what Erickson might do in such a case. He might prescribe a worse alternative to writing her term paper. Take a few minutes and see if you can recall other things she really dislikes that you might suggest she do instead.

Sally: You mean other things she might dislike more than writing the paper? Well, one thing she really hates doing is talking on the telephone. It doesn't matter who initiates the call, and it is worse yet if she is 'supposed' to call someone. Perhaps I could assign her to call one of her friends who is especially talkative instead of doing her paper. During the time she normally has scheduled for writing, she will be required to telephone someone and talk for twenty minutes.

Fritz: That's exactly right.

In this case Jenny cooperated by actually making several phone calls. This showed that a part of her did indeed not want to do the term paper which the therapy reinforced by agreeing that it was all right to postpone writing it. The part that did want to write the paper was reinforced by having her speak on the telephone, an action she truly disliked. By permitting both sides to live side by side in actuality permitted Jenny to integrate and resolve these two aspects of her life in a natural unity, in turn permitting her to write the paper in actuality. By prescribing a worse alternative to Jenny, this paradoxically made writing a paper much easier as it was a pleasure when compared to talking on the telephone (Zeig, 1980).

Anchoring

In one of the supervisory sessions, Sally had no specific problems to present with any of her clients. Fritz asked her if she was formally using patterns of anchoring with any of her clients and whether she had learned of these patterns (Bandler & Grinder, 1979). The answer was "no" to both questions. Fritz asked Sally if she had any anxieties she would like to address therapeutically herself. Sally agreed that her fear of talking in front of her classmates caused anxiety.

Fritz explained that anchoring any one element of an experience will bring back the entire experience (Bandler & Grindler, 1979). The senior author demonstrated the process by asking Sally to recall vividly a time when she was anxious while speaking in front of the class. Sally was able to feel that particular anxiety strongly. Fritz then "anchored" that feeling on her left knee by building an association between his touch of Sally's knee and her experience of anxiety. Next, Fritz directed Sally to recall vividly an episode where she felt extremely competent. When she reported that she was experiencing that feeling, he anchored it to her right knee. Fritz then touched both of her knees at the same time. Sally, unable to select which "anchor" to respond to experienced a "neutral-izing" sensation. Fritz informed her that this phenomenon was called "collapsing the anchors" (Bandler & Grindler, 1979). By demonstrating the use of anchoring with a real anxiety that Sally had, Fritz more effectively demonstrated the usefulness of this tool.

As homework, Sally was encouraged to read literature describing anchoring (Bandler & Grindler, 1979; Yapko, 1984). Her anxiety level did subjectively diminish significantly the next time she had to speak in front of her class. She also began to use this type of intervention with some of her clients.

Spatial Reorientation

Sally: Susan has been in therapy for three months, yet she is unable to talk about her experiences growing up in her family.

Fritz: What do you mean, "unable?"

Sally: She says she cannot remember much about her childhood and there probably is nothing significant there to consider anyway.

Fritz: You've been seeing her regularly for three months. One way to interrupt her restricted way of dealing with you about these issues is to disrupt her pattern in relation to the place she is at with you in therapy by shifting her spatial orientation. She's used to doing things in certain ways, at certain times. If those patterns are interrupted, her resistance may be as well (Haley, 1973).

Sally: She always sits in the same chair in the office.

Fritz: Exactly.

Sally: That is an interesting idea. I'll let you know what happens.

Three weeks later, Sally reported the following:

Sally: I did some spatial reorientation with Susan and the results are interesting. I decided to use another office for the next visit with her. She was unusually verbal and articulate. One thing she described related to her early family life. Although her parents were divorced and she visited her father's house often, she never passed stories from one parent's family to the other. She further stated that the family members all admired her for not talking. I asked her when she remembered these facts. She said she 'just remembered it'.

"It appears that shifting her spatial orientation with regard to my office may in fact have helped her. Of course I can't be sure that was the cause or that something she hadn't contributed to her remembering. But, it did happen when we changed offices. It was as though we had left some family resistances in the old office and she was able to begin talking about her position in her family from a more distant, objective position. Our stereotyped patterns of interaction changed with the new environment."

Synesthesia

Sally reported that she was having a problem formulating an intervention for her client, Kathy. Kathy presented with the complaint of having difficulty falling asleep. She reported to Sally that she has a very strong fear of a robber sneaking in through her bedroom window and attacking her with a knife. She obsesses over that image often, agitating herself, resulting in a lack of sleep.

Fritz used this case to teach Sally a method of altering someone's fear through the use of "synesthesia." Synesthesia refers to the ability of sensory discriminations originating in one sense modality to evoke patterned perceptual experiences in another sense modality (Gordon, 1978). By changing the experience in one modality, the other sense modality can also be affected in the change.

Fritz suggested that Kathy describe in detail what the fear feels like, i.e., where and how the tension manifests itself, and other such sensory description variables. Sally is then to ask Kathy to visualize that tension as a corresponding picture in her mind. When that picture of fear is clear, Sally can change it in some way that seemingly makes psychological sense. The corresponding fear may change accordingly since it is often easier to change a picture of the fear rather than changing the fear itself. This may be especially true of a kinesthetic fear that, though objectively is groundless, had been felt strongly for a long time.

Sally returned the following week with the report that Kathy has visualized her tension, felt acutely in her back, as a coat of armor complete with pointed edges and made of hard metal. Sally had Kathy imagine this coat of armor as a gold one, whose metal was soft instead of hard.

Instead of sharp edges, they were to be rounded. She instructed Kathy to imagine this new golden armor every night when she got into bed.

A few months later in a follow-up session, Kathy reported that she had lost her fear of being attacked and that her insomnia had disappeared. With the change of the picture, she began looking forward to seeing herself nightly in this golden suit of armor and began to fantasize herself in exciting adventures. The fear of the robber just seemed to vanish. By changing the visual modality's imagery, her kinesthetic sense of fear also changed from one of fear to one of adventure.

Summary

Clinical supervision is a process whereby the supervisee has an opportunity to integrate theory with practice and to relate new experiences to an experienced supervisor who has previously dealt with similar situations. Just as one needs a positive therapeutic alliance in order to succeed with a client, one can benefit greatly from a similar therapeutic and educational supervisory alliance.

Fritz ws able to use many of his therapy techniques in a new context. He enjoyed seeing the personal growth that Sally showed during the year, and further felt heartened by the positive outcome of Sally's cases. These are two of the most important possible outcomes for a supervisor.

Sally was equally appreciative of her in-vivo education of strategic intervention techniques. By discovering the hypnotic and strategic patterns in the context of supervision, she had an opportunity to both clinically apply and personally experience the effectiveness of the techniques described in this chapter.

There are many different tools that are relevant to the practice of clinical supervision. The authors believe that strategic intervention used in supervision, i.e.: "strategic supervision," is a most powerful approach that may be used for supervision of therapists in training as well as for peer supervision.

References

Bandler, R. & Grindler, J. (1979). *Frogs into Princes*. Moab, Utah: Real People Press.
Bandler, R. & Grindler, J. (1976). *The Structure of Magic*. (Vol. II.) Palo Alto CA.: Science & Behavior Books Inc.
Gordon, D. (1978). *Therapeutic Metaphors*. Cupertino, CA.: Meta Publications.
Haley, J. (1973). *Uncommon Therapy*. New York: W.W. Norton & Co.
Kopp, S. (1971). *Guru*. Palo Alto CA.: Science & Behavior Books Inc.

Kopp, S. (1977). *Back to One,* Palo Alto CA.: Science & Behavior Books Inc.
Watzlawick, P. Weakland, J. & Fisch, R. (1974). *Change.* New York: W.W. Norton & Co.
Yapko, M. (1984). *Trancework.* New York: Irvington Publishers.
Zeig, J. (Ed.). (1980). *A Teaching Seminar with Milton H. Erickson.* New York: Brunner/Mazel Inc.

Ericksonian Approaches with Language and Learning Disordered Children

By
Diane Yapko, M.A.

It is well known that using language strategically and modifying treatment approaches to the individual needs of a client was Milton Erickson's forte. Ericksonian literature abounds with information on the strategic use of language (Zeig, 1980; Bandler & Grinder, 1975; Grinder & Bandler, 1981). However, there is a striking absence of information in the literature on Ericksonian approaches on how to intervene with individuals whose primary deficit involves language, that is, the language learning disordered population. Although there are adults who have language and learning disabilities, the focus of this paper is on children and adolescents. These children may have difficulty processing or comprehending language, they may have difficulties with language expression, or they may have difficulties using language for the purposes of problem solving and learning. Whatever language based problem they may suffer, these children are frequently referred to psychotherapists for the behavioral manifestations of the language based problem rather than for treatment of the language or learning disorder itself. Such children are frequently referred to a psychologist, psychiatrist or physician with one or more of the following typical presenting complaints. "My child doesn't listen to me and he frequently misbehaves," or "My child is lazy," or "My child is doing poorly in school and I know he could do better if he just tried" (Wiig & Semel, 1984).

Since the presenting complaints (i.e., overt dysfunctional patterns) may seem quite unrelated to the true underlying cause(s), it is important to differentiate the child who is having difficulties which are precipitated or maintained by language-learning problems from the child who does not have a language based problem. This is a necessary step in order to design appropriate interventions that can maximize treatment results and effect desired change.

The purpose of this paper is twofold: 1) to help clinicians recognize language-learning disordered children in order to make appropriate referrals, and 2) to help clinicians modify their treatment strategies by identifying specific Ericksonian approaches which can either foster or inhibit rapport with the language-learning disordered child.

Historically, there has been controversy concerning the terminology used to describe language and learning disabilities. Throughout this paper however, the terms disability, disorder and dysfunction will be used interchangeably in order to refer to a discrepancy between performance and apparent ability. The terms language and learning will be paired throughout this paper in order to incorporate the language component of learning disorders.

The term "learning disability" is defined by the National Joint Comittee for Learning Disabilities (NJCLD) as:

> . . . a generic term that refers to a heterogeneous group of disorders manifested by significant difficulties in the acquisition of listening, speaking, reading, writing, reasoning, or mathematical abilities. These disorders are intrinsic to the individual and presumed to be due to central nervous system dysfunction. Even though a learning disability may occur concomitantly with other handicapping conditions . . . or environmental influences. . ., it is not the direct result of those conditions or influences. (Hammill, Leigh, McNutt, & Larsen, 1981, p. 336. In Mercer, C., 1983, p. 42).

According to the above definition, the terms learning disability (LD) and minimal brain dysfunction (MBD) may be thought of as synonymous since MBD is defined as ". . . a disorder of behavioral and perceptual-cognitive functioning that is assumed to involve some impairment of the central nervous system" (Weiner, 1982, p. 128). As Weiner pointed out, however, not all children with MBD develop learning disabilities. Therefore, MBD is a broader, more inclusive term featuring learning disabilities as the most common consequence (Weiner, 1982).

Characteristics

The process of learning can be thought of as occurring in four stages: attending, perceiving, organizing and retrieving. As Yapko (1984) pointed out:

First there must be some degree of *attentiveness* to the material to be learned. Second, there must be some method of bringing the material from the outside world into the internal world. One's *senses* . . . are the means for gathering information from the world around us. . . . Third, there must be some method for organizing the *information* . . . (and) Fourth, . . . there must be some method for being able to *retrieve* the information from within as necessity dictates (p. 70).

The following characteristics of language-learning disorders can interfere with the learning process at one or more of the above four stages.

Attentional Deficits

One of the most common characteristics of the language-learning disordered child is a difficulty in focusing and maintaining attention. As one child explained, "Doc, I'll tell you just what my head is like. It's like a television set. Only one thing, it's got no channel selector. You see, all the programs keep coming over my screen at the same time" (Levine, 1984, p. 3). For these children, selective attention is an arduous task. Their ability to discriminate relevant from non-relevant information is poor. They are easily distracted by internal or external stimuli. Because these children are tuning in and out, their performance is consistently inconsistent. For this reason, they may perform adequately on one task but not the next, or they may perform poorly on one day but not the next. Because of their apparent ability to perform appropriately on some occasions, they are expected to do so all the time. Hence, parents and teachers often simplistically assume that these children are lazy and could do better if they "just tried," rather than understanding that there is a subtle handicap present which affects the way such a child's brain organizes his or her ability to concentrate.

Hyperactivity and impulsivity are also frequently associated with attentional deficits. Hyperactivity generally refers to an excess of nonpurposeful motor activity. These children are fidgety, seemingly unable to sit or stand still, and are in constant motion. One unfortunate consequence of this behavior is that it makes them more accident prone (Wiig & Semel, 1984; Mercer, 1983).

Impulsivity refers to the child's inability to control or plan an action to say or do something. These children frequently do things quickly without regard for consequences. Due to the impulsivity and tendency toward emotional excitability, these children essentially have little self-control and a low frustration tolerance. They may have quick changes in mood from temper tantrums and tears to giggling and laughing. These emotional displays are generally inappropriate to the circumstances (Wiig & Semel, 1984).

Spatial Orientation and Perceptual Disorders

Children with language-learning disorders frequently have deficits in spatial orientation and perception. They appear lost in time and space (Wiig & Semel, 1984). Spatial and temporal concepts such as *above, below, next-to, behind, yesterday, tomorrow, next week, and right vs. left* are just a few examples of the concepts which can create perceptual havoc for these youngsters. A poor body image in space arising from spatial perceptual difficulties may manifest itself as clumsiness. Clumsiness is defined by five components: misjudging (over-or under-doing), poor timing (too fast or slow), not looking, not listening, and not being able to coordinate several things at once (U.S. Department of Health and Human Services Publication NO. 80-825, 1980). The latter characteristic, not being able to coordinate several things at once, is a primary component of sensory integrative dysfunction. According to Ayres (1972):

> Disorders consistently observed in learning disabled children that are suggestive of inadequate sensory integration in the brain stem are immature postural reactions, poor extraoculary muscle control, poorly developed visual orientation to environmental space, difficulty in the processing of sounds into percepts, and the tendency toward distractibility (p. 342).

A language-learning disabled child's ability to integrate information from more than one modality is frequently impaired. This is clearly demonstrated by poor visual-motor integration processes necessary for learning to write, poor auditory integrative abilities which are correlated with reading success, and the decrease in test performances which are noted when these children are required to process information from various modalities. Weiner (1982) stated that 75% of these children score one year or more below age level in copying designs from the Bender-Gestalt test of visual motor functioning. "They are often inept at putting blocks or puzzles together and slow to master the intricacies of buttoning buttons, drawing circles, and catching a ball . . .(p. 133)." These abilities require a fine motor control that is impoverished in the language-learning disordered child.

Memory Deficits

As previously mentioned, retrieving information is a necessary step in the learning process. However, language-learning disabled children often have difficulties in this area (Hallahan & Kauffman, 1982). They do not spontaneously use the necessary strategies for retrieval such as grouping information according to some classification or chunking information in order to remember a list of unrelated items. In addition, language-learning disordered children may have difficulty retrieving information due to their impoverished language skills. They may simply not possess the verbal mediation skills necessary for storing and retrieving information. For this reason, auditorily presented information may be particularly difficult to organize and remember.

Language Disorders

Language disorders can be independent of, or an integral part of a learning disability. "Language based learning disabilities" is a term used to describe children whose learning dysfunction can be attributed to a deficit in language (Wiig & Semel, 1984).

Language is comprised of three distinct components described by Bloom and Lahey (1978) as 1) content, 2) form, and 3) use. "Content" refers to the meaning of an utterance, "form" refers to syntax, (i.e., grammar), and "use" refers to the social-pragmatic aspect of language.

Content may be broken down into three component parts: phonology, morphology and semantics. "Phonology" refers to the sound system. A phoneme is a unit of sound. For example the word *boat* has 3 phonemes: /b/ /o/ and /t/. Learning disabled children's deficits in phonology relate to difficulty with discrimination of similar sounding phonemes (auditory) or similar looking phonemes (visual).

"Morphology", the second component of the content of language refers to the smallest unit of meaning. For example, the word *boxes* has 2 morphemes, *box* and *es* where *box* is the free morpheme (root word containing meaning and stands alone) and *es* is the bound morpheme (prefixes and suffixes which carry meaning by virtue of their attachment to a root word) and in this example means "more than one."

According to Wiig, Semel and Crouse (1973), morphological problems associated with learning disabled children include an inability to appropriately apply morphological rules for the third person singular of verbs (e.g., adding *es* to form plurals), possessives (e.g., adding 's and s'), adjectival inflections (e.g., adding *er* and *est*) and irregular past tense verbs (e.g., "rided" for "rode").

"Semantics," the third component in the content of language, refers to word meanings and is the symbolic aspect of language. For example, *chair* means "a piece of furniture one sits on." When the name "Milton" is added (e.g., Milton's chair), the concept of possession is added. "Thus, semantics requires an accurate and broad understanding of word categories . . . and their relationships, as well as an understanding of multiple word meanings and figurative language (Mercer, 1983, p. 252)."

Although many language-learning disabled children develop adequate vocabularies, their ability to acquire multiple meanings is often impoverished (Bryen, 1981). For example, a child may define the word *diamond* in a limited context of a shape and not incorporate the precious stone dimension.

In addition to a limited capacity to comprehend multiple meanings, language-learning disabled children tend to literally interpret figurative language (Wiig & Semel, 1984). This literal interpretation applies to idioms (e.g., "My father hit the roof"), metaphors (e.g., "Cold as a stone"), and proverbs (e.g., "Strike while the iron is hot"). A more detailed discussion of the language-learning disordered child's deficits in the areas of semantics, syntax and pragmatics will be presented later in this chapter.

The second component of language described by Bloom and Lahey (1978) is "form," or syntax. In English, the structure of a sentence (form) is critical in deciphering its meaning. For example, "The boy hit the ball" and "The ball hit the boy" have two very different meanings based on word order (grammar). Syntactical deficits in language-learning disordered children may include problems with comprehension of sentences, negative, passives, semantic mood and sentence repetition. Examples of these errors are summarized in Table 1.

The third, and final component of language is "pragmatic," that is, how an individual *uses* the language available to him. Hartzell (1984) pointed out that learning disabled children differ from their 'normal' peers on three dimensions of communicative competence (pragmatics): 1) adapting communicative intentions to the listener and situational characteristics, 2) conveying and comprehending information and 3) initiating and maintaining conversation (i.e., asking questions).

Particularly because language-learning disabled children have difficulty adapting their speaking style to the listener (Soenksen, P., Flagg, C., and Schmits, D., 1981), pragmatic deficits can interfere significantly

TABLE 1

Surface structure of difficult sentence for LD child	Deficit area	Reference
"The car is not bigger than the truck"	Decreased comprehension of negated statement involving a comparison between 2 objects.	Wiig & Semel, 1976
"I will be going", "I will go", "I think I will be going", "I think I may go".	Decreased comprehension of syntactic mood inferred from verbs (will, think, may).	Wiig & Semel, 1976
"Sally was hit by Sue." Was Sue hit? Learning disabled children frequently respond "yes."	Decreased comprehension of passive sentence structure.	Wiig & Semel, 1980
"The cups and a saucer were left on the table."	Decreased ability to accurately repeat a sentence containing plurals articles and prepositions.	Menyuk & Looney, 1972

with social competence and acceptance. This issue is discussed in the next section.

Social/Emotional/Behavioral Deficits

Bryan (1978) studied social relationships and verbal interactions of learning disabled children and found that:

> . . . learning disabled children experience difficulties in social development, interpersonal relationships, and perceiving and understanding others' affective states. It is also quite clear that teachers, peers, and even strangers make negative evaluations of these children. The source of difficulty for LD children's interpersonal problems seems to rest in their comprehension of nonverbal communication, their affective involvements with others, and their expressive language ability—what they say and how they say it (p. 66).

Hartzell (1984) discussed some special problems in working with language-learning disordered adolescents. As he acknowledged, it may be difficult for many people to accept the need for help, and the adolescent who is suspicious of dependent relationships, and needs to prove his or her independence is no different. Therapy with such individuals may be especially difficult and may even seem like wasted effort on a resistant client. "Because adolescents may express fear and resentment in unconscious ways, it is helpful for . . . clinicians to be aware of these behaviors and to recognize their significance" (p. 6). Such patterns are common among adolescents in general, making it even more difficult to be aware of the possibility of an underlying language-learning disability.

Hartzell identified denial, manipulation and acting out as common defenses against help. "Acting out" is a way of expressing anger. Anger may be demonstrated passively by losing or forgetting an assignment, or missing an appointment. Actively expressing anger may be through school vandalism, fighting with peers and arguing with teachers, parents and clinicians.

Denial and manipulation may be viewed on the same defensive continuum. In denial, the child rejects help because the language-learning problem is not yet acknowledged and accepted. Manipulation, on the other hand, involves acknowledging and using the problem as an excuse for not meeting expectations (e.g., "How can you expect me to mow the lawn when I spend so much time at therapy?").

Depression, especially in later adolescence, is another experience commonly observed in this population. Depressive characteristics commonly include: feelings of sadness, negativism, lethargy, social withdrawal, sleep disturbances, and eating disorders (Hartzell, 1984).

Psychosomatic complaints are also common in adolescents who have language-learning disabilities. Headaches and stomach aches are the most frequently observed manifestations and may interfere with attending school or appointments (Hartzell, 1984).

In summary, the learning disabled individual exhibits behavioral impairments which may include: attentional deficits, hyperactivity, distractability, impulsivity and emotional excitability. The perceptual-cognitive characteristics include deficits in: perception, spatial orientation, visual-motor coordination, sensory integration, memory, and language. Last, but not least, the social-emotional characteristics include: interpersonal difficulties, aggressive behavior, lack of self control, and depression.

Adapting Ericksonian Approaches to the Language-Learning Disordered Child

The previous section of this chapter described the common characteristics of the language-learning disordered child in order to better help clinicians recognize these children in their clinical practices. If a child demonstrates several of the characteristics described, appropriate referrals for assessment can be made to Speech-Language Pathologists, Neuropsychologists or learning disability specialists. Although Erickson believed it was not always necessary to know the cause of a disorder in order to treat the symptom, such knowledge *is* essential when dealing with language-learning disabled children in order to strategically use approaches which will maximize treatment results. In addition, as Erickson has stated (Zeig, 1980), he would use the information which his clients provided in order to make some generalizations about their experiences and thus become more aware and tuned into their "map" of the world. Knowing that a child is language-learning disabled can provide a clinician with an ample amount of information for extrapolating the kinds of experiences likely to be present in the child's personal history. That is, the clinician can be aware of the common characteristics which a language-learning disabled youngster exhibits (discussed in the previous section of this paper), and from these, he or she can likely assume that episodes of failure and rejection are not uncommon experiences for these children. The clinician can then generalize that a poor self-esteem is a probable component in the child's internal map. Such generalizations allow for more subtle means of confirming the suspicion than directly confronting the emotionally charged issues. Use of such generalizations by Erickson seemed to give him the mystique of being a "mind-reader" (Yapko, 1985).

In working with children, and specifically language-learning disordered children, flexibility becomes an integral part of a clinician's demeanor. The language-learning disordered child frequently needs repetition of ideas in different formats in order to understand the presented information. Flexibly shifting strategies from a primarily verbal modality to other modalities is a required skill for the clinician working with language-learning disordered children. Using multi-modality approaches will frequently facilitate a child's ability to comprehend information. A creative source for generating such strategies may be found in being able to regress to your own childhood which may facilitate ideas about what children are interested in doing and thinking about.

This section will present some ideas on how to modify Ericksonian approaches when working with language-learning disordered children. Modifying the use of language and, specifically, the use of metaphor and figurative language will be discussed. Additionally, a consideration of homework assignments and confusion techniques will be presented.

Language Modifications

A cornerstone of Ericksonian teachings is the belief that it is necessary to meet the client at his or her frame of reference. This is especially true of the language-learning disordered child because of the language deficits they may exhibit. Adapting one's language to the language-learning disordered client is an integral part of the individual approach to therapy.

Understanding and producing multiple word meanings is a problem for language-learning disabled children. Their reference for a word is usually limited to a single experience with that word, and consequently they have a difficult time generalizing that specific information to another context. This is demonstrated repeatedly in English with homonyms or homophones and homographs. According to the Random House Dictionary of the English Language (1968), a homophone is "a word pronounced the same as, but differing in meaning from another, whether spelled the same way or not. . ." For examples consider the words *"bare and bear"* or *"not and knot."* Although normal adults would assume that the contextual cues would clear up any discrepancy in meaning, language-learning disabled youngsters have difficulty with this aspect of language. A homograph is defined in the Random House Dictionary of the English Language (1968) as "a word of the same written form as another but of different origin and meaning. . . ." For example, *blow* as in *"Blow* up my balloon," or "The fighter got quite a *blow*." A sample list of homophones and homographs is provided in Appendix A.

This information becomes important when talking with a language-learning disabled youngster if the clinician's message is to be comprehended. Imagine that a young boy's frame of reference for the word *"bear"* is a big, brown, grizzly animal that lives in the woods. Further imagine that you, as the clinician, begin to use the relaxing imagery of a beach scene as a means to engage the child's attention and relax him. Using your best hypnotic approach you say "I wonder if you can imagine yourself on the beach, seeing the ocean and hearing the waves crash on the shore as you walk and feel the hot sand on your *bare feet*." Remember, *spelling is not important at this point because the message is being received auditorily, and the child only has an animal as his frame of reference for the word he hears as "bear."* You can easily imagine the disruption of concentration when your client begins to imagine large, brown, hairy feet at the end of his legs as he walks on the beach!

There are several possible causes attributed to the language-learning disordered child's limited ability to comprehend multiple word meanings. Wiig and Semel (1980) summarized them as follows: 1) being rigid and inflexible, 2) adhering to the most frequent and/or concrete word meaning, 3) limited ability to symbolize and conceptualize, and 4) perceptual adherence to one reference.

The need to recognize the individual's limited frame of reference for words with multiple meanings is evident in the following anecdote. A young girl who had a congenital anomaly and looked like a hunchback reluctantly went to a school dance with some friends. As she stood by herself against a back wall, a boy came over to her. He had previously been in a car accident and had one eye surgically removed. The boy asked the girl "Would you like to dance?" She responded "Would I!" and he angrily retaliated with "Hunchback!" and walked away. The young boy had heard the words *would I* as *wood eye* and incorrectly assumed the girl was making fun of him.

In addition to deficits in the comprehension of multiple word meanings, the language-learning disordered child may have difficulty with verbs, adjectives, adverbs, prepositions, and pronouns. This information becomes important as the clinician strategically chooses the words which are best suited for the given situation.

Verbs can create difficulties for the learning disabled child because they may describe complex actions or movements which the child hasn't learned motorically or conceptually (Wiig & Semel, 1980). These may include verbs such as *balancing, bouncing, crouching,* and *swaying.* In addition, discrimination problems may interfere with correct interpretation of phonetically similar verbs, e.g. *bring-ring, spell-sell, driving-diving, growing-groaning*. It is especially important to clearly articulate words which begin with a consonant cluster or blend in order to maximize the child's ability to discriminate what is being said.

Problems with adjectives include perceiving and differentiating spatial meanings, temporal meanings, attributes and qualities (Wiig & Semel, 1980). Examples of words to be aware of when talking with language-learning disabled children include: *long, short, tall, thin, wide, narrow, near, far, first, last, sweet, sour, smooth, rough, mad, sad, surprised* and *angry*. This list is by no means inclusive, rather it provides the clinician with some sample guidelines and hopefully generates a new awareness of concepts which may create difficulty for their language-learning disordered clients.

Adverbs are another area of semantics which are often misinterpreted. Wiig and Semel (1980) report that problems with adverbs seems to reflect difficulties with the

> . . . grammatical classification and interpretation of adverbs
> derived from adjectives. These difficulties affect adverbs derived
> from adjectives by adding *'ly,* such as *"quickly," "slowly,"*
> and *"quietly."* (p. 92).

These are terms frequently used by the clinician who utilizes hypnosis and should be considered as potentially confusing to the language-learning disordered client.

Prepositions may confuse language-learning disordered children for a variety of reasons. These include: problems with understanding reference points in space (e.g., *in, on, under, behind*), changes in direction (e.g., *left, right,* and phrases such as *run over to school, run down to the store),* spatial and temporal uses (e.g., *On* Sunday, *Around* noon). Prepositions can create misunderstanding in idiomatic expressions like "She looks *up* to me," and "She looked *into* the matter." Personal, reflexive, demonstrative, indefinite and negative pronouns may also cause some confusion for the language-learning disabled client.

Figurative language is yet another area in which language-learning disordered children typically experience confusion. This is primarily due to their literal interpretation of word meanings and inability to generalize and abstract meaning.

> In order to understand figurative relationships, you must discern
> changes in meaning, significance, and use of specific words,
> phrases, or sentences and translate the concrete word meanings

into generalized, abstract concepts . . . the words in idioms, metaphors, and proverbs must be translated into nonreferential, abstract, and generalized concepts (Wiig & Semel, 1980, p. 106)

Although language-learning disabled children frequently understand the individual words in an idiom, they tend to interpret only the literal, concrete meaning of the words when they are embedded in figurative language. For example, if one were working with a language-learning disordered boy, he might mention that he got his report card and failed all his classes. After talking about what the child has to say about his grades, and knowing that his mother has been very anxious about his disability, the clinician may spontaneously say, "I imagine that made your mother just *fall apart.*" One need not be surprised if the child wants to call home and hear his mother's voice. After all, he may be imagining the literal interpretation of that common expression! Another clinician's response may be "I bet your father *hit the roof.*" The literal interpretation of that idiom creates a very different picture than the abstract, figurative meaning. Unfortunately, a language-learning disabled youngster may not ask for clarification and so the clinician ay not know whether the child pictured his father being very angry or literally hitting the roof.

Literal interpretation of language is not uncommon in this population. Erickson, and others, have associated literalness with the presence of a hypnotic state. (Yapko, 1984). A question such as "Do you mind telling me your name?" may be received by the language-learning disabled client and the response may be a literal, "no," rather than responding with his name. This would *not* be an indication of the hypnotic state in these individuals.

Metaphors

There have been several studies on how "normal" children develop metaphoric understanding (Billow, 1975; Winner, Rosenstiel, & Gardner, 1976). It is beyond the scope of this paper, however, to address the developmental aspects of metaphoric acquisition. More importantly, for purposes of this discussion, the clinician should be aware of some limitations which the language-learning disabled child may encounter when attempting to comprehend a well intentioned clinician's metaphor.

It may be helpful to distinguish the traditional meaning of a metaphor from the Ericksonian meaning of metaphor. Metaphor in the traditional sense means "the application of a word or phrase to an object or concept it does not literally denote, in order to suggest comparison with another object or concept. . . ." (Random House Dictionary, 1968). In Ericksonian circles, the term metaphor has been distorted to become synonymous with story telling.

Metaphor as story telling is an approach which can be used with the language-learning disordered child as an excellent way to obtain and maintain attention (providing the metaphor [story] is interesting to that child). It should be pointed out, however, that expecting the language-learning disabled youngster to infer or generalize that information to some more meaningful event in his life is *a horse of a different color*. As previously mentioned, these individuals have difficulty making inferences, generalizing information or dealing with abstraction. If this factor is taken into account, metaphors may be meaningfully used. If this factor is not taken into account however, the therapeutic efforts may be marginal at best.

The Neuro-linguistic Programming model (Bandler & Grinder, 1979) has helped make many clinicians aware of the importance of different sensory modalities in processing information. For the language-learning disabled youngster, this takes on a different meaning, discussed in an earlier section of this chapter as sensory integration. In order to maximize the benefit of the stories which clinicians create, they should use as many modalities as possible in their delivery. Movement for these children is a necessary component for learning.

> Since sensory and motor development are aspects of neural processing and of the development of thinking and reasoning skills, young children should be given as many opportunities to move in as many ways as possible. (Williams, 1983, p. 150)

This may best be done by having the child act out the story or part of the story whenever possible.

As the Ericksonian clinician becomes more aware of the characteristics of the language-learning disabled youngster it should seem apparent that confusion techniques would not be the best of methods to employ with these individuals. In addition, homework assignments should be very creative if compliance is expected. These children have had very little success in the past and the clinician's assignments should naturally be ones in which the child can experience success. The reader is referred to the chapter on children in *Uncommon Therapy* (Haley, 1973) for examples of how Erickson motivated his younger clients to experience success.

Conclusion

The intent of this paper was to introduce the clinician who works from an Ericksonian perspective to the world of the language-learning disabled child. By developing a greater awareness for this population, clinicians will hopefully begin to modify their techniques and adapt them according to the individual needs of these children. A major theme evident throughout this chapter concerns the appropriateness of Ericksonian approaches for the language-learning disabled population. Erickson's innovative use of language patterns presupposes a "normal" unconscious mind that can process multiple and symbolic meanings inherent in metaphors, behavioral prescriptions, and other Ericksonian approaches to hypnosis and psychotherapy. The very patterns that can foster broader patterns of functional living in most people can have a negative effect on the language-learning disabled population. Thus, sensitivity to the deeper issues associated with this population can lead to more in-depth assessment of individuals with presenting complaints that may reflect a language-learning disorder. Once confirmed or ruled out, treatment can proceed with a larger degree of certainty about the appropriateness of interventions chosen.

References

Ayres, A. (1972). Improving academic scores through sensory integration. *Journal of Learning Disabilities, 5,* 338-43.

Bachara, G. & Zaba, J., (1978). Learning disabilities and juvenile delinquency. *Journal of Learning Disabilities, 11,* 242-46.

Bandler, R. & Grindler, J. (1975). *Patterns of the hypnotic techniques of Milton H. Erickson, M.D.* (Vol. I). Cupertino, Ca.: Meta Publications.

Bandler, R. & Grindler, J. (1979). *Frogs into princes.* Moab, Utah: Real People Press.

Billow, R. (1975). A cognitive developmental study of metaphor comprehension. *Developmental Psychology, 11,* 415-23.

Bloom, L. & Lahey, M. (1978). *Language development and language disorders.* New York: John Wiley & Sons.

Bryan, T. (1978). Social relationships and verbal interactions of language disabled children. *Journal of Learning Disabilities, 11,* 58-66.

Bryen, D. (1981). The language and learning problems. In A. Gerber & D. Bryen (Eds.), *Language and learning disabilities.* Baltimore: University Park Press.

Bush, C. (1979). *Language remediation and expansion.* Tucson, Az.: Communication Skill Builders, Inc.

Grinder, J. & Bandler, R. (1981). *Trance-formations.* Moab, Utah: Real People Press.

Griffiths, A. (1978). *Teaching the dyslexic child.* Novato, Ca.: Academic Therapy.

Haley, J. (1973). *Uncommon therapy.* New York: Norton.

Hallahan, D. & Kauffman, J. (1978). *Exceptional children: Introduction to special education* (2nd ed.). Englewood Cliffs, N.J.: Prentice Hall.

Hartzell, H. (March, 1984). The challenge of adolescence. *Topics in Language Disorders,* 1-9.

Lane, B. (1980). The relationship of learning disabilities to juvenile delinquency: Current status. *Journal of Learning Disabilities, 13,* 425-34.

Levine, M. (1984). The medical forum. In *The Harvard Medical School Health Letter.* Vol. IX, No. 11.

Menyuk, P. & Looney, P. (1972). A problem of language disorder: Length versus structure. *Journal of Speech and Hearing Research, 15,* 264-79.

Mercer, C. (1983). *Students with learning disabilities* (2nd ed.). Columbus, Oh.: Charles E. Merrill Publishing Company.

Senf, G. (1973). Learning disabilities. *Pediatric Clinics of North America, 20,* 607-40.

Solaksen, P., Flagg, C. & Schmits, D. (1981). Social communication in learning disabled students: A pragmatic analysis. *Journal of Learning Disabilities, 14,* 238-86.

Torgeson, J. & Kail, R. (1980). Memory processes in exceptional children. In B.K. Keogh (Ed.), *Advances in Special Education: Basic constructs and theoretical orientations.* Greenwich, Ct.: J.A.I. Press.

U.S. Department of Health & Human Services. (1980). "Plain talk about children with learning disabilities." Publication No. 80-825. Rockville, Md.

Weiner, I. (1982). *Children and adolescent psychopathology.* New York: John Wiley & Sons.

Wiig, E. & Semel, E. (1976). *Language disabilities in children and adolescents.* Columbus, Oh.: Charles E. Merrill Publishing Company.

Wiig, E. & Semel, E. (1984). *Language assessment and intervention for the learning disabled* (2nd ed.). Columbus, Oh.: Charles E. Merrill Publishing Company.

Wilgosh, L. & Paitich, D. (1982). Delinquency and learning disabilities: More evidence. *Journal of Learning Disabilities, 15,* 278-9.

Williams, L. (1984). *Teaching for the two-sided mind.* Englewood Cliffs, N.J.: Prentice Hall.

Winner, E., Rosenstiel, A. & Gardner, H. (1975). The development of metaphoric understanding. *Developmental Psychology, 12,* 289-97.

Yapko, M. (1984). *Trancework: An introduction to clinical hypnosis.* New York: Irvington.

Yapko, M. (1985). The Erickson hook: Values in Ericksonian approaches. In J. Zeig (Ed.) (pp. 266-281). *Ericksonian psychotherapy* (Vol. I). New York: Brunner/Mazel.

Zeig, J. (Ed.) (1980). *A teaching seminar with Milton H. Erickson.* New York: Brunner/Mazel.

Ziegler, R. (1981). Child and context: Reactive adaptations of learning disabled children. *Journal of Learning Disabilities, 14,* 391-93.

Appendix A:
Homophones and Homographs

HOMOPHONES: Words that sound alike but are spelled differently.

Spelling of word	Meaning of word
allowed	permitted
aloud	audible
board	lumber
bored	uninterested
carrot	vegetable
carat	weight of metal
die	expire
dye	color
heard	listened
herd	group of animals
scene	setting
seen	viewed
stair	step
stare	look intently

HOMOGRAPHS: Words that look the same but have several meanings.

Spelling of word	Meaning of word
arms	body parts weapons
bank	land along a river financial institution
blow	hard hit send forth a stream of air
blue	color feeling down
fast	speedy go without food
rose	flower stand up (past tense)
shark	large meat-eating fish dishonest person

Words that look alike and sound alike but have different meanings.
Clinicians must learn to articulate clearly if they want a particular word
to be heard correctly and therefore correctly interpreted.

affect/effect	quiet/quite
all ready/already	suppose/supposed
formally/formerly	than/then
picture/pitcher	use/used

References

Bush, C. (1979) **Language Remediation and Expansion.** Communication Skill Builders, Inc. Tuscon, Arizona.

Fry, E., Polk, J., and Fountoukidis, D. (1984) **The Reading Teacher's Book of Lists.** Prentice-Hall, Inc. Englewood Cliffs, New Jersey.

INVITED ADDRESS

Parts Work: The Neverending Story

by
Paul M. Carter, Ph.D.

This is a speculative paper in which I invite you to wonder along with me through some observations, dreams, thoughts, and a story or two. My major premises are that somehow *everything* we do is important and that the things we call "sick," "crazy," or "bad" are necessary parts of "our whole story." This is a theme that is being expressed today by more and more people in many diverse fields of exploration. Working with this theme as an ongoing guide in therapy as well as in life is not always an easy matter, and seems to require a certain "spiritual confidence" or faith in the basic intelligence of the universe. In so far as we can do this, our lives become a neverending story of growth and learning.

In terms of a modus operandi for people helpers, the process could involve the following series of steps: 1) Observe what is going on. 2) Accept what is going on without framing it positively or negatively. 3) Develop and expand what is going on. 4) Allow balancing parts to come out. 5) Validate all parts as well as the process of developing and balancing.

The most basic idea we're working with here is to be willing to develop ongoing patterns without evaluating them. We're assuming that we can get to where we want to go by using what's already here. Let me begin with a basic example from someone outside the field of psychotherapy which illustrates this most natural process of learning.

The following anecdotal case report was related to me by a student of Dr. Moshe Feldenkrais. Apparently, there was a successful European pianist who had heard that Feldenkrais had been of great help to other musicians and so went to Israel to see him. His problem was this: Though already a well-known conductor and pianist, he found himself incapable of learning a new piece of music in less than two years' time. As hard as he'd tried for years to improve this, two years seemed to be his minimum time for adding a new piece of his repertoire. The man was so involved in his particular framework for learning that he had become incapable of effectively using his abilities fully, as was soon demonstrated to him.

When he met with Feldenkrais, he had with him the score of a new piece he wanted to learn, which Feldenkrais promptly asked him to bring out. Feldenkrais had the man sight read the entire piece in his mind, listening to each passage as he looked at it. Being a conductor, he was quite capable of doing this. Feldenkrais then handed him a pencil and asked him to read through the piece again, this time marking out his very favorite phrases. When he had finished, Feldenkrais asked the gentleman to sit down at the piano and play just those few phrases which he had marked out as most pleasing to his ear. He did so with ease. Feldenkrais then instructed him to play the note before and the note just after each of his favorite phrases, which he also did with ease. After mastering that, Feldenkrais asked him to continue building in that fashion, adding just one note before and one note after each of his favorite phrases each time he played through the score. Feldenkrais did nothing else. The man learned his piece in less than a month.

This is a beautiful example of beginning with the smallest bit you can do well and slowing developing that into the larger whole. In the same way, you can start with the smallest bit of a whole person that is working—positively or negatively—and through the development of it come out into the larger whole person once again. It is this process of going from the whole to a part and back to the whole again which I am calling The Neverending Story. It is through this process of breakdown, separation, and reintegration, like the breaking down of the piece of music, the separating out of a few phrases, and the slow note-by-note reintegration of the whole piece, that we all learn and grow through the movements of our own life stories.

In the book called *The Neverending Story* by Michael Ende, the land of Fantastica, a symbolic representation of the unconscious, is being devoured by the great Nothing, a symbolic representation of the idea that nothing exists beyond what can be perceived by the five physical senses, as in behaviorism. The mythic child hero, Atreyu, is sent by the Childlike Empress of Fantastica on a journey of many challenges, allegedly to discover how to save the Childlike Empress and Fantastica from the spreading plague of the Nothing. Atreyu discovers that Fantastica can only be saved when the Childlike Empress is given a new name and that this can only be done by a human living beyond the boundaries of Fantastica. Since Fantastica has no boundaries, he returns to the Empress at the end of his journey believing himself failed in his mission to save Fantastica. Before he tells her a single word of his quest, she tells him he has done well, to which he responds that it is not so, that he has failed, and there is no hope. . . .

A long silence followed. Atreyu buried his face . . . and his whole body trembled. How would she react? With a cry of despair, a moan, . . . anger? Atreyu couldn't have said what he expected. Certainly not what he heard. Laughter. A soft, contented laugh. . . . Then he heard her say: "But you've brought him with you."

Atreyu looked up. "Who?"

"Our savior."

He looked into her eyes and found only serenity. She smiled again.

. . . He stammered. . . ., "I . . . no, really . . . I don't understand."

"I can see that by the look on your face," she said. "But whether you understand or not, you've done it. And that's what counts, isn't it?"

"I saw him," she went on, "and he saw me."

"When?" Atreyu asked.

"Just as you came in. You brought him with you."

Involuntarily Atreyu looked around.

"Then where is he? I don't see anyone but you and me."

"Oh, the world is full of things you don't see. You can believe me. He isn't in our world yet. But our worlds have come close enough together. . . . He will be with us soon and then he will call me by the new name that he alone can give me. Then I shall be well, and so will Fantastica."

As the Childlike Empress was speaking, Atreyu raised himself with difficulty. . . . "Then you've known my message all along? What Morla the Aged One told me in the Swamps of Sadness, what the mysterious voice of Uyulala in the Southern Oracle revealed to me—you knew it all?"

"Yes," she said. "I knew it before I sent you on the Great Quest."

Atreyu gulped.

"Why did you send me then? What did you expect me to do?"

"Exactly what you did," she replied.

"In that case," he said angrily, "it was all unnecessary. There was no need of sending me on the Great Quest. . . . But after all I've been through I hate to think that you were just having a joke at my expense."

The Childlike Empress's eyes grew grave.

"I was not having a joke at your expense, Atreyu," she said. "I am well aware of what I owe you. All your sufferings were necessary. I sent you on the Great Quest—not for the sake of the message you would bring me, but because that was the only way of calling our savior. He took part in everything you did, and he has come all that long way with you. You heard his cry of fear. . . . You entered into his image and took it with you, and he followed you, because he saw himself through your eyes. And now, too, he can hear every word we are saying. He knows we are talking about him, he knows we have set our hope in him and are expecting him. Perhaps he even understands that all the hardship you, Atreyu, took upon yourself was for his sake and that all Fantastica is calling him. . . ."

"Do you understand now, Atreyu," she asked, "why I had to ask so much of you? Only a long story full of adventures, marvels, and dangers could bring our savior to me and that was your story." (Ende, 1979, pp. 145-147).

The savior who was referred to in the above excerpt is a human child named Bastian who, in *The Neverending Story,* is reading the book called *The Neverending Story,* which describes Atreyu's quest. He is a symbolic representation of the Self. This passage tells us that, like Atreyu-Bastian, the purpose of our journey is not to discover something we don't already know, but rather to have a way of remembering and using what we do already know. It is my suggestion that disease is simply a part of our journey. Its general purpose is to awaken us and to involve the Self more fully in responding to our needs so that we grow toward wholeness. Like Atreyu, we may not be able to see just who and what we need to help us; but by going through the process of life, including what we call "disease" and "pain," we seem to learn and grow and to emerge more involved and connected with ourselves than we had been. And like Atreyu, we do not discover something that is not in some way already existent and known, but rather our disease and pain stimulates us to reconnect more fully with that which we have simply forgotten, dissociated, and left behind. It is rather like Erickson's saying, "I'm not asking you to use a skill that you don't have. I'm only asking you to be willing to use a skill which you have but don't know you have." The therapist's task, then, becomes one of developing the story in such a way as to help the client know and use his own resources and the ones around him more fully.

There are certainly numerous examples from Erickson's work of his reflecting back his client's behaviors or developing them through some real life task or story in such a way as to involve the client more fully. Erickson talked about these interventions as the need for the patient to see his own behavior and the need to get the patient involved and active in his own therapy. Likewise, one of the greatest values of hypnosis in therapy is in the heightened intensity of experiential involvement produced by the trance. Like the involvement of the human child, Bastian, that saves Fantastica in *The Neverending Story*, it is this fuller involvement of the client in therapy, developed through therapeutic tasks, stories, and trance, that leads to learning and growth in the human world.

The part of this natural process of learning, living, and growing with which most of us seem to have difficulty is accepting and developing parts of the "story" that we pre-judge to be "bad," "sick," and "crazy." Yet, it is exactly these "negative" parts that have the most immediate potential for more fully involving the client and other parts of the client's system in therapy. We need to be willing to develop the awareness, expression, meaning, and direction (instruction) of these so-called "bad" parts so that their value becomes clear and integration of the Self becomes possible. To illustrate how this may be done, I will describe three cases from my own studies.

Some years ago I met a nine-year-old girl whom I'll call Theresa. She had been involved in fights at school and was frightening some of the other children, not to mention her teachers and parents, by making marks on her arms, drawing her own blood, with the school compass. It was reported to me that she talked to herself a lot, sometimes quite loudly and angrily, and seemed to be quite successful in beating up other children, even those larger than herself. Her father told me he knew Theresa was "a good kid" but was afraid she had a "bad self-image." According to him, the school psychologist had labeled Theresa a child schizophrenic and had suggested the possibility of hospitalization. Both Theresa's parents and teachers were expressing the fear that she was becoming unmanageable. My challenge was to find a way to develop Theresa's abilities before some of these labels became too fixed and unmanageable.

When I first saw her, I noticed immediately that Theresa was a child in a lot of pain and that she looked, physically as well as emotionally, very similar to her father. She was feeling quite destructive that day, so I encouraged her to have a good tantrum on my bed, and then we continued working with her anger through some drawing. She loved drawing cats and dogs and identified herself immediately with a cat and her father with a dog. She went into quite some detail drawing a cartoon sequence of a cat destroying a dog in a fight. She enjoyed pointing out to me the claw marks and pools of blood, which she had made quite graphic. I began to notice Theresa's tension lessening and what felt like a sense of appreciation developing between us. At this point, I asked Theresa to close her eyes and just sit quietly while imagining a cat she really liked sitting on her lap. She had an easy time enjoying that feeling. I told her that it could become difficult to know just where the cat's feelings stopped and hers began. She assured me she had no difficulty with *that* and sat very contentedly for a few minutes with a beautiful smile purring through her whole face.

Here we can see how the development of what other people were calling "bad" and "crazy" was already beginning to transform. As work progressed with Theresa over several months, her anger was developed more fully, which led to her learning other means of separating herself, relaxing, and appreciating herself. It also awakened Theresa's parents, with my assistance, to the idea that they needed help with their own frustrations and angers, which they had been working out solely through Theresa. Greater acceptance of anger and the complementary need for appreciation in this family was the key to its transformation and Theresa's improvement in school.

A second case which illustrates this process involved a fifty-year-old man named John. John was a person many people had referred to as "a little crazy" and sometimes "very crazy." One moment he would be very quiet and removed and the next instant would explode into another's conversation with loud exclamations seemingly non sequitur to any current interaction. In response to someone's question about what he was trying to say or what he wanted, he would talk angrily about "flowers in the heavens" or something equally bizarre, and then just as suddenly would start mumbling to himself and making discounting gestures with his hands. As far as I knew, he had never physically accosted anyone, though his physical tension and sudden wild gesturing intimated violence and was certainly successful in keeping people away from him.

I first met John when he began coming to my training groups to learn hypnosis and family therapy. He was working with disturbed children, with whom he had an unusually good rapport and much success in therapy. In observing client families we brought to the group, John was always very accurate and vivid in his descriptions of the covert aggressions and alienation of particular family members. But because of his unusual style of communicating, John was quickly labeled the group "weirdo," with the result that only one person in the 15-member group was willing to work with him when we separated into pairs for training exercises. This was our unconscious group modeling of covert aggression and alienation of a family member.

Over the course of the training, I often demonstrated that John was responsive to playful and oppositional communications which matched his style. If I asked him to relax, John would find himself growing painfully tense. So, to develop relaxation and a pleasant childhood memory, I would ask John to be tense and on guard, not to relax or take a deep, easy breath, and above all to allow no memory of a pleasant childhood experience to enter his mind. I would smile pleasantly and John would smile mockingly as he breathed deeply, relaxed, and described a flash of some meaningless image of himself as a child being tossed playfully in the air by his father. I made note that so long as I made no attempt to change his oppositional style, we progressed excellently, and from time to time John would change his style by himself.

At the end of the two-year training period, most of the group's members had learned to "put up" with John and yet were still experiencing a lot of frustration with him. I kept telling individual members that their frustration was not exclusively John's fault nor was it their own, but rather was the result of their belief that they needed to change John rather than to develop his abilities. This, by the way, is one of the major problems engendered whenever we label someone "sick" or "bad." These labels initiate and condone a relationship wherein our approach to the person so labeled implies "You have to change and I don't." The basis of this system and any change that results from it is one of invalidation and alienation. This type of relationship does not provide a very solid foundation for learning. As a more effective alternative, I am suggesting that we accept all parts of a person as being of value and important in the whole process. Rather than implying, "You have to change and I don't," this approach implies, "Let's develop all of our parts. We don't know yet just how they are valuable, but let's find out." Validation and co-operation are the hallmarks of this system.

On the final weekend of the training, I decided it was time to work with the "crazy" part of our group. I asked John to sit in front of the group and tell me what he thought was limiting him the most, what was "really killing him." This is something he had talked about. He said, "It's this suppression," describing it with both his hands pushing down with extreme pressure while he blew out his breath loudly. In John's opinion, this came from his father's suppression of almost any verbal or nonverbal expression he had tried in childhood or adulthood. Hoping to find some ways in which the group could support him while simultaneously developing the group's responses to John, I had the whole group come around him and push down on him, mirroring John's particular expression of suppression, so that all of a sudden there were twelve people pushing on this man physically and exhaling loudly. Now, John was an incredibly strong person, as are many people who have lived with his kind of experiences. He started to laugh somewhat strangely, so I had a few of the people mirror his laugh and remarked that the laughter was another good suppression technique. We just took whatever he gave and gave it back to him. After a while he started to cry, so we started to cry with him; then he became very quiet and still and developed a very deep trance. Any time you feed back to people everything they're doing really completely, they'll go into a very deep trance—perhaps because there's nothing else left to do! At this point, I asked everyone to sit down and be at ease and gave John a suggestion to dream a dream in which he began to see what the value of his suppression was. I suggested he could develop this awareness in his night dreams and then we completed the day's work with a peaceful group induction.

John came back the next day and said to the group, "I failed." John and I had an agreement. As you may recall, whenever I told him to relax, he went tense, so I knew what he was saying to me now.

I said, "Oh, great, what did you see?"

He said, "Well, I saw . . . it's really stupid. I saw this giant sun. . . ."

And I said, "Okay. Everyone in the group become the sun." This was a pretty flexible group by this time, so everyone experienced themselves as the sun and felt what it's like to be the sun, first by sitting in trance and then standing and moving as the sun. Then I said, "Okay, what do you notice?" Different people said they felt power, strength, warmth, and energy and then I noticed something, too. I noticed that nobody can get close to the sun. This was certainly an important dimension and value of John's suppression. You can't get close to the sun, can you? It's a fantastic thing. In addition to this power, this incredible energy, I asked people to identify with this other dimension of suppression which was a feeling of "You can't touch me." Feel that for a second; it's a wonderful experience. "You can't touch me. There's nothing you can do that can affect me. I am invulnerable. No attack can damage me. I am truly safe." You could send off the entire world arsenal of nuclear warheads to the sun and they wouldn't even get close. (Come to think of it, that might not be a bad idea. . . .). That's how powerful the sun is. That's how powerful the indestructible part of each of us is. John had represented this part as suppression, his father, and the sun. (Sounds like the Trinity, doesn't it?)

The remainder of the day was spent developing and integrating a balance to the powerful sun. As a group, we came up with the image of a soft, lonely child to stand for our need and ability to be vulnerable, touchable, and a part of others. We spent some time working to accept and define some ways for each of us to continue developing these complementary parts. Although John had a long way to go to fully accept and integrate both the power and invulnerability of a sun and a touchable receptivity of a child, he was quite changed by his experiences. Most remarkable was his calm acceptance of touch and appreciation from others. Prior to this weekend, in response to a message of appreciation or a compliment, I had only seen John frown, shake his head, hold his breath, contradict the message, and sometimes get quite angry. I found his change amazing. As for the rest of the group, this work with John was one of the highest and most important experiences of the entire training. It all came out of the "weirdo," John, and our willingness to develop the "craziness," the suppression, and the balancing part of the soft, lonely child, which we came up with as a result of developing the powerful suppression.

A final example of a "bad" part of a person leading that person back to his own wholeness was the case of a colleague of mine named George who told me that he had one major problem. He felt that no matter how good he became at anything, he never really experienced complete confidence in himself. In fact, it seemed the more successful he was, the worse his problem became. He was already a successful family practitioner with a full practice and an excellent reputation. He was also beginning to teach classes and, although he was being successful and knew he was good, he was beseiged by what he described as a very painful self-criticism. Not only was this process preventing him from enjoying his life, but he also feared that it would soon begin to make him fail in his work. It was with this fear that he approached me for some help. I was quite happy to explore this with him as I'd felt something uncomfortable in George's confident demeanor ever since we had met and become friends.

I told George I'd pretend to be him—his cool, successful part—and he should ruthlessly criticize me in the same way that his inner voice criticized him. Thus we began our role-play. I started talking to him about how well I was doing and how happy I was with my first teaching experiences, when George interrupted me and began to pick me apart piece by piece, with tremendous confidence I might note. He was saying things to me like, "You don't know what you're talking about. Who the hell do you think you are. You're just a big, pompous ball of hot air. You're full of it!" As I tried to maintain the good, cool, calm composure that I'd seen in George so many times, George got more intense and colorful in his criticisms. "You think you're like God Almighty, with all your great stories and grandiose new intervention techniques!"

At this point I raised my voice and asked him, "Okay, so you don't like how I am. How do you want me to be?"

In the same loud, confident tones he had been using throughout this dialogue, only now with the sarcasm sounding more like compassion, George responded, "I just wish you'd stop trying to be somebody bigger than you are and just appreciate being yourself. Just be yourself!" I was surprised and George was stunned at discovering the intentions of this part of himself. The very part of himself that he had blamed for disturbing his confidence, let alone his enjoyment of himself and his successes, was in the end wanting to find a way for him to appreciate himself.

I have actually seen this many times since, that the intention of the critical part is appreciation. All that is spoken is the criticism, but the essence of the part is simply trying to make things into or return things to a state which he is capable of appreciating. This is often the case with a highly critical parent who is desperately trying to find a way to appreciate his child, not to mention himself, with whom he feels he is losing all understanding and connection. Now George's problem could be much more effectively described. He needed to find a way to balance a desire to improve himself and expand his professional horizons with his need to just appreciate himself as he already was. Instead of a "good" part and a "bad" part, he now had two important dimensions of his whole self to enjoy and support. Developing his parts within this more accepting framework made it possible for George to enjoy a much more powerful confidence based on the integration of seemingly opposite parts. This integration came from his willingness to develop more fully a part he had been certain was "bad" and "screwing up" his life.

For the past several years, I have been working on a manuscript, *The Parts Model,* in which I describe in detail how to develop difficult parts and their complements and reintegrate them into a whole. Repeated experiences like those with George, Theresa, and John led me to the following conclusion, which I will quote from my manuscript:

As I look back on my experience of working with this model for nearly six years now, there is one conclusion in particular that stands out. It is a rather paradoxical one, naturally. I say naturally because scientists, artists, and lay people alike are finding nature to be inherently paradoxical. What I have found is this: It is indeed the most negative and debilitating parts of a person which contain the seed (germ) of his greatest support. A pine seed, through the mystery of its genetics, acts to control, attract, and organize the appropriate nutrients from its environment to germinate and grow into a magnificent tree. The most negative part of a person, like the seed, can act as a magnet, attracting to itself the exact kind of love, support and nurturance that it needs, thus becoming a splendid symbol of the very love, support, and nurturance that it needed.

As with the seed, all that is needed to fulfill this incredible potential is the right environment. For the pine seed, that means soil with the right nutrients, sunshine, water, temperate zone, and ecosystem. For the evolving human, we are still discovering the necessary ingredients of that environment. With my clients, I have seen many important ingredients: love, acceptance, challenge, touch, vision, humor, trust, structure, and non-structure.

What I have suggested here is a very different view of illness. I am suggesting that illness and problems are a means we have to effect positive transformations. Within the framework of the Parts Model, all problems become a way of developing your parts and coordinating their mutual support. This is done through the development of greater awareness of all parts and the acceptance and integration of all parts. As Moshe Feldenkrais wrote:

lThe few exceptional men who really sought peace and true brotherly love reached this condition by perfecting their awareness, not by suppressing their passions. (Feldenkrais, 1972, p. 172).

I believe our common task is to stop invalidating our parts by calling them wrong, sick, or crazy and to begin the process of valuing and utilizing all our parts. It is an out-of-date belief that says we can't all live together. (Carter, 1983, pp. 181-3).

In this paper, I have discussed what I call the natural process of learning and growth through the acceptance, development, and validation of what is already occurring. I have focused on the therapeutic importance of learning to accept what may be labeled as "bad" parts and, through several case presentations, have shown how the development of a "bad" part is critical to growth and transformation.

As I have mentioned before, I know that accepting some parts can be very difficult, especially when we find them in our own home. Acceptance is great in theory, but when that kid gets drunk and ruins *my* car and *my* family, when this disease ruins all my great plans, my work, my sport, my everyday life, when those people hold *our* people hostage, then it's not so simple to consider helping those parts develop. We are mostly trained to be strong and healthy and to resent any uninvited intrusion into our system, yet it is this very dissociation from difficult parts that gives them their power to intrude and seemingly to break us. The next time you meet a part you consider bad, instead of saying "no" to it, try saying, "I don't know (no). I don't know how you are important or what you may help me with, but let's find out." When I began working with Theresa, George, and John, I had no idea what would develop. All I had was that funny kind of "spiritual confidence," what Erickson referred to as trusting your unconscious, what some call faith in God, what I sense as the basic correctness of all that is here. Armed with this knowledge, when we develop any part we will be ready to notice its value. Disease is the message that there are parts and needs that we have been ignoring and must attend to in order to become healthy again. These parts are physical and psychological and social and spiritual. I am suggesting that we can value both our strength and our weakness, our friends and our enemies. Both are important. In our strength we act and create, but it is through our weakness that we grow and become strong. Through the whole the neverending process of strength breaking down through weakness building us back up into strength, we become complete, powerful with no need to prove our power, a humble power, a peaceful warrior, a whole piece of the whole.

References

Carter, P. (1983). *The parts model: A formula for integrity.* Unpublished doctoral dissertation. International College.

Ende, M. (1979). *The neverending story.* New York: Penguin Books.

Feldenkrais, M. (1972). *Awareness through movement.* New York: Harper & Row.

Index

AUDIO VISUAL DEMONSTRATIONS

• The Artistry of Milton H. Erickson   In this two-part presentation, Milton H. Erickson elegantly demonstrates the clinical techniques in hypnosis that made his therapy so effective.   2 videos, 104 minutes,
Milton Erickson and *Herbert Lustig* $400

• A Primer of Ericksonian Psychotherapy   Recorded in professional television facilities, this thirty-two minute long videotape provides invaluable guidance to students of Erickson's clinical genius.
Milton Erickson and *Herbert Lustig* $150

• The Reverse Set in Hypnotic Induction   A forty-five minute audio-visual presentation of a youthful Erickson.   This is a valuable study of his earlier methods.
Milton Erickson $185

• Trancework: A Demonstration of Hypnotic Patterns   A sixty minute videotape illustrating basic principles and some of the different patterns inherent in the use of clinical hypnosis.   Includes demonstrations of indirect induction, age regression, and glove anesthesia. *Michael Yapko* $225

All tapes are in color, except   Please specify mode
The Reverse Set of Hypnotic Induction.   BETA, VHS, or PAL

PSYCHOTHERAPY BOOKS FROM IRVINGTON

• **Ericksonian Hypnosis: A Handbook of Clinical Practice**
Lee C. Overholser $29.95

• **Experiencing Hypnosis: Therapeutic Approaches to Altered States**
Milton Erickson & Ernest Rossi [cassette]   39.50

• **Family Therapy and Social Change**   Neil Solomon [cassette]   28.50
• **Hypnotic and Strategic Interventions**   Michael D. Yapko, Ed.   39.50
• **Hypnotic Methods in Non-Hypnotic Therapies**   Aaron Hoorwitz   29.50
• **Hypnotherapeutic Techniques**   John G. Watkins   39.50
• **Hypnotherapy: An Exploratory Casebook**
Milton Erickson & Ernest Rossi [cassette]   39.50

• **Hypnotherapy for Troubled Children**   Robert E. Duke [cassette]   29.95
• **Hypnotic Realities: Induction of Clinical Hypnosis and Forms**
of Indirect Suggestion   Milton Erickson, Ernest & Sheila Rossi [cassette] 29.95

• **Hypnotic Techniques for Increasing Self-Esteem**
Ronald A. Steffenhagen, Ed.   29.50

• **Rituals in Psychotherapy**   Onno Van der Hart   27.50
• **Time Distortion in Hypnosis**   Linn F. Cooper & Milton Erickson   29.50
• **Trancework: An Introduction to Clinical Hypnosis**
Michael D. Yapko [cassette]   38.50

• **We, The Divided Self**   John G. Watkins & Rhonda L. Johnson [cassette] 29.50
• **The Wisdom of Milton H. Erickson**   Ronald A. Havens   39.50
  [cassette] includes audio cassette

ALSO FROM IRVINGTON

HYPNOTIC AND STRATEGIC INTERVENTIONS: PRINCIPLES AND PRACTICE
Edited by Michael D. Yapko

Contains papers given at the First Annual Conference on Hypnotic and Strategic Interventions, hosted by the Milton H. Erickson Institute of San Diego. These provocative essays address a variety of theoretical and practical issues in hypnotherapy. Authors include Michael Yapko, Ernest Rossi, Christopher Beletsis, Paul Carter, and Mark Reese. Introduction by Jeffrey Zeig. $39.50

HYPNOTHERAPEUTIC TECHNIQUES
by John G. Watkins

An authoritative, practical and comprehensive handbook of clinical hypnosis by a leading expert in the field. Includes many case studies. Illustrated. $39.50

HYPNOTIC METHODS IN NON-HYPNOTIC THERAPIES
by Aaron Hoorwitz

A practical book showing the nature and value of hypnotic methods in day to day psychological practice. Includes numerous case studies.
$29.50